Organizational Behavior

The State of the Science

SERIES IN APPLIED PSYCHOLOGY

Edwin A. Fleishman, George Mason University
Series Editor

Psychology in Organizations: Integrating Science and Practice
Kevin R. Murphy and Frank E. Saal

Teamwork and the Bottom Line: Groups Make a Difference
Ned Rosen

Patterns of Life History: The Ecology of Human Individuality
Michael D. Mumford, Garnett Stokes, and William A. Owens

Work Motivation
Uwe Kleinbeck, Hans-Henning Quast, Henk Thierry, and Harmut Häcker

Human Error: Cause, Prediction, and Reduction
John W. Senders and Neville P. Moray

Contemporary Career Development Issues
Robert F. Morrison and Jerome Adams

Personnel Selection and Assessment: Individual and Organizational Perspectives
Heinz Schuler, James L. Farr, and Mike Smith

Justice in the Workplace: Approaching Fairness in Human Resource Management
Russell Cropanzano

Organizational Behavior: The State of the Science
Jerald Greenberg

Organizational Behavior

The State of the Science

Edited by

Jerald Greenberg
The Ohio State University

LEA LAWRENCE ERLBAUM ASSOCIATES, PUBLISHERS
1994 Hillsdale, New Jersey   Hove, UK

Lawrence Erlbaum Associates, Inc., Publishers
365 Broadway
Hillsdale, New Jersey, 07642

Cover design by Kate Dusza

Library of Congress Cataloging-in-Publication Data

Organizational behavior : the state of the science / edited by Jerald
   Greenberg.
      p.   cm. — (Series in applied psychology)
   Includes bibliographical references and index.
   ISBN-0-8058-1214-8 (c). — ISBN 0-8058-1215-6 (p).
   1. Organizational behavior. I. Greenberg, Jerald. II. Series.
HD58.7.O732 1994
302.3′5—dc20   93-50638
                                                            CIP

Books published by Lawrence Erlbaum Associates are printed on acid-free
paper, and their bindings are chosen for strength and durability.

Printed in the United States of America
10 9 8 7 6 5 4 3 2 1

CONTENTS

v

FOREWORD

There is a compelling need for innovative approaches to the solution of many pressing problems involving human relationships in today's society. Such approaches are more likely to be successful when they are based on sound research and applications. This *Series in Applied Psychology* offers publications that emphasize state-of-the-art research and its application to important issues of human behavior in a variety of societal settings. The objective is to bridge both academic and applied interests.

The present volume deals with the field of organizational behavior (OB), which has been developing rapidly over a number of years. The empirical bases, theoretical development, and methodological foundation of OB have been evolving. Certainly, the field has changed dramatically. It appears timely for an assessment of these developments. This book brings together a set of original chapters by prominent scholars in the field of OB. They examine some historical roots of the field and evaluate its present status and needs for future directions. Special focus is on a critical self-eamination of the field's value and worth as a scientific and practical endeavor. The book is essential reading for teachers, researchers, consultants, and managers who deal with the complex issues involved in understanding and managing organizations.

—Edwin A. Fleishman, Editor
Series in Applied Psychology

PREFACE

As scientists toil in the fields of their disciplines, they only infrequently enjoy opportunities to step back from their work to assess where their efforts have taken them. The everyday pressures to produce and publish the next scholarly advance makes such self-reflection a luxury that scientists rarely can afford. Yet, it is clear that the practice of assessing a field's scientific progress is critical if it is to have any hope of making meaningful advances.

Indulging in self-reflection is particularly important in a rapidly growing science such as organizational behavior (OB). The field of OB has certainly changed dramatically from the time-and-motion studies of the 1930s to the sophisticated computer models of human behavior in the workplace that we see today. In view of such rapid progress, the time has come for a systematic self-examination of the state of the field of OB. Where has it been, where it is now, and where is it going? Questions such as these are bound to raise the self-consciousness of organizational scholars, causing them to question the field's values and its worth as a scientific and practical endeavor. As painful as the process may be, a critical self-assessment of the state of OB is absolutely essential if the field is to prosper and make meaningful advances in behavioral science and in the welfare of individuals and society.

This is a collection of essays by the field's most highly regarded scholars— experts who have contributed widely to the field of OB, and who were invited to share their thoughts about its past, present, and future. By presenting their ideas about the state of the field, the discipline as a whole is invited to engage in critical self-reflection. Toward this end, the volume focuses on five spheres of activity that represent the major activities of those interested in OB: micro (individual level) processes, macro (organizational level) processes, research methodology, teaching OB, and practicing OB. Taken together, the contributions provide rich avenues of critical self-assessment for the field. The result, I believe, is a book that promises to make introspection among OB researchers, teachers, and practitioners less of a luxury and more of a necessity.

—Jerald Greenberg

1

THE COGNITIVE REVOLUTION IN ORGANIZATIONAL BEHAVIOR

Daniel R. Ilgen
Debra A. Major
Spencer L. Tower
Michigan State University

To say that there has been a cognitive revolution in organizational behavior (OB) is to misspeak; to date, it has been little more than a minor skirmish. But a cognitive revolution is occurring all around. The 1990s have been designated "the decade of the brain." What many of us knew as experimental psychology is now cognitive psychology. In some senses, this cognitive psychology includes many of the classic topics of sensation, perception, learning, and memory. In others, it has been dramatically transformed, both in the way that key constructs are viewed and in the way that research is done. A new discipline, cognitive science, has evolved that spans the boundaries of chemistry, biology, psychology, philosophy, mathematics, physics, computer science, and anatomy (Simon, 1992). In 1991, the Academy of Management established a new cognitive interest area for those concerned with cognitive processes across the whole spectrum of organizational phenomena. The adoption of cognitive constructs into a wide variety of disciplines has been so pervasive that to ask what is *not* cognitive is a reasonable question. The field of OB has not escaped the influence of cognitive points of view nor has the field been transformed or absorbed by such views.

When cognitive constructs are addressed within OB, they tend to be treated in one of two ways. The first begins with the cognitive theory and translates its constructs into organizational ones. Klein's (1989) control theory of work motivation was a good example of this. Working from classical control theory models, Klein added variables and reinterpreted behavioral theory related to control mechanisms in ways that fit organizational phenomena. Few or no changes were suggested in basic control theory constructs; the modifications provided were simple translations of key constructs into organizationally relevant terms. The end product was the same theory, in Klein's case, control theory, with an organizational twist.

The second approach is to begin and end with some particular organizational phenomenon. To this, cognitive constructs relevant to the phenomenon are brought to bear. Cognitive processes are used as explanatory constructs for understanding the organizational issue of interest. The extensive work on cognitive influences in performance appraisal follows the latter strategy. This work begins with the organizational phenomenon of appraising other individuals in a formal appraisal system and introduces cognitive variables likely to influence the rater's ability to observe, remember, recall, and record the performance of other individuals (Ilgen, Barnes-Farrell, & McKellin, 1993). In contrast to the first approach where the focus is on the cognitive theory, the second remains on the organizational phenomenon.

Taken together, the two orientations toward cognitive processes in organizations create the matrix depicted in Table 1.1 with theories of cognitive processes as rows and organizational topics to which they have been applied as columns. Checks indicate that a number of studies exist within that content area. Whether one chooses to view the set from the standpoint of the rows (the first approach described earlier) or the columns (the second approach) is immaterial; both are legitimate.

In 1989, there were two major reviews of the cognitive research in OB. One chose to organize the literature by cognitive theories (Ilgen & Klein, 1989) and the other by organizational topics (Lord & Maher, 1989). In the remainder of this chapter, we first briefly describe the primary cognitive theories and processes that have been invoked to address organizational phenomena. With these as background, we then provide a selected review and commentary on cognitively oriented organizational behavior topics. These reviews will be followed with an overall evaluative discussion of the role and nature of cognitive processes in OB.

COGNITIVE THEORIES AND PROCESSES COMMONLY INVOKED IN ORGANIZATIONAL BEHAVIOR

Control Theory

Control theory is a classic cybernetic model adapted to human behavior. According to the theory, the fundamental building block of all action is the feedback loop (Weiner, 1948). At its most basic level, the feedback loop is a simply input -> process -> output system with a feedback mechanism that routes outputs back into the system as inputs. Four elements are essential to all feedback loops. These are: (a) inputs sensed by the system, (b) a goal or standard, (c) a comparator that compares the inputs to the standard, and (d) some output that is responsive to the results of the comparison.

Carver and Scheier (1981) piqued the interest of behavioral scientists in control theory as a human behavior model. They adapted many of the basic model

TABLE 1.1
Areas of Cognitive Research on Organizational Behavior Phenomena

| | Organizational Topics | | | | |
Cognitive Theories	Training	Performance Appraisal	Decision Making	Motivation	Leadership
Control Theory	✓	✓		✓	
Social Cognition					
Attribution Theories		✓			
Subjective Expected Utility	✓				

elements to take into account behavioral science data. For example, they abandoned the notion of a simple standard provided a priori to a person. Instead, they imbedded the standard in a hierarchy of goals/standards. Goals in the hierarchy varied along a continuum of abstraction from general overarching goals (e.g., be a hard worker) to specific concrete ones (e.g., complete four units by noon Friday). From this hierarchy, a standard is believed to be selected at any particular time as the one that guides the person's behavior. Building on the work of Carver and Scheier (1981), Lord and Hanges (1987) and others (e.g., Klein, 1989) offered further refinements designed to fit behaviors of interest in organizational settings more closely. In general, there has been a great deal of acceptance of control theory as a valuable model for thinking about behavior in organizations, although the theory is not without its critics (e.g., Locke, 1991a).

Social Cognition

Social cognition represents the purest form of the cognitive influences on OB. Social cognition is concerned with the processing and representation of information about individuals and groups (Wyer & Srull, 1986). As with any cognition, the primary concerns are with the way that information is obtained, represented in memory, recalled, and integrated with other information. The source of input information may either originate in the person's environment or come from the person's own memory. Social cognition restricts the domain of information of interest to that dealing with social cues. Such a restriction alters cognitive processing somewhat due to unique characteristics of social cues. But, at the general level, the processing of social cues is believed to be much like the processing of many other forms of information.

Without implying that information processing within persons is compartmentalized or occurs in an orderly linear sequence, social cognitive models typically break down the process into sensing or gathering information, encoding it, storing it in memory, and retrieving it from memory. Around this basic process an elaborate set of theories is woven (e.g., Wyer & Srull, 1986). A full development of the state of the literature at this time is far beyond the scope of this chapter. We mention only two key processing issues as background for discussion later in the chapter.

One key characteristic is an organizing structure. Information does not exist as separate elements in memory, nor is it perceived or recalled as independent pieces. Rather, people organize information in some sense. Different labels for the organizing structures are given by different theorists. For example, some people talk of *mental models* (e.g., Johnson-Laird, 1983) and others speak of *schema* and *prototypes* (e.g., Wyer & Srull, 1986). Although these three are not identical, they all serve much the same function; they organize information into meaningful wholes that influence all phases of information processing.

A second common distinction is made between conscious and unconscious (i.e., *controlled* and *automatic*) processing (Langer, 1978). This distinction stresses that it is not necessary for people to be aware of all their cognitive processing. Sometimes individuals are aware of how they handle information cognitively (controlled) and other times they do it unconsciously (automatic). At any given time, both controlled and automatic processing are likely to occur. The distinction between the two types of processing is important for training, differentiating experts from novices and many other conditions important in organizations. Controlled and automatic processes are relevant for all cognitive phenomena; they are not limited to social cognition.

Attribution Theory

Attribution theory focuses upon a limited set of cognitions—beliefs about the causes of performance. The theoretical bases for most work in organizational behavior on performance attributions is that of Weiner (1974, 1980, 1985, 1986). It is proposed that individuals evaluate the performance of others and themselves not only on the basis of performance level (high or low), but also on the evaluators' beliefs about the causes of performance. In an early version of the theory, Weiner classified stability and internality to be causes of performance in a two-dimensional space. Four prototypical causes of performance were located in the space by dichotomizing both the stability and internality dimensions. These four were: ability, task difficulty, effort, and luck. Later elaborations of the model (Weiner, 1985, 1986) added perceptions of controllability to the two-dimensional model. Extensive research indicated that the extent to which people believed performers could control their level of performance operated somewhat independently of stability and internality, and that the inclusion of the control dimension added to the predictability of the model.

The implications of attribution theory to OB are obvious. Concerns for performance pervades much of the work in the field, both an individual's performance and the responses of others to that performance. Because attributions about the causes of performance influence both the level of performance and evaluations of performance quality, attribution theory has played a major role in the OB literature.

Subjective Expected Utility (SEU)

The final set of cognitive theories or models to be mentioned here is much more diffuse than the previous models. It includes a wide variety of models and theories that share the common characteristic of viewing behavior as a function of some conscious consideration of its value or utility. The best known of these in the OB area is Vroom's (1964) expectancy theory. Viewed as a model of motivation, it is based on the assumption that individuals cognitively evaluate alternative courses of action and choose actions on the basis of their subjective utility. More recent models have elaborated upon many of the expectancy theory variables and processes. (See Kanfer, 1990 and 1992, for excellent reviews and integrations of these theories and models.) In all cases, the elaborations maintain central cognitive constructs and processes that lead to choices among alternative courses of action. Choices to devote time and effort to particular causes of action are believed to result from the conscious consideration of the utility or value of alternatives as seen by the person making the choice. Although research on expectancy based models has been moderately supportive (Mitchell, 1974), these models have been criticized for their over reliance upon rationality and high levels of cognitive activity (Staw, 1980).

Goal setting theory also represents a cognitively oriented theory that can be fit within an expectancy X value framework, but it is often treated as an independent theory of organizational behavior. For goal setting, the behaviors of interest are narrowly defined as those related to task performance. A person's level of task performance is assumed to be most directly affected by his or her intended level of performance. Goals are intentions. Of all the cognitively oriented theories, goal setting is most closely aligned with OB, although the notion that intentions guide behavior permeates much of psychology (Dweck, 1992; Pervin, 1992). The work on goal setting theory is most frequently credited to Locke and Latham. Their work and the works of others over the last 20 to 25 years is summarized in their latest book entitled, *A Theory of Goal Setting and Task Performance* (Locke & Latham, 1990).

COGNITIVE INROADS IN ORGANIZATIONAL BEHAVIOR

Performance Appraisal

Much of the cognitive research in OB has focused on the way in which individuals evaluate others' performance (Lord & Maher, 1989). Three sets of issues dominate performance appraisal research from a cognitive perspective. The first is concerned with rating errors. The dominant errors are those of rating persons too leniently or harshly (leniency errors), failure to differentiate among various facets of performance by simply forming an overall evaluation (halo error), and a restriction of the range of performance levels considered (range restriction). It was hoped that an understanding of raters' cognitive processes would lead to the discovery of ways to reduce or eliminate rating errors.

In our opinion, the research in this area has made some major contributions but not in the ways that were intended. An implicit assumption behind interest in rating errors was that the errors represented an inability of raters to produce accurate ratings. Cognitive research has shown that this assumption often is wrong, particularly as it relates to halo errors. Conducting research under conditions where the levels of ratee performance are known, it has been possible to assess the accuracy of ratings and to compare accuracy to errors. A recent meta-analysis of research with both accuracy and error measures showed little or no correspondence between the two sets of measures (Murphy & Balzer, 1989). Patterns of responses that look like errors may, in fact, reflect valid ratings of the actual performance (Hulin, 1982; Murphy & Reynolds, 1988). Training to reduce errors may actually have the unintended consequence of reducing rather than improving accuracy (Hedge & Kavanagh, 1988). Thus, cognitive research modified our views about the meaning of performance rating errors and raised serious questions about both the need and the methods used to eliminate such "errors" as typically measured.

A second cluster of cognitive research has taken a more expansive approach to performance appraisal by attempting to increase understanding of the whole appraisal process. The overarching model assumes that (a) raters perceive information about the person being evaluated, (b) process that information, (c) recall the information, and (d) use that recalled information to evaluate the person (Ilgen & Feldman, 1983). Research has been conducted on all phases and the interaction among the phases. Some recent examples of such research are briefly mentioned.

Steiner and Rain (1989) varied the effectiveness of a lecturer's video performance over four time periods. Subjects rated each episode immediately following its viewing and gave an overall evaluation at the end. Results showed that recent poor performance was given the most weight in evaluations and that inconsistent performance information made it difficult for raters to form general impressions of the person.

Research on the way information is encoded and stored in memory clearly supports the conclusion that raters form general impressions about ratees. These impressions serve to organize the evaluations (Ilgen & Klein, 1989; Lord & Maher, 1989). Yet, these general impressions do not necessarily represent accurate mappings of information observed or not observed on the ratees. Some have shown that these impressions are consistent with attributional theory hypotheses about raters' beliefs about the reasons for performance (Martin & Klimoski, 1990). Comparisons of information processing models, which assume raters gather information about others and then somehow combine that information at some later time, to impression formation models continue to support the latter rather than the former model (Lance, Woehr, & Fisicaro, 1991). The impression formation models assume that general impressions are formed rather quickly and later information is fit to the general impressions. Other research that focuses on the output (i.e., recall and evaluation) finds that the amount of decay in recall is affected by the time delay between observation and recall (Murphy, Philbin, & Adams, 1989) as well as patterns of performance information over the time observed (Karl & Wexley, 1989). Having raters complete diaries about ratees across the time period over which they are observed may reduce some of the cognitive processing losses of information over time (DeNisi, Robbins, & Cafferty, 1989).

Finally, cognitive process research has clearly established that the very nature of the evaluations that are obtained depend upon the setting and conditions under which the ratings are obtained. The most frequent setting condition explored is that of the rating's purpose (Murphy et al., 1989).

Cognitive research on performance appraisal has been criticized for making little contribution to the improvement of performance appraisals in organizations (Murphy & Cleveland, 1991). In our opinion, this criticism is both valid and misdirected. It is valid in that the recent research has offered no major fixes for the problems observed in performance appraisal ratings presently in use. However, we believe it is misguided for two reasons. First, the research never was intended to offer direct solutions to appraisal systems in use. It was intended to gain an understanding of how raters process information about ratees. In this respect, much has been learned. Some of this has significant impact on practice, such as the finding that impressions drive ratings so that it is unrealistic to expect raters to gather information about others without evaluating this information immediately. Another contribution includes work that implies typical indices of rating errors do not necessarily imply inaccuracies in rating. To criticize the work for not having accomplished a broader purpose solely within the practice domain is premature. Such criticism fails to recognize that the primary goal of the performance accuracy research was to understand factors that influenced individuals' ability to provide accurate ratings of others. This ability was seen as a necessary but not sufficient condition for accurate performance appraisals in organizations. The fact that accuracy is not sufficient for effective performance appraisals in use in organizations is not a fault of accuracy research or of the fundamental assumption of accuracy's necessary but not sufficient role in appraisals.

Second, criticisms of performance accuracy research underestimate the value of learning what is *not* important. Accuracy research has contributed by identifying limits of performance appraisal practices. In learning more about how raters process information, it is clear that the information processing part of the rating task is not likely to be the major area in which problems with ratings arise (Ilgen et al., 1993). The political environment (Longnecker, Gioia, & Sims, 1987) and other conditions are likely to control much of the important nonvalid variance in ratings (Ilgen et al., 1993; Milkovich & Wigdor, 1991; Murphy & Cleveland, 1991). To the extent that cognitive work shifts attention from rater rating ability and the characteristics of rating scales, it has contributed to the potential improvement of a common and important organizational practice.

Motivation

There continues to be much cognitive research directed at understanding work motivation, that is, understanding what energizes and directs individual's behavior as well as what influences its persistence. Several insightful overarching and integrative motivational views with a cognitive orientation have recently appeared in literature. Klein's (1989) model parsimoniously blended various theories of motivation with elements of control theory. This metatheory brought together work in the areas of expectancy, attribution, feedback, and goal-setting. The broad emphasis on cognitive dynamics and theories in the process of discrepancy reduction is a welcome departure from control theory's (Carver & Scheier, 1981; Weiner, 1948) long-standing, and frequently critiqued, mechanical and static image.

Locke's (1991b) metatheory is a sequential model of motivation that incorporated many of the major cognitive theories of motivation. Locke calls the stage in which action is given purposeful direction, the "motivation hub." Influential concepts within this hub include goals and intentions, self-efficacy and expectancy, as well as performance attributions. Reactions to rewards and perceptions of satisfaction are also prominent factors impacting the person's motivation. Volition fits, directly or indirectly, in all stages of the model and the individual's values serve as the "motivational core" guiding action.

Although Deci (1992) criticized the goal setting theory of Locke and Latham (1990) for its failure to specify the origin of goals, the criticism appears to demand more from the theory than the authors intended. That is, the emphasis of the goal theory of Locke and Latham is on the effects of goals, not the source of them. Thus, the theory should be judged against its intended objectives rather than the preferences of others for the theory.

Another integrative model is that of Kanfer (Kanfer, 1990, 1992; Kanfer & Ackerman, 1989). Kanfer builds on those theories that view motivation as resource allocation (Atkinson & Birch, 1970; Naylor, Pritchard, & Ilgen, 1980) where the primary resources are time and effort. In addition to making more explicit the means by which people change their overall level of motivation, valuable contributions were added by acknowledging the impact of individual differences on performance and highlighting the benefit of distinguishing between distal and proximal motivational processes. Finally, the motivational problem is viewed as one that goes on over time. This is in contrast to much of the research on motivation that is cross-sectional and static.

Beach and Mitchell (Beach, 1990; Beach & Mitchell, 1987; Mitchell & Beach, 1990) proposed image theory in reaction to the over rationalized SEU models of motivation but without abandoning some of the percepts of these views. They argued that most decisions do not result from a careful weighing of the gains and losses associated with choices. They suggested that, when faced with a need for a decision, individuals size up the situation by comparing it to previous situations that they have encountered. Based on the degree of match of the new to the old, courses of action are chosen. When there is a good fit of the new to the old, people tend to choose routines or courses of action similar to what worked in the past without giving much thought to all the pluses and minuses of the choice. When the initial comparison leads to a bad fit, more rational, controlled cognitive processes are activated. Image theory provides a description of a flow chart model of the motivational process that demands far less active cognitive processing than typical SEU theories without abandoning the belief that SEUs play some role in motivation. Although the existence of data supporting the theory is limited at this time due to the recency of the model's appearance in the literature, it deserves watching.

Finally, there is a growing awareness of the need to consider the interface between learning and motivation. The boundaries of these two processes have always been blurred with theories in each domain sharing similar constructs (Kanfer, 1991; Kanfer & Ackerman, 1989). Dweck's (1992) work clearly showed that framing learning situations as achievement versus performance tasks can influence performance of the task. Ackerman and Kanfer's work (Ackerman, 1987; Kanfer & Ackerman, 1989) integrated abilities (typically the domain of learning theorists) with motivation into a common resource model of perform-ance. Both of these lines of research suggest that much can be gained by treating motivation and learning as interdependent effects on performance rather than independent ones, as has been done in the past.

Training

Training is, by its very nature, concerned with learning, and much of learning is cognitive. The greatest recent strides have been made in understanding the differences in the ways that experts and novices solve problems. It is generally accepted that experts store information in memory and apply knowledge differently than novices (see Chi, Glaser, & Farr, 1988 for a summary and review of this literature). Using what is known about the way experts process information, an emerging line of research focuses on underlying cognitive principles of successful training and transfer. Both training and transfer are viewed as schema-based processes (Phye, 1989, 1990). Empirical work has demonstrated that effective training is the result of activating the appropriate general schema for learning and using feedback and practice to induce a more specific procedural schema (Phye, 1989). Empirical evidence suggests that successful transfer of training depends upon similar processes (Phye, 1990).

Fisk and Gallini (1989) contended that rule-based training that activates both general and specific procedural schemata should be more effective than training that focuses solely on specific subskills. Rule-based training focuses on the underlying principal or general rule (e.g., If x, then do y.). Fisk and Gallini tested their hypothesis using rule-based and non-rule-based training programs for arithmetic skills. As predicted, individuals who received rule-based training demonstrated greater transfer and were also able to assess their own proficiency levels more accurately than those in the non-rule-based training condition.

It is important to note that the type of research conducted by Fisk and Gallini (1989) is possible because of the substantial body of basic research on expert and novice differences. Experts' cognitive processes are more automatic, whereas novices engage more effort in controlled processing. Rule-based training is believed to focus attention on the commonalities of problem solving that drive automatic processing. Non-rule-based training focused at the subskill level demands more controlled processing and fosters learning at that level. Leigh and McGraw (1989) were able to map the commonalities in the procedural knowledge of successful sales people. They suggested that such commonalities could be used to derive activity based scripts that would be useful in training new sales-people.

Bringing cognitive concepts to bear on long-standing training methods in use has resulted in new training methodologies that have potential to be as effective as they are innovative. Gist (1989), for example, derived a cognitive modelling training method by applying cognitive principles to the long-standing practice of behavioral modelling. Cognitive modelling focuses on teaching the thoughts or mental statements that occur during the performance of a given activity and then utilizing similar self-instructional thoughts. Results suggest that the method promoted both skill learning and efficacy building. Preliminary work on matching training methods and models to individual learning styles has also yielded encouraging results (Sein & Robey, 1991; Sims & Sims, 1991).

In summation, the cognitive perspective has not revolutionized the training field, but its impact is becoming increasingly apparent. It is especially exciting to see that the cognitive approach is beginning to yield meaningful practical applications. Equally heartening is the effort that has been made to merge ideas derived from the cognitive literature with well established training principles.

Decision Making

The cognitive literature has influenced the decision making literature in a variety of ways. The cognitive perspective has been used successfully to describe decision processes and study decision making effectiveness. However, theoretical devel-opments of the types that have made their way into OB often are not sufficiently refined to address specific individual decisions. This point is addressed later.

Concepts from the cognitive literature have been useful in describing decision making processes and determining effectiveness. For instance, describing decision strategies in terms of elementary information processes (EIPs) or component parts has provided insight into their relative effectiveness (Bettman, Johnson, & Payne, 1990). By summing the EIPs for each strategy, Bettman et al. (1990) were able to accurately predict differences in response time and subjective effort across decision strategies.

The notion of cognitive feedback has also proven useful. Cognitive feedback involves supplying decision makers with an information processing "scorecard" of previous decisions. Feedback includes the relative weights a decision maker gave to different informational cues and the efficacy of those weights in terms of decision accuracy. Harmon and Rohrbaugh (1990) found that providing cognitive feedback to every individual of a decision making group resulted in greater individual learning and increased efficiency in reaching consensus. At the individual level, negative cognitive feedback has been linked to increased use of evaluations, greater strategy processing, and increased variety in cognitive processing, whereas positive feedback is associated with decreased strategy processing and increased use of scripts (Wofford & Goodwin, 1990).

Recent theoretical developments, although interesting and creative, are presently too preliminary to have had much of an impact on applied decision literature. For example, Porac and Howard (1990) applied the "mental model" notion to the organizational level issue of competitor definition. They argued that the information processing demands associated with identifying and implementing competitive strategies exceed the cognitive capacities of organizational decision makers. As a result, decision makers seek to simplify the competitive environment by using a mental model of competitors. Although Porac and Howard (1990) worked through five propositions to explain how these mental models develop and change, their hypotheses have yet to be tested.

Wood & Bandura (1989b) sought to examine organizational functioning from the perspective of social cognitive theory. Their model attempted to explain decisions made by managers in terms of triadic reciprocal causation (i.e., the interaction of behavioral, cognitive, and affective factors). Based on preliminary tests using business students working in a simulated organization exercise, Wood and Bandura (1989a) concluded that managers form efficacy schema through experience and that performance becomes more strongly regulated by these self-conceptions over time. Although intriguing, the results are far from conclusive.

The examples cited above illustrate theories at their initial stages of development. Though they show promise and have the potential to make meaningful contributions to the decision making literature, further refinement is required. Beach and Mitchell's image theory (Beach, 1990; Mitchell & Beach, 1990) represents a clear case of such refinement. The model attempts to capitalize on the formal models of decision making and the growing literature on the limitations of human decision makers. Beach's recent book explicitly addresses decision making in organizations (Beach, 1990). Mitchell and Beach (1990) extended image theory, focusing more directly on treatment of automatic decision making and intuition.

Leadership

In the leadership area, the influence of the cognitive approach is most clearly focused on leadership perceptions (see Ilgen & Klein, 1989 and Lord & Maher, 1989 for reviews). Research along this line continues to develop. By far the most inclusive treatment of these issues is a book by Lord and Maher (1991b) that focused on leadership strictly from a cognitive perspective and supported the position with a great deal of research by Lord and his students, as well as others over the last few years. Maurer and Lord (1991), for example, studied the impact of extraneous cognitive demands on impression formation and leader perception. They found that irrelevant cognitive demands can deflect the leader's amount of information processing capacity allocated to the task of impression formation. They concluded that leadership perceptions may be processed automatically—without deliberate consideration—within organizational settings where cognitive demands tend to be high. These conditions lead to a greater likelihood of prototypical impressions being selected.

Others have also taken up the study of perceptions as they relate to leadership. One notable example took a cognitive approach to a long-standing issue in the leadership literature, perceptions of the physical attributes of leaders (Cherulnik, Turns, & Wilderman, 1990). Using photographs of male and female leaders and nonleaders, they found that naive observers were able to make differential and appropriate attributions of leadership status and related personality traits. In addition, a separate group of subjects rated the leaders as more attractive and more mature looking than nonleaders. Cherulnik et al. (1990) contended that their study demonstrates the importance and potential accuracy of schema-based attributions in leader emergence and the significant role of appearance cues in the attribution process.

As established cognitive theories in the leadership literature are being elaborated and tested, new theories concerning contemporary leadership topics are beginning to emerge. An excellent example is Shaw's (1990) cognitive categorization model for the study of intercultural management. The model focuses on the interaction between an expatriate manager and subordinates from the host country. Culture is contended to have a significant impact upon the content and structure of schemas for both leaders and subordinates. Shaw also posited that task demands and the extent of cultural differences interact to determine the extent to which information processing is automatic or controlled. Under normal task demands, greater cultural differences are expected to result in more controlled processing. However, under high task demands, greater cultural differences are expected to result in more automatic processing. The model appears to have implications for the convergence of cognitive structures through intercultural dynamics.

We are confident that the cognitive focus on leadership perceptions will continue to develop and that Lord and Maher's book (1991b) will prove to be a useful tool in that endeavor. It is also likely that contemporary leadership topics (e.g., cross-cultural, team leadership) will be influenced by the cognitive literature.

CRITIQUE OF COGNITIVE ORGANIZATIONAL BEHAVIOR RESEARCH

Nature of Contributions

Ilgen and Klein (1989) described three ways in which cognitive constructs work their way into OB. First, they appear in descriptive research illustrating that behaviors from the OB domain are consistent with constructs from the cognitive literature. Second, research on basic cognitive constructs is conducted within the domain of OB. Independent of the domain, the research itself makes contributions to the understanding of cognition. Finally, cognitive constructs and the research on them within OB can be useful for guiding and changing policies and practices affecting people in organizations. These three modes are labeled demonstrative, theory, and application contributions. Ilgen and Klein concluded that almost all work through 1988 was demonstrative and that cognitive research in OB was unlikely to make much of a contribution to OB or to behavioral science if it did not advance beyond demonstration.

Today, our view is one of reserved optimism. On the one hand, the literature since 1988 remains largely demonstrative, and we are no more convinced of the long-term value of a demonstrative science than previously. On the other hand, there has been a significant increase in the amount of work that has the potential for contributing to theory and application. Theoretically, research and writing from an organizational perspective on self-regulation (Bandura, 1991; Wood & Bandura, 1989b), control theory (Hollenbeck, 1989; Klein, 1989), switching mechanisms from controlled to automatic processing (Maheswaran & Chaiken, 1991) decision making (Bettman et al., 1990; Harman & Rohrbaugh, 1990), and leadership (Lord & Maher, 1991b) has contributed to the understanding of basic cognitive processes. In all cases, there was a greater awareness of the context in which cognitive processes took place. In addition, cognitive research in OB has explored more completely the impact of individual's past experience on cognitions.

Although all cognitive theories clearly recognize that cognitive processing is dependent upon individuals' interactions with their environment and on their past experience (Gardner, 1985; Medin & Ross, 1990), in the body of empirical research on which the basic theories are based, contexts are limited primarily to the laboratory, and the time frame rarely extends beyond a single session. As a result, in spite of the richness of the theories, the data are limited. Organizational behavior, because of the varied contextual settings to which the field is targeted, demands that research within its domain be context sensitive. This sensitivity can be addressed by the research settings or by the demand that researchers confront external validity issues regardless of setting. In addition, because persons populating organizations interact in those settings over time periods extending over years and even decades, OB research must also be sensitive to the cumulative effects of past behavior on present and future beliefs and actions. To a limited extent, the cognitive research in OB is speaking to the context and past history of individuals as these conditions impact on cognitive processes. It remains to be seen to what extent others interested in cognitions outside the OB area are listening. If they are not, the fault lies more in the listener than the research itself.

Application contributions also have resulted, but these come more indirectly than theoretical ones. That is to say, rarely is cognitively oriented research done within a particular practice or application. Rather, information is gained from research that has practice implications, and it finds its way into practice to the extent that applications are affected by what is learned from the research. Performance appraisals are a good case in point. Here, work on the cognitive processing of raters has clearly established that raters form general impressions of ratees, and ratings on appraisal forms are best viewed as reconstructions from the general impressions than "objective" reports of observed events (Ilgen et al., 1993). This conclusion is not based directly on work done on performance appraisal systems in practice. Rather, the work is done in the laboratory and other controlled settings. Yet, the consistency of the finding that ratings are impression driven should work itself into application, even though the data on how impressions affect ratings was not generated under conditions of application. In a similar fashion the limitations in cognitive processing described in image theory (Beach, 1990; Beach & Mitchell, 1990) and the extension of cognitive constructs to all phases of the leadership process by Lord and Maher (1991b) are likely to impact on practice even though the research that the theories are based on was not generated under practice conditions.

Limiting Conditions

In spite of some progress, there are a number of factors limiting the nature and quality of cognitive research in OB. Some of these are endemic to the topic and the discipline and others are due to the way in which research and theory building are conducted.

A primary limit stems from fundamental tensions between molar and molecular views of behavior intertwined with concerns for the ecological validity of research. Gardner's (1985) historical account of the cognitive revolution, described molecular approaches as those that focus on small scale units of analysis (bits of information, individual percepts, single associations that are briefly encountered) on the assumption that future work will advance by combining smaller units into more holistic theories. In contrast, proponents of the molar approach look at larger scale problems over more extended periods of time and invoke more expansive concepts such as schemas, frames, or strategies as explanations of behavior. The work of individual investigators typically can be located within a relatively narrow range along a molecular to molar continuum, and the reasons for location at a particular point are based on scientific strategy and personal preferences of the investigators themselves (Gardner, 1985).

When reviewing the field of cognitive science as a whole, Gardner (1985) made the interesting observation that molar research, in contrast to molecular research, tends to produce interesting demonstrations of cognitive phenomena rather than theory-enriching experiments. Given the wide range of units along the hypothetical molecular-to-molar continuum represented in the cognitive science literature addressed by Gardner (1985), cognitive research in organizational behavior is exclusively molar. In fact, most of this work would fall completely off the molar end of Gardner's scale. Thus, it is not surprising that Ilgen and Klein (1989) classified almost all of the cognitive research as almost exclusively demonstrative. Yet, Gardner's observations added a different twist to Ilgen and Klein's (1989) conclusions. Whereas Ilgen and Klein (1989) attributed the problem largely to the failure of researchers to look beyond the obvious, Gardner (1985) implied that the molar nature of the problems subjected to cognitive interpretations is likely to limit the nature of the approach that is taken to the topic.

Added to the molecular–molar distinction is the natural confound between research settings and molecularity. In general, the more molecular the research, the more likely that the research must be conducted under highly controlled laboratory conditions. As the conditions become more controlled and less natural, the questions of ecological validity (the ability of the research findings to generalize to settings other than the ones in which the data were collected) arise (Gardner, 1985; Medin & Ross, 1990). Debates and disagreements abound. In general, the more molar the researcher's orientation, the higher the level of dissatisfaction with the ecological validity of molecular research. In contrast, the more molecular a person's orientation, the more likely the person will have difficulty accepting a study's internal validity. (Internal validity refers to the extent to which observed conditions can be unambiguously attributed to particular causes.) The tensions between the molecular and the molar positions is a fact of life and not one that will disappear in the near future.

Another factor limiting the integration of cognitive sciences into the OB literature is a substantial discontinuity between the behavioral models that currently dominate the organizational behavior literature and the ones that are emerging from cognitive science. Organizational behavior models are, for the most part, serial. Variables are temporally ordered such that certain variables are predicted to influence other variables, and the influence is often unidirectional. That is, variable a is hypothesized to influence variable b rather than the reverse. Serial may also be bidirectional, typically viewed as reciprocal, with a influencing b to change it to b' and b' influencing a and creating a'. The sequence repeats over time as one state leads to another. By contrast, parallel processing goes on simultaneously.

As Lord and Maher (1991a) clearly described, human cognitive processing occurs both in serial and in parallel, and the data suggest that the latter condition is far more frequent than the former. Furthermore, many processes that were once described by serial models are now believed to be happening in parallel. For a simple example, consider the expectancy theory model that assumes beliefs exist about characteristics of behaviors, outcomes and contingencies between actions and outcomes and are then cognitively combined to form beliefs about utilities, generating affect (feelings) about particular conditions. Research would seem to imply that rather than being as clearly temporally ordered as implied by the model, people have feelings, beliefs and behaviors that are occurring simultaneously and mutually influencing each other. Because much of the current OB research is designed to address serial models, and the importance of the parallel models is being more clearly demonstrated in the recent cognitive literature, the mismatch between the models in use in OB and the emerging models of cognitive science is likely to retard effective integration of cognitive theory and research into the OB domain.

Finally, there is a limitation in the depth of knowledge of most scholars in OB with respect to the state of the cognitive sciences. Much of this is due to the rapid pace of advances in the cognitive sciences. It is also due, in part, to the fact that many of the advances are in areas that are molecular in nature, so they appear less relevant to OB. For whatever the reasons, there is a wide gap in understanding of the cognitive literature. Lord and Maher (1991a), in their chapter in the *Handbook of Industrial and Organizational Psychology*, made the size of this gap evident as they laid out some of the major dimensions of recent findings in the cognitive sciences and exposed disparities between these advances and both the topics and the approaches to these topics that are currently being addressed in OB.

Future Directions

As we mentioned earlier, we are encouraged by the progress in the cognitive area of organizational behavior research and theory over the last 3 years. Yet, the major advancements, in our opinion, are just beginning to appear. For such advancements to continue, we have four suggestions for continued progress.

First, there is a desperate need for a more complete understanding of the cognitive literature by organizational behavior researchers. Lord and Maher's (1991a) introduction and overview of major cognitive constructs and models provided an excellent starting point for developing an appreciation of recent findings in the cognitive sciences that are likely to impact on OB. At the same time, it exposed the shallowness of much of the work in organizational behavior that passes as cognitive. To be able to advance beyond the demonstrative stage, it is necessary that not only the common cognitive constructs (e.g., schema or prototypes) and processes (e.g., automatic and controlled) be brought into the discipline but also that the underlying paradigms and overarching models from which these constructs and processes are extracted be understood. At present, that understanding, or at least a recognition of that understanding, is less than it should be if major advances are to be made.

Second, we suggest that those in organizational behavior should capitalize on their long-standing interest and experience conducting research in which careful attention is paid to the context and the person's past history. As was mentioned earlier, cognitive models of memory and learning stress the importance of settings and individual past performance history, but research tends to be done almost exclusively in the laboratory with persons who participate in a single session. Organizational behavior research, on the other hand, has a long history of concern for field research and for attempting to construct laboratory research in such a way that its findings will generalize to the behavior of people in work organizations. This concern for settings and experience has the potential for making a unique contribution to cognitive research. Organizational behavior researchers, in many respects, are better prepared to address some of the problems associated with describing situations and developing indices of match than other behavioral scientists.

Third, more attention is needed on the role of computer models in behavioral research. A familiar term in the cognitive sciences is *cognitive architectures* (Lord & Maher, 1991a; Simon, 1992). Cognitive architectures are models of cognitive processes that are generated from knowledge of common mathematical models, computer modeling techniques, and the psychological and behavioral phenomena of interest. Based on a combination of these three, computer models are constructed of the psychological/behavioral phenomenon(a) of interest. These models are then "tested" in computer simulations and with behavioral studies. Through an iterative process of observing and taking discrepancies between simulation findings and those from the behavioral studies into account, the models are modified and refined to create better fits of the revised models to the observed behaviors to which they apply. The iterative process of matching computer models to observed behaviors is common in the cognitive science literature but uncommon in OB. A greater awareness of the potential of this procedure is needed in the latter discipline.

Finally, there is some value in recognizing the limits of cognitive contributions to OB research. In spite of the appeal of many of the labels and concepts in cognitive psychology for OB, the inherent location of OB at the far molar end of a molecular-to-molar continuum may mean that the setting restrictions on the field severely limits the kinds of cognitive issues that can be addressed and the way they can be addressed. If, for example, molar issues can be addressed only with demonstrative research, careful consideration must be given to how to incorporate cognitive work into the molar domain. Rather than conducting more and more demonstrations of transfer, it may be more valuable to move to application research or to drop back to more molecular levels in order to advance the field.

CONCLUSION

In all disciplines of human behavioral research, current theories and models of human behavior are being strongly influenced by the cognitive sciences. Organizational behavior is no exception. Yet, we concluded that much of the cognitive research in organizational behavior has suffered from two major limitations. First, initial cognitive research in OB has been demonstrative, showing only that the cognitive phenomena are applicable to organizational settings. Far too frequently research efforts are not carried on beyond these initial demonstrations. The failure to move beyond demonstrations occurs for many reasons. One likely reason is that researchers in the field are often not motivated to keep up with the rapid advancements in the basic cognitive literature, much of which is at a very micro level of analysis. Yet, as Lord and Maher (1991a) have shown, there is a great deal of the basic cognitive work that has potential for addressing important concerns in organizational behavior. Therefore, if the cognitive work in organizational behavior is to make a lasting contribution, it is going to need to become more immersed in the models and constructs of the basic disciplines from which it is drawn.

A second reason for the preponderance of demonstrative research is more fundamental to the nature of OB as a discipline and less easily changed, assuming the interest is to move away from primarily demonstrative research. In particular, as the cognitive constructs of interest operate at more molar levels, it is apparently more difficult to move research beyond the demonstrative stage. Evidence for this conclusion is provided by Gardner (1985) who also observed that the balance of research studies in the cognitive literature tipped toward the demonstrative type as one moved toward more inclusive constructs at the macro level. In Gardner's case, the macro end of the continuum was far more micro than is the case for most organizational research. Therefore, the level of the constructs that are typically of interest in OB may inhibit advancing from demonstrative forms of research.

Nevertheless, if advances are to continue, it is our opinion that more richly articulated theories of limited behavior domains in organizations with cognitive constructs must be developed and subjected to empirical investigation. We are encouraged by the fact that there is more evidence of such work in the last 4 years. Image theory (Beach, 1990; Mitchell & Beach, 1990) and Lord and Maher's (1991b) leadership theory are good examples of this work. In both, the authors have relied upon findings in the cognitive literatures and, at the same time, imbedded these findings in a well developed network of propositions that incorporate essential features of behavior in organizations by individuals who interact over time. Furthermore, the necessary concerns for situations/contexts, ecological validity and relatively long term relationships should position those in organizational behavior well for addressing the problems faced when attempting to incorporate situations and individuals' past history into cognitive models. All these factors lead to the conclusion that, although some changes are needed in the overall pattern of cognitive research and theory in organizations, there are some exciting theories to be pursued and there is potential for making contributions to both the OB literature, in particular, and there is cognitive science literature in general.

REFERENCES

Ackerman, P. L. (1987). Individual differences in skill learning: An integration of psychometrics and information processing perspectives. *Psychological Bulletin, 102*, 3–27.

Atkinson, J. W., & Birch, D. (1970). *The dynamics of action.* New York: Wiley.

Bandura, A. (1991). Social Cognitive Theory of Self-Regulation. *Organizational Behavior and Human Decision Processes, 50*, 248–287.

Beach, L. R. (1990). *Image theory: Decision making in personal and organizational contexts.* London: Wiley.

Beach, L. R., & Mitchell, T. R. (1987). Image theory: Principles, goals and plans in decision making. *Acta Psychologica, 66*, 201–220.

Beach, L. R., & Mitchell, T. R. (1990). Image theory: A behavioral theory of decisions in organizations. In B. M. Staw & L. L. Cummings (Eds.), *Research in organizational behavior* (Vol. 12, pp. 1–42). Greenwich, CT: JAI Press.

Bettman, J. R., Johnson, E. J., & Payne, J. W. (1990). A componential analysis of cognitive effort in choice. *Organizational Behavior and Human Decision Processes, 45*, 111–139.

Carver, C. S., & Scheier, M. F. (1981). *Attention and self-regulation: A control theory approach to human behavior.* New York: Springer-Verlag.

Cherulnik, P. D., Turns, L. C., & Wilderman, S. K. (1990). Physical appearance and leadership: Exploring the role of appearance-based attribution in leader emergence. *Journal of Applied Social Psychology, 20*, 1530–1539.

Chi, M., Glaser, R., & Farr, M. *The nature of expertise.* Hillsdale, NJ: Lawrence Erlbaum Associates.

Deci, E. L. (1992). On the nature and functions of motivation theories. *Psychological Sciences, 3*, 167–171.

DeNisi, A. S., Robbins, T., & Cafferty, T. P. (1989). Organization of information used for performance appraisals: Role of diary-keeping. *Journal of Applied Psychology, 74*, 124–129.

Dweck, C. S. (1992). The study of goals in psychology. *Psychological Sciences, 3*, 165–166.

Fisk, A. D., & Gallini, J. K. (1989). Training consistent components of tasks: Developing an instructional system based on automatic/controlled processing principles. *Human Factors, 31*, 453–463.

Gardner, H. (1985). *The mind's new science.* New York: Basic Books.

Gist, M. E. (1989). The influence of training method on self-efficacy and idea generation among managers. *Personnel Psychology, 42*, 787–805.

Harmon, J., & Rohrbaugh, J. (1990). Social judgment analysis and small group decision making: Cognitive feedback effects on individual and collective performance. *Organizational Behavior and Human Decision Processes, 46*, 34–54.

Hedge, J. W., & Kavanagh, M. J. (1988). Improving the accuracy of performance evaluations: Comparison of three methods of performance appraiser training. *Journal of Applied Psychology, 73*, 68–73.

Hollenbeck, J. (1989). Control theory and the perception of work environments: The effects of focus of attention on affective and behavioral reactions to work. *Organizational Behavior and Human Decision Processes, 43*, 406–430.

Hulin, C. L. (1982). Some reflections on general performance dimensions and halo rating error. *Journal of Applied Psychology, 67*, 165–170.

Ilgen, D. R., Barnes-Farrell, J. L., & McKellin, D. B. (1993). Performance appraisal process research in the 1980s: What has it contributed to appraisals in use? *Organizational Behavior and Human Decision Processes, 54*, 321–368.

Ilgen, D. R., & Feldman, J. M. (1983). Performance appraisal: A process focus. In L. L. Cummings & B. M. Staw (Eds.), *Research in Organizational Behavior, 5* (pp. 141–199). Greenwich, CT: JAI Press.

Ilgen, D. R., & Klein, H. J. (1989). Organizational behavior. *Annual Review of Psychology, 40*, 327–351.

Johnson-Laird, P. N. (1983). *Mental models: Toward a cognitive science of language, inference, and consciousness.* Cambridge, MA: Harvard University Press.

Kanfer, R. (1990). Motivation theory in industrial-organizational psychology. In M. D. Dunnette & L. M. Hough (Eds.), *Handbook of industrial and organizational psychology* (2nd ed.), (Vol. 1, pp. 75–170). San Diego, CA: Psychological Corporation.

Kanfer, R. (1992). Work motivation: New directions in theory and research. In C. L. Cooper & I. T. Robertson (Eds.), *International review of industrial and organizational psychology*, (Vol. 7, pp. 1–53). London: Wiley.

Kanfer, R., & Ackerman, P. L. (1989). Motivation theory and cognitive abilities: An integrative aptitude-treatment interaction approach to skill acquisition. [Monograph]. *Journal of Applied Psychology, 74*, 657–690.

Karl, S. A., & Wexley, K. N. (1989). Patterns of performance and rating frequency: Influence on the assessment of performance. *Journal of Management, 15* 5–20.

Klein, H. J. (1989). An integrated control theory of work motivation. *Academy of Management Review, 14*, 150–173.

Lance, C. E., Woehr, D. J., & Fisicaro, S. A. (1991). Cognitive categorization processes in performance evaluation: Confirmatory tests of two models. *Journal of Organizational Behavior, 12*, 1–20.

Langer, E. J. (1978). Rethinking the role of thought in social interaction. In J. H. Harvey et al., (Eds.), *New directions in attribution research* (Vol. 2). *Hillsdale, NJ: Lawrence Erlbaum Associates.*

Leigh, T. W., & McGraw, P. F. (1989). Mapping the procedural knowledge of industrial sales personnel: A script-theoretic investigation. *Journal of Marketing, 53*, 16–34.

Locke, E. A. (1991a). Goal theory vs. control theory: Contrasting approaches to understanding work motivation. *Motivation and Emotion, 15*, 9–28.

Locke, E. A. (1991b). The motivation sequence, the motivation hub, and the motivation core. *Organizational Behavior and Human Decision Processes, 50*, 288–299.

Locke, E. A., & Latham, G. P. (1990). *A theory of goal setting and task performance.* Englewood Cliffs, NJ: Prentice-Hall.

Longnecker, C. O., Gioia, D. A., & Sims, H. P., Jr. (1987). Behind the mask: The politics of employee appraisal. *Executive, 1*, 183–189.

Lord, R. G., & Hanges, P. J. (1987). A control systems model of organizational motivation: Theoretical development and applied implications. *Behavioral Sciences, 32*, 161–178.

Lord, R. G., & Maher, K. J. (1989). Cognitive processes in industrial and organizational psychology. In C. L. Cooper & I. T. Robertson (Eds.), *International Review of Industrial and Organizational Psychology 1989* (pp. 49–92). London: Wiley.

Lord, R. G., & Maher, K. J. (1991a). Cognitive theory in industrial and organizational psychology. In M. D. Dunnette & L. M. Hough (Eds.), *Handbook of industrial and organizational psychology, Volume 2, Second Edition* (pp. 1–62). Palo Alto, CA: Consulting Psychologist Press.

Lord, R. G., & Maher, K. J. (1991b). *Leadership and information processing: Linking perceptions and performance.* New York: HarperCollins.

Maheswaran, D., & Chaiken, S. (1991). Promoting systematic processing in low-motivation settings: Effect of incongruent information on processing and judgment. *Journal of Personality and Social Psychology, 61*, 13–25.

Martin, S. L., & Klimoski, J. J. (1990). Use of verbal protocols to trace cognitions associated with self and supervisor evaluations of performance. *Organizational Behavior and Human Decision Processes, 46*, 135–154.

Maurer, T. J., & Lord, R. G. (1991). An exploration of cognitive demands in group interaction as a moderator of information processing variables in perceptions of leadership. *Journal of Applied Social Psychology, 21*, 821–839.

Medin, D. L., & Ross, B. H. (1990). *Cognitive psychology*. New York: Harcourt Brace.

Milkovich, G. T., & Wigdor, A. K. (Eds.). (1991). *Pay for performance: Evaluating performance appraisal and merit pay*. Washington, DC: National Academy Press.

Mitchell, T. R. (1974). Expectancy models of job satisfaction, occupational preference and effort: A theoretical, methodological and empirical appraisal. *Psychological Bulletin, 81*, 1053–1077.

Mitchell, T. R., & Beach, L. (1990). '. . . Do I love thee? Let me count . . . ': Toward an understanding of intuitive and automatic decision making. *Organizational Behavior and Human Decision Processes, 47*, 1–20.

Murphy, K. R., & Balzer, W. K. (1989). Rating errors and rating accuracy. *Journal of Applied Psychology, 74*, 619–624.

Murphy, K. R., & Cleveland, J. N. (1991). *Performance appraisal: An organizational perspective*. Boston: Allyn & Bacon.

Murphy, K. R., Philbin, T. A., & Adams, S. R. (1989). The effect of purpose of observation on accuracy of immediate and delayed performance ratings. *Organizational Behavior and Human Decision Processes, 43*, 336–354.

Murphy, K. R., & Reynolds, D. H. (1988). Does true halo affect observed halo? *Journal of Applied Psychology, 73*, 235–238.

Naylor, J. C., Pritchard, R. D., & Ilgen, D. R. (1980). *A theory of behavior in organizations*. New York: Academic Press.

Pervin, L. A. (1992). The rational mind and the problem of volition. *Psychological Sciences, 3*, 162–164.

Phye, G. D. (1989). Schemata training and transfer of an intellectual skill. *Journal of Educational Psychology, 81*, 347–352.

Phye, G. D. (1990). Inductive problem solving: Schema inducement and memory-based transfer. *Journal of Educational Psychology, 82*, 826–831.

Porac, J. F., & Howard, T. (1990). Taxonomic mental models in competitor definition. *Academy of Management Review, 15*, 224–240.

Sein, M. K., & Robey, D. (1991). Learning style and the efficacy of computer training methods. *Perceptual and Motor Skills, 72*, 243–248.

Shaw, J. B. (1990). A cognitive categorization model for the study of intercultural management. *Academy of Management Review, 15*, 626–645.

Simon, H. A. (1992). What is an "explanation" of behavior? *Psychological Science, 3*, 150–161.

Sims, R. R., & Sims, S. J. (1991). Improving training in the public sector. *Public Personnel Management, 20*, 71–82.

Staw, B. M. (1980). Rationality and justification in organizational life. In B. M. Staw & L. L. Cummings (Eds.), *Research in Organizational Behavior* (Vol. 2, pp. 45–80). Greenwich, CT: JAI Press.

Steiner, D. D., & Rain, J. S. (1989). Immediate and delayed primacy and recency effects in performance evaluation. *Journal of Applied Psychology, 74*, 136–142.

Vroom, V. H. (1964). *Work and motivation*. New York: Wiley.

Weiner, B. (1974). An attributional interpretation of expectancy-value theory. In B. Weiner (Ed.), *Cognitive views of human motivation* (pp. 51–69). New York: Academic Press.

Weiner, B. (1980). *Human motivation*. New York: Holt, Rinehart & Winston.

Weiner, B. (1985). An attributional theory of achievement, motivation and emotion. *Psychological Review, 92*, 548–573.

Weiner, B. (1986). *An attributional theory of motivation and emotion*. New York: Springer-Verlag.

Weiner, N. (1948). *Cybernetics: Control and communication in the animal and the machine*. Cambridge: MIT Press.

Wofford, J. C., & Goodwin, V. L. (1990). Effects of feedback on cognitive processing and choice of decision style. *Journal of Applied Psychology, 75*, 603–612.

Wood, R. E., & Bandura, A. (1989a). Impact of conceptions of ability on self-regulatory mechanisms and complex decision making. *Journal of Personality and Social Psychology, 56,* 407–415.

Wood, R. E., & Bandura, A. (1989b). Social cognitive theory of organizational management. *Academy of Management Review, 14,* 361–384.

Wyer, R. S., & Srull, T. K. (1986). Human cognition in its social context. *Psychological Review, 93,* 322–359.

2

MOTIVATION THROUGH JOB DESIGN

Ricky W. Griffin
Texas A&M University

Gary C. McMahon
University of Southern California

Job design is one of the most discussed and studied concepts in the entire field of organizational behavior (O'Reilly, 1991). Indeed, job design has become one of the core topics, alongside the study of individual differences, motivation, leadership, group dynamics, and a few others, that comprises the fundamental literature in the field. This chapter summarizes the historical development of job design theory and research, describes current theory and research regarding job design, and suggests new directions that job design theory and research might more fruitfully pursue in the future.

THE NATURE OF JOB DESIGN

Although job design has a generally accepted meaning in the field, there is also some ambiguity as to its meaning. Thus, we begin by defining job design and highlighting its importance. We then discuss the motivational basis of job design and summarize early approaches to job design.

The Meaning of Job Design

Over the years, the term *job design* has been used interchangeably with terms such as task design and work design. In general, this usage is usually meant to convey an approach to structuring the individuals' jobs so as to optimize such organizational outcomes as efficiency, quality, and productivity with such individual outcomes as satisfaction, motivation, and personal growth. This perspective on jobs has generally been differentiated from attempts to better understand job properties for selection and training purposes (i.e., job analysis), compensation purposes (i.e., job evaluation), and efficiency purposes with little regard for humanistic consideration (i.e., human factors). In this chapter we use job design to refer to the study of jobs, tasks, and constellations of tasks that encompass properties, perceptions, and responses to properties and/or perceptions. It thus includes job enrichment, job enlargement, job characteristics models, and social information processing perspectives.

The Motivational Basis of Job Design

It is the motivational basis of job design that gives the topic its essential identity and focus. Although not every approach to job design deals with motivation, motivation is nevertheless one of the most common outcome variables studied in relation to jobs. Moreover, even perspectives that do not explicitly include motivation often consider performance, satisfaction, effort, and absenteeism, all of which can be linked with motivation. The goal of some approaches has been to learn how to design jobs so as to improve motivation. In other instances, the presumed relationship has been more indirect and the focus has been on improving related phenomena such as job satisfaction or organizational commitment.

Regardless of how it is cloaked, the basic thrust of most job design theory and research has rested on the premise that job design and motivation are linked. The implicit belief that has guided this work has been that the design of jobs can be altered so as to motivate job incumbents to work harder, do higher quality work, do more work, and be more satisfied as a result of having worked.

Early Approaches to Job Design

Although the historical details cannot be clearly documented, job specialization as expounded by Adam Smith (1776) was probably the first formal attempt to design jobs in the context of some framework of efficiency. Frederick Taylor's scientific management (Taylor, 1911) represented the first modern effort to design jobs to bring about some desired organizationally relevant outcome.

As some of the fundamental shortcomings of extreme specialization began to surface (i.e., boredom, low levels of job satisfaction and motivation), managers and researchers attempted for the first time to optimize organizational and individual considerations. Organizations experimented first with job rotation and then job enlargement in an effort to enhance employee satisfaction and motivation while simultaneously improving performance. Ultimately, however, researchers learned that these approaches to job design were so simplistic in their assumptions and operationalizations that they had very little real impact (see Griffin, 1982 for a review).

THE JOB ATTRIBUTES APPROACH

Herzberg's early work on job enrichment served to focus renewed attention on the importance of jobs in organizational settings (Herzberg, 1966, 1968). Most modern approaches to the study of job design, however, can trace their roots to early work that was concerned with identifying and studying job attributes. In a landmark study Turner and Lawrence (1965) studied and identified the effects of six job attributes—variety, autonomy, required social interaction, opportunities for social interaction, knowledge and skill required, and responsibility. They found that these attributes were positively associated with attendance but not satisfaction. Further analysis of their data led them to conclude that some employees were more satisfied with jobs with higher levels of these attributes, and other employees were less satisfied with the presence of those same attributes.

Hulin and Blood (1968) extended the role of individual differences by introducing the Protestant work ethic (Weber, 1947) constructed into the job design literature. Hackman and Lawler (1971) refined this construct by reframing it into a motivational context. They suggested that higher order need strength was the key moderator in the relationship between perceptions of task attributes and various outcome variables.

The task attributes approach reached its culmination with the development of the job characteristics model (Hackman & Oldham, 1976, 1980). The job characteristics theory suggests that five core job dimensions (skill variety, task identify, task significance, autonomy, and feedback) influence three critical psychological states (experienced meaningfulness of the work, experienced responsibility for outcomes of the work, and knowledge of the actual results of work activities). These states, in turn, are predicted to affect four outcome variables (high internal work motivation, high quality work performance, high satisfaction with the work, and low absenteeism and turnover). Employee growth need strength was predicted to moderate the relationships between core job dimensions and critical psychological states, and between the psychological states and the outcomes.

The job characteristics theory spurred a large body of research. Although much of this work was generally favorable (e.g., Orpen, 1979), it was also subject to criticism on a number of points. For example, as noted by Roberts and Glick (1981), the research evidence is often contradictory and most of it is subject to common-method variance problems. For example, most research on the job characteristics theory has relied heavily on a single instrument, the Job Diagnostic Survey (Hackman & Oldham, 1980). Still, the job characteristics theory has come to occupy a prominent niche in the organizational behavior literature (O'Reilly, 1991).

THE SOCIAL INFORMATION PROCESSING APPROACH

In response to criticism regarding the job characteristics theory, Salancik and Pfeffer (1977, 1978) proposed an alternative perspective on job design called the social information processing (SIP) view. Salancik and Pfeffer pointed out that existing models of job design are based on the assumption that individuals in organizations have fundamental needs they desire to satisfy and that properly designed jobs can be an important avenue for achieving need satisfaction. They argued against the validity of this assumption and also called into question the distinction between perceived and objective job properties. In particular, they argued that the social environment of people in organizations provides them with cues about which dimensions are salient and how those dimensions should be weighted and evaluated.

Several studies were conducted and published purporting to test the SIP approach (e.g., Griffin, 1983; O'Reilly & Caldwell, 1979; Weiss & Shaw, 1979). These studies usually provided subjects with social cues about the jobs they were performing and then assessed differences in perceptions and attitudes between those who received positive cues and those who received no cues or negative cues.

The results of this body of research were both encouraging and troubling. On the one hand, the SIP model received generally positive support (see Thomas & Griffin, 1983, for a review). On the other hand, little evidence was uncovered to refute the basic premises of the job characteristics theory.

To better assess the relative merits of the job characteristics theory and the SIP model, Griffin, Bateman, Wayne, and Head (1987) designed and conducted a sophisticated laboratory experiment to test both main and interactive effects of objective task properties and social cues about those tasks. The results provided reasonable support for both the job characteristics theory and the SIP approach. However, even stronger support was found for an interactive model that suggested that job characteristics and social cues work in concert to shape perceptions and attitudes.

In contrast to the job characteristics theory (cf. Griffin, 1991), however, there have been no long-term field studies of the social information processing model nor of the interactive model proposed by Griffin et al. (1987). Thus, field support for either the SIP model or a simple interactive model is unfortunately weak.

CONTEMPORARY PERSPECTIVES ON JOB DESIGN

During the past few years there have been several interesting and progressive attempts to re-energize the field of job design. Three recent developments in the job design literature will be discussed in this section.

First, we discuss the interdisciplinary approach to job design (Campion, 1988; Campion & Thayer, 1985). This approach focuses on the need to integrate the diverse views of and perspectives on job design from the fields of industrial engineering, industrial psychology, organizational behavior, human factors engineering, and work physiology.

Next, we examine an approach to studying job design called job-role differentiation (JRD). This approach was introduced and developed by Ilgen and

Hollenbeck (1992). The premise behind this perspective is the need to link role theory with job theory to allow for a more comprehensive study of work structures.

Finally, we summarize an integrated approach to job design proposed by Griffin (1987). This approach integrates the key aspects of the motivational models of job design into what the author describes as a midrange theory. The major contribution of this theory is the integration of job characteristics theory (Hackman and Oldham, 1976) and the social information processing model of Salancik and Pfeffer (1977, 1978).

The Interdisciplinary Approach

Campion and associates (e.g., Campion, 1988; Campion & Thayer, 1985) introduced the interdisciplinary approach to job design as a mechanism for integrating various schools of thought into a single job design literature. Campion has argued that there are actually several distinct approaches to studying jobs. Each of these approaches is supported by a separate discipline with its own body of literatures. The four distinct approaches that together comprise the interdisciplinary perspective are the motivational approach, the mechanistic approach, the perceptual-motor approach, and the biological approach.

The Motivational Approach. As described and defined by Campion & Thayer (1985), their motivational approach to job design is a view quite similar to the conceptualizations of job design developed from the organizational perspective. Grounded in the earlier work on job enrichment, job enlargement, and various characteristics of jobs, the motivational approach has primarily been developed within the domain and scope of organizational behavior and organizational psychology. The motivational approach has generally searched for job design constructs that will be correlated with such primary outcomes variables as satisfaction, motivation, involvement, absenteeism, and job performance.

Recent arguments from the motivational approach have suggested that if organizations attempt to make jobs more motivating by adding greater skill and ability requirements, the jobs may also have significantly longer training times and be more expensive and difficult to staff. Increased skill and responsibility requirements may also require higher compensation (Campion & Berger, 1990). Finally, motivating jobs may require such higher levels of involvement and commitment that employees may be faced with mental overload, stress, fatigue, and lower output quality.

The Mechanistic Approach. The mechanistic approach to job design draws primarily from the literature on industrial engineering. The early foundation of this approach was developed by Taylor (1911) and Gilbreth (1911) and included basic ideas and arguments from scientific management, time and motion study, and work simplification practices (Campion, 1988). The emphasis of this perspective has generally been on improving the efficiency with which jobs can be performed. Jobs that are constructed according to the mechanistic approach require less training and are less expensive to staff. In essence, the jobs are simplified and have lower levels of responsibility. With mental demands being lower, output quality may increase and compensation requirements may be reduced (Campion, 1989).

On the other hand, the mechanistic approach may carry with it additional costs. These costs include lower job satisfaction and motivation due to boredom brought on by repetitive, simple tasks. In addition, health problems may also result from the physical demands associated with repetitive, machine-paced work.

The Perceptual-Motor Approach. The perceptual-motor approach is derived from research on human factors engineering. This approach has its roots in experimental psychology, which tends to focus on job skills levels and information processing requirements. The perceptual-motor approach emphasizes the limitations and capabilities of job incumbents in their person-machine interactions. Campion and Medsker (1992) suggested that the researchers dealing with the perceptual-motor approach are more concerned with machinery and technology than are psychologists and are more concerned with abilities than are engineers.

The presumed benefits of the perceptual-motor approach include the increase in output quality and a predicted decrease in accident rates due to the emphasis on the reliability and safety of the job. The reduced mental demands of the job would also reduce employee stress and fatigue.

Campion and Medsker (1992) also noted that if the perceptual-motor approach is excessively applied, the costs might include lower satisfaction, lower motivation, and an increase in boredom. The reason for these costs is the lack of mental stimulation from the work, as the limit on a jobs' mental requirements is dictated by the least capable employee.

The Biological Approach. The biological approach stems from research on work physiology, ergonomics, biomechanics (body movements), and anthropometry (body sizes) (Campion, 1989). This approach focuses on designing jobs that have low levels of physical stress and physical discomfort. Although it is similar to the perceptual-motor approach in its focus on equipment and workplace considerations, the biological approach is differentiated by its focus on more physiological concerns based on ergonomics, whereas the perceptual-motor approach is more psychologically oriented based on human factors engineering.

Jobs designed from the biological approach may result in less fatigue and fewer physical injuries than jobs designed with no consideration for biological factors. Due to the reduction in occupational illness, there may also be an increase in job satisfaction and lowered absenteeism. The costs of jobs designed from the biological approach include the expense of equipment necessary to reduce the physical demands of work. In addition, jobs that have few physical demands may cause an increase in boredom and potentially have a negative impact on job performance and turnover.

Evident from the discussions of each approach, there are four hypothesized primary outcome variables (Campion, 1988). The motivational approach is associated with a satisfaction outcome, the mechanistic approach with an efficiency outcome, the perceptual-motor approach with a reliability outcome, and the biological approach is associated with a comfort outcome. Similar to the job characteristics theory, the interdisciplinary perspective was introduced in concert with a measurement instrument, the Multimethod Job Design Question-naire (MJDQ) (Campion, 1985). The current form of the instrument (MJDQ; Campion, 1988) is a 48-item, self-report questionnaire, which assesses the job elements associated with each job design approach. The measure has acceptable psychometric qualities (Campion, 1988; Campion & McClelland, 1991) and convergent and discriminant validity (Campion, Kosiak, & Langford, 1988) with the Job Diagnostic Survey (Hackman & Oldham, 1980).

The strength of the interdisciplinary approach is the simultaneous recognition it brings to somewhat competing job design approaches. Due to the state of the field of job design, researchers are being pushed to provide more integrated or sophisti-cated models of work systems. Industry has also recognized the competing disciplines when work models are attempted to be transferred to the workplace. As Campion (1988) previously pointed out, the competing theories can be found in the functional disciplines inside organizations. Organizational development consult-ants, human resource professionals, industrial engineers, and quality professionals all tend to be guided by their own set of job theories. The interdisciplinary model takes important first steps, from a research perspective, in recognizing the various schools of thought on job design and the various approaches that exist.

A weakness of the interdisciplinary approach is the challenge that exists for researchers to use the model. Many times we, as researchers, become "believers" in our own respective disciplines and tend to take sides (i.e., motivational proponents vs. efficiency proponents) as if we have a cause to protect. As stated earlier, for the field of job design to progress, we must start to understand and accept the complexities that alternative models provide. Each discipline has its own collection of research findings, some complement other approaches and some do not, but the field has matured to the point where it is shortsighted to ignore alternative theories, because they come from different disciplines other than our own.

A second weakness may be the theoretical grounding of the interdisciplinary approach. Future work may be necessary to improve the integration among the various approaches into a clear, understandable theoretical framework. Addition-ally, future theoretical development should include the recognition of individual differences and social cues that may impact individual perceptions of jobs.

Finally, as with other job design and organizational behavior research, measurement concerns also exist with the interdisciplinary model. The primary measurement instrument, the Multimethod Job Design Questionnaire (MJDQ), is self-report. As Campion and associates (cf. Campion & Thayer, 1985; Campion & McClelland, 1991) have attempted in recent work, other more "objective" measures should also be used in conjunction with the MJDQ. Future research using the Campion measures should also explore the problems associated with common method variance and item overlap.

The interdisciplinary approach offers an exciting integrative perspective that involves most major disciplines of job design. However, for this approach to be successful in the eyes of the research community, the model must become more widely accepted and used by researchers other than Campion and associates.

Job-Role Differentiation

Ilgen and Hollenbeck (1992) recently introduced an approach to the study of job design called job-role differentiation (JRD). This approach attempts to link, through clear differentiation, the often disparate literature on jobs and roles. The authors stated that JRD is an initial and necessary step in the process to fully integrate these two research domains.

An important assumption of JRD is the definitional distinction the authors make between jobs and roles. Relying on Blau and Scott's (1962) concept of prime beneficiaries and the idea of breaking jobs down into basic task elements (called the universe of task elements), the authors define jobs as "a set of task elements grouped together under one job title and designed to be performed by a single individual" (p. 173). Roles are defined as "larger sets containing emergent task elements plus those elements of the jobs that are communicated to the job incumbent through the social system and maintained in that system" (p. 174).

The authors suggested that jobs can be defined through objective task elements. However, jobs actually function in an environment only when additional task elements are added to the original elements that define the job. These additional or emergent task elements are specified by the social environment, as well as the job incumbent, and are described as subjective, dynamic, and specified by social sources beyond the prime beneficiaries. Therefore, work roles are differentiated from jobs by relegating only original task elements to jobs, and both original and emergent task elements to work roles.

The central argument is that the job design literature focuses too narrowly on the content of the elements called jobs. The authors define the job design literature quite narrowly, referring primarily to the job characteristics theory. The current study of job design emphasizes the physical demands of the task and the research focuses on establishing the objectivity of job perceptions. On the other hand, the role literature emphasizes the process whereby the expected set of behaviors called a role is established. The role literature tends toward the subjective reality that results from the process of sharing expectations between the role sender and the focal person.

Therefore, according to this logic, a job is regarded as a formal set of task elements influenced by an organization's prime beneficiaries. Roles include both formal and emergent task elements. An emergent task element may eventually evolve into a formal task element if there is consensus among members of a role set that the element is necessary or if the prime beneficiaries decide that the task should be formally established for all job incumbents.

Through a process of differentiation, the JRD approach is used to bridge the empirical and theoretical research on job design and roles. The concepts of *content* and *objectivity* from the job design literature are applied to the role literature. Process and social diversity in task expectations from the role literature are applied to the job design literature. By taking this approach, new perspectives are developed on a variety of overlapping issues in the job and role literatures. The authors propose an interesting argument for the fact that studying job design is a necessary but not sufficient condition for studying work structures. The same argument can be used for roles. These points provide the basis of this call to integrate job design and role theories.

The strength of the JRD approach to job design is the important, though not novel, call for integrating job and role literatures. The larger concern that this work focuses on is the need to understand the subjective realities that exist in jobs. The study of jobs from a strictly objective sense is quite antiquated. Campion's interdisciplinary approach, discussed earlier in this section, may be an early victim due to the model's highly objective slant. Ilgen and Hollenbeck provided a necessary contribution to the field by restating the need to perform research from both a subjective and objective framework.

An obvious weakness of the JRD approach is that the model doesn't go any further than making an argument for integrating role and job theories. Although the authors never claim to posit a theoretical model, an attempt to develop their ideas further may have been useful.

The Integrated Approach

In an effort to move the field of motivational job design ahead, Griffin (1987) introduced an integrated theory of task design. Figure 2.1 summarizes this integrated theory. The intent of the theory is to provide natural extensions to the dominant, though somewhat divergent, job characteristics theory (Hackman & Oldham, 1976) and social information processing approach (Salancik & Pfeffer, 1977, 1978).

The key concepts and variables of the theory are *job, role, task, perception, attitude,* and *behavior.* A job is defined by Griffin (1987) as the "array of elements and dimensions of the organization with which the individual comes into contact" (p. 94). A role is defined as the decision making latitude of the person performing the task. The task is defined as "the set of prescribed activities a person normally

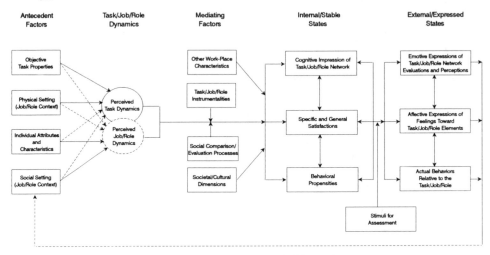

FIG. 2.1.   The integrated model of job design.

performs during a typical work period" (p. 94). Perception refers to the processes individuals use to become aware of, interpret, and organize information gathered through their senses. Attitudes are generalized feelings individuals have toward an object or referent, in this case, their jobs, roles, and tasks. Relevant behaviors include performance, absenteeism and turnover. In addition, individuals are assumed to have choices, within boundaries, regarding the levels of any possible behaviors.

The integrated theory develops four antecedent factors to understand job related phenomenona. These factors are the objective task properties, the physical setting, the individual attributes and characteristics, and the social setting. These antecedent factors are presumed to determine what Griffin referred to as task and job role dynamics. This set of dynamics is comprised of perceived dimensions of the task, the job and the work role.

The task and job role dynamics are the hypothesized to create three internal/ stable states. These internal/stable states include cognitive impressions of the task and job role, specific and general satisfactions, and behavioral propensities. The relationship between the perceived task and job role dynamics and the internal/ stable states is far from independent. For example, it is presumed to be mediated by a variety of factors including social comparison-evaluation processes, societal/ cultural dimensions, task and job role instrumentalities, and other workplace characteristics.

The internal/stable states are predicted to cause external-expressed states. These external-expressed states include emotive expressions of task and job role evaluations and perception, affective expressions of feelings toward task and job role elements and actual exhibited behaviors. Griffin (1987) stated the "actual correspondence between external/expressed and their analogous internal/stable states will be affected by mood, emotion, and other salient experiences, and will be mediated by the nature of the stimuli that elicits the expressed state to be made public" (p. 112).

As noted earlier, the integrated theory of task design was expressly introduced to extend and integrate the job characteristics theory and social information processing approach to job design. In contrast to the job characteristics theory, for example, the integrated model represents a comprehensive conceptualization of work design processes. The boundaries of the integrated theory are more encompassing and its potential for explaining workplace phenomena is greater. In comparison to the social information processing model, the integrated theory is far more precise and focused in its approach to task perceptions and attitudes (Griffin, 1987). The integrated theory provides a clearer specification and prediction of the construct relationships.

The integrated theory was introduced as an attempt to demonstrate how the two dominant motivational models of job design can be linked in such a way as to capitalize on their relative strengths, and with the assistance of other organizational concepts, overcome some of their relative weaknesses.

Griffin's integrated theory takes the necessary risks to provide a highly sophisticated model of motivational approaches to job design. The strength of the integrative approach is that it provides a well developed theory. In some ways the strength of the integrative model may also be its weakness. The model is so complex, researchers have been unable to move it forward. Future research relying on this model must show how to turn the propositions into testable hypotheses.

Summary

These three new developments in the job design literature have provided a renewed sense of interest to this very important area of organizational research. A variety of issues emerge, or re-emerge, from these latest developments. First, although the issue of objectivity has long been a concern in the motivational job design literature, these new developments push forward the philosophical debate between objective and subjective realities (Burrell & Morgan, 1979). Campion's interdisciplinary perspective fails to discuss the issue of objectivity, and therefore implies an objective reality of jobs. Both Griffin's integrated approach and Ilgen and Hollenbeck's JRD perspective emphasize the subjective, social reality of work structures.

Second, each new perspective is at a different stage of theoretical development. The interdisciplinary approach relies on theory from four major disciplines of job design research to develop a measurement tool. Ilgen and Hollenbeck's JRD approach calls for, but does not attempt, theory development to integrate the jobs and roles literature. Griffin offers the most completely developed theoretical model. However, it also suffers form being too general. Moreover, empirical assessment of this theory has been slow, perhaps due to the comprehensiveness of the model.

Finally, the most fascinating result that comes from these contemporary developments to the study of job design is the lack of an approach to overcome, or seriously challenge, the domination of the job characteristics theory. These developments, for one reason or another, have lacked the powerful influence that the original job characteristics theory (Hackman & Oldham, 1976) has had, and continues to have, for this area of research.

Most researchers would agree that the study of jobs is ripe for new ideas and conceptualizations. But these new ideas and conceptualizations are not likely to come at the expense of replacing a long-standing theory that has yet to be refuted (Griffin, 1991). A healthy outlook toward the future study of job design would be to understand these contemporary perspectives as extensions, rather than replacements or competing theories, to the knowledge gained over the past three decades of job design research.

NEW DIRECTIONS FOR JOB DESIGN THEORY AND RESEARCH

In this section we first outline some potentially fruitful new directions for both theory and research. We then focus on three specific perspectives on job design that will likely take on increasing importance in the next few years: group-based approaches to job design, information technology and job design, and international issues in job design.

New Directions for Theory Development

There are two quite different avenues for theory development that might be worth pursuing. The first is for continued midrange theory development work along the lines of the interdisciplinary approach, the job and role differentiation approach, and the integrated approach. Each of these approaches is essentially an extension of existing theory, and each is an effort to take two or more existing frameworks, theories, or models and combine them into a new one. The advantage of such an incremental approach is that the new models that emerge are somewhat more comprehensive than their predecessors. To the extent that the resulting synthesized models yield a more realistic model of job design phenomenon, they do a more effective job of capturing the nature of jobs and individual responses to those jobs. Moreover, each also capitalizes on the known strengths of their component models. On the other hand, these same models are also subject to the same basic weaknesses and shortcomings inherent in the original models from which they are derived.

At any rate, these models seem to hold enough promise to warrant additional attention. Indeed, one logical variation might be to investigate areas where the three existing combinational models might be merged to create a single new integrated model or meta-theory. For example, the work of Griffin and of Ilgen and Hollenbeck include both task and role variables. Similarly, the work of Griffin and of Campion and associates each include both perceptual and objective task elements. The virtue of a single overarching model is that it could focus research more efficiently on a single organizing framework. A major disadvantage of this approach, however, is that the resultant comprehensive model will include an accumulation of all the shortcomings and limitations inherent in each of the existing models used to create it. Also, job design researchers have had little success in testing or attempting to test integrated models in the past (e.g., Griffin, 1987; Salancik & Pfeffer, 1977, 1978).

An alternative direction for new theory would be to start from ground zero. Although existing job design theories, and those from which they were derived, yielded valuable insights into job design processes, they have also failed to completely capture the job design phenomenon. By essentially starting over, scholars could conceivably avoid the conceptual and empirical shortcomings of existing conceptualizations.

If this path were adopted, it would be most helpful to truly start with a blank slate. For example, several fundamental questions could be answered anew: What is a job? What is a task? What is work? How do people conceptualize jobs and work? What are the real antecedents and consequences of jobs, tasks, and work? Of course, this approach is a costly alternative in that a substantial body of existing work gets discounted or ignored altogether. Thus, a midrange approach could instead focus on identifying existing perspectives that could be recast into a job design framework.

Regardless of which direction job design theorists take, however, a lingering question that clearly needs to be addressed is the role of individual differences. Much of the early work dealing with task attributes had important individual difference constructs as a major component. Apparently because much of the empirical work assessing the job characteristics theory found little or conflicting support for the JCT's hypothesized individual difference effects (i.e., growth need strength), many researchers began to ignore or discount the individual difference component. Only recently have individual differences re-emerged as a central component in job design studies (e.g., Hunter, Schmidt, & Judiesch, 1990). The importance of individual differences in job design is intuitively appealing. If for no other reason than this, a more careful and thoughtful conceptualization of individual differences in job design can almost certainly be justified.

New Directions for Research

From a pure research perspective, several observations can also be established. Regardless of whether one takes an incremental or fresh perspective on job design theory, several specific directions can be identified. Foremost among these is measurement. Most research today continues to use the original Job Diagnostic Survey (JDS). Those studies that do not use the JDS usually use either a derivative of the original instrument or Campion's (1988) MJDQ.

More rigorous measures should probably include a self-development portion where job incumbents are allowed to formulate and express their own perceptions of jobs, as opposed to indicating how much of a researcher defined attribute is or is not present in the job. Moreover, future measuring devices need to include some component designed to assess critical elements of the social context within which the job is performed. That social information affects job perceptions and job related attitudes seems sufficiently well documented that not incorporating it seems to be a serious oversight. Depending on how individual differences are incorporated into future job design theory, their measurement may also need to be an integral part of measurement devices in the future.

One fundamental confound that continues to plague research in the job design area is the reliance on job incumbent generated perceptual data. To the extent that theory specifies variable or component based job perceptions, it obviously becomes necessary to measure those variables or components with perceptual apparatus such as questionnaires. But more objective components of theory should always be assessed with objective data of some sort, based on valid measurement strategies and assessed by someone other than job incumbents. Attitudinal outcome variables will also, of course, generally be measured by incumbents. But other outcomes such as performance, effort, and behavioral propensities need to be measured with data from sources other than job incumbents. Only if job design research begins to incorporate new and varied sources of data can it overcome its hallmark weakness of common method variance.

In addition to measurement improvement, researchers should also pursue stronger and more rigorous research designs. New and innovative research designs should also be explored. Several studies exist that rely on experimental designs (e.g., Staw & Boettger, 1990) and/or longitudinal designs (e.g., Griffin, 1991). However, important insights into job design processes may also come from designs that utilize participant observation, self-study, or other qualitative approaches.

Group-Based Approaches to Job Design

The primary focus of the study of job design has been at the individual level of analysis. Recent trends in organizations point to the widespread use of self-managed work teams (Manz & Sims, 1987), quality circles (Ledford, Lawler, & Mohrman, 1988) and other forms of group structures (Goodman, Ravlin, & Schminke, 1987). Due to this increased interest among practicing managers in using work teams, researchers are challenged to expand the job design domain to include group work design.

Debate continues over the most effective way to divide task objectives and associated rewards. For years the field of management was influenced by the scientific management approach, which stressed the need to break jobs down into their most simplistic pieces, and then group these task pieces to create a job. Current personnel management practices of job evaluation and analysis and performance appraisal still remain heavily focused on the individual job. The difference between individual job design and group work design is that the task or set of tasks is assigned to a group of individuals instead of a single individual. Therefore, the work group becomes the unit of performance and associated group controls and rewards must follow.

The literature in the area of group work design is unsurprisingly sparse. Almost all of our knowledge of group-based approaches comes form international studies (which will be discussed later in this section). However, Hackman (1987) provided an interesting insight into the area of group work design. Based on the collective knowledge of years of group research, he identified three primary group design variables.

First, the task itself must motivate group members. To produce a motivated group Hackman provided the following task conditions: (a) the group task should require members to use a variety of higher level skills, (b) the group task should be an identifiable, meaningful piece of work, with a visible outcome, (c) the outcomes of the group's work on the task should have significant consequences for other people, (d) the task should provide group members with substantial autonomy for deciding about how they go about doing the work, and (e) work on the task should generate frequent, accurate feedback about how well the group is performing (Hackman, 1987). This first variable, the task condition, is very similar to the seminal work of Hackman and Oldham (1980) discussed earlier in this chapter. The primary difference is simply that the traditional task characteristics or conditions are being applied at a group level of analysis as opposed to the individual level.

Second, group composition is critical to the effectiveness of the work group. The group should be composed of the right size and mix of members who possess the necessary task skills. Four conditions are delineated with regard to work group composition: (a) individual members should have high task-relevant expertise, (b) the group should just be large enough to perform the work, (c) members should possess interpersonal as well as task skills, and (d) group membership should be moderately diverse (Hackman, 1987).

Finally, group norms are critical to regulate group member behavior and to allow for flexibility in adapting alternative strategies to perform the work. Some form of group norm structuring will emerge in almost all work groups. When designing group work, careful attention should be given to the norm formation process to assure compliance to task-appropriate performance strategies (Hackman, 1987). It is imperative that the norm structure be understood by the work group and/or the managerial team in order to bring about necessary changes if the enforcement structure is dysfunctional to work group effectiveness (McMahan & Kacmar, 1991).

These three group work design variables are critical to achieving the process results necessary for group effectiveness. Hackman (1987) defined the process criteria as (a) having sufficient effort applied to the group task, (b) assuring sufficient knowledge and skill is applied to the group task, and (c) having task-appropriate performance strategies. In addition to the group work design factors just discussed, issues of organizational context and group synergy are necessary ingredients to the normative model of group effectiveness proposed by Hackman (1987).

The need for research in the area of group work design is tremendous. Industry continues to make attempts to redesign work around groups of individuals in efforts to improve productivity and boost quality and responsibility. One of the certainties in future job design research is the inclusion of group level studies.

Information Technology and Job Design

An extremely important area for future job design research concerns the impact of information technology on jobs and job incumbents. Some have stated that information technology (IT) may well be the single most important change affecting the modern day workplace (Gerstein, 1987). Turnage (1990) stated that the rise of automated systems has been compared to the tremendous impact of the Industrial Revolution. Information technology is hypothesized to produce significant impacts at the job and individual levels of analysis.

Zuboff (1985) described two primary types of information technology. First, those technologies that *automate* the task through computer software, hardware, and other mechanisms. Second, those technologies that *informate* the task by going beyond the physical automation stage and allowing the information to be processed and used by the end user. Beard (1991) defined the end user as a worker who interacts with computerized information technologies, but who is not a programmer or analyst. In essence, an automated technology is a necessary but not sufficient condition for an informated technology. Zuboff (1985, 1988) argued that an organization has considerable discretion over the way an information technology can be applied or implemented in the workplace. How to construct the jobs that result from the implementation of IT, is the decision of the job designers in the organization.

Parsons (1988) commented on the relative lack of empirical studies that have examined the changes produced as a result of IT and how they affect humans at work. However, some job design research has been conducted (e.g., Beard, 1991; Franz, Robey, & Koeblitz, 1986; Kling, 1978). These studies rely almost exclusively on the job characteristics theory and the use of the Job Diagnostic Survey. Attewell and Rule (1984), in a review of the information technology literature, found that most questions concerning the impact of IT cannot be answered based on current research. The results of the research that has been conducted reintroduces the traditional debate over the effect of technology on work and individuals (Mesthene, 1970). One argument is that technology is basically bad, in that it deskills the worker and reduces the importance of the individual. On the other hand, technology is viewed as good, in that it tends to upgrade or enrich the work and helps to advance society.

The impasse that exists in the empirical research to date further suggests that the depictions of information technology by Zuboff (1988) and Walton (1990) were accurate. It is the discretion that organization members possess and the decisions they make on how to apply IT in the workplace that creates the real opportunity for job design researchers. What are the effects on jobs and workers when IT is implemented given various organizational objectives? What are the job costs and benefits associated with different types of IT? The use of Campion's (1988) interdisciplinary model may be a fruitful avenue to pursue with regard to these questions. Campion's model focuses on a wider range of approaches and outcomes compared to the more traditional motivational approaches to job design.

Based on limited conceptual and empirical research concerning job design and IT, the need for rigorous, creative studies exists. The future challenges that face the field of job design, or even more the field of organizational behavior, rest in our ability as scholars to change with society and industry by increasing our understanding and predictive ability of organizational phenomena that affects people at work. This knowledge revolution (Drucker, 1988), in which IT is a major factor, is quite possibly the most important phenomenon in the workplace today.

International Issues in Job Design

Finally, international and cross-cultural issues will also become an increasingly important arena for future job design theory and research. Indeed, some of the most influential theory and practice of group based perspectives on job design comes from Europe. Beginning with the early work on sociotechnical systems theory (e.g., Rice, 1958; Trist & Bamforth, 1951), for example, researchers in Great Britain made significant advances. This tradition continues today with the work of Wall, Clegg, and their colleagues at the University of Sheffield (e.g., Wall, Corbett, Clegg, Jackson, & Martin, 1990). The autonomous work group experiments at the Volvo plant at Kalmar, Sweden also received widespread attention (Dowling, 1973) in this regard.

Aside from group-based approaches, however, other international and cross-cultural research on job design has been relatively narrow and restricted. For example, an increasingly common research approach is to take an existing model or instrument like the JDS and apply or administer it to samples of workers in different countries (cf. Birnbaum, Farh, & Wong, 1986). Although these approaches yield some interesting and preliminary insights, they should also clearly be treated as only a first step in understanding job design in different countries and/or cultures.

The basic shortcoming in international and cross-cultural comparisons is that little theoretical work has been done to better allow researchers to understand the validity of basic constructs across cultures. For example, by translating the JDS into different languages and having workers in different countries respond to its questions, it is clearly possible to get different sets of data from which comparisons can be drawn. Unfortunately, such a strategy presupposes that the underlying theoretical constructs, and thus the derived questions in the survey instrument, have meaning in those countries and cultures. Unfortunately, there is little or no theoretical evidence to support such an assumption.

Once again, the necessary starting point is theory. Scholars must start by carefully understanding what work and jobs mean to workers and managers in different cultures. If a job is something a person does to earn a living, the relevant attributes and outcomes of that job will be quite different from the situation where a job represents one's social position in a status hierarchy. Thus, theorists and researchers might be advised to first develop theoretical understanding of job design processes in a particular culture before starting to study them.

England and Harpaz (1990) have taken some promising first steps in this regard with their MOW (meaning of work) research. This and similar work has attempted to develop an understanding of how people in different cultures define work. As this understanding continues to evolve, researchers will be able to more effectively study job design in other countries.

In advancing this line of inquiry, however, researchers will need to seek the appropriate level of compromise between specificity and generalizability. For example, one approach is to study job design processes within a particular culture with such depth and specificity that true understanding of job design in that culture may be achieved. But if substantial cultural variations exist, it will be difficult, if not impossible, to generalize understanding between cultures. Thus, the challenge is to develop a framework for studying international job design processes that allows a meaningful degree of within-culture understanding while simultaneously providing meaningful channels for comparing and contrasting those processes across different cultures.

CONCLUSION

Job design continues to be a dominant area of interest for theorists and researchers interested in understanding human behavior and in organizations. Jobs are the window through which individuals perceive, experience, and contribute to organizations. Similarly, jobs are also the window through which organizations direct the work of individuals in productive ways, assess their value to the organization, and undertake efforts to motivate their behavior.

Just as organizations throughout the world are changing, so too are jobs within those organizations. The job characteristics theory provided a solid foundation for advancing work in this field. Unfortunately, recent attempts to extend and broaden these preliminary perspectives have yet to have a substantive impact on the field.

Although there are many avenues the field might fruitfully follow, perhaps the most logical ones extend to group-based work systems, information technology, and international and cross-cultural issues. Each of these areas is becoming more central to the work of most organizations today. Thus, linking them, either individually or together, with the fundamental relationships between people and their jobs, holds great promise for better understanding how organizations can become more effective.

ACKNOWLEDGMENTS

The authors would like to thank Mike Campion, Jennifer George, Jerry Greenberg, Greg Oldham, Anne O'Leary-Kelly, and Patrick Wright for their helpful comments on an earlier draft of this manuscript.

REFERENCES

Attewell P., & Rule J. (1984). Computing and organizations: What we know and what we don't know. *Communications of the ACM, 27,* 1184–1192.

Beard, J. W. (1991). *Information technology and task design: An examination of the impact of changes in task methods and social information on worker job characteristics perceptions, attitudes, and performance.* Unpublished doctoral dissertation, Texas A&M University, College Station, Texas.

Birnbaum, P. H., Farh, J. L., & Wong, G. Y. (1986). Job characteristics in Hong Kong. *Journal Of Applied Psychology, 71,* 598–605.

Blau, P. M., & Scott, R. S. (1962). *Formal organizations: A comparative approach.* New York: Chandler Publishing.

Burrell, G., & Morgan, G. (1979). *Sociological paradigms and organizational analysis.* London: Heineman.

Campion, M. A. (1985). The multimethod job design questionnaire (MJDQ). *Psychological Documents, 15,* 1.

Campion, M. A. (1988). Interdisciplinary approaches to job design: A constructive replication with extensions. *Journal of Applied Psychology, 73,* 467–481.

Campion, M. A. (1989). Ability requirement implications of job design: An interdisciplinary perspective. *Personnel Psychology, 42,* 1–24.

Campion, M. A., & Berger, C. L. (1990). Conceptual integration and empirical test of job design and compensation relationships. *Personnel Psychology, 43,* 525–553.

Campion, M. A., Kosiak, P. L., & Langford, B. A. (1988, August). *Convergent and discriminant validity of the Multimethod Job Design Questionnaire.* Paper presented at the 96th annual convention of the American Psychological Association, Atlanta, GA.

Campion, M. A., & McClelland, C. L. (1991). Interdisciplinary examination of the costs and benefits of enlarged jobs: A job design quasi-experiment. *Journal of Applied Psychology, 76,* 186–198.

Campion, M. A., & Medsker, G. L. (1992). Job design. In G. Salvendy (Ed.), *Handbook of industrial engineering* (2nd ed.) (pp. 145–173). New York: Wiley.

Campion, M. A., & Thayer, P. W. (1985). Development and field evaluation of an interdisciplinary measure of job design. *Journal of Applied Psychology, 70,* 29–43.

Dowling, W. F., Jr. (1973, Winter). Job redesign on the assembly line. *Organizational Dynamics,* pp. 51–67.

Drucker, P. F. (1988, January–February). The coming of the new organization. *Harvard Business Review,* pp. 45–53.

England, G. W. & Harpaz, I. (1990). How working is defined: National contexts and demographic and organizational roles influences. *Journal of Organizational Behavior, 11*, 253–266.

Franz, C. R., Robey, D., & Koeblitz, R. R. (1986). User response to an online information system: A field experiment. *MIS Quarterly, 10*, 29–42.

Gerstein, M. S. (1987). *The technology connection: Strategy and change in the information age.* Reading, MA: Addison-Wesley.

Gilbreth, F. B. (1911). *Motion study: A Method for increasing the efficiency of the workman.* New York: Van Nostrand.

Goodman, P. S., Ravlin, E. C., & Schminke, M. (1987). Understanding groups in organizations. In B. M. Staw & L. L. Cummings (Eds.), *Research in organizational behavior* (Vol. 9, pp. 121–173). Greenwich, CT: JAI Press.

Griffin, R. W. (1982). *Task design: An integrative approach.* Glenview, IL: Scott, Foresman.

Griffin, R. W. (1983). Objective and social sources of information in task design: A field study experiment. *Administrative Science Quarterly, 28*, 184–200.

Griffin, R. W. (1987). Toward an integrated theory of task design. In Staw, B. & Cummings, L. L. (Eds.), *Research in organizational behavior,* (Vol. 9, pp. 79–120). Greenwich, CT: JAI Press.

Griffin, R. W. (1991). Effects of work redesign on employee perceptions, attitudes and behaviors: A long-term investigation. *Academy of Management Journal, 34*, 425–435.

Griffin, R., Bateman, T., Wayne, S., & Head, T. (1987). Objective and social factors as determinants of task perceptions and responses: An integrated perspective and empirical investigation. *Academy of Management Journal, 30*, 501–523.

Hackman, J. R. (1987). The design of work teams. In J. Lorsch (Ed.), *Handbook of organizational behavior* (pp. 315–342). Englewood Cliffs, NJ: Prentice-Hall.

Hackman, J. R., & Lawler, E. E. (1971). Employee reactions to job characteristics. *Journal of Applied Psychology, 55*, 259–286.

Hackman, J. R., & Oldham, G. R. (1976). Motivation through the design of work: Test of a theory. *Organizational Behavior and Human Performance, 16*, 250–279.

Hackman, J. R., & Oldham, G. R. (1980). *Work design.* Reading, MA: Addison-Wesley.

Herzberg, F. (1966). *Work and the nature of man.* Cleveland, OH: World.

Herzberg, F. (1968, January–February). One more time how do you motivate employees? *Harvard Business Review,* pp. 53–62.

Hulin, C. L. & Blood, M. R. (1968). Job enlargement, individual differences, and worker responses. *Psychological Bulletin, 69*, 41–55.

Hunter, J. E., Schmidt, F. L., & Judiesch, M. K. (1990). Individual differences in output variability as a function of job complexity. *Journal of Applied Psychology, 75*, 28–42.

Ilgen, D. R., & Hollenbeck, J. R. (1992). The structure of work: Job design and roles. In M. Dunette & L. Hough (Eds.), *Handbook of Industrial and Organizational Psychology,* (Volume 2, pp. 165–207). Palo Alto, CA: Consulting Psychological Press.

Kling, R. (1978). *The impacts of computing on the work of managers, data analysts and clerks* [Working Paper, WP-78–64]. Public Policy Research Organization, University of California-Irvine.

Ledford, G. E., Lawler, E. E., & Mohrman, S. A. (1988). The quality circle and its variations. In J. P. Campbell & R. J. Campbell (Eds.), *Productivity in organizations* (pp. 255–294). San Francisco: Jossey-Bass.

Manz, C. C., & Sims, H. P. (1987). Leading workers to lead themselves: The external leadership of self-managing work teams. *Administrative Science Quarterly, 32*, 106–129.

McMahan, G. C., & Kacmar, K. M. (1991). The diagnosis of work group norms: Practical implications for change. *Journal of Organizational Change Management, 4*, 24–33.

Mesthene, E. G. (1970). *Technological change: Its impact on man and society.* Cambridge, MA: Harvard University Press.

O'Reilly, C. A. (1991). Organizational behavior. In M. R. Rosenweig & L. W. Porter (Eds.), *Annual Review of Psychology* (Vol. 42, pp. 427–458). Palo Alto, CA: Annual Reviews, Inc.

O'Reilly, C. A., & Caldwell, D. F. (1979). Informational influence as a determinant of perceived task characteristics and job satisfaction. *Journal of Applied Psychology, 64*, 157–165.

Orpen, C. (1979). The effects of job enrichment on employee satisfaction, motivation and performance: A field experiment. *Human Relations, 32*, 189–217.

Parsons, C. K. (1988). Information technology: Implications for human resource management. In G. R. Ferris & K. M. Rowland (Eds.), *Research in personnel and human resource management*, (Vol. 6, pp. 1–36). Greenwich, CT: JAI Press.

Rice, A. K. (1958). *Productivity and social organization: The Ahmedabad experiment*. London: Tavistock.

Roberts, K. H., & Glick, W. (1981). The job characteristics approach to job design: A critical review. *Journal of Applied Psychology, 66*, 193–217.

Salancik, G., & Pfeffer, J. (1977). An examination of need-satisfaction models of job attitudes. *Administrative Science Quarterly, 22*, 427–456.

Salancik, G., & Pfeffer, J. (1978). A social information processing approach to job attitudes and task design. *Administrative Science Quarterly, 23*, 224–253.

Smith, A. (1776). *An inquiry into the nature and causes of the wealth of nations*. Dublin: Whitestone.

Staw, B. M., & Boettger, R. D. (1990). Task revision: A neglected form of work performance. *Academy of Management Journal, 33*, 534–559.

Taylor, F. W. (1911). *The principles of scientific management*. New York: Norton.

Thomas, J., & Griffin, R. W. (1983). The social information processing model of task design: A review of the literature. *Academy of Management Review, 8*, 672–682.

Trist, E. L., & Bamforth, K. W. (1951). Some social and psychological consequences of the long-wall method of coal-getting. *Human Relations, 4*, 3–38.

Turnage, J. J. (1990). The challenge of new workplace technology for psychology. *American Psychologist, 45*, 171–178.

Turner, A. N., & Lawrence, P. R. (1965). *Individual jobs and the worker*. Cambridge, MA: Harvard University Press.

Wall, T. D., Corbett, J. M., Clegg, C. W., Jackson, P. R., & Martin, R. (1990). Advanced manufacturing technology and work design: Towards a theoretical framework. *Journal of Organizational Behavior, 11*, 201–219.

Walton, R. E. (1990). *Up and running: Integrating information technology and the organization*. Cambridge, MA: Harvard Business School Press.

Weber, M. (1947). *Theory of social and economic organization*. New York: Oxford University Press.

Weiss, H. M., & Shaw, J. B. (1979). Social influences on judgments about tasks. *Organizational Behavior and Human Performance, 24*, 126–140.

Zuboff, S. (1985). Technologies that informate: Implications for human resource management in the computerized workplace. In R. E. Walton & P. R. Lawrence (Eds.), *HRM trends and challenges* (pp. 103–139). Cambridge, MA: Harvard Business School Press.

Zuboff, S. (1988). *In the age of the smart machine: The future of work and power*. New York: Basic Books.

3

LEADERSHIP EFFECTIVENESS: PAST PERSPECTIVES AND FUTURE DIRECTIONS FOR RESEARCH

Robert J. House
University of Pennsylvania

Philip M. Podsakoff
Indiana University

Although systematic research into the topic of leadership is a product of the twentieth century, interest in identifying the properties that make leaders effective is almost as old as recorded history. Indeed, Bass and Stogdill (Bass, 1990) noted that discussions relating to leadership and leadership effectiveness can be found in the Greek and Latin Classics, the Old and New Testaments of the Bible, the writings of ancient Chinese philosophers, and in early Icelandic sagas. Part of the fascination with the topic of leadership undoubtedly relates to our desire to understand why it is that some men or women are more effective than others at leading groups, organizations, and/or societies. However, another more practical reason for the interest in leadership may be our desire to improve our ability or that of others to become more effective leaders in organizations.

The goal of this chapter is to examine some of the theory and research on the topic of leadership effectiveness. We begin our analysis by first providing a definition of leadership. This is followed by an examination of some of the past and present views on the topic. However, given the space limitations, our primary focus is to provide a discussion of important recent theoretical developments in the leadership domain that we believe will serve as the basis for future research.

DEFINITIONS OF LEADERSHIP

Given the amount of attention devoted to the topic of leadership, one might expect that there is common agreement on its definition. However, this is not the case, and as noted by Stogdill (1974), there appear to be almost as many

45

definitions of the phenomenon as there are researchers in the field. Indeed, Bass and Stogdill (Bass, 1990) noted that leadership has been variously defined in terms of group and social influence processes, exchange relationships, personality characteristics, the result of specific types of behaviors, and as the means to achieve organizational goals. Unfortunately, these different definitions have led some (e.g., Pfeffer, 1977) to conclude that our understanding of leadership is somewhat ambiguous and confusing.

Although we agree that the different definitions of leadership can result in some confusion, we nevertheless do feel that an examination of many of the definitions over the years indicates that there are some common threads among leadership researchers regarding the elements of leadership:

> Leadership may be considered as the process (act) of influencing the activities of an organized group in its efforts toward goal setting and goal achievement. (Stogdill, 1950, p. 3).

> Leadership . . . is the behavior of an individual when he is directing the activities of a group toward a shared goal. (Hemphill & Coons, 1957, p. 7).

> Leadership is both a process and a property. The process of leadership is the use of noncoercive influence to direct and coordinate the activities of the members of an organized group toward the accomplishment of group objectives. As a property, leadership is the set of qualities or characteristics attributed to those who are perceived to successfully employ such influence. (Jago, 1982, p. 315).

> Leadership is defined as the process of moving a group (or groups) in some direction through mostly noncoercive means. (Kotter, 1988, p. 5).

> Leadership is . . . defined in terms of a process of social influence whereby a leader steers members of a group towards a goal. (Bryman, 1992, p. 2).

Common to all of these definitions is the notion that leaders are individuals that, by their actions, facilitate the movement of a group of people toward a common or shared goal or objective. Thus, these definitions imply that leadership results from the interaction between individuals organized around some commonly agreed-upon mission or purpose. However, it is important to note that these definitions do not specify the specific nature of the actions taken by the leader, or of the goal to be attained. Therefore, the definitions permit the inclusion of leaders who serve the collective interests of groups of people, as well those who serve their own self-interests; a point that has been discussed recently in the leadership literature by Howell (1988), Hogan, Raskin, and Fazzini (1990), and House and Howell (1992), among others.

HISTORICAL PERSPECTIVES: WHERE WE HAVE BEEN?

Generally speaking, there have been three dominant approaches to the study of leadership during the past century: (a) those that focus on the personal attributes of leaders ("trait" or "personality" approaches), (b) those that focus on specific types of leadership behaviors ("behavioral" or "style" approaches), and (c) those that focus on the situation or context in which leaders interact with their followers ("situational" or "contingency" approaches). In the next section, we provide a brief historical examination of these approaches, and some of their contributions to our knowledge of leadership processes.

Trait Approaches

Leadership research from the turn of the century until the late 1940s was predominantly concerned with the identification of the traits or personality characteristics of leaders. According to Webster's (1983), a trait is defined as "a distinguishing quality or characteristic" of an individual. Thus, trait theories of leadership were aimed at identifying those specific qualities or characteristics of individuals who influence a group. Included in the categories of traits examined by researchers were *physical characteristics* such as the height, weight, physical stature, and personal appearance; *personality characteristics*, such as introversion-extroversion, dominance, self-confidence, emotional balance or control, and independence; *social characteristics* such as cooperativeness, interpersonal skills, sociability, tactfulness, and diplomacy; and *personal abilities and skills* such as intelligence, judgment, knowledge, and fluency of speech (cf. Stogdill, 1974; Bass, 1990).

However, a series of influential reviews published in the late 1940s by Gibb (1947), Stogdill (1948), and Jenkins (1947), casted serious doubts on the validity of trait approaches to leadership. Generally, these reviews failed to show any consistency in the pattern of relationships obtained between individual traits and leadership. Moreover, Stogdill (1948) concluded that if the trait studies provided any information regarding leadership at all, it was that the situation that the leader was in had a substantial amount of influence on the specific traits that were associated with leadership.

The reviews by Stogdill (1948), Gibb (1947), and Jenkins (1947), are often cited in the prevailing leadership literature as the reason for the disenchantment with trait approaches to leadership. However, there is growing evidence to suggest that the abandonment of trait approaches may be somewhat premature, if not misguided, for several reasons. First, it is important to note that Stogdill's own updated review of the trait literature from the period from 1949–1970 led to the conclusion that his earlier paper had probably underemphasized the possibility that certain traits exhibited by leaders appeared to be quite universal. Second, House and Baetz (1979) pointed out that Stogdill's (1948) summary of the trait literature was somewhat problematic, because many of the studies included in it were based on children and adolescent leaders. Moreover, House and Baetz noted that when such studies were omitted from Stogdill's review, the results tended to show a rather consistent set of relationships between some traits and follower's attributions of leadership and/or leadership emergence, with many correlations ranging from .40 to .50. Related to House and Baetz's point regarding the nature of the samples in many of the early trait studies, it is also worth noting that we know very little about the measurement properties of many of the trait measures used in these studies, and what we do know is not very encouraging. For example, many of the early trait studies provided only sketchy descriptions of the nature of the measures that were employed, and very few attempts were actually made to ensure that the measures used in these studies were valid measures of the traits assessed.

Recent studies reported in the literature (e.g., Kenny & Hallmark, 1992; Kenny & Zaccaro, 1983; Lord, DeVader, & Alliger, 1986; Zaccaro, Foti, & Kenny, 1991) that are less susceptible to the problems outlined above have indeed demonstrated the potential importance of traits to the leadership emergence process. For example, in a reanalysis of a study reported by Barnlund (1962) and Kenny and Zaccaro (1983) found that between 49% and 82% of the variance in leadership could be attributed to a stable characteristic of the emergent leader. They speculated that the underlying basis for this characteristic may involve behavioral flexibility and social sensitivity on the leader's part; a speculation that received support in a subsequent study conducted by Zaccaro et al. (1991). In an examination of the relationship between interpersonal sensitivity and perceived leader status across different group situations, these researchers found that 59% of the variance in leadership emergence was trait based, and suggested that behavioral flexibility and social perceptiveness were the underlying leadership traits that accounted for this variance.

Finally, additional evidence regarding the potential importance of traits to leadership has been reported in a recent paper by Lord et al. (1986). They conducted a meta-analysis of 35 studies reported by Mann (1959) and others dealing with six traits that were associated with follower attributions of leadership. Lord and his colleagues reported that three traits—intelligence, dominance, and masculinity— were all significantly associated with follower perceptions of leadership, and that adjustment also was very close to reaching statistical significance. Thus, contrary to what has been assumed in much of the leadership literature over the past few decades, there does appear to be growing evidence that there are some traits that are rather consistently associated with *perceptions* of leadership. *Perceptions* is an important qualifier here. For many (if not most) of the trait studies of leadership were designed to identify those characteristics of leaders that distinguish them from nonleaders, not to distinguish *effective* from *ineffective* leaders. Although the identification of those traits or characteristics that help individuals *emerge* as leaders is undoubtedly important to a comprehensive understanding of leadership phenomena in general, it is probably fair to say that the identification of those characteristics that are related to leadership *effectiveness* is more important in organizational contexts.

Behavioral (or Leadership Style) Approaches

Following the early disillusionment with the trait approaches to leadership, research from the early 1950s to the latter part of the 1960s tended to focus on the observable *behavior* of leaders, rather than their less directly observable traits or characteristics. During this period, the majority of leadership research focused on two related issues (Jago, 1982). The first of these was the identification of the categories or dimensions of leadership behavior or "style." The second issue was to determine which of these dimensions of leadership were the most important for distinguishing between effective and ineffective leaders. Although a number of empirical studies were reported during this period of time, it is probably fair to say that the most influential groups of studies were those conducted at Iowa, Ohio State University, and the University of Michigan.

One of the first systematic studies of leadership behavior was conducted by Lewin, Lippitt, and White (1939), under the auspices of the "Iowa Childhood Studies." These researchers were interested in examining the effects of two different styles of leadership behavior—autocratic and democratic leader behavior—on young boys who were members of two different clubs. Autocratic leaders were defined as those who directed all activities for the boys and made all decisions regarding the activities for them. Democratic leaders, on the other hand, were defined as those who served as coordinators of the boys' activities and allowed the boys to vote on most major decisions. In an attempt to insure that it was the behavior of the leader that caused the differences in the boys' responses and not the leader's personal traits or characteristics, the same leader was used in both clubs. The only difference was that the leader behaved autocratically with one group of boys and democratically with the other. In later studies (cf. White & Lippitt, 1960), these researchers not only examined the effects of autocratic and democratic leadership style, but also the effects of a *laissez faire* leader. Laissez faire leaders were described as those that basically took a "hands-off" approach to leadership and provided no form of guidance to the boys under their tutelage.

An examination by Lewin and his colleagues of the boys' groups attitudes and performance under the three leadership "styles" indicated that the boys: (a) were the least productive and expressed the worst attitudes when they interacted with a laissez faire leader; (b) expressed the most positive attitudes with a democratic leader; and (c) were the most productive in the presence of an autocratic leader. Interestingly, however, the results of their study also showed that although the boys led by a democratic leader tended to continue to perform their work when their leader was no longer in their presence; the boys led by the autocratic leader stopped working, argued, and began to exhibit a substantial amount of "horseplay" when their leader left the room. This latter finding seems to suggest that although autocratic leaders may "force" followers to perform when they are present, democratic leadership styles may result in more long-lasting attitude and behavioral changes.

The research conducted by Lewin and his colleagues depended primarily on observations by the researchers and conversations with the boys and their leaders. However, research conducted at Ohio State University employed a decidedly different methodological approach, one which has served as the "method of choice" in much of the subsequent leadership research. Many of the early efforts of the Ohio State researchers were devoted to the identification, operationalization, and validation of questionnaire measures of leader behaviors (cf. Halpin & Winer, 1957; Schriesheim & Stogdill, 1975; Stogdill, 1969; Stogdill & Coons, 1957). Although a number of different forms of behavior were identified in the early studies, the two major ones were called "initiating structure" (or *IS*), and "consideration" (or *C*). Leaders who exhibited initiating structure were defined as those who structured the work for their subordinates, and provided clear messages regarding the roles they expected their subordinates to perform. Leaders who exhibited consideration behavior, on the other hand, were described as those who demonstrated friendliness and a concern for the well-being of their subordinates.

Early studies conducted at Ohio State looked promising, and were taken by some researchers as evidence that these two dimensions of leadership were relatively independent and generally positively related to important outcome variables, such as group morale and effectiveness. Unfortunately, subsequent research has demonstrated that both of these conclusions were somewhat optimistic. For example, ensuing research on the psychometric properties of the IS and C scales has indicated that some versions of them generally produce significant positive relationships between the IS and C dimensions, (cf. Weissenberg & Kavanagh, 1972), and other versions of the scales generally produce significant negative relationships (cf. Schriesheim, House, & Kerr, 1976; Schriesheim & Kerr, 1977a) between these supposedly independent dimensions of leadership. Moreover, later research evidence also indicated that although the relationship between consideration and employee morale or satisfaction is generally positive, the relationship between consideration and group effectiveness, and the relationships between initiating structure and both group satisfaction and effectiveness is rather mixed. In some cases, initiating structure was positively related to group members' satisfaction and effectiveness, whereas in other cases just the opposite was true; suggesting that the *situation* or context that a leader is in may have a substantial impact on the effectiveness of the individual's behavior.

At about the same time that researchers at Ohio State University were examining the effects of leader initiating structure and consideration, important research on leadership was also being conducted at the University of Michigan. Although the early phases of this research (cf. Kahn & Katz, 1953; Katz, Maccoby, & Morse, 1950) tended to focus much attention on the differences produced by "general" versus "close" supervision, and "employee-centered" versus "production-centered" leadership styles; later phases of the research (cf. Bowers, 1975) identified and examined the effects of four dimensions of leadership: support, interaction facilitation, work facilitation, and goal emphasis. Unfortunately, research using the Michigan "four-factor" approach (cf. Bowers, 1975) did not prove all that much more promising than the research on the Ohio State leadership dimensions of initiating structure and consideration; although it must be acknowledged that the Michigan approach also did not generate nearly as many empirical tests as the Ohio State dimensions did.

Despite the relatively disappointing findings produced by the early behavioral approaches, we feel that their importance should not be underestimated. Indeed, these approaches have made several contributions to the study of leadership. For example, they were among the first approaches to attempt to incorporate the psychometric and methodological advances in the social sciences into the operationalizations and measurement of leadership dimensions. These approaches also clearly demonstrated that it was feasible to identify different behavioral dimensions of leadership; thereby suggesting that, in principle, it was possible to: (a) distinguish effective leaders from ineffective leaders on the basis of their *behavior*; and (b) *train* people how to be more effective leaders. Finally, it should be acknowledged that although the early behavioral approaches to leadership have not completely lived up to their promise in terms of providing the field with a unverisal theory of leadership, they have led to the identification and examination of other forms of leader behavior, such as leader reward and punishment behaviors (cf. Podsakoff, Todor, & Skov, 1982; Podsakoff, Todor, Grover, & Huber, 1984; Sims & Szylagyi, 1975; Szylagyi, 1980), and "transformational" or "charismatic" leadership behaviors (which we will return to later in this chapter), that have proven to be generally more predictive of leadership effectiveness.

Situational and Contingency Approaches

Much (although certainly not all) of the leadership research conducted up until the mid-1960s was decidedly atheoretical in nature. This probably resulted from the relatively inductive approach taken by the researchers at Ohio State and the University of Michigan. However, between the mid-1960s and the mid- to late 1970s, the study of leadership became more theory-focused. Although some of the theoretical developments during this time period related to the nature of the "transaction" (cf. Hollander, 1978; Hollander & Julian, 1968, 1969, 1970) or "exchange" (cf. Dansereau, Graen, & Haga, 1975; Graen & Cashman, 1975; Graen & Schiemann, 1978) that takes place between leaders and their followers, perhaps the greatest departure from earlier perspectives results from those approaches that explicitly recognized the potential moderating effect that situational variables might have on the relationships observed between leader traits or behaviors and subordinate outcome variables. Although several of these situational or contingency approaches to leadership exist, given our limited space, we focus on the two most prominent of them, Fiedler's contingency (or LPC) model (cf. Fiedler, 1967; Fiedler & Chemers, 1974) and House's (House, 1971; House & Dessler, 1974; House & Mitchell, 1974) path-goal approach.

Fiedler's contingency model was perhaps the first approach designed to incorporate specific aspects of the situation into a comprehensive theory of leadership. Fundamentally, this approach assumes that: (a) leaders have either a trait-based task-orientation or a trait-based relationship-orientation; (b) these trait-based orientations may be measured using an instrument called the least preferred co-worker (LPC) scale, and (c) a leader's effectiveness will depend on the appropriateness of the "match" between task or relationship orientation and the "favorableness" of the situation.

For Fiedler, situational favorableness is determined by three variables: leader-member relationships (good vs. bad), task structure (structured vs. unstructured), and position power (high vs. low). The most favorable situation for the leader is considered to be one in which he or she experiences good leader-member relationships, the subordinates perform structured tasks, and the leader enjoys high levels of position power. The least favorable situation, on the other hand, exists when the leader-member relationships are poor, the tasks performed by the subordinates are relatively unstructured, and the leader's position power is low. According to Fiedler (cf. Fiedler, 1967, 1971; Fiedler & Chemers, 1974), task-oriented leaders tend to be more effective when the situation they face is either highly favorable, or highly unfavorable; and relationship-oriented leaders tend to be more effective when the situation is moderately favorable.

Despite its ground breaking nature, Fiedler's model has received relatively strong criticisms (cf. Ashour, 1973; Schriesheim & Kerr, 1977a, 1977b; Vecchio, 1977) on several grounds. For example, several researchers (Ashour, 1973; Schriesheim & Kerr, 1977a, 1977b) questioned the underlying meaning and/or the potential lack of stability of the LPC scales. Related to this, is the fact that Fiedler's model appears to treat task- and relationship-orientation as existing on a uni-dimensional scale, rather than as multiple dimensions of leadership. Another criticism relates to the potential lack of independence between the LPC scale, and the leader-member relationship measure used in this line of research. Finally, Schriesheim and Kerr (1977a, 1977b), and Vecchio (1977, 1983) raised several questions regarding the nature of the evidence Fiedler cited as supportive of the model.

Unlike Fiedler's model, which is based on the interaction between *traits* and situational variables, House's (House, 1971; House & Dessler, 1974; House & Mitchell, 1974) path-goal approach focuses on the interaction of leadership *behaviors* and situational factors. Building on the premises of the expectancy model of motivation (Vroom, 1964), this theory suggests that effective leaders are ones that motivate subordinates by: (a) clarifying the paths by which the subordinates can attain their goals, and (b) increasing subordinates' personal payoffs once these goals have been reached.

Two categories of situation variables were identified in the original path-goal model (cf. House, 1971; House & Dessler, 1974; House & Mitchell, 1974). Broadly speaking, the first of these categories relates to personal characteristics of subordinates, including their needs, task-relevant skills, and their locus of control, although the second category relates to the subordinates' work environment, and includes the nature of the subordinates' task, the nature of their work group, and the formal authority system in the organization.

Although it is probably fair to say that the number of studies designed to test the path-goal approach are probably not as numerous as those that have been conducted to test Fiedler's model, the results of those studies that have been reported (cf. Schriesheim & Kerr, 1977a) provided only mixed support for the model. Although the original theory provided hypotheses regarding four different forms of leader behavior within the path-goal framework—instrumental leadership, supportive leadership, participative leadership, and/or achievement-oriented leadership, the majority of the studies that have been reported to test the model have only examined the instrumental and supportive leadership categories, and the measures used to assess instrumental leadership behavior in some of these studies have questionable validity (cf. Schriesheim & von Glinow, 1977). However, another possible reason for the relatively mixed support for the path-goal model may have been caused by the initial statements of the theory, which only identified a relatively small set of potential variables that might serve as moderators of the relationships between leader behaviors and subordinate outcome variables.

In an apparent attempt to remedy the latter problem, Kerr and Jermier (1978) identified a substantially expanded list of potential moderators of instrumental and supportive leader behaviors that they call "substitutes for" or "neutralizers of" leadership. According to Kerr and Jermier (1978) leadership "substitutes" are moderators that act in the place of a leader's behavior, and make it unnecessary; while "neutralizers" are moderators that counteract the effectiveness of a leader's behavior, and make it impossible for it to have an effect. Included among the potential substitutes and neutralizers of leader behavior identified by Kerr and Jermier are four *subordinate characteristics* (the subordinate's ability, experience, training, and knowledge; need for independence, professional orientation, and indifference toward organizational rewards), three *task characteristics* (routine, methodologically invariant tasks; intrinsically satisfying tasks; and task feedback), and six *organizational characteristics* (organizational formalization; inflexibility of rules; work group cohesion; amount of staff and advisory support; organizational rewards not controlled by the leader; and the degree of spatial distance between the leader and subordinates).

Unfortunately, recent tests (cf. Podsakoff, MacKenzie, & Fetter, 1993a; Podsakoff, Niehoff, MacKenzie, & Williams, 1993b) of the potential moderating effects of the substitutes variables did not prove all that more supportive than the tests of the path-goal moderators. Indeed, the recent studies reported by Podsakoff and his colleagues (Podsakoff et al., 1993a, 1993b) indicate that although the subordinate, task, and organizational characteristics identified by Kerr and Jermier (1978) tended to have significant *main effects* on employees' attitudes, role perceptions, and performance, few of the substitutes variables moderated the relationships between the leader behaviors and these subordinate criterion variables in a manner consistent with that specified by Kerr and colleagues (Howell, Dorfman, & Kerr, 1986).

SUMMARY AND CRITIQUE: TRADITIONAL THEORIES AND RESEARCH

The leadership theories and research reviewed in this chapter primarily emphasized the instrumental effect that leaders can have on follower perceptions and satisfaction, and follower and work-unit performance. With the exception of Fiedler's contingency theory (Fiedler, 1967), most of these theories focus almost exclusively on dyadic relationships between leaders and their followers, rather than relationships between leaders and organizational criteria. They focus on the ways that leaders can motivate followers and improve follower performance. Accordingly, effective leaders are viewed as those who perform such functions as clarifying follower expectations by providing psychological structure to the followers' environment, increasing follower abilities by coaching, making tasks more intrinsically satisfying through job enrichment, and making rewards received by followers contingent on effective follower performance through the use of performance appraisal systems and frequent performance related feedback.

However, with the exception of path goal theory (House, 1971; House & Mitchell, 1974), none of these theories explicitly address the effects of leaders on followers values, preferences, or intrinsic motivation. Personality characteristics and motives of both leaders and followers are also largely ignored by these theories. Indeed, to our knowledge, only the contingency theory of leadership (Fiedler, 1967) included leader personality characteristics and only the path goal theory (House & Mitchell, 1974) included follower personality characteristics. Moreover, these theories focus on leaders' effects on individual subordinates, small groups, and work units, and generally ignore how leaders affect total organizations or the environments in which organizations exist. As a result, the empirical tests of these theories have been based largely on samples of lower level managers, and almost exclusively concern supervision of followers. In addition, instrumental leadership theories stress the effects of leaders on follower cognitions, and the leader's ability to appeal to the rationality of followers; thus, implicitly these theories make strong rationality assumptions and ignore leaders' symbolic behavior and followers' unconscious motives. Finally, these theories ignore the possibility of conflict and political behavior in organizations, which often results from demands for change from organizational members other than the leader; thus, they are biased toward the status quo and incremental, rather than revolutionary, change.

Disenchantment

Because the trait, behavioral, and situational theories, when tested empirically, seldom accounted for more than about 10% to 12% of the variance in dependent variables, there emerged a rather general disenchantment with the study of leadership in the 1960s, which persisted well into the 1980s. It became fashionable to debunk leadership as a topic of scholarly or practical interest, and a number of scholars questioned whether leaders make a difference in organizational performance (cf. Hannan & Freeman, 1984; Lieberson & O'Connor, 1972; Meindl, Ehrlich, & Dukerich, 1985; Pfeffer, 1977; Salancik & Pfeffer, 1977). Although the bases of these arguments differ from one scholar to another, a common thread among them is that leaders have substantially less impact on organizational outcomes than generally assumed.

As a result of the disenchantment with leadership research and theory throughout the 1960s and 1970s, together with the introduction of new perspectives on leadership, a paradigm shift with respect to the study of leadership took place in late 1970s. As will be shown, despite the skepticism of those who expressed disenchantment with leadership research and theory, there is substantial evidence that leaders can significantly influence the performance and survival of complex organizations.

THE PARADIGM SHIFT

Since the mid-1970s, a number of theories have been advanced to explain how leaders can have major effects on the emotions, motives, preferences, aspirations, and commitment of followers, as well as on the structure, culture, and performance of complex organizations. These theories were variously labeled *charismatic leadership theory* (House, 1977; Conger & Kanungo, 1987, 1988), *transformational leadership theory* (Burns, 1978; Bass, 1985), and *visionary leadership theory* (Sashkin, 1988).

All of these theories have much in common. They all describe and contrast outstanding leaders with leaders who meet the normal requirements of positions of management, but are not considered to be outstanding leaders. In contrast to earlier theories that concern the effects of leaders on follower cognitions, satisfaction, and normal levels of performance, these newer theories take as their dependent variables a number of affective consequences. These affective consequences include: emotional attachment to the leader on the part of the followers; emotional and motivational arousal of the followers as a consequence of the leader's behaviors, and thus enhancement of follower valences and values with respect to the mission articulated by the leader; followers' self-esteem, trust, and confidence in the leader; and values that are of major importance to followers.

The leader behavior specified by this new genre of theory is also different. Whereas earlier theories described leader behavior in terms of leader-follower relationships (Graen & Cashman, 1975), providing direction and support (House, 1971), and reinforcement behaviors (Ashour & Johns, 1983; Podsakoff, Todor, Grover, & Huber, 1984; Podsakoff, Todor, Skov, 1982; Sims & Szylagyi, 1975), the new leadership paradigm emphasizes symbolic leader behavior, visionary and inspirational ability, non-verbal communication, appeal to ideological values, and the empowerment of followers by the leader. According to this new genre of theory, outstanding leaders transform organizations by infusing into them ideological values and moral purpose, thus inducing strong commitment, rather than by affecting the cognitions or the task environment of followers, or by offering material incentives and the threat of punishment.

We refer to this general class of leadership theory as outstanding leadership theory. We chose this general title because all of these theories are intended to account for, and differentiate, leaders who accomplish outstanding achievements from ordinary leaders who are either ineffective, or those who meet the normal requirements of their positions, but do not make outstanding achievements.

Leaders considered to be outstanding are those whose organizations accomplish ambitious and unusual objectives, such as major military victories and competitive gains, organizational turn-arounds from loss to profit, major organizational innovations, or substantial organizational growth beyond that of competitors. As of our last count, over 30 empirical studies have been conducted to test or shed light on these theories. We now present a brief summary of empirical findings, which collectively support this new genre of leadership theory.

THE TRANSFORMATIONAL EFFECTS
OF OUTSTANDING LEADERS

The various theories of outstanding leadership address a wide variety of intervening and dependent variables including followers' emotional and motive arousal; self-esteem; identification with the leader, the leader's vision, and the collective trust in and loyalty to the leader; experience in the meaningfulness of work; and changes in organizational practices, structure, culture, and performance. Because this list of effects is long and cumbersome, it is necessary to specify a set of criteria by which outstanding leaders can be identified. The criteria we specify here are the unique effects of such leaders. Thus, we assert that when one observes these effects as the consequence of a leader's intended behavior then that leader qualifies for the designation "outstanding."

With respect to their followers, "outstanding" leaders are expected to have at least three effects. First, as a result of the self-engagement, awareness of shared end values, and motive arousal induced by the leader, followers of outstanding leaders become committed to the vision of the leader. A sense of urgency and exhilaration is experienced by organizational members. Work becomes more meaningful and members experience satisfaction and a sense of self worth when goals are accomplished. Berlew (1974) described these phenomena in more detail. Second, House (1977), Burns (1978), and Bass (1985) proposed that such leaders motivate followers to transcend their own self-interests for the sake of the team, the organization, or the larger policy. Third, as a consequence of their collective orientation, followers become willing to engage in self-sacrificial behavior in the interest of the vision and the collective. Self-sacrificial behavior is likely to take the form of what Organ (1988) referred to as organizational citizenship behaviors. Organizational citizenship behaviors (*OCBs*) are behaviors that are above and beyond the duties normally found in one's job description, or normally expected of one. Podsakoff, MacKenzie, Moorman, and Fetter (1990) found that leaders who engage in transformational leadership practices (one form of outstanding leadership) have followers who more frequently engage in OCBs than leaders who do not engage in such practices.

The three classes of effects of outstanding leaders described above are the immediate effects of the leaders on their followers. These intervening variables mediate the relationships between outstanding leaders and the effects these leaders have on the organizations or collectivities they lead. These effects can be viewed as the ultimate dependent variables of the theories of outstanding leadership. Burns (1978), Bennis and Nanus (1985), Tichy and Devanna (1986), and Sashkin (1988) asserted that such leaders, have a transforming effect on the organizations that they lead, as well as on their followers. Theoretically, such leaders transform the strategies, the structural forms, the practices, and the cultures of organizations they lead to fit the demands of their environments to better achieve organizational goals.

Motivational Processes

None of the versions of outstanding leadership theory include an empirically supported motivational explanation to account for the rather profound effects of the theoretical leader behaviors on follower affective states. Further, there is disagreement among the authors who specify such motivational processes. Bass' (1985) version of transformational leadership theory rested on Maslow's hierarchical need theory. According to Bass (1985), transformational leaders induce followers to desire and pursue the higher order needs in Maslow's need hierarchy: the needs of self-esteem and self-actualization. Unfortunately, it is not clear exactly how this process works, as Bass provided no explanation of the mechanisms by which followers' needs are transformed from lower to higher levels in the hierarchy. Further, this explanation does not account for followers' identification with the collective, because this is an individually oriented theory nor does it account for followers' identification with the charismatic vision.

Conger and Kanungo (1987) argued that charisma is a function of the attributions made by followers. However, these authors did not specify the particular attributional processes, or the contextual conditionals that induce or facilitate follower attributions of charisma toward leaders. Nor do they link attributional processes to follower motivation, or identification with the charismatic vision or the collective.

Mullin's (1992) theory of charismatic influence asserts that the relationship between charismatic leaders and followers rests on shared end values. According to Mullin, charismatic leaders raise followers' awareness of important end values, values which are shared by followers but have become latent because the followers are either not consciously aware of such values, or have given up on their pursuit of these values because of oppression resulting from the existing social order. By internalizing the values of the charismatic vision, followers identify with the vision and mission, and with the collectivity, and thus become committed to collective interests rather than pursuit of their own self-interests.

House and Shamir (1993) offered a more complete theory to account for the motivational effects of charismatic leaders. According to this theory, individuals are assumed to be motivated by: behavior of leaders that arouse individuals' unconscious needs of affiliation, achievement, and social influence; deeply held end values and the recognition that these values are shared with the leaders; and behaviors of the leader which strongly engage followers' self-concepts, such that followers' evaluations of their self-worth are contingent on their identification with the leader's vision, mission, and the collectivity of others who also share the same values and are committed to the vision and mission specified by the leader. More specifically, House and Shamir (1993) argued that outstanding leaders have a positive effect on follower motivation by: (a) articulating a transcendent ideological goal that embodies end values that are congruent with the deeply held end values of followers; (b) engaging in behaviors that selectively arouse unconscious follower motives that are relevant to the accomplishment of the vision, thus increasing the degree to which follower self-evaluation is based on goal accomplishment; (c) expressing positive evaluations, confidence, and high performance expectations of followers, thus enhancing their self-esteem and sense of self-worth; (d) linking goals and efforts to valued aspects of the follower's self-concept, thus harnessing the motivational forces of self-expression, self-consistency, and further enhancing follower self-esteem and self-worth; (e) changing the salience hierarchy of values and identities within the followers' self-concept, thus increasing the probability that these values and identities will be implicated in action; and (f) emphasizing ideological and collective end values, thus encouraging a shift from instrumental to moral orientation, and from concern with individual gains to concern with contributions to the collective.

Both House and Shamir's (1993) theory and Mullin's (1992) theory accounted for the self-sacrificial behavior of followers and their identification with the vision and the collective. However, Fiol, Harris, and House (1992) provided some empirical evidence that is consistent with the House and Shamir theory, based on a content analysis of writings and speeches of all 20th-century U.S. presidents. Their findings suggest that charismatic presidents use rhetoric, which is consistent with the motivational processes specified by House and Shamir, more than noncharismatic presidents. We now turn to a discussion of the specific leader behaviors that have been hypothesized to activate the motivational processes and transformational effects of outstanding leaders previously described.

Outstanding Leader Behaviors

Outstanding leaders may lead informal organizations, social movements, political parties, or nation states, as well as formal organizations. Yet, a common set of behaviors have been shown to differentiate outstanding from ordinary leaders in all of these situations. We argue that the core set of leader behaviors described here are genotypic leader behaviors that are theoretically generic to outstanding leadership. However, their manifestations may vary from one leader to another, or from one situation to another. For example, although having a transcendent vision is the sine qua non of outstanding leadership, some leaders communicate their visions in a highly assertive, oratorical manner, with a high degree of emotional nonverbal expression, and other equally outstanding leaders communicate their vision in a mild, deliberate, soft-spoken manner. The essence of the vision is its content, and not the specific way it is communicated (Kirkpatrick, 1992). The following is a brief description of the theoretical leader behaviors specified by the various authors of theories of outstanding leadership.

Vision. Outstanding leaders articulate an ideological vision that is congruent with the dearly held values of followers, a vision that describes a better future to which the followers have a moral right. By claiming that followers have a right to attain the vision, the vision is made to embrace a set of ideological values that resonate with the values and emotions of followers. Examples include Martin Luther King's vision, which he expressed as a dream of a future America where everyone can live in equality and peace; and Gandhi's vision of a self-governed India in which Moslems, Hindus, and Christians would accept and respect each other and live in equality. Visions of outstanding leaders need not be grandiose. Leaders of industrial and government organizations often articulate visions of organizations that embrace such ideological values as honesty, fairness, craftsmanship, and respect for organizational members, customers, and the environment in which the organization functions (Berlew, 1974). Such visions can be formulated for entire organizations or for organizational subunits as well.

Passion and Self Sacrifice. House (1977) argued that charismatic leaders display a passion for and have a strong conviction in the moral correctness of their vision. Similarly, Weber (1947), Conger and Kanungo (1987, 1988), and Sashkin (1988) argued that charismatic leaders engage in outstanding or extraordinary behavior and make extraordinary self-sacrifices in the interest of their vision and the mission they lead. We believe that one potential manifestation of such passion is a willingness to take personal risks in support of the vision. As a test of this expectation, House and Shamir (1993) recently identified ten charismatic and ten noncharismatic third world leaders. These charismatic and the noncharismatic were matched by the size of the country they lead, continent, and historical period in which they were leaders. These leaders are listed in Table 3.1. Seven of the charismatic leaders did time in prison, whereas only two of the noncharismatic leaders did so. Clearly, doing time in prison reflects risk taking and self-sacrificial behavior that are sincere manifestations of the leaders' passion for the vision.

Confidence, Determination, and Persistence. Outstanding leaders display a high degree of faith in themselves and in the attainment of the vision they articulate. Theoretically, such leaders need to have a very high degree of self-confidence and moral conviction, because their mission usually challenges the status quo, and therefore is likely to offend those who have a stake in preserving the established order. Such people frequently possess considerable power to discipline and punish

TABLE 3.1
Third World Leaders

Leader	Nation
Charismatic	
Castro	Cuba
Peron	Argentina
Mkurman	Ghana
Ken Yatta	Kenya
Myere	Tanzania
Nassar	Egypt
Ataturk	Turkey
Nehru	India
Mao	China
Sukarno	Indonesia
Noncharismatic	
Trujillo	Dominican Republic
Betancourt	Venezuela
Vargas	Brazil
Tubman	Liberia
Gbote	Uganda
Moboto	Zaire
Nurial-Said	Iraq
Reza Shak Pahlavi	Iran
Synagman Rhee	Korea
Phipum	Thailand

others. Consequently, challenging the status quo frequently places outstanding leaders in precarious positions. Thus, outstanding leaders need to be exceptionally determined in order to persist in the face of high risks and major obstacles. The display of determination and persistence demonstrates courage, and conviction in the vision and mission, and thus inspires, empowers, and motivates followers.

Nelson Mandela chose to remain in prison after 20 years of incarceration in South Africa, rather than forswear the possible use of violence against apartheid in the interest of the peoples' "struggle" for equality. Very likely, this determination and persistence gained him a great deal of credibility as a leader who could be trusted to act in the interest of the vision and the mission he articulated. It also likely inspired and motivated the followers to persist in "the struggle" for equal treatment of Africans.

Image Building. Outstanding leaders are self-conscious about their own image. They recognize that they must be perceived by followers as competent, credible, and trustworthy. Many famous charismatic leaders deliberately cultivated their image. Both Hitler and Churchill practiced their speeches for long hours. A story about Churchill, perhaps apocryphal, is both amusing and illustrative.

Supposedly, Churchill was practicing a speech while taking a bath. His valet overheard him and asked, "Prime Minister are you calling for me?" Churchill replied, "No, I am not talking to you, I am addressing Parliament." General George Patton's attire also illustrates leader image building. When addressing infantry recruits, Patton would do so against the background of a large American flag, dressed with braids and medals of his accomplishments and victories, and a shiny helmet with four gold stars, carrying a cropping whip. U.S. generals are allowed to design their own uniforms. Patton's choice of attire also included horse racing jodhpurs and boots, and two pearl-handled six guns which were holstered to his hips—attire suitable for leading warriors into mortal battle.

Patton's speeches also illustrated how conscious he was of presenting an inspiring image to his followers. When speaking to the troops, his speeches were laced with profanity. However, when speaking to officers, his speeches would seldom include vulgarities, because he knew that the officers were generally better educated than the troops and would not find the profane language used with the troops to be acceptable (Blumenson, 1985). To the troops, he wanted to appear as a strong warrior. To the officers, he wanted to appear as a master of military strategy, and thus carried out his image building masterfully.

Role Modeling. Leader image building sets the stage for effective role modeling because followers identify with the values of role models who are perceived with a positive view (Bandura, 1986). Leader image building contributes to the followers' perception of the leader as competent, credible, trustworthy, and motivated to serve the rightful and moral interests of the mission and the collective. But image building is more than the way one dresses and practices speeches. It includes behaving in a way that sets a personal example of the beliefs and values inherent in the vision and the mission. The leader becomes a "representative character" (Bellah, Madsen, Sullivan, Swidler, & Tipton, 1985)—a symbol that brings together in one concentrated image the way people in a given social environment organize and give meaning and direction to their lives. The leader becomes an image that helps define the types of traits, values, beliefs, and behaviors it is good and legitimate for the followers to develop. Thus, the leader provides an ideal, a point of reference and focus for followers' emulation and vicarious learning.

Outstanding leaders ask a great deal of personal sacrifice, effort, and commitment from their followers. Outstanding leaders influence followers by personal example. They serve as a role model of the kind of behavior required to attain the vision. For example, Mahatma Gandhi consciously served as a role model of the values of his vision. He gave up a lucrative law practice and lived a life of poverty and forbearance and dressed in swaddling clothes to set a personal example of the behaviors that he believed were required of the Indian population if they were to be successful in establishing Indian autonomy from England. Followers learn vicariously the values and the kind of behavior required for the attainment of the vision as a result of the leader's personal example.

External Representation. Outstanding leaders act as the spokesperson for their organization and symbolically represent the organization to external constituencies. For example, Nelson Mandela has served as the spokesperson for the African National Congress (ANC), represents the ANC to the United Nations, and negotiates with the South African government for better, and equal, treatment of Black Africans. Such behavior serves, in part, to symbolically reinforce the leader's vision through repetition, to communicate the vision to others who are not part of the collective, and also to define the boundaries of the collective.

Expectations and Confidence Toward Followers. Outstanding leaders communicate high performance expectations of their followers, and strong confidence in their followers' ability to meet such expectations. They often invoke slogans that express their confidence in, and high esteem for, their followers. Black leaders assert that "Black is beautiful." Churchill praised the valor of The Royal Air Force's defense of London, and the courage of British citizens in World War II as "England's finest hour." Vince Lombardi, the legendary charismatic professional football coach who led both the Green Bay Packers and the Washington Redskins from the bottom of their leagues to become league champions, communicated his performance expectations of his teams with such well-known statements as "Winning isn't everything–it's the only thing," and "Any play can be the play that wins or loses the game. . . . Every player must give 100% on every play. . . . You must be in top condition to win. . . . Fatigue makes cowards of us all."

The combination of high expectations and confidence in followers expressed in such statements results in increased follower motivation and self-confidence. There is substantial evidence that followers rise to the challenge of high performance expectations of their leaders and sink to the despair of leaders who view them as incompetent or lazy (Eden, 1990; Farris & Lim, 1969; Korman, 1971; Rosenthal & Jacobson, 1968).

Selective Motive Arousal. Outstanding leaders selectively arouse those motives of followers that are of special relevance to the successful accomplishment of the vision and mission. McClelland (1985) and associates demonstrated that three unconscious motives have substantial effects on both short- and long-term behavior (McClelland & Boyatzis, 1982). The three motives identified by McClelland and associates are the affiliative, power, and achievement motives.

When task demands of subordinates require the assumption of calculated risks, achievement oriented initiative, the assumption of personal responsibility, and persistence toward challenging goals, the arousal of the achievement motive enhances intrinsic satisfaction and motivation and facilitates effective performance and goal attainment. When the task demands of subordinates require them to be persuasive, assert influence or exercise control over others, or be highly competitive or combative, the arousal of the power motive enhances intrinsic motivation and satisfaction and facilitates performance. When task demands require affiliative behavior, as in the case of tasks requiring cohesiveness, teamwork, and peer support, the arousal of the affiliative motive enhances intrinsic motivation, satisfaction, and performance. Thus, one of the major effects that charismatic leaders have on their followers is the arousal of motives that are especially relevant to the mission envisioned by the leader.

Such motive arousal is achieved differentially for each of the three motives. For example, the achievement motive has been aroused by suggesting to subjects that an experimental task is a measure of personal competence, or that the task is a standard that one can measure one's general level of ability against (cf. Heckhausen, 1967; McClelland, 1953, 1985).

The affiliative motive has been aroused by having fraternity members rate one another, while all were present, on a sociometric friendship index, while at the same time requiring each person to stand and be rated by the other members of the fraternity on a list of trait adjectives (Atkinson, Heyns, & Veroff, 1954; French & Chadwick, 1956; Shipley & Veroff, 1952).

The power motive has been aroused experimentally by: (a) evoking the image of, or reminding one of, an enemy; (b) having subjects observe the exercise of power by one person over another; or (c) allowing subjects to exercise power over another (Winter, 1973), and by showing subjects inspirational speeches such as John F. Kennedy's inaugural address (Steele, 1977).

If motives can be aroused so easily, under isolated laboratory conditions, within a few minutes by use of the appropriate experimental treatments by psychologists, it seems obvious, at least to us, that leaders can also arouse motives. Because outstanding leaders are viewed as credible, trusted, admired, and respected, they are able to have rather profound motive arousal effects on followers.

Frame Alignment. To persuade followers to accept and implement change, outstanding leaders engage in frame alignment. Frame alignment (Snow, Rochford, Worden, & Benford, 1986) refers to the linkage of individual and leader interpretive orientations, such that some set of followers' interests, values, and beliefs, and the leader's activities, goals, and ideology, become congruent and complementary. The term *frame* denotes "schemata of interpretation" that enable individuals to locate, perceive, and label occurrences within their life and the world at large (Goffman, 1974). By rendering events or occurrences meaningful, frames function to organize experience and guide action, whether individual or collective (see also Boal & Bryson, 1987).

Charismatic leaders engage in communicative processes that affect frame alignment and "mobilize" followers to action. For example, Fiol, Harris, and House (1992) found that those presidents who are considered charismatic, and rated as great, or near great, by present day political historians, engage in systematic frame alignment communications more frequently than less outstanding presidents. Specifically, early in their first terms, the presidents Theodore and Franklin Roosevelt, John F. Kennedy, and Ronald Reagan, used significantly more negative terms than other 20th century presidents who were not charismatic, to convince followers that conventional thinking and conventional solutions to problems are unworkable. These four presidents are recognized as charismatic leaders by a poll of prominent presidential historians taken by House, Woycke, and Fodor (1988). By using negative terminology early, these presidents attempted to "unfreeze" the attitudes of those who might oppose their policies. Outstanding presidents also invoked inclusive terms such as *we* or *us* to stress identification of followers with the collective, and abstract terms such as *distant goals, visions of the future,* and *positive attributes of the followers* to stress the values inherent in the vision.

Shamir et al. (1993) argued that charismatic, visionary, and transformational leaders engage in frame alignment by interpreting the present and past. They link present behaviors to past events by citing historical examples. They articulate an ideology clearly, often using labels and slogans and provide a vivid image of the future. Further, they amplify certain values and identities and suggest linkages between expected behaviors, the amplified values and identities, and their vision of the future (Willner, 1984).

Based on the previous discussion, Shamir, House, and Arthur (1993) suggested that messages of outstanding leaders, compared to the messages of ordinary leaders, include

1. More reference to values and moral justifications and less reference to tangible outcomes.
2. More reference to the collective and to collective identity.
3. More reference to history.
4. More reference to distal goals and less reference to proximal goals.

The findings by Fiol et al. (1992) suggested that outstanding leaders also systematically engage in more frame alignment than other leaders.

Inspirational Communication.   Outstanding leaders often, but not always, communicate their messages in an inspirational manner, using vivid stories, slogans, symbols, and ceremonies. John F. Kennedy appealed to American patriotism with his famous statement "Ask not what your country can do for you, but what you can do for your country." Franklin Roosevelt asserted that with the implementation of the New Deal "There will be chicken in every pot," and "Better times are just around the corner." However, not all outstanding leaders are assertive and macho in their mannerisms. Kirkpatrick (1992) has shown in a laboratory experiment that it is not the nonverbal behavioral of the leader that induces motivation on the part of followers, but rather the content of the leader's message. It is the congruence of the values of leaders and followers, and the appeal of the leader's vision that are motivational, rather than any specific mannerism. Mahatma Gandhi, Nelson Mandela, and Sister Teresa, are examples of soft-spoken, nurturing, and supportive outstanding leaders who appeal to followers on the basis of their vision and the values of the vision.

Leader Behaviors Not Associated with Outstanding Leadership. There are several leader behaviors or leader characteristics suggested by other theorists that we believe are associated with either ordinary or effective leadership but not uniquely associated with outstanding leadership. These are individualized consideration or personal orientation (Bass, 1985; Sashkin, 1988), environmental monitoring (Conger & Kanungo, 1988), intellectual stimulation (Bass, 1985), and adaptability (Sashkin, 1988). Following are our reasons for arriving at this conclusion.

Bass argued that individualized consideration is a transformational leader behavior, although Sashkin (1988) believed that personal communication and displaying respect toward followers are characteristics of visionary leaders. We see these and other supportive person and group oriented behaviors as rather normal behaviors of most effective leaders. Supportive leadership is necessary for leaders to be effective. However, we believe that individuals can engage in these behaviors to a great extent and still not be outstanding leaders. Clearly, the studies by Bass and associates demonstrate consistently that transformational leaders are perceived as high on individualized consideration by followers. The motivational analysis previously presented suggests that individualized consideration is seen by subordinates as a result of shared values and the belief that the leader has the interests of the collectivity strongly in mind. Scores on the individualized consideration scale most likely reflect not only the behaviors described by Bass' (1985) Multifacet Leadership Questionnaire (MLQ), but also the positive attributions by followers associated with the transformational relationship.

Conger and Kanungo's (1987, 1988) theory of charismatic leadership asserts that charismatic leaders are more sensitive to, and monitor, the environment more than noncharismatic leaders do. We do not view this is a distinction between outstanding and ordinarily effective leaders. We believe environmental sensitivity and monitoring are attributes of effective leaders in open systems in uncertain and changing environments. These behaviors are not interpersonally oriented, and we see no self-implicating or motive arousing effects on followers of environmental sensitivity and monitoring. Thus, we do not believe these attributes to be unique to charismatic leaders.

Furthermore, we do not see intellectual stimulation as a behavior that differentiates outstanding from other leaders. Several studies have revealed negative effects of intellectual stimulation on followers satisfaction, motivation, and trust (Bass, personal communication, March 4, 1991; Podsakoff et al. 1990). Finally, we do not see leader adaptability as a characteristic of outstanding leadership. Although this may be a desirable characteristic, it is likely that outstanding leaders are so committed to their vision and ideological value position that they are not likely to vary in this regard. This lack of adaptability is likely a result of their conviction in the moral correctness of their vision and values. Because lack of adaptability may in some circumstances be a liability to such leaders, we doubt that the leaders we describe as outstanding, or the leaders who have been found to be outstanding in prior research, are highly adaptable with respect to their vision or their value system. What is more likely is that such leaders are willing and able to maneuver within the broad limits of their vision and are therefore effective strategic problem solvers and tactical implementors or competitors.

PERSONALITY CHARACTERISTICS AND MOTIVES OF OUTSTANDING LEADERS

Theory

The 1976 theory of charismatic leadership (House, 1977) provided a preliminary description of personality characteristics of outstanding leaders. According to this theory, charismatic leaders (one form of outstanding leadership), have high self-confidence, high verbal ability, high need for influence or power, and exceptionally strong convictions in the moral correctness of their beliefs. Theoretically, such leaders need to have a very high degree of self-confidence and moral conviction because their mission is usually unconventional and likely to be resisted by those who have a stake in preserving the status quo. Consequently, outstanding leaders need to be exceptionally determined and able to persist in the face of high risks and major obstacles. Further, the display of confidence and determination inspires, and thus motivates and empowers followers.

According to House (1977), the ability to be verbally articulate is necessary for outstanding leaders to communicate their vision and mission in a compelling way to followers. We speculate that in addition to the above personality characteristics, outstanding leaders have the ability to be nonverbally expressive. Nonverbal expressiveness is the ability of an individual to change the mood of others by the use of gestures, and facial and bodily expressions. Friedman and his colleagues (Friedman, DiMatteo, & Taranta, 1980; Friedman & Riggio, 1981) showed that individuals vary on this ability, and that nonverbal expressiveness significantly enhances the impact of one's communication on the affective states of others. Thus, nonverbal expressiveness is a personality characteristic that allows leaders to have powerful effects on followers. House also argued that outstanding leaders need to derive satisfaction from the process of leading others and being influential. Thus, they need to have a high need for influence if they are to receive intrinsic satisfaction from leading and are to be sustained in the face of risks, obstacles, and hardship. We now review evidence relevant to the motives and personality characteristics of outstanding leaders.

Evidence

House, Spangler, and Woycke (1991), and Spangler and House (1991), assessed the motives and the personality traits of U.S. presidents. Outstanding (charismatic) presidents were personally more forceful and immoderate. They had more radical solutions to the country's problems, and were also more willing to take risks to accomplish their goals (Spangler & House, 1991).

Outstanding presidents were higher on the need for social influence and lower on the need for personal (as opposed to collective) achievement. High achievement motivation is associated with a preference for personal involvement in work, and thus results in centralization of decision making (Miller & Droge, 1986), close supervision, and meddling in tasks that are better performed autonomously by subordinates. The combination of high need for social influence and low need for personal achievement thus resulted in presidents engaging in behavior to accomplish their goals by influencing others rather than by personal actions and decisions.

Outstanding presidents were also lower than other presidents on the need for affiliation. Having a low need for affiliation allowed them to remain somewhat emotionally uninvolved and less intimate with their followers compared to other leaders. Consequently, it is likely that leaders who have less need for affiliation are better able to delegate authority to followers and monitor follower behavior with less emotional attachment than other leaders. High affiliation motivated presidents are more inclined to delegate on the basis of friendship relationships and favoritism and are less inclined to monitor and discipline followers when they engage in improprieties and scandalous behavior. The tendency for some presidents to become excessively intimate in their relationships with followers is illustrated by the famous statement, attributed to Harding, that "It's not my enemies who give me trouble, it's my goddamn friends [whom he appointed to high office] I can't control."

An interesting, and somewhat different picture of the outstanding leader personality can be drawn from informal product champions in industrial organizations (Howell & Higgins, 1990a, 1990b), military squad leaders in the Air Force Academy (Ross & Offermann, 1991) and midshipmen in the Naval Officer Academy (Rouse & Atwater, 1991). In these studies, outstanding leaders are differentiated from less effective leaders by several personality traits including cognitive (as opposed to unconscious) achievement orientation; strong tendencies to be creative, innovative, visionary, and inspirational; high levels of work involvement, energy, and enthusiasm; a strong propensity to take risks; being self-confident; a high need for social influence coupled with a strong concern for the moral and nonexploitative use of power in a socially desirable manner, willingness to exercise influence, but not to be dominant, tough, forceful, aggressive, or critical; strong inclinations to be confident in and encouraging toward followers, and show a developmental orientation towards followers; and tendencies to be nurturant, socially sensitive, and sensitive to, and considerate of, follower needs.

It is important to note that this is a composite description based on a number of studies, each of which used different trait constructs and measures. Consequently, none of the findings have been replicated in subsequent studies. It is possible that somewhat different traits are required for different contexts such as mass movements, military organizations, political parties, religious organizations, nation-states, and business organizations. In addition, the composite picture of outstanding middle and lower level leaders described above is most likely relevant to formal organizations in which followers are formally appointed subordinates of their leaders and have frequent face-to-face interactions with and are dependent on the leaders for social support, as well as inspiration.

We speculate that there are likely some generic personality characteristics that differentiate outstanding from less effective leaders. Some candidates have dispositional tendencies to be self-confident and confident of others; to have strong will and determination; to be optimistic with respect to one's view of human beings; to be nurturant and have a developmental orientation toward followers; and to have the capacity to experience passion for a cause and a high need for social influence.

Collectively, the findings from these studies indicate that outstanding leaders in complex organizations, including military educational institutions, do not fit the stereotype of a bold, forceful, assertive, and aggressive leader. Rather, the findings describe a leader who is sensitive to follower needs, nurturant, and developmentally oriented, more like Mahatma Gandhi rather than General George Patton or the outstanding U.S. presidents studied by House et al. (1991).

There are two possible explanations for these counter-intuitive findings. First, Bass (1985) and Sashkin (1988) argued that outstanding leaders are highly considerate of, and sensitive to, the needs of their followers. The above findings are consistent with this argument. Moreover, the path-goal theory of leader effectiveness (House, 1971) predicted that supportive leadership is most satisfying to followers under conditions of dissatisfying jobs, stress, or boredom. Accordingly, leaders who are more nurturant and less dominant, critical, and aggressive, would be predicted from the path-goal theory to produce more follower satisfaction under highly demanding and structured conditions such as those found in the Air Force and Naval Academies. Consistent with path-goal theory, it may well be that the manner in which outstanding leaders express their vision, communicate expectations of followers, show confidence in followers, and stimulate them intellectually varies with the situations and the kinds of organizations in which they function.

The second explanation for the somewhat counter-intuitive findings reported above is not inconsistent with the first. According to transformational theory, leaders in complex organizations are developmentally oriented, and foster follower independence rather than subservience. Bass (1985) contended that transformational (or outstanding) leaders even encourage followers to think for themselves to the extent that they become willing to openly question the leader's directions when in disagreement with the leader. Through coaching, questioning, and role modeling, the leader stimulates followers to question the status quo, to consider creative ways to tackle and solve problems on their own, and to solve future problems unforeseen by the leader. By creating learning opportunities for their followers, tailoring these learning opportunities to their needs, and providing social support conducive to learning, outstanding leaders build followers' self-confidence and self-reliance and foster their growth and independence in a collaborative way. Ultimately outstanding leaders create followers who are more capable of leading themselves.

SOCIAL DETERMINANTS OF OUTSTANDING LEADERSHIP

Weber (1947), House (1977), and Burns (1978) argued that charismatic leadership is born out of stressful situations facing followers. Theoretically, under such conditions there is a felt need on the part of followers for a courageous leader who will challenge the established order and offer a radical, or at least innovative, solution to the stressful conditions that followers experience. If a leader emerges who expresses sentiments that are deeply held by followers such a leader is likely to be viewed as outstanding. Because leaders' views are different from the established order, they place themselves in jeopardy and are thus likely to be perceived as courageous. Such personal risk taking adds credibility to the leader and causes followers to believe that the leader may bring about social change and thus deliver them from their plight.

In contrast, however, Shils (1965) argued that followers need not be in distress, and that the only requirement for the emergence of outstanding leadership is a transcendent ideological vision that expresses end values with which followers can identify. Consistent with Shils' position, several recent studies reported by Bass and colleagues (Bass, 1985) indicate that outstanding leaders can be found in many kinds of organizations, thus suggesting that follower stress may be a sufficient, but not a necessary condition, for the emergence of outstanding leaders.

Of course, this should not be taken to suggest that stress is unimportant to the emergence of outstanding leaders. Indeed, although stressful situations may not be a necessary condition for the emergence and effective performance of outstanding leadership, there are two empirical studies that demonstrate that stress indeed facilitates the emergence of outstanding leadership (House et al., 1991; Pillai & Meindl, 1991).

All scholars who have attempted to explain the phenomena of charismatic leadership agree that charisma, one form of outstanding leadership, must be based on the articulation of an ideological goal. Opportunity to articulate such a goal, whether in stressful or nonstressful situations, can thus be considered as one of the situational requirements for a person to emerge as an outstanding leader. House (1977) concluded from this line of reasoning that whenever the roles followers perform can be defined as contributing to ideological values held by followers, a leader can to some degree have a strong influence on the affective states of followers by stressing end values and engaging in the outstanding leader behaviors described earlier.

However, House (1977) also argued that there are some roles in society that do not lend themselves to ideological value orientation. These roles generally require highly routine, nonthinking effort in exclusively economic oriented organizations. It is hard to conceive of clerks or assembly line workers in profit making firms as perceiving their roles as ideologically oriented. However, the same work when directed toward an ideological goal could lend itself to charismatic (outstanding) leadership. For example, in World War II, "Rosie the Riveter" expressed the ideological contribution of an assembly line worker. And such menial work as stuffing envelopes frequently is directed toward ideological goals in political and religious organizations. Thus, it would appear that a necessary condition for a leader to have charismatic effects is that the role of followers be definable in ideological terms that are congruent with end values held by followers.

Shamir, House, & Arthur (1993) suggested additional social conditions that facilitate the emergence and effectiveness of outstanding leaders. They suggested that when the values of followers are likely to reflect the dominant values of society, at least in part, charismatic (outstanding) leadership is more likely to emerge and be effective when the organizational task is closely related to the dominant social values than when it is unrelated to such values or contradicts them. For example, they suggested that leaders are less likely to strongly influence the affective states of followers in the tobacco industry than in high technology industries whose tasks can be easily linked to values such as scientific progress and national pride.

Shamir et al. (1993) also argued that leaders are more likely to be viewed as outstanding and have strong affective influence under conditions that do not favor instrumental leadership—conditions under which goals cannot be clearly specified, the means for achieving goals is unclear, and objective or consensual ways of measuring performance are not available and leaders have little discretion about the allocation of rewards on the basis of follower performance.

Finally, House et al. (1991) found that the frequency of crises during U.S. presidential administrations was positively correlated with the degree to which the presidents were described in biographies as visionary, creative, and charismatic. Based on this finding they suggested that exceptional leadership is more appropriate under exceptional conditions that require exceptional efforts, behavior, and sacrifice by both leaders and followers.

EMPIRICAL EVIDENCE FOR OUTSTANDING LEADERSHIP THEORIES

To date, over 30 studies of the behavior and effects of outstanding leaders have been conducted. These empirical investigations of outstanding leadership have employed a variety of philosophy of science perspectives, research designs, and data collection methods, including case studies, longitudinal observational studies, field surveys, an analysis of behavior in a management game, laboratory experiments, qualitative and quantitative analyses of interviews, content analyses of historical archival information about U.S. presidents, and a large sample longitudinal analysis of the effects of outstanding leaders. Studies that have demonstrated support for the theoretical relationships between leader behaviors and follower responses have been conducted across a wide variety of samples, including students who served as laboratory subjects, military and industrial middle and lower level managers, world class national leaders, U.S. educational leaders, Asian Indian middle managers, Dutch supermarket managers, school principals in Singapore, top level executives, presidents of alcoholic rehabilitation organizations, managers of research and development organizations, and emergent informal project champions.

At present there is only one quantitative study that shows that leaders can profoundly effect total organizations in the ways predicted by the theories described earlier (Koh, Terborg, & Steers, 1991). However, there is an abundance of historical evidence from the sociological, political science, and historical literature (Burns, 1978), as well as qualitative evidence based from interviews (Bennis & Nanus, 1985), and observations (Roberts, 1985; Trice & Beyer, 1986) of chief executives of complex formal organizations.

There is a strong convergence of the findings of the studies previously cited. Collectively, the findings of all of these studies indicate that leaders who engage in the behaviors specified in charismatic, transformational, and visionary theories, and leaders with the motive profile specified by the leader motive profile theory, receive higher performance ratings, have more satisfied and more highly motivated followers, and are viewed as more effective leaders by their superiors and followers than others in positions of leadership. Further, the effect size of leader behavior on follower satisfaction and performance is consistently higher than prior field study findings concerning other leader behaviors. We now turn to a discussion of some of the limitations of this leadership paradigm.

SUMMARY AND CRITIQUE OF OUTSTANDING LEADERSHIP THEORY

As a class of theory, outstanding leadership has several limitations. First, these theories differ with respect to the leader behaviors that are asserted to effect follower affective states. These differences need to be reconciled or the contingencies under which the differing predictions hold need to be specified (see House & Shamir, 1992, for a theoretical attempt to integrate the leader behavior of charismatic, transformational, and visionary leader behaviors). There is also a modest controversy among the authors of theories of outstanding leadership concerning whether they are all essentially of the same genre, or whether there are meaningful differences among them.

Sashkin (personal communication, August 10, 1993) argued that charismatic theory refers to the "darker side of leadership" and accounts only for socially undesirable and destructive leadership. Howell and House (1992) disagreed, and suggested two kinds of charismatic leadership: personalized (self aggrandizing, exploitative, and authoritarian) and socialized (altruistic, collectively oriented, and egalitarian) leadership. Bass argued that transformational theory subsumes charismatic theory, but House and Shamir (1992) disagreed. House and Shamir (1992) saw transformational, charismatic, and visionary leadership as essentially the same, in that all of these theories take as their dependent variables the affective states of followers, and all of them stress leader behavior that is symbolic, and appeals to follower emotions.

House (1993) further argued that the measure (MLQ) that Bass (1985) used to empirically support transformational theory does not include all of the theoretical behaviors of charismatic leadership. For example, Curphy (1990) demonstrated empirically that the factorial structure of MLQ responses do not conform to the theoretical dimensions of transformational theory based on a sample of 11,000 respondents. Similarly, Podsakoff et al. (1990) also demonstrated that there are more dimensions of transformational leadership than those included in the MLQ, and these additional dimensions are more consistent with the arguments advanced by House (1977), than those of Bass (1985) or Bass and Avolio (1989).

These are rather minor differences among the theories and the opinions of the theorists. They are arguments over subsidiary definitions and fine tuning rather than arguments that are fundamental to the class of theory we refer to as outstanding leadership theory. However, more substantive differences do exist.

For example, the theories of outstanding leadership all offer inadequate or untested explanations of the process by which the theoretical leader behaviors are linked to and effect the affective states of followers. The theory of transformational leadership (Bass, 1985) rests on Maslow's theory of motivation which has been largely disproved by empirical tests (Wahba & Bridwell, 1975). Similarly, the charismatic theory advanced by Conger and Kanungo (1987) rested on an attribution explanation of the effects of charismatic leaders, which is not well explicated with respect to the specific attribution processes that are alluded to in the theory.

In addition, there is no explication of the processes whereby the leader behaviors specified by visionary theory (Bennis & Nanus, 1985; Sashkin, 1988), and the leader motives specified by the leader motive profile theory (McClelland, 1972), have their theoretical effects on either followers or larger units of analysis. The self-concept and motive arousal theory of motivation advanced by House and Shamir (1992), while more explicit, and more elaborate, remains to be refined and tested.

Further, there is little evidence that charismatic, transformational, or visionary leadership transforms individuals, groups, large divisions of organizations, or total organizations—or their environments—despite claims that they do so. The bulk of supportive evidence is cross-sectional in nature, and thus the transformations, or changes in individuals and organizations, asserted by the various theories of outstanding leadership are not well demonstrated empirically.

Only the theory advanced by House (1977) and extended by House et al. (1991) and Shamir et al. (1993) addressed the relationship of organizational context to emergence and effectiveness of outstanding leadership. Studies by Pillai and Meindl (1991) and House et al. (1991) showed that crises facilitate the emergence of charismatic leadership. Other than these two studies, there is no empirical evidence concerning the relationship between contextual social conditions and outstanding leadership emergence and effectiveness. Finally, theories of outstanding leadership have ignored political processes that occur within organizations, and need to be extended to describe how outstanding leaders deal with political opposition to their vision.

PRESCRIPTIVE IMPLICATIONS

Despite some of the limitations discussed previously, there are several interesting implications of outstanding leadership theory. First, there is the normative issue concerning both the appropriate means used and ends pursued by leaders who are capable of having such profound effects on followers, organizations, and societies. We argued that leaders can be judged as outstanding or ordinary on the basis of their effects. It is possible for personalized (self-aggrandizing, exploitative, authoritarian) leaders to cause followers to forego self-interest in the interest of the collective and the leader's mission. It is also possible for personalized leaders to cause socially undesirable changes in the culture, practices, and structures of the organizations they lead. The history of despots and dictators informs us of leaders who were outstanding in the sense that they were able to accomplish such effects, not only at the cost of their enemies, but also at the expense of their followers (Lindholm, 1990). Despite their socially undesirable behavior and self-aggrandizing motivation, some personalized leaders must be judged as outstanding according to the criteria of the effects they bring about—the profound effects they have on their followers and their organizations. Nevertheless, on moral grounds, we strongly believe that such personalized leaders are not appropriate when they employ personalized leadership or pursue self-aggrandizing ends.

The studies reviewed all demonstrate a high level of follower commitment to the values, mission, and goals of outstanding leaders. To the extent that the leaders' goals and values are congruent with organizational goals and values, outstanding leadership provides a strong link between organizational goals and member commitment to such goals. To the extent that the leaders' goals and values are in conflict with those of the organization, such as when leaders represent a challenge to the status quo. Charismatic leadership is likely to induce negative attitudes toward the organization and resistance to directives from management by organizational members. Thus, charismatic leadership is a strong force for or against member commitment to organizational goals. The major prescriptive conclusion to be drawn from this discussion is, as stated by

Hodgkinson (1983) "Beware Charisma! . . . But to beware does not necessarily mean or entail 'Avoid' . . . Be aware! Then choose" (p. 187).

Second, it may be possible to design assessment systems to identify and select individuals with potential to be outstanding leaders. Avolio, Waldman, and Einstein (1988) found that leaders who engaged in transformational and charismatic behavior in a realistic management simulation had teams that performed more effectively than teams led by transactional leaders. House, Howell, Shamir, Smith, and Spangler (1993) also demonstrated the superiority of charismatic leadership over transactional leadership with respect to U.S. presidents and middle managers, respectively. Because the behaviors that are characteristic of outstanding leaders are now well specified and empirically supported, it is possible to develop behavioral observation technologies, such as the management simulation used by Avolio et al. (1988). Such observation can then be used to identify and select outstanding leaders by observing their behavior in such simulations. Observations in management simulations can also provide the basis of feedback and coaching as well.

It may also be possible to identify potentially outstanding leaders through the use of personality tests. Spangler and House (1991) empirically demonstrated that U.S. presidential motives were predictive of presidential effectiveness and greatness. Similarly, Rouse and Atwater (1991), and Ross and Offermann (1991) demonstrated that there are a set of personality characteristics strongly associated with transformational and charismatic leader behaviors. These studies provide clues that can be used for the identification and selection of potential outstanding leaders. However, considerable work is yet required to develop and validate instruments that can be used in applied field settings.

Third, it may be possible to increase leader effectiveness by providing managers with behavioral training and role models intended to increase their ability to engage in the behaviors that differentiate outstanding from ordinary leaders. Again, behavioral observation of potential leaders in management simulations can be used to provide feedback and coaching. Further, a study by Howell and Frost (1989) demonstrated the possibility of training outstanding leaders. These authors demonstrated that selected individuals could be trained to engage in structured, supportive, and charismatic leader behaviors. However, the individuals who were trained were selected on the basis of their ability to engage in the various leader behaviors in role playing exercises. Their impact was observed in an experimentally isolated setting over a short period of time. We do not know whether outstanding leader behaviors can be acquired through training and applied to field settings, or whether behaviors acquired in this way would have the expected effects on followers in natural organizational settings over extended periods of time.

The development of outstanding leadership by the use of role models is also suggested by prior research. Bass, Waldman, Avolio, and Bebb (1987) found that middle and lower level managers' behavior can be predicted from the behavior of their superiors. Thus, a personal example set by one's superior provides a means by which leaders learn outstanding leader behavior through observation. Fourth, prior research (House, 1968) suggested the kinds of organizational policies, norms, and reward systems that need to be employed if outstanding leadership is to be practiced. There is substantial evidence that leadership practices reflect the practices of the organization in which the leader works and the practices of one's immediate superiors (cf. Fleishman, Harris, & Burtt, 1955; House, 1968; Sykes, 1962; Weiss, 1977).

If outstanding leadership is to be encouraged, it is necessary to provide role models, organizational norms, and supportive organizational practices. At a minimum, the behavior of higher level managers, performance appraisal and incentive systems, and management practices, policies, rules, and regulations, need to reflect the same values as the values that are implicit in the desired leader behavior if developmental efforts are to be effective in bringing about desired leader behavior.

FUTURE RESEARCH DIRECTIONS

The prescriptive implications described previously will require considerable research to develop and validate the necessary selection, training, and incentive systems. As argued earlier, there is an identifiable and definable set of genotypic processes in which outstanding leaders engage, but these processes are likely enacted in a variety of different phenotypic ways. The appropriateness of such enactments likely depends on contexts in which they occur and the expectations of followers. Historical accounts make it clear that both Gandhi and Patton were outstanding leaders, both engaged in the same genotypic processes of articulating a vision, demonstrating conviction in the correctness of their visions, showing confidence in themselves and their followers, taking extraordinary personal risks in the interest of the vision and the collectivity, communicating high performance expectations of their followers, and presenting themselves in a manner consistent with the mission they lead. Yet, the phenotypic expression by which they enacted such processes was strikingly different behaviorally. Clearly, substantial research will be required to explain and predict and phenotypic behavioral manifestations of the genotypic outstanding leadership processes identified in the numerous studies cited earlier. Further, additional research is required to determine why the phenotypic enactments of the genotypic outstanding processes differ across cultures and situations.

Research also needs to address the relationship between the behaviors which affect the motivational processes described, and instrumental leader behaviors that effect follower expectations of reward and punishment and cognitions and skills relevant to effective performance and satisfaction. Bass (1985) argued that the behaviors he labeled as transformational leader behaviors augment transactional leader behaviors. However, both dissonance theory (Aronson, 1980) and self-perception theory (Bem, 1982) suggested that transactional leader behaviors such as management-by-exception and contingent reward and punishment undermine engagement of follower self-concepts and discourage intrinsic follower motivation.

A related issue concerns the cognitive-instrumental skills required for leaders to be outstanding. Nadler and Tushman (1990) argued persuasively that charismatic leader behavior alone is inadequate, and that high level leaders need to have the skills to conceive and implement appropriate organizational infrastructures such as incentive, control, and support systems. It can be further argued that strategy formulation and implementation abilities are also required of high level leaders, and that inappropriate strategies are likely to lead to disastrous consequences, especially if the leaders who conceive of such strategies have powerful effects on the three core affective motivational processes described above. For example, both Napoleon and Hitler were able to strongly motivate their followers, but their strategies were flawed in that they underestimated the ability of the Russian army to prolong their invasions until the severe effects of Russian winters took their toll on the invading armies. Similarly, General George Custer underestimated the strength of the Sioux, only to incur the complete slaughter of his troops. Clearly, followers can be motivated to enthusiastically embrace flawed strategies that eventually lead to failure.

CONCLUSION: TOWARD A THEORY
OF EFFECTIVE LEADERSHIP

Our review of the theories and research in the leadership domain has, of necessity, been brief. As a result, we have not been able to discuss in detail all of the past or contemporary theories of leadership effectiveness. Nor have we been able to adequately review the impressive amount of empirical research that has been garnered to test these theories. However, our intent was not to provide a comprehensive review of all the literature on leadership effectiveness. Such an ambitious undertaking would require more space than the chapters represented in this book combined. Rather, our goal was to provide a selected review of the leadership literature, with particular emphasis on one emerging theory of leadership (outstanding leadership theory) that we feel holds much promise for our understanding of leadership effectiveness.

Taken in this light, we believe that this chapter represents a first step toward an integrated theory of outstanding leadership. The theory provides a basis for the identification and integration of leader behaviors that are generic to outstanding leadership and differentiate outstanding from ordinary leaders. The theory provides an explanation of how and why selected leader behaviors have such profound effects on the affective states of followers. Of course, additional research needs to be conducted to validate the theory, and to identify the antecedents to the emergence of outstanding leaders. Undoubtedly, such antecedents concern the personality characteristics of both leaders and followers, and the social conditions that give rise to, and facilitate or impede, the emergence and effectiveness of such leaders. Hopefully, the propositions advanced in this theory will be subjected to empirical tests, and additional propositions will be advanced to provide a more complete theory of outstanding leadership.

REFERENCES

Aronson, E. (1980). Persuasion by self justification: Large commitments for small rewards. In L. Festinger (Ed.), *Retrospections on social psychology* (pp. 3–21). New York: Oxford University Press.

Ashour, A. S. (1973). The contingency model of leadership effectiveness: An evaluation. *Organizational Behavior and Human Performance, 9*, 339–355.

Ashour, A. S., & Johns, G. (1983). Leader influence through operant principles: A theoretical and methodological framework. *Human Relations, 36*, 603–626.

Atkinson, J. W., Heyns, R. W., & Veroff, J. (1954). The effect of experimental arousal of the affiliation motive on thematic apperception. *Journal of Abnormal and Social Psychology, 49*, 405–410.

Avolio, B. J., Waldman, D. A., & Einstein, W. O. (1988). Transformational leadership in a management game simulation, *Group and Organization Studies, 13*, 59–80.

Bandura, A. (1986). *Social foundations of thought and action: A social cognitive theory.* Englewood Cliffs, NJ: Prentice-Hall.

Barnlund, D. C. (1962). Consistency of emergent leadership in groups with changing tasks and members. *Speech Monographs, 29*, 45–52.

Bass, B. M. (1985). *Leadership and performance beyond expectations.* New York: The Free Press.

Bass, B. M. (1990). *Bass and Stogdill's Handbook of Leadership Theory, Research, and Managerial Applications* (3rd ed). New York: The Free Press.

Bass, B. M., & Avolio, B. J. (1989). Potential biases in leadership measures: How prototypes, leniency, and general satisfaction relate to rating and rankings of transformational and transactional leadership constructs. *Educational and Psychological Measurement, 49*, 509–527.

Bass, B. M., Waldman, D. A., Avolio, B. J., & Bebb, M. (1987). Transformational leadership: The falling dominoes effect. *Group and Organization Studies, 12*, 73–87.

Bellah, R. N., Madsen, R., Sullivan, W. M., Swidler, A., & Tipton, S. M. (1985). *Habits of the heart: Individualism and commitment in American life.* New York: Harper & Row.

Bem, D. J. (1982). Self-perception theory. In L. Berkowitz (Ed.), *Advances in experimental social psychology* (Vol. 6, pp. 2–62). New York: Academic Press.

Bennis, W., & Nanus, B. (1985). *Leaders: The strategies for taking charge.* New York: Harper & Row.

Berlew, D. E. (1974). Leadership and organizational excitement. *California Management Review, 17*, 21–30.

Blumenson, M. (1985). *Patton: The man behind the legend.* New York: William Morrow.

Boal, K. B., & Bryson, J. M. (1987). Charismatic leadership: A phenomenological and structural approach. In J. G. Hunt et al. (Eds.), *Emerging Leadership Vistas.* (pp. 11–25). Lexington, MA: DC Heath.

Bowers, D. G. (1975). Hierarchy, function, and the generalizability of leadership practices. In J. G. Hunt & L. L. Larson (Eds.), *Leadership frontiers* (pp. 167–180). Kent, OH: Kent State University Press.

Bryman, A. (1992). *Charisma & leadership in organizations.* London: Sage.

Burns, J. M. (1978). *Leadership.* New York: Harper & Row.

Conger, J. A., & Kanungo, R. A. (1987). Towards a behavioral theory of charismatic leadership in organizational settings. *Academy of Management Review, 12,* 637–647.

Conger, J. A., & Kanungo, R. S. (1988). Behavioral dimensions of charismatic leadership. In J. A. Conger & R. N. Kanungo (Eds.), *Charismatic Leadership: The elusive factor in organizational effectiveness.* (pp. 78–97). San Francisco: Jossey-Bass.

Curphy, G. J. (1990). *An empirical study of Bass' (1985) theory of transformational and transactional leadership.* Unpublished doctoral dissertation, University of Minnesota.

Dansereau, F., Graen, G., & Haga, W. J. (1975). A vertical dyad linkage approach to leadership within formal organizations. *Organizational Behavior and Human Performance, 13,* 46–78.

Eden, D. (1990). *Pygmalion in management.* Lexington, MA: DC Heath.

Farris, G. F., & Lim, F. G. (1969). Effects of performance on leadership, cohesiveness, influence, satisfaction, and subsequent performance. *Journal of Applied Psychology, 53,* 490–499.

Fiedler, F. E. (1967). *A Theory of Leadership Effectiveness.* New York: McGraw-Hill.

Fiedler, F. E. (1971). Validation and extension of the contingency model of leadership effectiveness: A review of empirical findings. *Psychological Bulletin, 76,* 128–148.

Fiedler, F. E., & Chemers, M. M. (1974). *Leadership and effective management.* Glenview, IL: Scott, Foresman.

Fiol, C. M., Harris, D., & House, R. (1992). *Charismatic leadership: Strategies for effecting social change.* Working Paper, University of Colorado at Denver.

Fleishman, E. A., Harris, E. F., & Burtt, H. E. (1955). *Leadership and supervision in industry.* Columbus, Ohio: Bureau of Educational Research, Ohio State University.

French, E. G., & Chadwick, I. (1956). Some characteristics of affiliation motivation. *Journal of Abnormal and Social Psychology, 52,* 296–300.

Friedman, H. S., DiMatteo, M. R., & Taranta, A. (1980). A study of the relationship between individual differences in nonverbal expressiveness and factors of personality and social interaction. *Journal of Research in Personality, 14,* 351–364.

Friedman, H. S., & Riggio, R. E. (1981). Effect of individual differences in nonverbal expressiveness on transmission of emotion. *Journal of Nonverbal Behavior, 6,* 96–104.

Gibb, C. A. (1947). The principles and traits of leadership. *Journal of Abnormal and Social Psychology, 42,* 267–284.

Goffman, E. (1974). *Frame analysis.* Cambridge, MA: Harvard University Press.

Graen, G., & Cashman, J. F. (1975). A role making model of leadership in formal organizations: A developmental approach. In J. G. Hunt & L. L. Larson (Eds.), *Leadership Frontiers.* (pp. 143–165). Carbondale, IL: Southern Illinois University Press.

Graen, G., & Schiemann, W. (1978). Leader-member agreement: A vertical dyad linkage approach. *Journal of Applied Psychology, 63,* 206–212.

Halpin, A. W., & Winer, B. J. (1957). A factorial study of the leader behavior descriptions. In R. M. Stogdill & A. E. Coons (Eds.), *Leader behavior: Its description and measurement* (pp. 39–51). Columbus: Ohio State University, Bureau of Business Research.

Hannan, M., & Freeman, J. (1984). Structural inertia and organizational change. *American Sociological Review, 49,* 149–164.

Heckhausen, H. (1967). *The anatomy of achievement motivation.* New York: Academic Press.

Hemphill, J. K., & Coons, A. E. (1957). Development of the leader behavior description questionnaire. In R. M. Stogdill & A. E. Coons (Eds.), *Leader behavior: Its description and measurement.* (pp. 6–38). Columbus: Ohio State University, Bureau of Business Research.

Hodgkinson, C. (1983). *The philosophy of leadership.* New York: St. Martin's Press.

Hogan, R. T., Raskin, R., & Fazzini, D. (1990). The dark side of leadership. In K. E. Clark & M. B. Clark (Eds.), *Measures of leadership.* (pp. 343–354). West Orange, NJ: Leadership Library of America.

Hollander, E. P. (1978). *Leadership dynamics: A practical guide to effective relationships.* New York: The Free Press.

Hollander, E. P., & Julian, J. W. (1968). Leadership. In E. F. Borgatta & W. W. Lambert (Eds.), *Handbook of personality theory and research*. Chicago: Rand McNally.

Hollander, E. P., & Julian, J. W. (1969). Contemporary trends in the analysis of leadership processes. *Psychological Bulletin, 71*, 387–397.

Hollander, E. P., & Julian, J. W. (1970). Studies in leader legitimacy, influence, and innovation. In L. Berkowitz (Ed.), *Advances in experimental and social psychology* (Vol. 5., pp. 33–69). New York: Academic Press.

House, R. J. (1968). Leadership training: Some dysfunctional consequences. *Administrative Science Quarterly, 12*, 556–571.

House, R. J. (1971). A path goal theory of leader effectiveness. *Administrative Science Quarterly, 16*, 321–338.

House, R. J. (1977). A 1976 theory of charismatic leadership. In J. G. Hunt & L. L. Larson (Eds.), *Leadership: The cutting edge* (pp. 189–207). Carbondale, IL: Southern Illinois University Press.

House, R. J. (1993). A theory of outstanding leadership [Working paper]. Wharton School of Business, University of Pennsylvania.

House, R. J., & Baetz, M. L. (1979). Leadership: Some empirical generalizations and new research directions. In B. M. Staw (Ed.), *Research in Organizational Behavior, 1*, 341–423.

House, R. J., & Dessler, G. (1974). The path-goal theory of leadership: Some post hoc and a priori tests. In J. G. Hunt & L. L. Larson (Eds.), *Contingency Approaches to Leadership* (pp. 29–55). Carbondale, IL: Southern Illinois University Press.

House, R. J., & Howell, J. M. (1992). Personality and charismatic leadership. *Leadership Quarterly, 3*, 81–108.

House, R. J., Howell, J. M., Shamir, B., Smith, B., & Spangler, W. D. (1993). *Charismatic leadership: A 1993 theory and five empirical tests.* [Working paper]. The School of Business Administration, The University of Western Ontario, London, Ont.

House, R. J., & Mitchell, T. R. (1974). Path-goal theory of leadership. *Journal of Contemporary Business, 3*, 81–97.

House, R. J., & Shamir, B. (1993). Toward the integration of transformational, charismatic and visionary theories of leadership. In M. Chemmers & R. Ayman (Eds.), *Leadership: Perspectives and research directions* (pp. 81–107). New York: Academic Press.

House, R. J., Spangler, D. W., & Woycke, J. (1991). Personality and charisma in the U.S. Presidency: A psychological theory of leader effectiveness. *Administrative Science Quarterly, 36*, 364–396.

House, R. J., Woycke, J., & Fodor, E. M. (1988). Charismatic and non-charismatic leaders: Differences in behavior and effectiveness. In J. A. Conger & R. N. Kanungo (Eds.), *Charismatic leadership: The elusive factor in organizational effectiveness* (pp. 98–121). San Francisco: Jossey-Bass.

Howell, J. M. (1988). Two faces of charisma: Socialized and personalized leadership in organizations. In J. A. Conger & R. N. Kanungo (Eds.), *Charismatic Leadership* (pp. 213–236). San Francisco: Jossey-Bass.

Howell, J. P., Dorfman, P. W., & Kerr, S. (1986). Moderator variables in leadership research. *Academy of Management Review, 11*, 88–102.

Howell, J. M., & Frost, P. J. (1989). A laboratory study of charismatic leadership, *Organizational Behavior and Human Decision Processes, 43*, 243–269.

Howell, J. M., & Higgins, C. A. (1990a). Champions of technological innovation, *Administrative Science Quarterly, 35*, 317–341.

Howell, J. M., & Higgins, C. A. (1990b). Leadership behaviors, influence tactics, and career experiences of champions of technological innovation. *Leadership Quarterly, 1*, 249–264.

Howell, J. M., & House, R. J. (1992). *Socialized and personalized charisma: An essay on the bright and dark sides of leadership.* Unpublished manuscript, School of Business Administration, The University of Western Ontario.

Jago, A. G. (1982). Leadership: Perspectives in theory and research. *Management Science, 28,* 315–336.

Jenkins, W. O. (1947). A review of leadership studies with particular reference to military problems. *Psychological Bulletin, 44,* 54–79.

Kahn, R. L., & Katz, D. (1953). Leadership practices in relation to productivity and morale. In D. Cartwright & A. Zander (Eds.), *Group dynamics* (pp. 554–571). New York: Harper & Row.

Katz, D., Maccoby, N., & Morse, N. (1950). *Productivity, supervision, and morale among railroad workers.* Ann Arbor: University of Michigan, Survey Research Center.

Kenny, D. A., & Hallmark, B. W. (1992). Rotation designs in leadership research. *Leadership Quarterly, 3,* 25–41.

Kenny, D. A., & Zaccaro, S. J. (1983). An estimate of the variance due to traits in leadership. *Journal of Applied Psychology, 68,* 678–685.

Kerr, S., & Jermier, J. M. (1978). Substitutes for leadership: Their meaning and measurement. *Organizational Behavior and Human Performance, 22,* 375–403.

Kirkpatrick S. A. (1992). *Decomposing charismatic leadership: The effects of leader content and process on follower performance, attitudes, and perceptions.* Unpublished doctoral dissertation, University of Maryland.

Koh, W. L., Terborg, J. R., & Steers, R. M. (1991, August). *The impact of transformational leaders on organizational commitment, organizational citizenship behavior, teacher satisfaction and student performance in Singapore.* Paper presented at The Academy of Management Meetings, Miami, FL.

Korman, A. K. (1971). Expectancies as determinants of performance. *Journal of Applied Psychology, 55,* 218–222.

Kotter, J. P. (1988). *The leadership factor.* New York: The Free Press.

Lewin, K., Lippitt, R., & White, R. K. (1939). Patterns of aggressive behavior in experimentally created social climates. *Journal of Social Psychology, 10,* 271–299.

Lieberson, S., & O'Connor, J. F. (1972). Leadership and organization performances: A study of large corporations. *American Sociological Review, 37,* 117–130.

Lindholm, C. (1990). *Charisma.* Cambridge, MA: Basil Blackwell.

Lord, R. G., DeVader, C. L., & Alliger, G. M. (1986). A meta-analysis of the relation between personality traits and leadership perceptions: An application of validity generalization procedures. *Journal of Applied Psychology, 71,* 402–410.

Mann, R. D. (1959). A review of the relationship between personality and performance in small groups. *Psychological Bulletin, 56,* 241–270.

McClelland, D. C. (1953). *The achievement motive.* New York: Appleton-Century-Crofts.

McClelland, D. C. (1972). What is the effect of achievement motivation training in the schools? *Teachers College Record, 74,* 129–145.

McClelland, D. C. (1985). *Human motivation.* Glenview, IL: Scott, Foresman.

McClelland, D. C., & Boyatzis, R. (1982). The leadership pattern and long term success in management. *Journal of Applied Psychology, 67,* 737–743.

Meindl, J. R., Ehrlich, S. B., & Dukerich, J. M. (1985). The romance of leadership. *Administrative Science Quarterly, 30,* 788–802.

Miller, D., & Droge, C. (1986). Psychological and traditional determinants of structure. *Administrative Science Quarterly, 31,* 539–560.

Mullin, R. (1992). An end-value theory of charismatic influence [Working Paper]. College of Business and Economics, Central Missouri State University.

Nadler, D. A., & Tushman, M. L. (1990). Beyond the charismatic leader: Leadership and organizational change, *California Management Review, 32,* 77–97.

Organ, D. W. (1988). *Organizational citizenship behavior: The good soldier syndrome.* Lexington, MA: DC Health.

Pfeffer, J. (1977). The Ambiguity of Leadership. *Academy of Management Journal, 2,* 104–112.

Pillai, R., & Meindl, J. R. (1991). The effects of a crisis on the emergence of charismatic leadership: A laboratory study. *Best Paper Proceedings: Annual Meeting of the Academy of Management, Miami*, 420–425.

Podsakoff, P. M., MacKenzie, S. B., & Fetter, R. (1993a). Substitutes for leadership and the management of professionals. *Leadership Quarterly, 4*, 1–44.

Podsakoff, P. M., MacKenzie, S. B., Moorman, R. H., & Fetter, R. (1990). Transformational leader behaviors and their effects on followers' trust in leader, satisfaction, and organizational citizenship behaviors. *Leadership Quarterly, 1*, 107–142.

Podsakoff, P. M., Niehoff, B. P., MacKenzie, S. B., & Williams, M. L. (1993b). Do substitutes for leadership really substitute for leadership? An empirical examination of Kerr and Jermier's situational leadership model. *Organizational Behavior and Human Decision Processes, 54*, 1–44.

Podsakoff, P. M., Todor, W. D., Grover, R. A., & Huber, V. L. (1984). Situational moderators of leader reward and punishment behaviors: Fact or fiction? *Organizational Behavior and Human Performance, 34*, 21–63.

Podsakoff, P. M., Todor, W. D., & Skov, R. (1982). Effects of leader contingent and noncontingent reward and punishment behaviors on subordinate performance and satisfaction. *Academy of Management Journal, 25*, 810–821.

Roberts, N. C. (1985). Transforming leadership: A process of collective action. *Human Relations, 38*, 1023–1046.

Rosenthal, R., & Jacobson, L. (1968). *Pygmalion in the classroom: Teacher expectation and pupils' intellectual development*. New York: Holt, Rinehart & Winston.

Ross, S. M., & Offermann, L. R. (1991, April). *Transformational leaders: Measurement of personality attributes and work group performance*. Paper presented at the annual meeting of the Society for Industrial Organizational Psychology, St. Louis, MO.

Rouse, P. E., & Atwater, L. E. (1991, April). Using the MBTI to understand transformational leadership and self perception accuracy. Paper presented at the annual Society for Industrial and Organizational Behavior, St. Louis, MO.

Salancik, G. R., & Pfeffer, J. (1977). Constraints on administrator discretion: Limited influence of mayors on city budgets. *Urban Affairs Quarterly, 12*, 475–498.

Sashkin, M. (1988). The visionary leader. In J. A. Conger & R. A. Kanungo (Eds.), *Charismatic leadership: The elusive factor in organizational effectiveness*, (pp. 122–160). San Francisco: Jossey-Bass.

Schriesheim, C. A., House, R. J., & Kerr, S. (1976). Leader initiating structure: A reconciliation of discrepant research results and some empirical tests. *Organizational Behavior and Human Performance, 15*, 297–321.

Schriesheim, C. A., & Kerr, S. (1977a). Theories and measures of leadership. In J. G. Hunt & L. L. Larson (Eds.), *Leadership: The cutting edge* (pp. 9–45). Carbondale, IL: Southern Illinois University Press.

Schriesheim, C. A., & Kerr, S. (1977b). R.I.P. LPC: A response to Fiedler. In J. G. Hunt & L. L. Larson (Eds.), *Leadership: The cutting edge* (pp. 51–56). Carbondale, IL: Southern Illinois University Press.

Schriesheim, C. A., & Stogdill, R. M. (1975). Differences in factor structure across three versions of the Ohio State leadership scales. *Personnel Psychology, 28*, 189–206.

Schriesheim, C. A., & von Glinow, M. A. (1977). Tests of the path-goal theory of leadership: A theoretical and empirical analysis. *Academy of Management Journal, 20*, 398–405.

Shamir, B., House, R. J., & Arthur, M. (1993). The motivational effects of charismatic leadership: A self-concept based theory. *Organization Science, 4*, 577–594.

Shils, E. A. (1965). Charisma, order, and status. *American Sociological Review, 30*, 199–213.

Shipley, T. E., & Veroff, J. (1952). Projective measure of need for affiliation. *Journal of Experimental Psychology, 43*, 349–356.

Sims, H. P., Jr., & Szylagyi, A. D. (1975). Leader reward behavior and subordinate satisfaction and performance. *Organizational Behavior and Human Performance, 14*, 426–438.

Snow, D. A., Rochford, E. B., Worden, S. K., & Benford, R. D. (1986). Frame alignment processes, micromobilization, and movement participation. *American Sociological Review, 51,* 464–481.

Spangler, W. D., & House, R. J. (1991). Presidential effectiveness and the leadership motive profile. *Journal of Personality and Social Psychology, 60,* 439–455.

Steele, R. S. (1977). Power motivation, activation, and inspirational speeches. *Journal of Personality, 45,* 53–64.

Stogdill, R. M. (1948). Personal factors associated with leadership: A survey of the literature. *Journal of Psychology, 25,* 35–71.

Stogdill, R. M. (1950). Leadership, membership and organization. *Psychological Bulletin, 47,* 1–14.

Stogdill, R. M. (1969). Validity of leader behavior descriptions. *Personnel Psychology, 22,* 153–158.

Stogdill, R. M. (1974). *Handbook of leadership: A survey of theory and research.* New York: The Free Press.

Stogdill, R. M., & Coons, A. E. (1957). *Leader behavior: Its description and measurement.* Columbus: Ohio State University, Bureau of Business Research.

Sykes, A. J. M. (1962). The effect of a supervisory training course in changing supervisors' perceptions and expectations of the role of management. *Human Relations, 15,* 227–243.

Szylagyi, A. D. (1980). Causal inferences between leader reward behavior and subordinate goal attainment, absenteeism, and work satisfaction. *Journal of Occupational Psychology, 53,* 195–204.

Tichy, N. M., & Devanna, M. A. (1986). *The transformational leader.* New York: Wiley.

Trice, H. M., & Beyer, J. M. (1986). Charisma and its routinization in two social movement organizations. In B. M. Staw & L. L. Cummings (Eds.), *Research in organizational behavior* (Vol. 8, pp. 113–164). Greenwich, CT: JAI Press.

Vecchio, R. P. (1977). An empirical examination of the validity of Fiedler's model of leadership effectiveness. *Organizational Behavior and Human Performance, 19,* 180–206.

Vecchio, R. P. (1983). Assessing the validity of Fiedler's contingency model of leadership effectiveness: A closer look at Strube and Garcia. *Psychological Bulletin, 93,* 404–408.

Vroom, V. H. (1964). *Work and motivation.* New York: McGraw-Hall.

Wahba, M., & Bridwell, L. (1975). Maslow reconsidered: A review of the need hierarchy theory. *Organizational Behavior and Human Performance.*

Weber, M. (1947). *The theory of social and economic organization.* (T. Parsons, Ed.; A. M. Henderson & T. Parsons, Trans.) New York: The Free Press. (Original work published 1924)

Webster's New Twentieth Century Dictionary, Unabridged, 2nd ed. (1983). New York: Simon & Schuster.

Weiss, H. M. (1977). Subordinate imitation of supervisor behavior: The role of modeling in organizational socialization. *Organizational Behavior and Human Performance, 19,* 89–105.

Weissenberg, P., & Kavanagh, M. J. (1972). The interdependence of initiating structure and consideration: A review of the evidence. *Personnel Psychology, 55,* 119–130.

White, R. K., & Lippitt, R. (1960). *Autocracy and democracy: An experimental inquiry.* New York: Harper & Row.

Willner, A. R. (1984). *The spellbinders: Charismatic political leadership.* New Haven: CT: Yale University Press.

Winter, D. G. (1973). *The power motive.* New York: The Free Press.

Zaccaro, S. J., Foti, R. J., & Kenny, D. A. (1991). Self-monitoring and trait-based variance in leadership: An investigation of leader flexibility across multiple group situations. *Journal of Applied Psychology, 76,* 308–315.

4

ORGANIZATIONAL ATTACHMENT: ATTITUDES AND ACTIONS

Thomas W. Lee
Terence R. Mitchell
University of Washington

Similar to the employee who pauses to evaluate one's job with respect to progress toward personal and occupational goals, this chapter pauses, metaphorically, to assess the research on employee attachment to the organization. Rather than being evaluated by personal standards, the research on organizational attachment is evaluated against the scientific criteria of theoretical grounding, empirical inquiry, and paradigmatic improvement. Judgments on the quality, meaning, and promise for new research directions will be liberally offered. As such, our attention focuses primarily on academically oriented research and theory, and only secondarily on intervention based or practitioner focused approaches. Although organizational attachment is the general domain, the research and theory connecting job attitudes to withdrawal behaviors constitute the chapter's more specific focus. Though other work attitudes and behaviors will be considered, our immediate attention centers on job satisfaction, organizational commitment, turnover, and absenteeism. Moreover, the chapter does not focus on the research directed toward these variables in isolation. We are mainly concerned with the research that links the attitudes of job satisfaction and organizational commitment with the withdrawal behaviors of turnover and absenteeism. Following, five major sections are presented toward this end. First, the focal work attitudes of job satisfaction and organizational commitment and the primary withdrawal behaviors of turnover and absenteeism are defined. Second, the extensive literature on organizational attachment is summarized through four themes drawn from this research. Third, we express our opinions about these themes. Fourth, several current research topics that are not commonly associated with employee withdrawal are shown to be relevant for understanding the withdrawal process. The integration of these topics with the theory on organizational attachment suggests some new research directions. Finally, some concluding thoughts are offered.

DEFINITIONS

Job Satisfaction

In the discipline's early years, job satisfaction referenced virtually all feelings about the job, including affect, desire to change jobs, and relative comparisons of one's own feelings to the hypothetical feelings of other people (Herzberg, Mausner, & Snyderman, 1959). Over the years, the concept of job satisfaction has received greater, though gradual, specification. For example, Vroom (1964) added specification by stating ". . . job satisfaction . . . refer[s] to affective orientations on the part of the individual toward work roles which they are presently occupying." (p. 99). A few years later, Smith, Kendall, and Hulin (1969) added still more specification by stating "Job satisfactions are feelings or affective responses to facets of the situations" (p. 6) . . . and "a function of the perceived characteristics of the job in relation to an individual's frame of reference" (p. 12). With perhaps the most detailed specification, Locke (1976) stated "Job satisfaction may be defined . . . as a pleasurable or positive emotional state resulting from the appraisals of one's job or job experiences" (p. 1300) . . . and "results from the attainment of values which are compatible with one's needs" (p. 1328).

When taken together, three themes may characterize the conceptualization and understanding of job satisfaction. First, employees usually have both an overall evaluative reaction to their jobs, as well as a set of more focused reactions to the jobs' specific facets. Furthermore, the overall evaluation should correlate quite highly, in general, with the sum of these facet based satisfactions. Second, these evaluative reactions result from perceived discrepancies involving various needs or wants. That is, dissatisfaction should occur when employees perceive substantial differences between what one feels he or she *should* receive and what one *does* receive from the job. Finally, these reactions are heavily determined by one's framing of the situation in terms of time and context. Job satisfaction involves responses to prior or current facets of the work situation, as well as projected reactions to future events and conditions, which have been called anticipated job satisfaction (Mobley, Griffeth, Hand, & Meglino, 1979).

Organizational Commitment

In the discipline's early years, organizational commitment was not a common term. Rather, portions of the modern day meaning of commitment (defined later) were more readily captured by concepts like personnel and organizational loyalties

(Barnard, 1938), organizational identity (Simon, 1945), and identity (March & Simon, 1958). Over the years, taxonomies have sought to capture the inherent complexity of employee loyalty and corporate identification. For example, Etzioni (1961) proposed that commitment could be based on moral involvement, economically rational calculation, or exploitive relations among individuals. A few years later, Kanter (1968) proposed that commitment could be derived from the personal sacrifices one makes toward an organization's survival, cohesion between an individual and other people in the company, and acceptance of the firm's norms. In what was a dominant conceptualization for perhaps 15 years, Porter and his colleagues proposed that organizational commitment involved the internalization of the company's goals and values, a willingness to exert considerable effort on behalf of the firm, and a desire to remain a member (Mowday, Steers & Porter, 1979).

More recently, organizational commitment has been summarized into pairs of distinctive dimensions. One pair consists of attitude (Staw, 1977) and behavioral commitment (Salancik, 1977). Attitudinal commitment refers to the employee's internalization of the organization's goals and values. It includes the notions of organizational loyalty and company identity and is virtually identical to Porter's first dimension. Behavioral commitment refers to specific characteristics surrounding a given decision to join an organization. If the decision to join can be characterized as volitional, explicit, public, relatively irrevocable, and insufficiently justified, the decision is said to be more binding than otherwise. A second pair of dimensions consists of affective and continuance commitment (Meyer & Allen, 1984). Like attitudinal commitment, affective commitment also refers to the employee's internalization of the organization's goals and values and is virtually identical to Porter's first dimension. Continuance commitment refers to the intendedly rational comparison of the costs and benefits associated with staying or leaving the company and appears to be very similar to Etzioni's (1961) second dimension, namely, economically rational calculation. Finally, O'Reilly and Chatman (1986) proposed psychological and instrumental attachment. Psychological attachment appears to be identical with attitudinal and affective commitment and again refers to the internalization of the organization's goals and values. Instrumental attachment appears to be similar to continuance commitment and Etzioni's (1961) calculative dimension. When taken together, the discipline seems to have defined organizational commitment as involving two primary dimensions, namely, psychological and instrumental attachment.

Turnover

Within the discipline, the majority of the research on turnover has focused on the employee's volitional departure from the organization. Moreover, the volitional nature of turnover has been most often theorized as a simple unidimensional concept. The prevailing theories (e.g., Mobley, 1977; Price & Mueller, 1986; Steers

& Mowday, 1981) posited that turnover results from a decision to stay or leave, which is, in turn, based on the major antecedents of job satisfaction and perceived alternatives. Over the years, a few scholars have sought to expand the volitional aspect of turnover. For example, Dalton, Krackhardt, and Porter (1981) discussed the circumstances under which turnover can be functional versus dysfunctional and avoidable versus unavoidable. Jackofsky and Peters (1984) argued for the meaningful distinction between inter and intraorganizational turnover. Despite these efforts to broaden the focus, the unidimensional nature of voluntary turnover remains the discipline's dominant conceptualization.

Absenteeism

Whereas the research on job satisfaction, organizational commitment, and turnover have been largely theory based and cumulative, the research on absenteeism has evolved along three somewhat distinct and relatively separate lines (Rhodes & Steers, 1990). One line has been intervention based; a second has been measurement oriented; and the third has been theory driven. As a result, the definition of absenteeism has not evolved as systematically as that of job satisfaction, organizational commitment, and turnover.

In many organizational settings, absenteeism is often interpreted as an indirect indicator of more serious managerial problems (e.g., lost production, additional labor costs). Quite understandably, many published studies, as well as internal technical reports, describe interventions aimed at managing absenteeism (e.g., Frayne & Latham, 1987). Understanding and defining absenteeism in a precise and agreed upon manner, however, often receives only passing attention in these more intervention based studies.

Another sizable portion of the research literature involves discussions of definitions and measurement. For example, Atkin and Goodman (1984) discussed the ambiguities involved with absenteeism's definition and measurement (e.g., excused versus unexcused absences, how to handle chronic or long term illness). Landy, Vasey, and Smith (1984) identified the statistical problems commonly encountered when analyzing absence data. Several theorists (Ilgen, 1977; Latham & Pursell, 1975, 1977) debated whether researchers should address attendance or absenteeism. More recently, Rhodes and Steers (1990) summarized the many operationalizations of absenteeism. To date, however, absenteeism has been most commonly operationalizations in terms of (a) *magnitude* (i.e., the total number of hours absent in a given time period divided by the total number of employees), (b) *frequency* (i.e., the number of absence events regardless of duration for a given period of time), and (c) *duration* (i.e., the total number of days absent divided by the total number of scheduled work days).

Simultaneously occurring with the intervention-based and measurement-oriented studies, there have been efforts at theorizing about absenteeism. Unfortunately, these theoretical efforts have been quite different and do not represent a clear accumulation of knowledge. For example, Steers and Rhodes (1978) theorized about the causes of attendance rather than absenteeism, whereas Hulin (1991) theorized about a general withdrawal construct with absenteeism as only one of several behavioral outcomes. In a very innovative approach (detailed following), Fitchman (1989) theorized about "absence spells" rather than the more common conceptualizations of duration and frequency. When taken together, the discipline has still not reached agreement on how best to conceptualize absenteeism. Correspondingly, the discipline has not approached agreement on how to measure absenteeism as well.

Employee Attachment: Where Has Organizational Behavior Been? Even a casual survey of the research and theory on employee attachment reveals a substantial body of literature. As one indication of this magnitude, literature reviews on employee attachment appear with great regularity. From our reading of this literature, four major themes might effectively summarize the research. After presenting these themes, commentary will be offered in the next section.

Theme 1: Testing and Improving the Majors Model of Turnover

Some researchers continued to test the major psychological models of turnover (e.g., Mobley, 1977; Price & Mueller, 1986; Steers & Mowday, 1981). In general, these models suggest that job dissatisfaction results in lower organizational commitment, which then leads to various withdrawal cognitions (e.g., "thinking of quitting"). Furthermore, these withdrawal cognitions are theorized to precede a search for and examination of job alternatives, which in turn produce the intent to stay or leave. Finally, actual staying or leaving follows. In comparison to research reported in the late 1970s and early 1980s when these theories were developed, subsequent work has been more comprehensive. Whereas Mobley, Horner, and Hollingsworth (1978) tested a shortened version of the Mobley (1977) model, for example, Hom, Griffeth, and Sellaro (1984) tested the complete theory. Similarly, Stumpf and Hartman (1984) and Lee and Mowday (1987) reported fairly comprehensive tests of the Steers and Mowday (1981) model. More recently, researchers have also sought to improve upon the major models. Based on their comprehensive test, for instance, Hom et al. (1984) proposed an alternative formulation to the Mobley (1977) model. In subsequent research, Hom and Griffeth (1991) and Hom, Caranikas-Walker, Prussia, and Griffeth (1992) sought to validate their alternative model by applying very rigorous structural equation analysis.

Theme 2: Alternative Antecedents to Turnover

In addition to inquiry on formal turnover models, other researchers explored the role of job performance as an antecedent to employee turnover. Dreher (1982), for example, argued for the moderating effects of job performance on the relationships between attitudes and turnover. In particular, Dreher suggested that better performing employees tend to stay when they work in a performance–contingent reward system and it is difficult to communicate to a perspective employer their level of past performance. In contrast, better performing employees tend to leave when they work in a nonperformance–contingent reward system and they can unambiguously communicate to a prospective employer their level of past performance. Under other conditions, Dreher suggested no systematic relationships. Other researchers have considered not only the costs but the benefits of turnover as well. For example, Dalton, Krackhardt, and Porter (1981) and Dalton and Tudor (1982) discussed how avoidable versus unavoidable and functional versus dysfunctional turnover might be integrated into the research. In other words, these researchers explored issues of optimal, as opposed to absolute, levels of turnover.

Theme 3: Method

In a summarizing commentary on the "state of the science" in withdrawal research, O'Reilly (1991) judged that "While these [theory-based and substantive] studies add useful increments to our knowledge about absenteeism and turnover, perhaps the most interesting developments in this area have been methodological . . . [that is, applications of] . . . survival analysis and event history models. . . . (p. 442). For example, O'Reilly cited Morita, Lee, and Mowday (1989) on turnover and Harrison and Hulin (1989) on absenteeism as novel analytical demonstrations.

Theme 4: A General Withdrawal Construct

Hulin and associates (Hulin, 1991; Hulin, Roznowski, Hachiya, 1985; Roznowski & Hulin, 1992; Rosse & Miller, 1984) advocated an "organizational adaptation/withdrawal model." At the model's core, researchers are advised to move *away* from a narrow focus on specific attitude–behavior relationships (e.g., commitment–turnover) and *toward* a broader orientation concerned with the relationship between job- or work-role satisfaction and a general withdrawal construct. The general withdrawal construct includes the set of intentions to reduce job inputs, increase job outcomes, reduce work-role inclusion, and change work roles. Withdrawal would be negatively associated with job satisfaction. Moreover, the construct would also include the set of behaviors that correspond to a given intention. For example, increases in job outcomes can correspond to the employee's stealing from the company; reduction in job inputs can correspond to the employee's taking 3-hour lunches each day; reduction in work-role inclusion can correspond to the employee's absenteeism or turnover; and changes in work roles can correspond to the employee's transferring to another work group.

A COMMENTARY ON THE CURRENT PERSPECTIVES OF EMPLOYEE ATTACHMENT

With key terms defined and major research themes summarized, we now offer a commentary on the attachment literature. In addition, we suggest immediate directions for the current research. In the section that follows our suggestions, we propose new and perhaps unusual departures for the research. As such, we try to answer the question of where the research on employee attachment should go next.

Job Attitudes

Agreeing with O'Reilly (1991), much of the research on job attitudes has focused on the development and validation of measurement instruments and the identification of antecedents and consequences of these attitudes. Certainly, the field will only benefit from better measures of job attitudes, and such empirical calibration of tools must continue, of course. Nonetheless, a topic's core should not focus on instrumentation. The intellectual excitement generated by a research topic should focus on the quality of its underlying theory and empirical research. In other words, a topic's intellectual standing should be judged on its theory development, the theoretical grounding of its empirical research, and the reciprocal influences between theory and research.

In our reading of the literature, the discipline appears to be moving away, albeit too slowly perhaps, from the empirically driven search for cross sectionally measured correlates of job attitudes, and the subsequent post hoc classification of these variables as antecedents or consequences. In its place, the discipline appears to be advancing toward the documentation of more theoretically specified and a priori classified antecedents and consequences. In our judgment, the "attitude portion" (as opposed to the "withdrawal behaviors portion") of the research on employee attachment appears quite healthy. In particular, Mathieu and Zajac (1990) provided a comprehensive summary of the research on organizational commitment, and Cranny, Smith, and Stone (1992) provided a comprehensive review of the research on job satisfaction.

The good health of the attitude side in withdrawal research is evident on a number of fronts. For example, researchers have begun to study the development (or process) of commitment over time, with particular interest in the period of organizational entry. Meyer, Bobocel, and Allen (1991) compared the validity of three dimensions of behavioral commitment (labeled retrospective rationality because it focused on the interpretation of one's own behavior) and the employee's judgments about decision quality (labeled prospective rationality because it focused on the judgments about predicting future reactions). Retrospective and prospective rationality were measured prior to organizational entry and correlated to later affective and continuance commitment, measured three times after entry. Meyer et al. (1991) found that prospective rationality more validly predicted affective and continuance commitment than retrospective rationality. Lee, Ashford, Walsh, and Mowday (1992) provided evidence for the construct validity of an individual's commitment propensity and demonstrated its subsequent influences in the commitment–turnover process. In particular, Lee et al. (1992) found that commitment propensity, measured prior to organizational entry, was significantly predictive of one's initial and subsequent organizational commitment, measured five times after entry. Moreover, initial commitment was found to be very strongly associated with subsequent tenure in the organization.

Researchers also have started to examine relationships between job attitudes and other measures of affect. A considerable amount of intellectual effort has been directed toward understanding expressed emotions (i.e., behaviors enacted to intentionally convey a specific emotion to a client, a customer, or an observer; Rafaeli & Sutton, 1989), positive affectivity (i.e., an employee's good feelings about the job; Isen & Baron, 1991), affective events (i.e., emotionally significant events; Weiss, Nicholas, & Link, 1992), and negative affectivity (i.e., a state of neuroticism, emotional instability, bad feelings about the job, and poor self-concept; Burke, Brief, & George, 1991) as well as the situational versus dispositional basis for work related affect, like job satisfaction (Keller, Bouchard, Arvey, Segal, & Dawis, 1992). Parenthetically, it should be noted that positive and negative affectivity have been most often conceptualized as separate dimensions and not as different ends of a single continuum (Clark & Watson, 1988), though others have disagreed (Judge, 1992).

One question that needs to be examined is how affective events, expressed emotions, and positive and negative affectivity relate to the attachment literature. An initial issue is to determine whether the constructs of job satisfaction and organizational commitment can be clearly distinguished from that of affective events, expressed emotion, and positive and negative affectivity. Otherwise, an older construct might be reinvestigated under a new label (i.e., "old wine in a new bottle"). Moreover, the temptation might then arise to articulate small, virtually meaningless, and empirically inseparable, though logically consistent, differences between the older and newer labels.

Although a detailed discussion is beyond the scope of the present chapter, we offer the following observations. First, in comparison to job satisfaction, expressed emotions would seem to be a separate construct. Whereas satisfaction involves affective and evaluative reactions to a job or its aspects, expressed emotions are not theorized to involve psychological responses to the job. Expressed emotions are theoretically independent of felt emotions and affect. Second, positive and negative affectivity, in contrast, are defined to include feelings about the job and, therefore, a substantial overlap with job satisfaction must be expected. Third, in comparison to organizational commitment, expressed emotions again would seem to be a separate construct. Whereas organizational commitment involves company loyalty and the calculation of benefits versus costs, expressed emotions are not theorized to involve calculative or underlying psychological processes. Fourth, positive and negative affectivity, in contrast, would seem to have a modest overlap with organizational commitment (but less than with satisfaction); that is, one's loyalty, mental calculations, and general framing of the work situation would seem to be biased by one's basic feelings about the job. Finally, affective events are seen as momentary reactions to specific events that happen on the job. These reactions have been shown to be independent influences on job satisfaction when compared to more traditional cognitive evaluations (Weiss et al., 1992).

Furthermore, the various job attitudes might be arrayed by their possible dispositional versus situational basis as a useful heuristic. Figure 4.1 depicts our interpretation of this hypothetical array. At one end of a continuum, affective events and expressed emotions appear as primarily situationally based (Rafaeli & Sutton, 1987; Weiss et al., 1992); that is, these feelings and behaviors are enacted only under specific contextual circumstances. At the other end of the continuum, positive and negative affectivity have been most often conceptualized as primarily dispositionally based (Clark & Watson, 1991). Job satisfaction and organizational commitment (i.e., psychological and instrumental attachment) appear as somewhere in between. Traditionally, job satisfaction has been viewed as situationally based, but recent evidence suggests at least some dispositional basis (e.g., Arvey, Bouchard, Segal, & Abraham, 1989; Keller, Bouchard, Arvey, Segal, & Davis, 1992). Thus, we place job satisfaction slightly away from the situational end of the continuum.

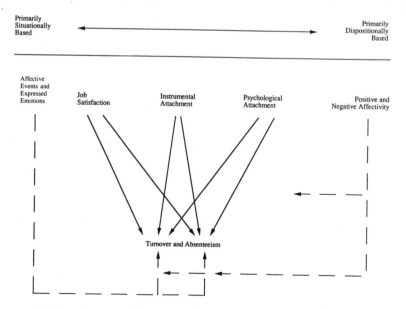

FIG. 4.1. Hypothetical relations among attitudes and withdrawal behaviors.

To our knowledge, serious discussions about commitment's situational versus dispositional basis have not been published, though there may be some evidence that commitment is more situationally, than dispositionally, determined. Lee et al. (1992), for example, indirectly addressed this issue. In a field situation that tightly constrained the variation of individual attitudes and behaviors, organizational commitment was demonstrated to effect systematically subsequent turnover. These authors concluded that, in less constraining situations, organizational commitment would most likely result from the interaction of situation and dispositions. Thus, we place organizational commitment between job satisfaction and affectivity on our continuum.

Returning to the earlier question, how might affective events, expressed emotions, and affectivity be integrated into the relationships between job attitudes and withdrawal behaviors? The solid lines in Fig. 4.1 show the connections from job satisfaction and organizational commitment to turnover and absenteeism that have been reliably documented. The broken lines represent our speculations about the relationships that connect affective events, expressed emotions, and affectivity to turnover and absenteeism. In particular, we speculate that affective events and expressed emotions have no direct effects on either turnover or absenteeism; however, we suggest that affective events, expressed emotions, and affectivity can combine *interactively* to influence the likelihood of subsequent withdrawal. More specifically, we hypothesize that, if either dispositional affectivity or affective events are inconsistent with expressed emotions, cognitive dissonance will occur (Festinger, 1957), and the likelihoods for turnover and absenteeism should increase.

Withdrawal Behaviors

Turnover.   Despite attempts to broaden the research (e.g., Dalton & Tudor, 1982; Jackofsky & Peters, 1983), researchers in OB have maintained a fairly tight focus on the voluntary dimension of turnover. As a result, the discipline can offer good quality advice on why and how employees elect to quit the company in general (e.g., Lee & Mitchell, 1994; Mobley, 1977), but the discipline may have very little advice to offer if attention turns to other dimensions of withdrawal (Hulin, Roznowski, & Hachiya, 1985). Thus, the discipline might be fairly criticized as knowing a great deal about a limited portion of a larger organizational phenomenon. Certainly, research on the voluntary dimension of turnover should continue, but studying other dimensions of turnover and withdrawal may now be timely.

Although discussed further in the next major section, withdrawal researchers might be well advised to broaden their basic and grounding disciplines. That is, withdrawal researchers draw ideas almost exclusively from social and organizational psychology (e.g., beliefs, attitudes, and behavioral intentions). In addition to psychology, research in labor economics and organizational sociology might be considered for additional ideas and traditions on the dimensions of turnover. Within these other disciplines, for example, complementary concepts and research can be found under such labels as job mobility (Hachen, 1992), internal labor markets (Althauser, 1989), and job shifts (Halaby, 1988). From these alternative labels, specific terms for additional turnover dimensions might be "involuntary exits" (e.g., firing), "intrafirm mobility" (e.g., transfer; though organizational behavior has a small literature on transfer; Lee & Johnson, 1994; Pinder & Walter, 1984), "upward authority mobility" (e.g., promotions within or between companies), and movement between companies but within the same internal labor markets. All of these terms describe people leaving their current job with varying degrees of choice. That is, volition ranges from full choice (e.g., voluntary turnover) to negotiated decisions (e.g., transfers and promotions) to nonvolitional (e.g., firing). Investigating the antecedents and consequences to these decisions might prove to be a useful extension to the turnover research.

Absenteeism. The theory-based research on absenteeism appears to have slowed somewhat, although work by Harrison and Hulin (1989) and by Fitchman (1989) represented very impressive and welcome exceptions. Moreover, the general focus appears to be shifting toward intervention-based studies that are often based on a patchwork of ideas. As a result, absenteeism may be increasingly conceptualized in a company specific manner, and a general definition may become even more elusive. As an alternative, researchers might focus more specifically on multiple definitions of absenteeism. In addition to Fitchman's (1989) absence spells, researchers might simultaneously study absence cultures (Chadwick-Jones, Nicholson, & Brown, 1982), absence duration and frequency, and types of absences. Through multiple specifications, contingency models may evolve that have greater applied value than many current applications.

Methods in Withdrawal Research

Agreeing with O'Reilly (1991), the innovation in withdrawal research has been methodological rather than substantive in the last several years. Although a vibrant research area must continually improve its tools, a focus on methods may represent at least some degree of intellectual stagnation. Nonetheless, improvement in methods has suggested an enhanced likelihood for more powerful empirical results. Thus, it may be useful to comment on some traditional and more recent tools.

Two Variable Case. In the simplest case, interest may focus on the strength of association between two categorical variables (e.g., gender and turnover). Most commonly, a contingency, crosstabulation, or mobility table would be compiled, and a chi-square, a Yule's Q, or an odds ratio would be calculated as an indicator for the strength of association. In an equally simple case, interest may focus on the bivariate relationship between a continuous and categorical variable (e.g., satisfaction and turnover). Most commonly, a point biserial correlation would be calculated and provide information on mean difference in the continuous variable when grouped by the categorical variable (i.e., stayer versus leaver). Although technically incorrect, many applied statisticians suggest a "conventional wisdom" that unless the proportion of leavers is less than 20% or greater than 80%, the product moment correlation is typically a sufficiently good substitute for the point biserial correlation. In our experience, we agree with the conventional wisdom.

Multiple Categorical Variables. When interest shifts to the estimation of association among *three or more* categorical variables (e.g., gender, college graduate, turnover), multiple contingency tables could be compiled but would quickly become unwieldy. Instead, the general log-linear model might become the analytical method of choice. Somewhat analogous to an analysis of variance model, the log-linear model expresses the frequency of each cell from a hypothetical set of contingency tables as a function of each categorical variable and their relationships. For each cell in the hypothetical contingency table, an estimated frequency can be compared to an actual frequency, and an index for the goodness of fit can be estimated. The relationships between conditions (or cells) can be estimated by comparing the various goodness of fit indicators.

Categorical and Continuous Variables. When interest shifts to estimating the effects of a combination of categorical or continuous (e.g., gender and organizational commitment) on a categorical dependent variable (e.g., turnover), a special case of the log-linear model, logistic regression, might become the analytical method of choice. The logistic model applies a logit transformation to the outcome variable that stretches out the categorical dependent variable. The "linearized" dependent variable is then regressed onto the similarly transformed set of predictors in a manner analogous to ordinary least squares regression.

Dynamic Effects. Recently, the attachment research has begun to move beyond simple predictive designs involving categorical dependent variables. That is, the predictors are typically collected cross sectionally at time one, and the criterion data are commonly collected over the next several months (see Peters & Sheridan, 1988, for discussion of these design issues). More recent research, for example, has involved repeated waves of survey data (Hom & Griffeth, 1991), time until the turnover event (Lee, Ashford, Walsh, & Mowday, 1992), multiple absence events (Fitchman, 1989), and the instanteous probability of an employee quitting (O'Reilly, Caldwell, & Barnett, 1989). A common element of the more recent research has been the attention to the timing of events; that is, theoretical interest has directly focused on when the withdrawal occurs. As such, survival analysis may be appropriate for the recent interest on time base withdrawal (Morita et al., 1989, 1993).

Summary

The research on employee withdrawal constitutes normal science (Kuhn, 1970). The discipline is indeed making small incremental gains in our understanding of the withdrawal process (O'Reilly, 1991). Although valid, the current approach results in only a limited proportion of explained criterion variance. What may be needed to explain additional criterion variance, is a dramatic shift in the way we think about job attitudes and behaviors.

RECOMMENDATIONS ON FUTURE OB PERSPECTIVES OF EMPLOYEE ATTACHMENT

In the previous section, our commentary on the current body of knowledge stayed within the bounds of the dominant paradigm. As a result, incremental and normal science was suggested through our recommendations for immediate research directions. In this section, we seek to move beyond the established paradigm through a discussion of four major issues. As before, we again offer our commentary. First, the role of time in the withdrawal process is considered. Second, the concept of employee embeddedness, conceptualized as person, task, and organization "fit," is addressed. Third, the nonregularity of withdrawal phenomena is discussed. Finally, we ask questions about job attitudes as dependent variables and withdrawal behaviors as independent variables.

The Role of Time

Work attitudes, like job satisfaction and organizational commitment, and events, like absenteeism and turnover, develop and occur over time. As a result, many scholars have made calls for more longitudinal research aimed at capturing these dynamic processes. These calls, however, tend to be methodologically, as opposed to theoretically, based. Of course, the reverse should hold. The passage of time should be a substantive part of our withdrawal theories. Correspondingly, the duration of measurement for any relevant constructs could then be determined by theory, rather than the researcher's convenience. In some cases, job attitudes and withdrawal behaviors occur smoothly, gradually, and monotonically; in other cases, distinctive stimuli punctuate these occurrences. Any substantive withdrawal theory must deal directly with how these processes unfold over time. Moreover, a theory should address how contexts and employees change over time, with some changes being systematic and others being random.

As noted, most theories of attachment adopt some variant of a negative attitude causing subsequent employee withdrawal. In some theories, job satisfaction (e.g., March & Simon, 1958), organizational commitment (e.g., Mowday, Porter, & Steers, 1982), or both (e.g., Steers & Mowday, 1981), are highlighted. Similarly, some models highlight turnover (Mobley, 1977), absenteeism (e.g., Steers & Rhodes, 1978), or multiple withdrawal behaviors (e.g., Hulin, 1991). Unfortunately, most theories do not directly address the time dimension of the withdrawal phenomena. Recently, however, the issues of absenteeism (Fitchman, 1984, 1989) and turnover (Lee & Mitchell, 1991, 1994) were directly addressed. These dynamic issues may serve as useful models for the theoretical treatment of time. Their ideas are summarized below.

Fitchman's Theory on Absenteeism. In the research on absenteeism, Fitchman (1984) offered an innovative and a fundamental shift that may change the way scholars approach the phenomena. Rather than dissatisfaction (or weak commitment) causing absences, Fitchman argued that attention should focus on two larger, competing, and simultaneously occurring sets of motivations and rewards. The first set involves forces compelling (i.e., rewarding) an employee to attend work, and the second set involves alternative forces compelling an employee to attend to nonwork activities (i.e., rewards foregone by attending work). By focusing on these simultaneously occurring and competing forces, the immediate issue for researchers becomes *when* does the employee shift from attendance to nonattendance.

According to Fitchman (1989), the magnitude for the motivational forces to attend work decreases over time and eventually reaches some asymptotic level. In other words, the reward value for coming to work on a given day decreases as the number of consecutive days an employee has already come to work increases, until some base level is eventually reached. Simultaneously, the magnitude for the motivational forces to attend to the nonwork alternatives increases over time, particularly when there has been little or no opportunity to attend to these nonwork activities. At some point, the attraction to attend to nonwork activities may exceed the attraction to attend work, and absenteeism occurs. In turn, when the attraction to attend work exceeds the attraction to attend to nonwork activities, the absence spell ends. Furthermore, the more dissatisfying the job, the more attractive nonwork activities should be. As a result, the strength of an attendance spell should decrease with time.

In sum, the research on absenteeism needs a new theory that incorporates time as a substantive feature. Fitchman's innovative ideas both complement existing theory and offer a fundamentally different direction for the research. Empirically, these dynamic processes can be readily assessed with survival models.

Lee and Mitchell's Theory on Turnover. Unquestionably, the dominant paradigm on turnover originates from March and Simon's (1958) *decision to participate.* In brief, the decision to participate results from the perceived ease and desirability of movement. Historically, the perceived desirability of movement has been conceptualized as job satisfaction, and the perceived ease of movement has been conceptualized as perceived job alternatives. In our judgment, all major psychological models of turnover have incrementally built upon the decision to participate (e.g., Hom et al., 1984; Mobley, 1977; Mobley et al., 1979; Price & Mueller, 1986; Steers & Mowday, 1981).

Recently, Lee and Mitchell (1991) suggested that Beach's (1990) image theory offers a theoretical alternative to the decision to participate. Further, Lee and Mitchell (1994) proposed the "unfolding model of employee turnover" for understanding dynamic processes. In particular, the unfolding model seeks to expand the research from an emphasis on affect-driven turnover to a broader paradigm. Based on image theory, retention and turnover were theorized to result from judgments about the "fit versus misfit" of the one's values, goals, and progress towards those goals, with each judgment constituting a specific image for an individual. Moreover, the unfolding model specifies a mechanism, called the "shock to the system," that prompts the onset of three of four distinctive decision paths. Over time, all four decision paths describe the process by which an employee decides to stay or leave.

In the first decision path, Lee and Mitchell theorized that a shock to the system elicits a memory probe for the recollection of a virtually identical shock and situation, and an acceptable response. If a shock, a situation, and an acceptable response are recalled, the recollected response (e.g., staying or leaving) is enacted. If a highly similar memory cannot be recollected, another decision path is initiated.

In the second decision path, a shock to the system prompts the reassessment of the employee's basic attachment to the organization. That is, the employee focuses on how much he or she wants to stay a member of the company. Moreover, the reassessment occurs when there is no specific alternative in mind and results in the binary outcome of staying or quitting. The specific process for this reassessment is theorized to be image theory's "compatibility test" (Beach, 1990) and involves judging the shock, the situation, and three specific images for compatibility or fit. The first image involves one's personal values; the second image concerns the employee's goals; and the third image deals with the progress toward goal attainment. If the shock, situation, and images fit together, the employee stays; if the shock, situation, and images do not fit, the employee simply quits.

In the third decision path, a shock to the system prompts the assessment of whether the employee could form a basic attachment to another organization. That is, the employee focuses on how much he or she wants to leave. Note that these assessments occur when there are specific alternatives in mind. The process for this assessment is theorized to involve three sets of decisions. First, image theory's compatibility test (Beach, 1990) is again conducted. Because the focus is on leaving rather than staying, the outcome of this compatibility test differs from that of the second decision path. Whereas the immediate outcome in the second decision path was staying versus leaving, the immediate outcome to the first compatibility test in decision path 3 is to stay for a fit decision versus some level of disaffection for a not fit decision. When disaffection occurs for a not fit decision, a search for alternatives is undertaken. The second set of judgments in decision path 3 applies the compatibility test to the located alternatives. Because alternatives are assessed in this second compatibility test in decision path 3, a judgment of not fit leads to deletion of the located alternative from further consideration; in contrast, a judgment of fit leads to the decision to analyze further the particular option. In other words, the second compatibility test produces a set of options that are positioned for more rigorous scrutiny. The final set of judgments is called the profitability test (Beach, 1990) and involves the intendedly rational analyses of a surviving alternative's subjective expected utility for the employee. The option that is judged to maximize one's preferences is selected. In sum, a shock to the system prompts two compatibility and one profitability tests, leading, in turn, to the decision to stay or quit for a specific alternative.

In the fourth decision path, no shock to the system prompts scripted behaviors (decision path 1), reassessment of one's attachment to the current organization (decision path 2), or assessment of whether an attachment could form with another firm (decision path 3). Instead, the organizational life is perceived as ongoing with few distinguishing demarcations. Over time, some employees will come to reassess their basic satisfaction with the job. Rather than prompted by a shock to the system, this reassessment begins randomly and occurs gradually. The unfolding model holds that, in the absence of a shock to the system, relative job dissatisfaction leads, in sequence, to lower organizational commitment, more job search activities, greater perceived ease of movement, stronger intention to quit, and higher probability of actual turnover.

In sum, the research on employee turnover needs new theory that incorporates time as a substantive feature. Acknowledging considerable personal bias, the unfolding model complements and fundamentally differs from existing theory (e.g., Hulin, 1991; Mobley, 1977) and research (e.g., Hom & Griffeth, 1991). Moreover, the statistical tools are available to empirically test the unfolding model's many binary judgments (e.g., Huslid & Day, 1991).

Employee Embeddedness

In this section, we address how employees are embedded within their contextual surroundings and how such embeddedness might affect organizational attachment. In particular, we suggest that employees' attitudes and behaviors are strongly influenced by the (a) *homogeneity* between an individual and his or her colleagues, (b) *interdependence* among job tasks, and (c) *fit* between a person's skills and characteristics, and the requirements of the job.

Homogeneity. A decade ago, Pfeffer (1983) noted that the already large amount of literature on employee turnover focused almost exclusively on the individual-level decision to quit. In particular, job attitudes were considered the main determinant of employee withdrawal. Organizational researchers seemed to hold little interest in viewing employee attachment and withdrawal as a more systemic concept. As a result, Pfeffer (1983) called for attention to the effects of the employees' demographic distributions on numerous organization outcomes. In short, Pfeffer drew attention to organizational demography. Gradually, organizational researchers have begun to respond to Pfeffer's (1983) call, albeit too slowly in our judgment. In the literature on organizational attachment, for example, O'Reilly, et al. (1989) found that age and tenure similarity were positively associated with social integration, which, in turn, lead to decreased individual turnover. Jackson et al. (1991) reported that dissimilarity among top management teams in terms of age, tenure, education, college major, military experience, alma mater, and career experiences predicted individual turnover and that team heterogeneity on these characteristics strongly predicted group turnover rates.

From the research in organizational sociology, demography has a long and rich tradition. Pfeffer and associates (e.g., Wagner, Pfeffer, & O'Reilly, 1984) did the discipline of organizational behavior a great service by bringing this body of knowledge to our collective attention. In our judgment, the promises of organizational demography to the research on employee attachment are twofold. First, our conceptualization of many seemingly "common" variables like employees' attitudes, age, tenure, and location can be expanded. In addition to individual self-reports (e.g., an employee's current age), researchers can approach these variables in terms of different aggregates' mean, standard deviation, and explicit distribution form (e.g., employees' similarity). Second, different patterns and conceptualizations of common variables imply the consideration of different functional relationships between these variables and withdrawal behaviors. Rather than linear associations, step functions, reversals in slopes, and various interactional forms beyond the standard multiplicative ANOVA type can be considered (Terborg, 1981). In short, one potentially valuable contribution of organizational demography might be as a prompt for alternative thinking about common variables and how homogeneous or heterogeneous patterns of these variables might affect employee attachment.

Further, a more inclusive way to think about homogeneity among employees comes from the theory and research in organizational demography (Pfeffer, 1983), job design (Hackman & Oldham, 1980), social information processing (Salancik & Pfeffer, 1978), interactional psychology (Schneider, 1983), and organizational design (Thompson, 1967). Based on these areas, we confidently assert that within organizations, (a) employees vary in their attitudinal and demographic similarity with other people; (b) a job's tasks and events vary in their similarity to tasks and events on other jobs; and (c) the context for these employees and jobs vary in their similarity across the organization. In other words, settings, employees, and tasks and events vary in their similarity. However, the research on employee attachment has not seriously addressed the issues of similarity across situations, people, and jobs. Based on our discipline's larger literature, we suggest that similarity should be included in the research on employee attachment. Furthermore, it seems timely to insert the organization's complexity back into our thinking about attachment.

As a start, Fig. 4.2 provides a simple heuristic device to structure one's thinking about similarity. For the sake of conceptual simplicity, work settings, employees, and tasks and events are dichotomized into similar versus dissimilar, resulting in eight cells. Cell 1 signifies the most similarity in work settings, employees, and tasks and events, and cell 8 represents the least similarity, with the remaining cells varying in their degree of similarity. For each cell, one might ask how job attitudes and withdrawal behaviors might be related. For example, the high similarity in settings, employees, and tasks and events represented by cell 1 suggests minimal variance in job attitudes (as well as employee's demographic characteristics); as a result, empirical relationships between job attitudes and withdrawal behaviors may be virtually nonexistent. Rather than focus on individual level attitude–turnover associations, for instance, researchers might be well advised to turn their attention to aggregate level attitude–turnover rate associations under cell 1 conditions (e.g., average levels for work groups; Terborg & Lee, 1984). In contrast, the minimal similarity in settings, employees, and tasks and events represented by cell 8 suggests maximal variance in job attitudes; as a result, relationships between job attitudes and withdrawal behaviors may be quite prevalent under cell 8 conditions.

Our point is that researchers of employee attachment should begin to incorporate the larger organization's complexity into their thinking. Figure 4.2 simply represents one way to heuristically structure thinking on this issue.

Interdependence. A second aspect of embeddedness may be captured by task interdependence, which has been defined in many ways (Brass, 1981; Kiggundu, 1983; Thompson, 1967). At one end of a continuum, task inde-

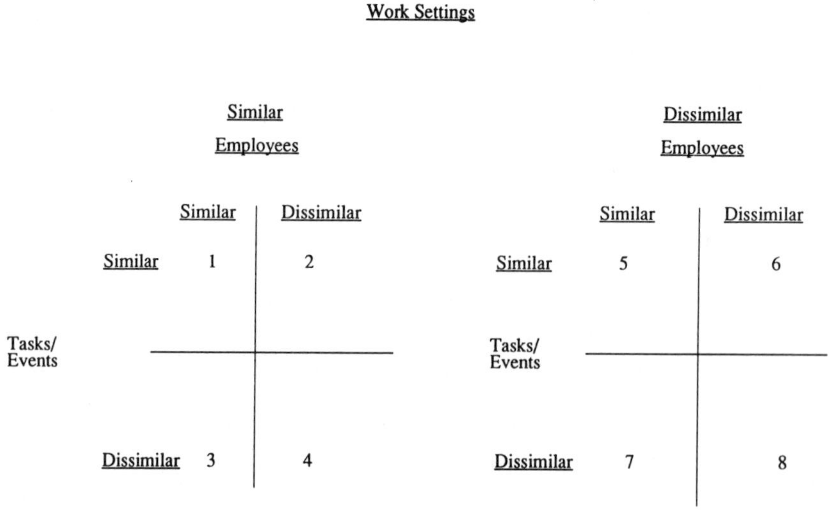

FIG. 4.2.   Similarity and interdependence of settings, employees, and tasks/events.

pendence refers to employees working alone; at the other end, complete interdependence refers to employees having the same goals, working together, and exchanging resources and information. Varying degrees of interdependence refer to the extent (a) goals are held in common; (b) employees' physical proximities are close; and (c) resource and information exchanges occur routinely.

As presented here, interdependence involves the nature of the exchange relationships between employees; that is, people need others, and others need them. In the general literature from organizational behavior, interdependence is most often associated with task attributes, with much attention focused on its motivational properties (Mitchell & Silver, 1990) or its impact on employee attachment (Hackman & Oldham, 1980). It is our belief that different types of interdependence may result in different levels of job attitudes and withdrawal patterns. As a general hypothesis, we suggest that interdependence is positively associated with job satisfaction and organizational commitment and negatively associated with turnover and absenteeism.

Fit. The third aspect of embeddedness refers to how well an employee fits with the job and organization. Much like organizational versus psychological climates (James, L. R., James, L. A., & Ashe, 1990), the job and context represent a more or less constant fixture to most individuals. As such, both job and organization context can be thought of as relatively stable for an employee. Researchers might consider how employees "fit" into these relatively constant work contexts, and whether fit might affect employee attitudes and withdrawal behaviors (e.g., O'Reilly, Chatman, & Caldwell, 1991).

For purposes of discussion, fit is conceptualized as involving an employee's feelings of congruity, consonance, or comfort with the job and organizational context, and preferences to remain in that context. As a general hypothesis, we would expect that the greater the fit, the more positive will be one's job satisfaction and organizational commitment and the lower the likelihood for turnover and absenteeism. Note that this general hypothesis treats worker's attitudes and behaviors as direct outcomes of fit. As another general hypothesis, we would also expect that, in addition to direct effects, fit would also have a strong indirect effect on employee withdrawal behaviors via job attitudes.

Returning to Fig. 4.2, another heuristic purpose can be suggested. In particular, Fig. 4.2 allows for the more specific question of *how* an employee's fit within a given cell might affect job attitudes and withdrawal. Note that cell 1 represents similarity on the three dimensions in Fig. 4.2, and cells 2, 3, and 5 represent similarity on two of the three dimensions. Moreover, cells 5, 6, and 7 signify similarity on only a single axis, and cell 8 signifies similarity on none. By questioning employees about their comfort and preference levels for the eight cells, sources for the fit versus not-fit in a particular cell could be determined. We speculate that the magnitudes of the direct and indirect effects of fit on turnover and absenteeism may vary systematically by the source of fit (or misfit).

Nonregularity

Within the major models of employee withdrawal, systematic patterns and slowly developing processes are most often implied. For example, Mobley (1977) has theorized that employees systematically evaluate, in sequence, their current job, the cost of searching for alternatives, and the comparison between the located alternatives and their current jobs; eventually, employees make decisions about staying or leaving. In a similar fashion, Steers and Mowday (1981) theorized that an employee's expectations, values, organizational experiences, and job performance combine to affect job satisfaction, organizational commitment, and job involvement. In sequence, these affective responses to the job combine with nonwork influences to affect the behavioral intention to stay or leave, which, in turn, directly predicts actual staying or leaving.

In our reading of the academic and managerial literatures and in our first-hand organizational experiences, there are no compelling reasons to restrict one's thinking to the systematic patterns and often slowly developing regularities frequently implied in many withdrawal models. As noted, external events often prompt the onset of these withdrawal processes (e.g., Lee & Mitchell's shock to the system, 1994; Rosse & Miller's stimulus event, 1984; Weiss et al.'s affective event, 1992). Reactions to these prompts, like lowered job attitudes and increased stress, absenteeism, or turnover, may occur in bursts or spurts, rather than in simply linear changes. For example, IBM announced quite suddenly in 1991 that, within 12 moths, the corporate human resource function was to be restructured into a wholly owned subsidiary, called Workforce Solutions—An IBM Company, and relocated to four sites in the nation. Moreover, only a portion of those currently working in human resources would be asked to join and relocate to the newly formed subsidiary company. Just as suddenly, according to our informal sources, stress increased and commitment decreased across broad segments of the human resource function. These suddenly changing and quickly spreading levels of higher stress and lower commitment (i.e., a burst) may have caused large numbers of employees to search for alternative jobs and/or to quit (often times immediately or via Lee & Mitchell's second decision path). Furthermore, to the extent that substantial similarity (or personnel homogeneity) exists across identifiable groups within a firm, burst or spurts in attitudinal and behavioral reactions among employee groups would seem more likely (i.e., a social contagion spreads among these employees).

Certainly, our traditional models (e.g., linear functions) and tools (e.g., ordinary least squares or logistic regression) could be applied to situations characterized by bursts and spurts. One potential problem, however, is that researchers might be forcing traditional (and ill-fitting) conceptual models and tools to nontraditional situations. As a result, researchers may study these phenomenon quite inefficiently (e.g., linear correlations would be quite low) or miss the burst or spurt entirely. Bursts and spurts in attitudinal and behavioral reactions to prompting events (e.g., shocks to the system) may be more effectively studied by models that describe discontinuous functions. In particular, catastrophe models describe several families of discontinuous functions and may represent a near optimal technology to describe and understand bursts and spurts. In sum, alternative theories (Lee & Mitchell, 1994; Rosse & Miller, 1984) and tools (e.g., catastrophe theory) would seem to allow researchers to approach quite readily bursts and spurts in employee reactions.

Proactive Versus Reactive Evaluations and Actions: Broadening the Causal Chain

Much of the research implies that employees are somewhat passive and reactive. That is, people are most often theorized to feel some level of disaffection and usually react by withdrawing. Correspondingly, researchers treat job attitude as the independent variable and employee withdrawal as the dependent variable. What if, however, employees are proactive? For example, some people create their own shocks to the system by constantly asking for a pay raise or monitoring the job market because they do not want to miss a potential opportunity. Some people increase their satisfaction by personalizing their working conditions and job tasks. Some people test the organization's limits by taking (too) many absences. As such, it may be useful to consider, on occasion, withdrawal (broadly defined) as a process that is initiated by the employee rather than a reaction to existing environments and circumstances.

In addition, some employees closely monitor the behaviors and situations of their co-workers. That is, they are immediately aware of the feelings and behaviors of people who are withdrawing from the organization. For example, Brockner and associates studied the feelings of survivors to company lay offs (e.g, Brockner, Grover, Reed, DeWitt, & O'Malley, 1987). In general survivors reacted most negatively when they identified with the leavers and perceived them to be poorly treated. Furthermore, when survivors perceived that the organization demonstrated a commitment to the dismissed people (i.e., caretaking activities like severance pay and outplacement counseling), the survivor's commitment to the organization increased.

In a similar vein, one can reverse the idea of organizational commitment. Instead of assessing the employee's commitment to the organization, we might study how much the organization is committed to the employee. For example, research by Eisenberger, Huntington, Hutchinson, and Sowa (1986) linked the construct of perceived organizational support, which focuses on the employees' perception that the organization is genuinely concerned about them, to job satisfaction and organizational commitment.

Carrying the chain of causality further, researchers have begun to study the consequences of employee lay offs on *subsequent* attitudes and feelings. For example, Leana and Feldman (1992) studied the reactions and coping behaviors of people who lost their jobs. Reactions to job loss included perceptual changes (e.g., the individual's personal explanation for why and how the job loss occurred, the meaning of work in one's life), emotional distress, and physiological problems. Furthermore, two broad classes of coping behaviors were identified. For some, coping focused on eliminating or changing the source of stress itself; these individuals engaged in activities such as retraining, job searches, and relocation efforts. For others, coping focused on alleviating the consequences or symptoms of stress; these individuals engaged in activities such as applying for government assistance, receiving counseling, and involvement in public relief programs.

In research streams by Brocker and by Leana and Feldman, the approaches to employee turnover and its effects are innovative and insightful. Yet, only the surface of these issues have been studied. For example, the psychological and calculative commitment for people *waiting* to be recalled from a lay off might be studied. In addition, the organizational commitment, job satisfaction and likelihood of absences for people actually *recalled* from one or more lay offs might also be studied. In short, reversing the traditional notions about job affect causing employee withdrawal and extending the causal chain to consider proactive causes of attitudes and consequences of withdrawal behaviors might be valuable research activities.

CONCLUSION

In this chapter, we reflected on an active and enduring body of research and theory. In general, we perceived a reasonably sound and methodologically rigorous body of knowledge that is fairly well grounded in theory. Moreover, the likelihood for continued vitality of the topic seems quite high. At the very least, consistent and incremental gains in our knowledge seem assured because of the wide array of ongoing research activities. In addition, some new and different theories may be sufficiently innovative to stimulate more nontraditional research directions. These new orientations focus on broadening our understanding of employee attachment to the organization. Attachment is seen as occurring over a period of time and not necessarily as a smooth and easily predictable process. Job attitudes and behaviors are seen as resulting from a broad array of factors, such as the contextual variables reflecting employee embeddedness. Moreover, the causal chain has been extended to include events antecedent to job attitudes and subsequent to work behaviors. We feel that these new orientations are important to the field of OB behavior. Further, we hope that this chapter serves as a catalyst for more innovative theory and research on employee withdrawal processes.

AUTHORS' NOTE

We thank *Jerry Greenberg* and *Rick Mowday* for their helpful comments on earlier versions of this chapter.

REFERENCES

Althauser, R. P. (1989). Internal labor markets. In W. R. Scott (Ed.), *Annual review of sociology* (pp. 143–161). Palo Alto, CA: Annual Reviews, Inc.

Arvey, R. D., Bouchard, T. J., Segal, N. L., & Abraham, L. M. (1989). Job satisfaction: Environmental and genetic components. *Journal of Applied Psychology, 74,* 187–192.

Atkin, R. S., & Goodman, P. S. (1984). *Methods of defining and measuring absenteeism.* In P. Goodman & R. Atkin (Eds.), *Absenteeism* (pp. 47–109). San Francisco: Jossey-Bass.

Barnard, C. I. (1938). *The functions of the executive.* Cambridge: Harvard University Press.

Beach, L. R. (1990). *Image theory: Decision making in personal and organizational contexts.* Chichester, England: Wiley.

Brass, D. J. (1981). Structural relationships, job characteristics, and worker satisfaction and performance. *Administrative Science Quarterly, 26,* 331–348.

Brockner, J., Grover, S., Reed, T., DeWitt, R., & O'Malley, M. (1987). Survivors' reactions to layoffs: We get by with a little help from our friends. *Administrative Science Quarterly, 32,* 526–541.

Burke, M. J., Brief, A. P., & George, J. M. (1991). *The role of negative affectivity in understanding relationships between self reports of stressors and strains: A comment on the organizational literature* [Working Paper #91–HRMG–10]. Freeman School of Business, Tulane University.

Chadwick-Jones, J. K., Nicholson, N., & Brown, C. (1982). *Social psychology of absenteeism.* New York: Praeger.

Clark, L. A., & Watson, D. (1988). Mood and the mundane: Relations between daily life events and self-reported mood. *Journal of Personality and Social Psychology, 54,* 296–308.

Clark, L. A., & Watson, D. (1991). General affective dispositions in physical and psychological health. In C. Snyder & D. Forsyth (Eds.), *Handbook of social and clinical psychology* (pp. 221–245). New York: Pergamon.

Cranny, C. J., Smith, P. C., & Stone, E. F. (1992). *Job satisfaction.* Lexington, MA: Lexington.

Dalton, D. R., Krackhardt, D. M., & Porter, L. W. (1981). Functional turnover: An empirical assessment. *Journal of Applied Psychology, 66,* 716–721.

Dalton, D. R., & Tudor, W. D. (1982). Turnover: A lucrative hard dollar phenomena. *Academy of Management Review, 7,* 212–218.

Dreher, G. F. (1982). The role of performance in the turnover process. *Academy of Management Journal, 25,* 137–147.

Eisenberger, R., Huntington, R., Hutchinson, S., & Sowa, D. (1986). Perceived organizational support. *Journal of Applied Psychology, 71,* 500–597.

Etzioni, A. (1961). *A comparative analysis of complex organizations.* New York: The Free Press.

Festinger, L. (1957). A theory of cognitive dissonance. Stanford, CA: Stanford University Press.

Fitchman, M. (1984). A theoretical approach to understanding employee absence. In P. Goodman & R. Atkin (Eds.), *Absenteeism* (pp. 1–46). San Francisco: Jossey-Bass.

Fitchman, M. (1989). Attendance makes the heart grow fonder: A hazard rate approach to modeling attendance. *Journal of Applied Psychology, 74,* 325–335.

Frayne, C. A., & Latham, G. P. (1987). Application of social learning theory to employee self management of attendance. *Journal of Applied Psychology, 72,* 387–392.

Hachen, D. S. (1992). Industrial characteristics and job mobility rates. *American Sociological Review, 57,* 39–55.

Hackman, J. R., & Oldham, G. R. (1980). *Work redesign.* Reading, MA: Addison-Wesley.

Halaby, C. N. (1988). Action and information in the job mobility process. *American Sociological Review, 53,* 9–25.

Harrison, D., & Hulin, C. (1989). Investigations of absence taking using Cox regression. *Journal of Applied Psychology, 74,* 300–316.

Herzberg, F., Mausner, B., & Snyderman, B. B. (1959). *The motivation to work.* New York: Wiley.

Hom, P. W., Caranikas-Walker, Prussia, G. E., & Griffeth, R. W. (1992). A meta-analytical structural equation analysis of a model of employee turnover. *Journal of Applied Psychology, 77*(6), 890–909.

Hom, P. W., & Griffeth, R. W. (1991). Structural modeling test of a turnover theory: Cross sectional and longitudinal analyses. *Journal of Applied Psychology, 76*, 350–366.

Hom, P. W., Griffeth, R. W., & Sellaro, C. L. (1984). The validity of Mobley's (1977) model of employee turnover. *Organizational Behavior and Human Performance, 34*, 141–174.

Huslid, M. A., & Day, N. E. (1991). Organizational commitment, job involvement, and turnover; A substantive and methodological analysis. *Journal of Applied Psychology, 76*, 380–391.

Hulin, C. L. (1991). Adaptation, persistence, and commitment in organizations. In M. Dunnette & L. Hough (Eds.), *Handbook of industrial and organizational psychology* (Vol. 2, 2nd ed. pp. 445–506). Palo Alto, CA: Consulting Psychologists Press.

Hulin, C. L., Roznowski, M., & Hachiya, D. (1985). Alternative opportunities and withdrawal decisions: Empirical and theoretical discrepancies and an integration. *Psychological Bulletin, 97*, 233–250.

Ilgen, D. R. (1977). Attendance behavior: A reevaluation of Latham and Pursell's conclusions. *Journal of Applied Psychology, 62*, 230–233.

Isen, A. M., & Baron, R. A. (1991). Positive affect as a factor in organizational behavior. In L. Cummings & B. Staw (Eds.), *Research in organizational behavior* (Vol. 13, pp. 1–54). Greenwich, CT: JAI Press.

Jackofsky, E. F., & Peters, L. H. (1983). Job turnover versus company turnover: Reassessment of the March & Simon participation hypothesis. *Journal of Applied Psychology, 68*, 490–495.

Jackofsky, E. F., & Peters, L. H. (1984). The hypothesized effects of ability in the turnover process. *Academy of Management Review, 8*, 46–49.

Jackson, S. E., Brett, J. F., Sessa, V. I., Cooper, D. M., Julin, J. A., & Peyronnin, K. (1991). Some differences make a difference: Individual dissimilarity and group heterogeneity as correlates of recruitment, promotions, and turnover. *Journal of Applied Psychology, 76*, 675–689.

James, L. R., James, L. A., & Ashe, D. K. (1990). The meaning of organizations: The role of cognition and values. In B. Schneider (Ed.), *Organizational climate and culture* (pp. 40–84). San Francisco: Jossey-Bass.

Judge, T. A. (1992). The dispositional perspective in human resources research. In G. Ferris & K. Rowland (Eds.), *Research in personnel and human resources management* (Vol. 10, pp. 31–72). Greenwich, CT: JAI Press.

Kanter, R. M. (1968). Commitment and social organization: A study of commitment mechanisms in utopian communities. *American Sociological Review, 33*, 499–517.

Keller, L. M., Bouchard, T. J., Arvey, R. D., Segal, N. L., & Dawis, R. V. (1992). Work values: Genetic and environmental influences. *Journal of Applied Psychology, 77*, 79–89.

Kiggundu, M. N. (1983). Task interdependence and job design: Test of a theory. *Organizational Behavior and Human Decision Processes, 31*, 145–172.

Kuhn, T. S. (1970). *The structure of scientific revolutions (2nd ed.).* Chicago: University of Chicago Press.

Latham, G. P., & Pursell, E. D. (1975). Measuring absenteeism from the opposite side of the coin. *Journal of Applied Psychology, 60*, 369–371.

Latham, G. P., & Pursell, E. D. (1977). Measuring attendance: A reply to Ilgen. *Journal of Applied Psychology, 62*, 234–236.

Leana, C. R., & Feldman, D. C. (1992). *Coping with job loss.* Lexington, MA: Lexington.

Lee, T. W., Ashford, S. A., Walsh, J. P., & Mowday, R. T. (1992). Commitment propensity, organizational commitment and voluntary turnover: A longitudinal study of organizational entry processes. *Journal of Management, 18*, 15–32.

Lee, T. W., & Johnson, D. R. (1994). Reactions to job transfer by job type and career stage. *Journal of Business and Psychology, 8*, 377–390.

Lee, T. W., & Mitchell, T. R. (1991). The unfolding effects of organizational commitment and anticipated job satisfaction on voluntary employee turnover. *Motivation and Emotion, 15*, 99–121.

Lee, T. W., & Mitchell, T. R. (1994). An alternative approach: The unfolding model of voluntary employee turnover. *Academy of Management Review, 19*(1), 51–89.

Lee, T. W., & Mowday, R. T. (1987). Voluntarily leaving an organization: An empirical investigation of Steers and Mowday's model of turnover. *Academy of Management Journal, 30*, 721–743.

Locke, E. A. (1976). The nature and causes of job satisfaction. In M. Dunnette (Ed.), *Handbook of industrial and organizational psychology* (pp. 1297–1349). Chicago: Rand McNally.

March, J. G., & Simon, H. A. (1958). *Organizations.* New York: Wiley.

Mathieu, J. E., & Zajac, D. M. (1990). A review and meta-analysis of the antecedents and correlates, and consequences of organizational commitment. *Psychological Bulletin, 108*, 171–194.

Meyer, J. P., & Allen, N. J. (1984). Testing the "side-bet" theory of organizational commitment: Some methodological considerations. *Journal of Applied Psychology, 69*, 372–378.

Meyer, J. P., Bobocel, D. R., & Allen, N. J. (1991). Development of organizational commitment during the first year of employment: a longitudinal study of pre- and post-entry influences. *Journal of Management, 17*, 717–733.

Mitchell, T. R., & Silver, W. S. (1990). Individual and group goals when workers are interdependent: Effects on task strategies and performance. *Journal of Applied Psychology, 75*, 185–193.

Mobley, W. H. (1977). Intermediate linkages in the relationship between job satisfaction and employee turnover. *Journal of Applied Psychology, 62*, 237–240.

Mobley, W. H., Griffeth, R. W., Hand, H. H., & Meglino, B. M. (1979). Review and conceptual analysis of the employee turnover process. *Psychological Bulletin, 86*, 493–522.

Mobley, W. H., Horner, S. O., & Hollingsworth, A. (1978). An evaluation of precursors to hospital employee turnover. *Journal of Applied Psychology, 63*, 408–414.

Morita, J. G., Lee, T. W., & Mowday, R. T. (1989). Introducing survival analysis to organizational researchers: A selected application to turnover research. *Journal of Applied Psychology, 74*, 280–292.

Morita, J. G., Lee, T. W., & Mowday, R. T. (1993). The regression analog to survival analysis: A selected application to turnover research. *Academy of Management Journal, 36*, 1430–1464.

Mowday, R. T., Porter, L. W., & Steers, R. M. (1982). *Employee organization linkages.* New York: Academic Press.

Mowday, R. T., Steers, R. M., & Porter, L. W. (1979). The measurement of organizational commitment. *Journal of Vocational Behavior, 14*, 224–247.

O'Reilly, C. A. (1991). Organizational behavior: Where we've been, where we're going. In M. R. Rosenzweig & L. W. Porter (Eds.), *Annual review of psychology* (pp. 427–458). Palo Alto, CA: Annual Reviews, Inc.

O'Reilly, C. A., Caldwell, D. F., & Barnett, W. P. (1989). Work group demography, social integration, and turnover. *Administrative Science Quarterly, 34*, 21–37.

O'Reilly, C. A., & Chatman, J. A. (1986). Organizational commitment and psychological attachment: The effects of compliance, identification, and internalization on prosocial behavior. *Journal of Applied Psychology, 71*, 492–499.

O'Reilly, C. A., Chatman, J. A., & Caldwell, D. F. (1991). People and organizational culture: A profile comparison approach to assessing person-organization fit. *Academy of Management Journal, 34*, 487–516.

Peters, L. H., & Sheridan, J. E. (1988). Turnover research methodology: A critique of traditional designs and a suggested survival model alternative. In G. Ferris & K. Rowland (Eds.), *Research in personnel and human resources management* (Vol. 6, pp. 231–262). Greenwich, CT: JAI Press.

Pfeffer, J. (1983). Organizational demography. In L. Cummings & B. Staw (Eds.), *Research in organizational behavior* (Vol. 5, pp. 299–357). Greenwich, CT: JAI Press.

Pinder, C. C., & Walter, G. A. (1984). Personnel transfers and employee development. In K. Rowland & G. Ferris (Eds.), *Research in personnel and human resources management* (Vol. 2, pp. 187–218). Greenwich, CT: JAI Press.

Price, J. L., & Mueller, C. W. (1986). *Absenteeism and turnover of hospital employees.* Greenwich, CT: JAI Press.

Rafaeli, A., & Sutton, R. I. (1987). Expression of emotion as part of the work role. *Academy of Management Review, 12,* 23–37.

Rafaeli, A., & Sutton, R. I. (1989). The expression of emotion in organizational life. In L. Cummings & B. Staw (Eds.), *Research in organizational behavior* (Vol. 11, pp. 1–42). Greenwich, CT: JAI Press.

Rhodes, S. R., & Steers, R. M. (1990). *Managing employee absenteeism.* Reading, MA: Addison-Wesley.

Rosse, J. G., & Miller, H. E. (1984). Relationship between absenteeism and other employee behaviors. In P. Goodman & R. Atkin (Eds.), *Absenteeism* (pp. 194–228). San Francisco: Jossey-Bass.

Roznowski, M., & Hulin, C. (1992). The scientific merit of valid measures of general constructs with special reference to job satisfaction and job withdrawal. In C. Cranny, P. Smith, & E. Stone (Eds.), *Job satisfaction.* Lexington, MA: Lexington.

Salancik, G. R. (1977). Commitment and control of organizational behavior and belief. In B. Staw & G. Salancik (Eds.), *New directions in organizational behavior* (pp. 1–54). Chicago: St. Clair Press.

Salancik, G. R., & Pfeffer, J. (1978). A social information processing approach to job attitudes and task design. *Administrative Science Quarterly, 23,* 224–254.

Schneider, B. (1983). Interactional psychology and organizational behavior. In L. Cummings & B. Staw (Eds.), *Research in organizational behavior* (Vol. 5, pp. 1–32). Greenwich, CT: JAI Press.

Simon, H. A. (1945). *Administrative behavior.* New York: The Free Press.

Smith, P. C., Kendall, L. M., & Hulin, C. L. (1969). *The measurement of satisfaction in work and retirement.* Chicago: Rand McNally.

Staw, B. M. (1977, August). *Two sides of commitment.* Paper presented at the annual meeting of the Academy of Management, Orlando, FL.

Steers, R. M., & Mowday, R. T. (1981). Employee turnover and post decision accommodation processes. In L. Cummings & B. Staw (Eds.), *Research in organizational behavior* (pp. 235–282). Greenwich, CT: JAI Press.

Steers, R. M., & Rhodes, S. R. (1978). Major influences on employee attendance: A process model. *Journal of Applied Psychology, 63,* 391–407.

Stumpf, S. A., & Hartman, K. (1984). Individual exploration to organizational commitment or withdrawal. *Academy of Management Journal, 27,* 308–329.

Terborg, J. T. (1981). Interactional psychology and research on human behavior in organizations. *Academy of Management Review, 8,* 569–576.

Terborg, J. T., & Lee, T. W. (1984). A predictive study of organizational turnover rates. *Academy of Management Journal, 27,* 793–810.

Thompson, J. D. (1967). *Organizations in action.* San Francisco: McGraw-Hill.

Vroom, V. (1964). *Work and Motivation.* New York: Wiley.

Wagner, W. G., Pfeffer, J., & O'Reilly, C. A. (1984). Organizational demography and turnover in top-management groups. *Administrative Science Quarterly, 29,* 74–92.

Weiss, H. M., Nicholas, J., & Link, C. (1992). *Affective and cognitive influences on job satisfaction* [Working Paper]. Purdue University, West Lafayette, IN.

5

PERSPECTIVES ON ORGANIZATIONAL CHANGE: EXPLORING MOVEMENT AT THE INTERFACE

Robert E. Quinn
Joel A. Kahn
Michael J. Mandl
The University of Michigan—Ann Arbor

> *To Schwenk, vortices meant instability, and instability meant that flow was fighting an inequality within itself, and inequality was archetypal. The rolling eddies, the unfurling of ferns, the creasing of mountain ranges, the hollowing of animal organs all followed one path, as he saw it . . . The inequalities could be slow and fast, warm and cold, dense and tenuous, salt and fresh, viscous and fluid, acid and alkaline. At the boundary, life blossoms.*
> —Gleick, 1987, p. 198

INTRODUCTION

This chapter begins with a brief review of four perspectives on organizational change. They are: organizational development, strategic choice, resource dependence and institutional theory, and population ecology. This chapter argues that researchers tend to seek new knowledge more often through differentiation within perspectives than they do by integrating across perspectives. The former practice tends to lead toward routinization and more systematic analysis. The latter practice tends toward creative conceptualization and new direction.

The purpose of this chapter is to help students of organizational change to consider the interface between perspectives and the potential for integrating across the tensions in the interface more frequently. To assist the reader, the chapter reviews some basic principles of polarity theory, and argues that new directions often emerge from cross boundary thinking, particularly when polarities are encountered and the relationships between them are reconceptualized. A researcher can reconceptualize a relationship between polarities by: (a) accepting and differentiating the polar elements; (b) integrating through considering the role of time in the relationship; or (c) altering the perspective or level of analysis that each element is seen to operate at.

With these three procedures as conceptual categories, recent trends in the organizational change literature are examined. Particular emphasis is placed on the volition-constraint polarity. In conclusion the chapter reviews some of the existing problems in the change literature and illustrates how the polar perspective might facilitate the process of reconceptualizing the starting assumptions in the field.

FOUR PERSPECTIVES IN ORGANIZATIONAL CHANGE LITERATURE

There are many perspectives that guide research efforts in the change literature. We begin this chapter with a brief review of four perspectives that we think set the foundation for much of the current work in organizational change. These are organizational development, strategic choice, resource dependence and institutional theory, and population ecology. In this section, we briefly review each of the four. For insights on other possible perspectives on change see Goodman and Kurke (1982).

Organizational Development

The planned change, or organization development, literature has benefited from a number of reviews including Friedlander and Brown, 1974; Beer, 1976; Alderfer, 1977; Faucheux, Amado, and Laurent, 1982; Beer and Walton, 1987; Mirvis, 1988, 1990; Porras & Robertson, 1992; Porras and Silver, 1991. From these reviews a fairly consensual history can be ascertained.

As a field, organizational development (OD) has always had a focus on application, that is, on designing and executing interventions in human systems. According to Mirvis (1988), the early literature tended to describe interventions, internal to the organization, that sought to increase cohesion. Over time, the literature became less focused on the micro level and eventually came to include interventions focused at the interorganizational level. The target focus expanded from philosophy and process, to technology and structure, then to strategy. Interventions sought to not only achieve cohesion, but also identification and community and coherence and cooperative competition. Over time the literature has become increasingly rigorous (Alderfer, 1977). Attention has focused on evaluations of interventions, general frameworks of change, and propositional inventories. Of particular recent interest is the research on radical change and organizational transformation (Porras & Silver, 1991).

From a general view, organizational development is an optimistic field that assumes that change can be created and positively directed. Although OD tends to include some concerns for external factors, it tends to be more micro and more internal than some of the other perspectives that will be considered. Traditionally OD has seen the change process as incremental, but it now includes the notion of radical change. It also differs from other perspectives in that the literature is tied directly to a field of practice. It therefore seeks to develop prescriptive propositions to guide the change process.

Strategic Choice

Child (1972) emphasized the role of strategic choice in organizational change and adaptation. Child, like Chandler (1962), posited that organizations change, or fail to change, primarily because of the strategic choices made by organizational decision makers. Early strategic choice theorists argued that management possessed significant latitude in shaping its own fate. In a review of three perspectives (environments, technology, and size) concerning the determinants of variation in organizational structure, Child (1972) argued that none adequately accounted for the importance of the "agency of choice" by power players within organizations. He contended that, although these perspectives drew attention to potential constraints in structural variation, they all over-emphasized the deterministic nature of contextual factors in shaping variation and change. In contrast, Child argued, organizational decision makers have opportunities to: select types of environments in which to participate; influence conditions within existing environments; alter the type of technologies and structures employed; and make tradeoffs in performance standards. In essence, the organization's "dominant coalition" can, despite contextual constraints, change both its organization's structure and its environment. Work in this vein emphasizes the "free" nature of organizational change.

Resource Dependence and Institutional Theory

Our brief review of resource dependence focuses on Pfeffer and Salancik (1978) and Aldrich and Pfeffer (1976). The concept of resource dependence centers around the fact that organizations are not self-sufficient and therefore, by definition, must interact with and rely on the external environment to exchange resources. This reliance creates a dependency that drives organization action. Although the environment is the source of contingencies and constraints, it is not viewed as eliminating adaptation possibilities. The resource dependence approach "portrays the organization as active, and capable of changing, as well as responding to the environment. Administrators manage their environments as well as their organizations, and the former activity may be as important, or even more important, than the later" (Aldrich & Pfeffer, 1976, p. 83). Because the resource dependence model posits power to the organization in controlling its own survival, it affords more significance to the environment in posing constraints and in influencing decisions than does the strategic choice perspective. In a broad sense, organizational change is seen as a response to contextual dependencies, and the framework suggests a number of strategies (i.e., mergers, buffering, etc.) that organizations can employ to either change the nature of their environment or adapt to a changing environment.

Institutional theory provides an alternative perspective that also emphasizes the influence of the organizational environment in adaptation. Where the dependency perspective posits resource needs and effective performance as the constraining force, institutional theorists (DiMaggio & Powell, 1983; Meyer & Rowan, 1977) emphasized the social and cultural pressures that organizations face to conform to established norms (Scott, 1987). Under this perspective, the extent to which organizations are open to change depends on the degree to which social and economic exchanges are institutionalized. For recent theory and empirical work on organizational change within the institutional perspective, see Powell & DiMaggio (1991).

Population Ecology

Whereas the perspectives reviewed to this point posit individual organizational adaptation, the ecological perspective posits selection at the population level as the prime force for change. The population ecology or natural selection model of organizations is rooted in the traditions of biology (i.e., Darwin) and human ecology (i.e., Hawley). Hannan and Freeman (1977) and Aldrich (1979) applied ecological and natural selection concepts to organization–environment dynamics. The population ecology framework applies to whole populations of organizations rather than to individual firms. In sharp contrast to the strategic choice perspective, Hannan & Freeman (1977) argued that organizations develop "core" characteristics early in their life, and because of a variety of inertial forces, possess limited ability to adapt to changing environments. Individual managers do not affect organizational survival or adaptation in any significant way. Organizational ecologists therefore do not concern themselves with individual firms; instead, they focus on variety and change in populations of organizations as they evolved over time (Freeman, 1982). Population ecology seeks to explore survival and change in populations through the study of differential birth and death rates associated with natural selection. In their review of organization–environment relationships, Aldrich and Pfeffer (1976) and later Aldrich (1979) explicated the natural selection model. The model consists of a three stage process: (a) *variation*, the presence of different organizational forms; (b) *selection*, the process by which the environment differentially selects some forms over others (forms that are not selected are eliminated during this stage); and (c) *retention*, the process by which selected forms are preserved and reproduced. Because the original work was concerned with population level change, ecologists have recently begun to investigate change within populations. We have sought simply to outline the origins of the population ecology framework as it relates to organizational change; for a review of empirical research see Singh and Lumsden (1990).

THE FOUR PERSPECTIVES AND WITHIN BOUNDARY THINKING

The previously mentioned perspectives define four ways of thinking about organizational change. They have different foci and different assumptions. They can, in the order of their earlier presentation, be arrayed along several dichotomous dimensions. On a micro–macro dimension, for example, we would find the following array: organizational development, strategic choice, resource dependence, and population ecology. The same order would follow on such axes of bias as the following: prescriptive–descriptive, internal–external, and volition–constraint. The placement of the perspectives along these dimensions provides some sense of the conceptual boundaries that define the frameworks.

As with all boundaries, if taken to the extreme, they close the system and make it less relevant. Closed conceptual systems, like closed biological systems, tend to move toward equilibrium and then decay. Each of the above perspectives can be critiqued in terms of this tendency.

Because the OD perspective is the oldest, and perhaps the most in danger of losing vitality, we will use it as a point of illustration. We will then consider a potential remedy for the loss of vitality in organization development, in particular. We specifically consider it but the general arguments about boundaries apply to all four perspectives in general. Organizational development does, however, as in the case of each perspective, have unique features. The most extreme point of bias in OD is its emphasis on practice and application.

Within Boundary Thinking: OD As An Illustration

In a recent review, Porras and Silver (1991) noted that much literature continues to be published in traditional OD, but that the field has moved from "energetic adolescence" to "sedate maturity," and "major new insights are rare." This evaluation is consistent with our own.

In a world characterized by "hyperchange" the demand for new ideas and competent intervention skills is intense. Yet, with some limited exceptions, the traditional field of OD is in serious question. Quinn (1990), for example, reporting on an assessment of the Executive Committee of the Organization Development Division of the Academy of Management, argued that the interface between theory and practice is decaying badly, and the decay is reflected in both the practice and the literature of OD.

Organizational development has become traditionalized, and the radical zest of early years of OD has long disappeared. Worse still, there is a crisis of legitimacy. This is particularly reflected in the disappearance of programs in business schools offering training in the practice of planned change. Even the departments that once specialized in such training, have tended to modify their educational programs in favor of more mainline efforts in organizational behavior and organizational theory. By making such changes they are less likely to face questions from other disciplines about the "appropriateness" of their work. Given the change in these programs, there are simply few or perhaps no academic places for new students to go and be trained in the practice of OD.

In a similar vein, the literature itself tends to suffer. For a variety of reasons, including legitimacy, many of the more scholarly writers in the field take a secondary identity in OD while taking a primary identity in organizational behavior or organizational theory. The literature is further hurt by the fact that many of the practitioners of OD get trapped in their own competencies. They bring the tools they have mastered to those markets that desire the tools. They then write papers reporting the application of the same intervention in a continuous string of new settings. The resulting insights are incremental at best. The papers often are narrowly focused, lack rigor, and rehash old ideas. Quinn (1990) argued that there is a great need to bring increased energy to the field. As with organizations, that energy was most likely to be found at the interface between organizational development and other areas of research on change.

In considering the above proposal, Weick (1990) undertook an analysis of the potential interface of organization development and organization theory. He concluded that the interface was potentially fruitful for both organization development and organization theory. Organization development people, Weick argued, are in an ideal position to do problem finding, to examine the phenomena of organizational life from a close view, to experience the richness of organizational life, and to understand the high variety language there associated. In doing so, they are in a position to reexamine the ground of organizational theory. Cited were a number of OD practitioners who have been able to translate their high variety observations into the low variety language of *Administrative Science Quarterly*, and thus impact organization theory.

Weick (1990) saw a need for more attention at the interface. Organization theorists suffer from a tendency towards novelty through differentiation and are not oriented toward integration. The practice oriented focus of OD can help with the task of integration, by posing criteria, identifying silly questions and saying "when to stop." The potential fruitfulness of the interface lies in communication and debate that leads to the uncovering of implicitly shared foundational beliefs. Such communication can lead OD people to look more carefully, and organization theory people to think more precisely. Weick called for the development of a high variety language that will help to preserve "fresh nuances" in the observation of organizational change. Weick (1990) stated, "If we want to tackle problems of paradox, polarity, and opposition with more intelligence, then we will have to do some language work" (p. 23).

The above observations of Quinn and of Weick about the interface of OD and organizational theory also apply to the boundary relationships between all four of the perspectives. As defined bodies of knowledge, the perspectives will continue to be routinized. Many papers will be written at the center of each perspective, but they will very likely be of ever less impact on people broadly interested in the issue of organizational change. The excitement will occur at the boundaries of these and other perspectives. Here there will be transformations. These researchers will differentiate by integrating the differences that occur across the boundaries rather than differentiating within a perspective. Weick suggested that such attempts can be facilitated by some language work—the creation of tools that will help people to "look again" and see differently. In the next section we will explore such a tool.

ON SEEING CHANGE: SOME PRINCIPLES
OF POLARITY THEORY

Polarity theory is evolving from a number of roots in the social science literature (Aram, 1976; Bobko, 1985; Cameron, 1986; Evans & Doz, 1989; Hampden-Turner, 1981; Quinn, 1988; Quinn & Cameron, 1988; Quinn & Kimberly, 1984; Quinn & Rohrbaugh, 1983; Quinn, Spreitzer, & Hart, 1992; Smith & Berg, 1987; Srivastva, Fry, & Associates, 1992; Watzlawick, Weakland, & Risch, 1974). It is an emerging perspective that differs from the four perspectives discussed earlier. It is a tool for seeing polar elements and the connections between the elements. It is particularly useful for looking at change because it helps the observer to notice connections assumed away by other perspectives. In looking at the relationships between the four perspectives in this chapter, it serves as a meta-frame, a tool for finding, understanding and reframing the paradoxical elements in the interfaces between perspectives. It is a language for differentiating by integrating across differences. Here we will present some key principles of polarity theory.

Principle 1.   Energy is found in simultaneity. The quote at the outset of this chapter is from Gleick's (1987) review of the chaos theory. In physical systems, chaos theorists find vortices, instabilities, and inequalities that are associated with change. These have a polar structure in that they are "slow and fast, warm and cold, dense and tenuous, salt and fresh, viscous and fluid, acid and alkaline" (Gleick, 1987, p. 198). It is at the boundaries, where these polar elements meet and interpenetrate, that energy increases and "life blossoms."

The same observation can be made for conceptual systems, in that great breakthroughs are often associated with the insight that conceptual opposites, like motion and rest or love and hate, are operating simultaneously (Rothenberg, 1979). Likewise, in social systems, Munch (1981, 1982) observed that new levels of development are a function of the interpenetration of opposites. By integrating the highly differentiated subsystems in some positive way, a creative tension emerges and new patterns or systems develop. Munch observed that opposite subsystems come together, elevating the amount of tension that can be tolerated while each subsystem retains its individual autonomy.

Principle 2. Imbalance has pathological consequences (Hampden-Turner, 1981). Principle 1 suggests that creative energy and new forms emerge when oppositions are joined in a reinforcing tension system. The two elements are integrated while retaining their differentiation. At the physical, social, or conceptual level, such tension systems are easily distorted. Just as humans require stress, but suffer when there is too little or too much, so it is with other types of systems. The overemphasis on one element in the tension system leads to distortion of the creative tension, and to decay rather than growth. Faerman and Quinn (1988) and Quinn (1988) provided a framework illustrating the creative balance between cohesion and achievement, and between continuity and change, that are necessary in the organizing process. They identify the organizational pathologies that occur when any of the four are over emphasized while de-emphasizing the polar value.

Principle 3. The problem of imbalance, at the social level, takes root in the implicit assumptions of social actors. Discourse is possible because of commonly shared conceptual differentiations. In purposive action, a differentiated position becomes the starting point of a given logic. This logic, or starting point, ignores or negates opposing values, and eventually the problems of imbalance emerge and self-reinforcing patterns of decay tend to follow. Because the problem is lodged in the assumptions being made by the focal person or group, and not in the logic that follows from the assumptions, the cause of the problem is attributed elsewhere. The problem is impermeable to rational instruction and must be resolved through reframing.

Principle 4. The discovery or stimulation of creative energy systems requires the reframing of imbalanced oppositions. This principle suggests a value, at the conceptual level, in the surfacing and reframing of implicit theoretical assumptions. A theorist, for example, might argue passionately about the virtues of equality, participation and cohesion, and the vices of hierarchy. In so doing, the oppositions are imbalanced along a positive-negative dimension. Here the assumed (or sometimes explicit) opposite of equality, participation and cohesion is domination. One must ask, however what the positive opposite of equality is. This frustrating question might lead to a reframing. If hierarchy is differentiated from the negative domination, it may be seen as a positive form of order with important virtues. The theorist may then be able to envision the interpenetration of hierarchical order with equality, participation, and cohesion. Such an organization, one that is both hierarchical and participative, might have extraordinary capabilities.

Such an organization, however, would exist where we normally cannot see, at the juxtaposition of positive opposites. It would be an outlier at the extreme end of two measures that we would not ordinarily think to consider at the same time.

Consider, for example, the work of Womack, Jones, and Ross (1990). They examined a sample of automobile plants along the conceptually opposing dimensions of production cost and product quality. Here two opposite hypotheses exist: increases in quality drive up the cost of production; and, quality is free. Hypothesizing either a negative (quality is costly) or a positive (quality is free) relationship, they found neither. The lack of a correlation led them to look at their data again. In doing so, they found that a few plants were outliers. These had both low cost and high quality. When these outliers were removed from the analysis, the negative relationship emerged. In fact, both hypotheses were true. In traditional plants, quality drives up cost. In less traditional plants, using different assumptions of managing and organizing, costs go down and quality goes up. The discovery of the latter point led to some of their most insightful conclusions.

Principle 5. There are techniques to facilitate reframing and increase our understanding of polarities (Van de Ven & Poole, 1988). The first is to simply live with contradiction, to recognize that the world is contradictory. This approach often results in high differentiation and sometimes conflict. The second technique is to alter the perspective or level of analysis. In the auto study, for example, the researchers produced a paradoxical finding that two opposing hypotheses were true. This logical problem however is resolved by moving from the financial–technical level, to the organizational level, and realizing that two different organizing processes are in play. The third technique is to consider time. One element in a polarity may hold at time one, and the other at time two. In this solution one element may impact the context in which the other operates, one may create the context necessary for the other, or each may mutually influence the other. This third approach also suggests that a paradox that exists because of a logical flaw in theory or assumptions may be resolved by the introduction of new terms or new logic.

EXPLORING THE OPPOSITIONS BETWEEN PERSPECTIVES: CURRENT TRENDS

Earlier we identified some of the oppositions that differentiate the four perspectives on change that we considered at the beginning of this chapter. These include, among others, constraint and volition, micro and macro, prescription and description. These partially serve as conceptual boundaries. In this section, we consider some current research that is occurring at the interface of these boundaries. We use the principles of polarity theory to frame the discussion. Because the volition–constraint dichotomy is particularly salient in recent theoretical discussions, we give it central emphasis. We undertake this exercise to illustrate the type of approach that we hope will come to play an increasing role in research on organizational change, that is, research that seeks to see and explore the tensions and connections between polar elements.

Accepting and Differentiating

The advances within each of the four perspectives can, in part, be attributed to the clarity of their assumptions about the forces of individuals and environments in shaping organizational characteristics, about the appropriate level of analysis for investigating or making change, and about the relative capacities of organizations to change. The distinctiveness of the underlying assumptions has also fostered vigorous debate, and the perspectives have tended to isolate researchers from one another. In the future we can expect much work to continue within each of these perspectives.

It is already evident, however, that some researchers have begun to question the validity of their competing assumptions. In particular, theorists have begun to examine their assumptions about organizations' abilities to change. Although the resource dependence (Pfeffer & Salancik, 1978) and institutional perspectives (Tolbert & Zucker, 1983; DiMaggio & Powell, 1983) have, to some extent, recognized the simultaneity of volition and constraint, still others have also begun to explore this notion. Researchers in OD and in strategic choice, have begun to explore how organizations may be constrained in capacities for change. Organizational ecologists, by contrast, have begun to explore the nature of conditions that may promote organizational change. Because it is too soon to posit any convergence (let alone synthesis) of these broadly disparate theories, there is clear interest in exploration of the boundaries and limits of the heretofore distinct positions. Hambrick and Finkelstein (1987), for example, offered one of the first moves at some reconciliation of extreme positions in their paper on managerial discretion, what they termed "a bridge between polar views of organizational outcomes" (p. 369). They focus on managers as the key to bridging the views of organizations as unconstrained in their abilities to respond to environmental change and the views that emphasize constraint. Examining factors of personal discretion and environmental forces, they conclude that when factors conspire to increase managerial discretion, the probability of organizational change increases; when factors conspire oppositely, the probability declines. Thus, organizations are not simply free to change or wholly constrained from change. The probability of change depends on a complex confluence of factors that pertain to the particular organization in its particular industry and time. In other words, organizations have no perfect freedom to change because their managers are not perfectly free to perceive, conduct, or implement changes. (See Finkelstein & Hambrick, 1990, and Lawless & Finch, 1989, for related empirical studies.)

A general retreat from the strong assumption of freedom in strategic activity has also been recently sounded by Hrebiniak and Joyce (1985) and Mintzberg (1990). Hrebiniak and Joyce argued forcefully that "classifying change as either organizationally or environmentally determined is misleading and diverts research inquiry away from the critical interactive nature of organization–environment relationships in the adaptation process" (1985, p. 336). They suggested that choice and determinism are not opposite ends of one continuum, but rather are two variables that should be examined in interaction.

Mintzberg (1990) also took what he called "the design school" (e.g., Andrews, 1971) of strategic management to task for many of its basic, underlying assumptions. Excessive emphasis on how to design organizations to fit their environments, he argued, ignores the existence of emergent—that is, not designed—strategies. It ignores the influence of structure on strategy (Chandler, 1962). Moreover, it typically excludes from consideration any actors other than the chief executive. Mintzberg argued further that there exists a constraint on design. He stated, "the more clearly articulated the strategy, the more deeply imbedded it becomes in the habits of the organization as well as the minds of its strategists" (1990, p. 184).

Overall these arguments bespeak a growing concern of strategic management theorists for conditions under which organizations may be constrained from responding to environmental change. There is movement in the debate about organizational capacities for change. As summarized by Hambrick and Finkelstein (1987, p. 370) ". . . population ecologists increasingly acknowledge the possibility of intentional change . . . [and strategic choice theorists] seem to be more receptive to a view that at least some organizations are incremental, inertial, and bound up by their internal consistencies."

Integrating by Considering Time

The movement by ecologists that Hambrick and Finkelstein referenced began with a relaxation of their stance on structural inertia (Hannan & Freeman, 1984, 1989). Although relative inertia, that is, that organizations do not change as quickly as environments, is still central to ecological theory, there appears to be an emerging emphasis on investigating change within population. This movement is represented in papers by Singh, Tucker and Meinhard (1988); Delacroix and Swaminathan (1991); and Haveman (1992). These authors, all dedicated ecologists, take up the question of when, that is, under what conditions, organizations may be likely to alter their core organizational activities.

Singh, Tucker, and Meinhard (1988) investigated the influence of government legislation on rates of change in organizational features of voluntary service organizations in Canada. Specifically, they found an increase in the probability of core feature change associated with the occurrence of changes in legislative periods. From an ecological perspective, this study is significant in that its findings support a contention that organizations do respond to changing environmental conditions.

Delacroix and Swaminathan (1991) raised a similar question in their study of changes in California wineries over the period 1946 through 1984. They examined the effect of changes in resource scarcity and munificence on a variety of organizational characteristics. Specifically, they hypothesized that greater environmental variation (i.e., uncertainty, frequency, and amplitude of change in wine consumption) would be associated with a higher likelihood of organizational change. Although rates of organizational change were found to be lower for older and larger organizations (in support of inertia theory), the findings did reveal a significant response of organizations, overall, to changes in environmental conditions. These authors examined the nature of organizational response and found that changes occurred in what they considered to be relatively minor or peripheral domains of organizational activity. This study thus raises an additional, and largely unexamined question about relevant areas of activity over which change should be substantively investigated.

Finally, Haveman (1992) explained that the test of inertia as a key premise of ecological theory must involve investigation of change under conditions where organizations are faced with change or probable death. Haveman studied changes in the market domains of savings and loan organizations over the period 1977 through 1987. Findings revealed that changes in the technological and competitive environment led to substantial changes in the core activities of California savings and loan associations. Further, Haveman found that most core changes (especially those that built on established competencies) made in response to the fundamental environmental shifts improved financial performance, and several changes enhanced survival chances. Haveman concluded that inertial pressures are weakened when environmental conditions change rapidly and substantially, because in such cases the population may face extinction.

Although these ecologists focus their attention on rates of change at the population, not the organization, level of analysis, their findings indicate increasing acceptance of the argument that organizations can, under some conditions, alter important characteristics of form. Although inertia is not, in general, refuted by the results of these studies, its strength and generality are muted. Thus, as with the strategic management theorists reviewed in the previous section, we see movement toward investigation of when organizations may likely change their activities and when they are more strongly constrained from change. Some researchers have specifically tested competing theories of organizational change, that is, ecological versus adaptation models (Ginsberg & Buchholtz, 1990; Singh, House, & Tucker, 1986). The findings of these studies lend credence to the argument that the various perspectives are indeed complimentary (also see Scott, 1987).

In considering the use of time to explain constraint and volition, a highly related and very important stream of literature should also be reviewed. Here time is used to integrate stability and revolutionary change and has direct implications for volition and constraint. Punctuated–equilibrium theorists (Miller & Friesen, 1984; Tushman & Romanelli, 1985) described organizations as proceeding alternatively through convergent periods (i.e., relatively long periods of incremental change that support established strategies, structures, and cultures), and reorientations (i.e., short periods of discontinuous change during which strategies, structures, and cultures are fundamentally altered). Convergent periods are characterized by inertial forces and incremental changes that serve to reinforce the current strategic orientation and to impede radical change. Reorientations are characterized as radical, discontinuous change in the core features of the organization. According to these theorists, especially Tushman and Romanelli (1985), organizations do not often engage in reorientation. Inertia prevents change as a routine response of organizations to changing conditions. Organizational change must occur as a radical, discontinuous intervention on ongoing activities precisely because inertia is strong. Only when the risks of sustaining current, established activity patterns are very great do organizations tend to change. Punctuated equilibrium models, then, seek to explain change in the presence of strong organizational inertia.

Gersick (1991) elaborated this model, especially its emphasis on inertia, ascribing "deep structure" to organizational systems and understandings. According to Gersick, deep structure represents the established design of organizational activities, that is, "the set of fundamental 'choices' that a system has made. . . . The activity patterns of a system's deep structure reinforce the system as a whole, through mutual "feedback loops" (Gersick, 1991, pp. 15–16). Similarly, Miller (1990) posited that the punctuated process is inherent in the nature of organizations. He argued that four common organizational configurations differ in their receptiveness to first-order changes but because of system interconnectedness, each resists second-order changes, making them prone to long periods of momentum punctuated by brief periods of revolution. Gersick also pointed out that punctuated equilibrium models have been recently explicated over a wide variety of scientific disciplines and levels of organizational analysis. Gersick characterized the familiar arguments of Kuhn (1970) about the structure of scientific revolutions as representing basically a punctuated equilibrium model. Gersick's own work (Gersick, 1988; Gersick & Hackman, 1990) on time and transitions in group problem solving sessions also emphasized a deep resistance toward change and, when change finally occurs, a discontinuous change process.

What we see by considering time is that there are pockets, moments, or eras, when change is more or less likely to occur. We see some attempts at theoretical convergence, and we note that history itself is confounded with this convergence. Hyperchange has permeated the world. In response, even the giant firms with all their inertia have begun to change, and small organizations, with all their flexibility, are themselves looking for routines, habits, and niches, to hold on to. All of this is to say that the nature of organizations is changing, so we should only expect that traditional theoretical boundaries must be explored and altered. This recent work also has suggested that longitudinal studies of organizational change afford opportunities for insight that are not available in static cross-sectional studies. We hope and expect that future research will increasingly employ a longitudinal approach.

Alter the Perspective or Level

Another technique for fruitfully engaging the tensions at the boundaries of volition and choice polarity is to alter the perspective or level. We may, for example, be able to more creatively see the polarity by becoming more micro or more macro. Here we consider recent examples of both perspectives.

The Micro Perspective. The volition–choice dichotomy can be reframed within the strategic choice perspective by turning to an even more microperspective. Hambrick and Mason (1984), for example, pointed out that organizations do not simply respond to environmental change. Some person must first perceive the need for change. Here, the perceptions, interpretations, and role of the transformational leader or executive team become more relevant.

Three recent streams of literature place senior executives at the pivotal point of interface between the environment and the organization and between the organization in its history and in its future. One stream of literature focuses on the capacities of leaders to envision a future organization and to translate that vision, via symbolic communication and persuasion, into the very fabric of new organizational arrangements and understandings. This stream of literature, like the planned-change literature, concentrates on the methods of change. Another stream of literature, developing principally within the strategic management perspective, emphasizes the background characteristics of senior executives, for example, their education, functional specialties, and prior experience in general management, as filters on the kinds of environmental information that executives will attend to and the nature of responses they are likely to implement. Finally, a third stream of literature emphasizes characteristics of organizations as wholes, and their leaders in particular, as interpretive systems that identify and understand information from the environment.

The Visionary or Transformational Leader. In the last 15 years, the interest in the notion of the charismatic or transformational leader has increased dramatically. A well recognized book by Burns (1978) stimulated considerable interest in the topic, as did the empirical work of Bass and his associates (see Bass, 1985).

To understand the intense interest in this area, however, one must also look at the world of practice. In recent years, the transformation to a global society has placed enormous competitive pressure on organizations of all kinds. In order to perform in the age of hyperchange, organizations have to become ever more responsive. The problem is that organizations are not predisposed to change. Indeed, the primary purpose of organizational structures is to produce predictable behaviors. Given the power of such structures, it is not unusual for organizations to evolve to the point where more emphasis is placed on the needs of internal constituents than on the needs of external constituents. As organizations have come to confront this problem, the need for leaders who can bring deep change has intensified. The desire for information on how to stimulate organizational transformations has increased (Bass, 1985; Tichy & Devanna, 1986).

In an integration of the literature, Conger (1989) argued that there are four stages of charismatic behavior. In stage one, the leader detects opportunities or deficiencies in the present situation, shows high sensitivity to constituents needs, and formulates an idealized strategic vision. In stage two, the leader communicates the vision, articulates what is unacceptable in the status quo and shows the vision to be the most attractive alternative, and provides motivation to follow the vision. In stage three, the leader builds trust through success, expertise, personal risk taking, self-sacrifice, and unconventional behavior. In the fourth stage, the leader demonstrates the means to achieve the vision through modeling, empowerment, and unconventional tactics.

In this literature, the charismatic or transformational leader is the agent of change. The leader has the capacity to see the organization from a larger perspective, to articulate a new vision, and to present that vision so as to capture the imagination of those people who are invested in the status quo. Clearly, the assumption is that one highly gifted person can, in fact, bring significant change to the organization. Interestingly, the underlying steps of vision, trust, and risk are not unlike the processes underlying many of the central strategies in the OD literature.

Executives as Perceptual Filters. In pointing out that some person must first perceive the need for change, Hambrick and Mason (1984) focused on top management teams as critical in the perceptual process, because these individuals possess sufficient power to implement organizational change. Hambrick and Mason argued that strategic choice may exist, but because it has a behavioral component, the choice will, to some extent, reflect the "idiosyncracies" of top management teams. These idiosyncracies serve to filter and distort the decision maker's perception. According to Hambrick and Mason, executives vary substantially in the kinds of information they routinely perceive. Based on characteristics such as age, education, and functional experience, executives will best understand and consider only certain information in the environment to be important. As a consequence of this filtered perception, executives will perceive needs for change and project possible change responses only within a limited cognitive frame. Thus, strategic choice, although it may be informed by environmental conditions, is constrained by the backgrounds and experiences of organizational executives.

Drawing on the theoretical thrust of Hambrick and Mason, several empirical studies have recently examined how particular background characteristics of executive teams influence organizational change. For example, the results of two studies (Bantel & Jackson, 1989; Wiersema & Bantel, 1992) supported the claim that diversity in top managements' cognitive perspectives might facilitate adaptation. However, two other studies in this vein (Finkelstein & Hambrick,

1990; Fredrickson & Iaquinto, 1989) that examined the impact of team tenure on change, suggest that the longer top teams are in place, the less likely they are to engage their organization in change. This particular finding may be related to the notion that, through time, executives' capacities for change may decrease as a result of their commitment to previous courses of action (Staw, 1981; Staw & Ross, 1987). Taken together these studies support the view that organizational capacities, perceptions, and outcomes are associated with the demographic characteristics of top management teams.

Recent research (Walsh & Fahey, 1986; Walsh, Henderson, & Deighton, 1988), although it is not as clearly grounded in the strategy literature, made a related point about the filtering effect of decision makers' perceptions on possibilities for organizational change. Walsh and Fahey (1986) introduced the concept of "negotiated belief structure" to help explicate the process of strategy making and the content of strategic choice. The negotiated belief structure represents the cognitive orientation within the strategy making group and is formed through the interaction of personal beliefs and political forces. The group's belief structure serves to filter the type of information considered and acted upon and to affect the type of action taken. Walsh and Fahey contended that whether or not organizations change, and the direction of change, are a function of the decision makers' negotiated belief structure.

Starbuck and Milliken (1988) equated perceptual filters, in part, to what executives *notice*. "Noticing is influenced by perceivers' habits, their beliefs about what is, and their beliefs about what ought to be" (Starbuck & Milliken, 1988, p. 46). These authors linked the idea of noticing to Weick's (1979) concept of enactment. All of this suggests that people's beliefs and expectations serve to define what parts of the environment are relevant.

The importance of arguments about executives as perceptual filters on strategic choice cannot be overestimated. First, the recognition of a perceptual agent in the matching of organizational characteristics to environmental conditions offers a beginning, even if only in a limited way, for exploration of organizational change processes. The theoretical way is at least left open for examination of how the perceptions of executives may be translated within existing organizational activity patterns. As Walsh and Fahey argued, "the concept of a negotiated belief structure is pivotal to furthering our understanding of the linkages between strategic decision process and content" (1986, p. 336). Second, and perhaps more important, this view of executive perceptions as a critical filter on important information fundamentally alters the question of which organization–environment fits may be achieved. Where choice was once considered to exist over the entire realm of environmental possibility, today it is understood and investigated as constrained by the perceptions of executives. Organizations may still be rather free to change (although some, i.e., Starbuck, 1983, remain pessimistic in this regard), but their possibilities for change are more limited.

Managers as Interpreters. A related but still different view of the role of executive leadership in organizational change is offered in a series of papers by Dutton and colleagues (Denison, Dutton, Kahn, & Hart, 1992; Dutton & Dukerich, 1991; Dutton & Duncan, 1987a, 1987b; Jackson & Dutton, 1988). Building on the work of Daft and Weick (1984), who emphasized the organization itself as an interpretation system, Dutton and others proposed that a major reason organizations respond differently to changes in the environment involves how issues are triggered and interpreted by decision makers. For example, in Jackson and Dutton (1988), whether an issue is categorized as a threat or opportunity to the organization is an important predictor of the organization's response. More generally, Dutton and Duncan (1987b) described the strategic planning process itself as shaping the interpretations of issues that executives are able to make about possible courses of strategic change.

Interpretative studies of response to change draw on three critical assumptions: a) organization members enact the reality they inhabit and use different frames of reference to make sense of events; b) individuals share their frames of reference within the organization, creating a cognitive consensuality; and c) the views of managers are particularly salient, because managers appear to be at the heart of the cognitive shifts that occur during organizational change (Isabella, 1990). Empirical evidence supporting differential responses to acquisitions, executive succession, quality process deployment, (Isabella, 1990), social responsibility (Dutton & Dukerich, 1991), foreign direct investment (Denison, Dutton, Kahn, & Hart, 1992), and technological innovation (Ginsberg & Venkatraman, 1992) based upon decision makers' interpretations of these issues, continues to accumulate.

In moving to the microperspective on leadership we find three perspectives, which themselves range from more micro to more macro. They provide some useful insights on the volition–choice polarity. The leaders-as-visionaries perspective emphasizes the need for a strong individual who can both develop and implement a new vision. The executives-as-perceptual-filters view addresses the question of how leaders may arrive at a particular vision, focusing especially on the backgrounds of executives as filters on processing of environmental information. The managers-as-interpreters view emphasizes the role of the established organization as a strong influence on the nature of problem or response that can be legitimate within the institutionalized scheme of understanding. Taken together, the three perspectives suggest that the senior executive is both influential and constrained.

The Macro Perspective

While the above efforts reframed volition and constraint by moving to the micro level, the work of Ford and Backoff (1988) and of Thompson (1988) made a dramatic impact by reframing the change process at the macro level. They did this by bringing the notions of trialectics (Ichazo, 1982) to organizational studies. The level of analysis here is not individual or organizational, but universal. Ford and Backoff (1988) discussed three points of view: formal logic excludes paradox and denies change; dialectics embraces paradox and sees the constant progression of change; trialectics "harnesses the permanence of formal logic and the endless change of dialectics into a logic of cycles and process" (p. 99). The key is process. No things exist that are not process. As Ford and Backoff (1988) wrote, "Things, such as people, organizations, rocks, trees, electrons, atoms, planets, and galaxies are names given to abstractions of what is an identifiable and relatively constant pattern from a process of movement and transformation extending over the whole universe. What appears as static is, in fact, a dynamic foci of many processes" (p. 99).

In the trialectics approach, the relatively constant foci are seen as material manifestation points or MMPs. They are neutral points where energy is retained. In viewing change, it is the MMPs that get altered, they are what changes. In trialectics all change is discontinuous. It involves mutation from one MMP to another. Gradual increases in quantity do not necessarily lead to changes in quality. Perceptions of the change process depend on the assumed scale. The finer grained the time scale, the less perceptible the jump. According to trialectics, opposites do not exist in nature, but are a product of the human perceptual system. "Apparent" opposites are complementary in nature. They are poles in a circuit of dynamically balanced flows of energy. Change happens not because of conflict between opposites in nature, but because of equilibrium, or the balanced circulation of energy. Here, it is the stability of process that brings change. The disruption of the balance, however, leads to the emergence of a new MMP. Liquid turns to gas. This happens because the energy of one MMP is attracted to a higher or lower MMP in a larger system that fixes the relationships. The energy of the seed can transfer to the plant in terms of growth or to the soil in terms of decomposition.

Trialectics is highly compatible with the notion of coevolution and this has implications for the volition–constraint issue. A human system is like a raft being steered in a rapidly changing river. At the moment the decision is made on direction, the situation changes simultaneously. Macro and micro systems are evolving together. They are not necessarily causing each other but they are linked by a series of mutual feedback loops that operate simultaneously. Ford and Backoff (1988) argued that all action is impacted by all changes prior to and during the action. This involves all micro and macro structures. For this reason "organizations do engage in strategic choice (the choice of action being taken) and they are subject to natural selection (the consequence of action)—a natural selection that they have themselves helped to create" (Ford & Backoff, 1988, p. 110).

In this perspective, everything is dynamically connected to everything else. Organizations both create and are created by the environment. By changing themselves, they change the environment. Likewise, the executive is connected to all. When things go wrong and the executive separates self from systems and prescribes change, the results are often disastrous because the executive is not outside the system looking in (Hurst, 1986). This point has led Thompson to conclude that the most powerful tool of change is not argument, reason, or method, but relationship, and that trialectics may not be so much about ways of thinking, but about ways of being, and better modes of acting within those relationships (Thompson, 1988).

CONCLUSION

There have been numerous reviews of the change literature. The concluding sections of these reviews are often similar in their criticisms. In one of the most recent reviews, for example, Fry and Srivastva (1992) argued that there is a convergence in previous reviews that suggests our models of change are ahistorical and acontextual. Building on this theme, they make five points of criticism: *First,* studies of change analyze episodes about a change. They tend not to analyze across a sample of changes. The models that result are linear and sequential. Hence, it is not recognized that change can be both desired and resisted, spontaneous and planned, linear and untidy. *Second,* studies of change seldom take a broad enough time frame to take into account alternative explanations of cause or to consider the extended outcomes. Hence, most models of change move from the present to the future. The fact that history greatly influences the array of choices about the future is often ignored. Ignoring the role of history makes it difficult to understand such things as the degree of readiness for change. *Third,* most studies exclude more contingencies than they include. They assume away context. In fact, there are very few absolutes or universal truths in the change process, and context matters. Here the bias toward American assumptions also becomes a point of criticism. *Fourth,* our frames for understanding are very limited. Much of the work is based on either–or assumptions that tolerate little ambiguity. More complex thinking is seen in various contingency approaches and multivariate analyses. The field, they argued, will benefit from moving to still more complex approaches where "pluralism is accepted as a condition . . . but intellectual standards and reasoned commitment are . . . paramount" (Srivastva & Fry, 1992, p. 8). *Fifth,* studies of change tend to be deterministic and outcome oriented. There is more emphasis on closed system assumptions than there is on the open system notion of equifinality. Because of the focus on desired outcomes, much energy goes into understanding how to overcome resistance to change. Little goes into mobilizing energy or understanding that even when we stay the same we are in fact changing.

From analyses such as these, come some predictable recommendations. Develop more complex designs that analyze across samples, utilize an extended chronological perspective, take more sophisticated approaches to context and ambiguity, and take more account of the dynamics of change.

From our review, we see a special need for studies accounting for context and exploring process. Organizational context matters tremendously when considering questions of change. We must ask "under what conditions do my assumptions hold?" This does not simply mean that we qualify our findings with basic generalization disclaimers, but rather we should examine very thoughtfully and carefully the conditions under which our broader theoretical assumptions apply. For example, ecologists ask "under what conditions do assumptions regarding inertia hold?" When asking these questions, we encourage researchers to look outside their own boundaries. Before asking, and especially before answering questions concerning organizational change, look to the world around you. Observe and reflect on both history and current events. If we look around broadly, could we advocate polar statement such as, organizations never transform, or could we ever say that they do so freely? Further, many of our theoretical concepts assume process but do not explicate it in any detail. But, as the notion of trialectics suggests, all is process. Even what appears static can be seen as dynamic. Organizational change is fundamentally an issue of process. As seen in the work of punctuated equilibrium theorists, even periods of inertia are characterized by change—only, change is moving in a direction that reinforces the status quo. In light of the basic point that change is process, we find relatively few studies that actually explore processes of organizational change (for recent exceptions see Child & Smith, 1987; Dutton & Dukerich, 1991; Pettigrew, 1987). Studies exploring process undoubtedly require researchers to employ a fine-grained research approach.

We endorse recommendations for increased complexity and sophistication. We, however, would also argue for increased simplicity. One theme in this chapter is to "look again," to return to the classic phenomena and the classic analyses and see them from a new frame. In doing so, we encourage the researcher to differentiate by integrating across boundaries. Finding the boundaries is not as easy as it seems. It requires that the researcher "look again" at his or her own natural language. What words are most valued? What words are negatively defined? After identifying the key words, search for positive opposites and look for ways to reframe. What does it mean, for example, to have a clear hierarchy with high commitment and participation? What happens when predictability and spontaneity interpenetrate? What new words or concepts might emerge from such thinking?

Such advice is abstract. Let us conclude with an example, by returning to a classic paper in the field of planned change. Chin and Benne (1976) identified the three general strategies of planned change. The rational empirical approach is tied to expertise and the notion of finding and communicating facts. It takes root in science and in liberal education. The assumption about change is that the communication of facts will bring change in behavior. The power–coercive approach is tied to more sociopolitical traditions and the distribution of rewards. The assumption is that change follows the coercive manipulation of rewards, or the application of force. The normative-re-educative approach assumes that humans are embedded in strongly held behavior patterns for complex reasons. From this perspective the communication of facts are likely to bring resistance rather than compliance. Conveying the scientific fact that smoking is related to cancer, is unlikely to stimulate quitting in someone addicted to the habit. What is required is the building of trusting relationships, and participation in the exploration and recreation of context.

If we analyze and compare each of the three general strategies, we find positive opposition between the rational-empirical and the normative-re-educative approaches. The underlying assumptions in each are highly contrasting. The former seeks control and values the use of analysis, information, expertise, and authority. The latter seeks development and values hope, involvement, faith, and trust. Each works under specified conditions and each fails when those conditions are not met.

The power–coercive approach takes an external focus on the target of change, values assertiveness and conflict, and looks to pressure the target of change, through positive or negative rewards, into compliance. This approach also works under specified conditions but fails in alternative conditions. Where, however, is the positive opposite of this approach? Is there a viable strategy of change that was missed entirely in the classic paper? Can the logic of the present chapter lead us to discover the potential empty set? We think so.

In applying the principles of this chapter one would begin to look for opposite values that are positively defined. Here the focus would be internal, with the change agent looking to modify self while putting a premium on freedom of choice for other people. Influence would derive not from coercion but from personal attraction and role modeling. Here power derives from the moral force of high integrity. The change agent has influence because the change agent makes personal sacrifice to personify the most central values of integrity and principle driven behavior. The target of change eventually alters behavior out of attraction and choice.

The above approach might be called the self-modification strategy (see Quinn, 1988). It would complement the rational-empirical and normative-re-educative strategies while it would contrast with the power–coercive. The newly articulated strategy might help to understand the power of many of the great transformational leaders such as Gandhi, whom Benne and Chin place in the power–coercive strategy. The last sentence is important. The change efforts of Gandhi, for example, can be fruitfully analyzed from opposing perspectives. More complexly, Gandhi's power may be best understood, not from one or the other, but the fact that it crosses or interpenetrates both general strategies. Such analyses might be fruitful for nearly every topic of change research.

REFERENCES

Aldrich, H. E. (1979). *Organizations and environments.* Englewood Cliffs, NJ: Prentice-Hall.

Aldrich, H. E., & Pfeffer, J. (1976). Environments of organizations. In R. H. Turner & J. F. Short, Jr. (Eds.), *Annual Review of Sociology* (Vol. 2, pp. 79–105). Palo Alto, CA: Annual Reviews Inc.

Alderfer, C. P. (1977). Organization development. In M. R. Rosenzweig & L. W. Porter (Eds.), *Annual Review of Psychology* (Vol. 28, pp. 197–223). Palo Alto, CA: Annual Reviews Inc.

Andrews, K. R. (1971). *The concept of corporate strategy.* Homewood, IL: Irwin.

Aram, J. D. (1976). *Dilemmas of administrative behavior*. Englewood Cliffs, NJ: Prentice-Hall.

Bantel, K. A., & Jackson, S. E. (1989). Top management and innovations in banking: Does the composition of the top team make a difference? *Strategic Management Journal, 10,* 107–124.

Bass, B. M. (1985). *Leadership and performance beyond expectations*. New York: The Free Press.

Beer, M. (1976). The technology of organization development. In M. Dunnette (Ed.), *Handbook of industrial and organizational psychology* (pp. 937–993). Chicago: Rand McNally.

Beer, M., & Walton, A. E. (1987). Organization change and development. In M. R. Rozenzweig & L. W. Porter (Eds.), *Annual Review of Psychology* (Vol. 38, pp. 339–367). Palo Alto, CA: Annual Reviews Inc.

Bobko, P. (1985). Removing assumptions of bi-polarity: Towards variation and circularity. *Academy of Management Review, 11,* 99–108.

Burns, J. M. (1978). *Leadership*. New York: Harper & Row.

Cameron, K. S. (1986). Effectiveness as paradox. *Management Science, 32,* 539–553.

Chandler, A. (1962). *Strategy and structure: Chapters in the history of the industrial enterprise*. Cambridge, MA: MIT Press.

Child, J. (1972). Organizational structure, environment and performance: The role of strategic choice. *Sociology, 6,* 1–22.

Child, J., & Smith, C. (1987). The context and process of organizational transformation—Cadbury Limited in its sector. *Journal of Management Studies, 24,* 565–593.

Chin, R., & Benne, K. D. (1976). In W. G. Bennis, K. D. Benne, R. Chin, & K. E., Corey (Eds.), *The planning of change* (3rd ed. pp. 22–45). New York: Holt, Rinehart, & Winston.

Conger, J. A. (1989). *The charismatic leader: Behind the mystique of exceptional leadership*. San Francisco: Jossey-Bass.

Daft, R., & Weick, K. (1984). Toward a model of organizations and interpretation systems. *Academy of Management Review, 9,* 284–296.

Delacroix, J., & Swaminathan, A. (1991). Cosmetic, speculative, and adaptive organizational change in the wine industry: A longitudinal study. *Administrative Science Quarterly, 36,* 631–661.

Denison, D., Dutton, J., Kahn, J., & Hart, S. (1992). *Seeing through the lens of experience: Global business experience and CEO's interpretations of foreign direct investment* [Working Paper]. University of Michigan.

DiMaggio, P. J., & Powell, W. W. (1983). The iron cage revisited: Institutional isomorphism and collective rationality in organizational fields. *American Sociological Review, 48,* 147–160.

Dutton, J. E., & Dukerich, J. M. (1991). Keeping an eye on the mirror: Image and identity in organizational adaptation. *Academy of Management Journal, 34,* 517–554.

Dutton, J. E., & Duncan, R. B. (1987a). The creation of momentum for change through the process of strategic issue diagnosis. *Strategic Management Journal, 8,* 279–295.

Dutton, J. E., & Duncan, R. B. (1987b). The influence of the strategic planning process on strategic change. *Strategic Management Journal, 8,* 103–116.

Evans, P. A. L., & Doz, Y. (1989). The dualistic organization. In P. A. L. Evans, Y. Doz, & A. Laurent (Eds.), *Human resource management in international firms: Change, globalization, innovation*. London: Macmillan.

Faerman, S. R., & Quinn, R. E. (1988). Effectiveness: The perspective from organizational theory. *The Review of Higher Education, 9,* 83–100.

Faucheux, C., Amado, G., & Laurent, A. (1982). Organizational development and change. In M. R. Rosenzweig & L. W. Porter (Eds.), *Annual Review of Psychology* (Vol. 33, pp. 343–370). Palo Alto, CA: Annual Reviews Inc.

Finkelstein, S., & Hambrick, D. C. (1990). Top-management-team tenure and organizational outcomes: The moderating role of managerial discretion. *Administrative Science Quarterly, 35,* 484–503.

Ford, J. D., & Backoff, R. H. (1988). Organizational change in and out of dualities and paradox. In R. E. Quinn & K. S. Cameron (Eds.), *Paradox and Transformation: Toward a theory of change in organization and management* (pp. 81–122). Cambridge, MA: Ballinger.

Fredrickson, J. W., & Iaquinto, A. L. (1989). Inertia and creeping rationality in strategic decision processes. *Academy of Management Journal, 32*, 516–542.

Freeman, J. (1982). Organizational life cycles and natural selection processes. In B. Staw & L. L. Cummings (Eds.), *Research in Organizational Behavior* (Vol. 4, pp. 1–32). Greenwich, CT: JAI Press.

Friedlander, F., & Brown, L. D. (1974). Organization development. In M. R. Rosenzweig & L. W. Porter (Eds.), *Annual review of psychology* (Vol. 25, pp. 313–341). Palo Alto, CA: Annual Reviews Inc.

Fry, R. E., Srivastva, S. (1992). Continuity and change in organizational life. In R. E. Fry, S. Srivastva, & Associates (Eds.), *Executive and organizational continuity: Managing the paradoxes of stability and change*, (pp. 1–24). San Francisco: Jossey-Bass.

Gersick, C. J. G. (1991). Revolutionary change theories: A multilevel exploration of the punctuated equilibrium paradigm. *Academy of Management Review, 16*, 10–36.

Gersick, C. J. G. (1988). Time and transition in work teams: Toward a new model of group development. *Academy of Management Journal, 31*, 9–41.

Gersick, C. J. G., & Hackman, J. R. (1990). Habitual routines in task-performing groups. *Organizational Behavior and Human Decision Processes, 47*, 65–97.

Ginsberg, A., & Buchholtz, A. (1990). Converting to for-profit status: Corporate responsiveness to radical change. *Academy of Management Journal, 33*, 445–477.

Ginsberg, A. & Venkatraman, N. (1992). Investing in new information technology: The role of competitive posture and issue diagnosis. *Strategic Management Journal, 13*, 37–53.

Gleick, J. (1987). *Chaos: Making a new science.* New York: Viking.

Goodman, P. S., & Kurke, L. B. (1982). Studies of change in organizations: A status report. In P. S. Goodman and Associates (Eds.), *Change in organizations* (pp. 1–46). San Francisco: Jossey-Bass.

Hambrick, D., & Finkelstein, S. (1987). Managerial discretion: A bridge between polar views of organizational outcomes. In L. L. Cummings & B. Staw (Eds.), *Research in Organizational Behavior* (Vol. 9, pp. 369–406). Greenwich, CT: JAI Press.

Hambrick, D., & Mason, P. (1984). Upper echelons: The organization as a reflection of its top managers. *Academy of Management Review, 9*, 193–206.

Hampden-Turner, C. (1981). *Maps of the mind.* New York: MacMillan.

Hannan, M. T., & Freeman, J. (1989). *Organizational ecology.* Cambridge, MA: Ballinger.

Hannan, M. T., & Freeman, J. (1984). Structural inertia and organizational change. *American Sociological Review, 49*, 149–164.

Hannan, M. T., & Freeman, J. (1977). The population ecology of organizations. *American Journal of Sociology, 82*, 929–965.

Haveman, H. A. (1992). Between a rock and a hard place: Organizational change and performance under conditions of fundamental environmental transformation. *Administrative Science Quarterly, 37*, 48–75.

Hrebiniak, L. G., & Joyce, W. F. (1985). Organizational adaptation: Strategic choice and environmental determinism. *Administrative Science Quarterly, 30*, 336–349.

Hurst, D. (1986). Why strategic management is bankrupt. *Organizational Dynamics*, Autumn, 4–27.

Ichazo, O. (1982). *Between metaphysics and protoanalysis.* New York: Arica.

Isabella, L. A. (1990). Evolving interpretations as a change unfolds: How managers construe key organizational events. *Academy of Management Journal, 33*, 7–41.

Jackson, S., & Dutton, J. (1988). Discerning threats and opportunities. *Administrative Science Quarterly, 33*, 370–387.

Kuhn, T. S. (1970). *The structure of scientific revolution.* Chicago: University of Chicago Press.

Lawless, M. W., & Finch, L. K. (1989). Choice and determinism: A test of Hrebiniak and Joyce's framework on strategy-environment fit. *Strategic Management Journal, 10*, 351–365.

Meyer, J. W., & Rowan, B. (1977). Institutionalized organizations: Formal structure as myth and ceremony. *American Journal of Sociology, 83*, 340–363.

Miller, D. (1990). Organizational configurations: cohesion, change, and prediction. *Human Relations, 43*, 771–789.

Miller, D., & Friesen, P. (1984). *Organizations: A quantum view.* Englewood Cliffs, NJ: Prentice-Hall.

Mintzberg, H. (1990). The design school: Reconsidering the basic premises of strategic management. *Strategic Management Journal, 11*, 171–195.

Mirvis, P. H. (1988). Organizational development: Part I—An evolutionary perspective. In *Research in organizational change and development* (Vol. 2, pp. 1–57). Greenwich, CT: JAI Press.

Mirvis, P. H. (1990). Organizational development: Part II—A revolutionary perspective. In *Research in organizational change and development* (Vol. 4, pp. 1–66). Greenwich, CT: JAI Press.

Munch. (1981). Talcott Parsons and the theory of action I. The structure of the Kantian core. *American Journal of Sociology, 87*, 709–739.

Munch. (1982). Talcott Parsons and the theory of action II. The continuity of action. *American Journal of Sociology, 88*, 771–826.

Pettigrew, A. M. (1987). Context and action in the transformation of the firm. *Journal of Management Studies, 24*, 649–670.

Pfeffer, J., & Salancik, G. R. (1978). *The external control of organizations.* New York: Harper & Row.

Porras, J. I., & Robertson, P. (1992). Organization development. In M. Dunnette & L. M. Hough (Eds.), *Handbook of industrial and organizational psychology* (2nd ed.) (pp. 719–822). Palo Alto, CA: Consulting Psychological Press.

Porras, J. I., & Silver, R. C. (1991). Organization development and transformation. In M. R. Rosenzweig & L. W. Porter (Eds.), *Annual review of psychology* (Vol. 42, pp. 51–78). Palo Alto, CA: Annual Reviews Inc.

Powell, W. W., & DiMaggio, P. J. (Eds.). (1991). *The new institutionalism in organizational analysis.* Chicago: The University of Chicago Press.

Quinn, R. E. (1988). *Beyond rational management: Mastering the paradoxes and competing demands of high performance.* San Francisco: Jossey-Bass.

Quinn, R. E. (1990). Call for papers: A larger perspective. In R. W. Boss (Ed.), *Academy of Management O.D. Newsletter* (Winter, pp. 4–5). The O.D. division of the Academy of Management.

Quinn, R. E., & Cameron, K. S. (1988). *Paradox and transformation: Toward a theory of change in organization and management.* Cambridge, MA: Ballinger.

Quinn, R. E., & Kimberly, J. R. (1984). Paradox, planning and perseverance: Guidelines for managerial practice. In J. R. Kimberly & R. E. Quinn (Eds.), *New futures: The challenge of managing corporate transitions* (pp. 295–314). Homewood, IL: Irwin.

Quinn, R. E., & Rohrbaugh, J. (1983). A spatial model of effectiveness criteria: Toward a competing values approach to organizational analysis. *Management Science, 29*, 363–377.

Quinn, R. E., Spreitzer, G. M., & Hart, S. L. (1992). Integrating the extremes: Crucial skills for managerial effectiveness. In S. Srivastva & R. E. Fry (Eds.), *Executive and organizational continuity: Managing the paradoxes of stability and change* (pp. 222–252). San Francisco: Jossey-Bass.

Rothenberg, A. (1979). *The emerging goddess.* Chicago: University of Chicago Press.

Scott, W. R. (1987). *Organizations: Rational, natural, and open systems.* Englewood Cliffs, NJ: Prentice-Hall.

Singh, J. V., House, R. J., & Tucker, D. J. (1986). Organizational change and organizational mortality. *Administrative Science Quarterly, 31*, 587–611.

Singh, J. V., & Lumsden, C. J. (1990). Theory and research in organizational ecology. In W. R. Scott & J. Blake (Eds.), *Annual Review of Sociology* (Vol. 16, pp. 161–195). Palo Alto, CA: Annual Reviews Inc.

Singh, J. V., Tucker, D. J., & Meinhard, A. G. (1988, August). *Are voluntary organizations structurally inert? Exploring an assumption in organizational ecology.* Paper presented at the Academy of Management Annual Meeting, Anaheim, CA.

Smith, K. & Berg, D. (1987). *Paradoxes of group life.* San Francisco: Jossey-Bass.

Srivastva, S., Fry, R. E., & Associates. (1992). *Executive and organizational continuity: Managing the paradoxes of stability and change.* San Francisco: Jossey-Bass.

Starbuck, W. H. (1983). Organizations as action generators. *American Sociological Review, 48,* 91–102.

Starbuck, W. H., & Milliken, F. (1988). Executives' perceptual filters: What they notice and how they make sense. In D. Hambrick (Ed.), *The executive effect: Concepts and methods of studying top managers* (pp. 35–65). Greenwich, CT: JAI Press.

Staw, B. M. (1981). The escalation of commitment to a course of action. *Academy of Management Review, 6,* 577–587.

Staw, B. M., & Ross, J. (1987). Understanding escalation situations: Antecedents, prototypes, and solutions. In B. Staw & L. L. Cummings (Eds.), *Research in Organizational Behavior* (Vol. 9, pp. 39–78). Greenwich, CT: JAI Press.

Thompson, M. P. (1988). Being, thought, and action. In R. E. Quinn & K. S. Cameron (Eds.), *Paradox and transformation: Toward a theory of change in organization and management* (pp. 123–136). Cambridge, MA: Ballinger.

Tichy, N., & Devanna, M. A. (1986). *The transformational leader.* New York: Wiley.

Tolbert, P. S., & Zucker, L. G. (1983). Institutional sources of change in the formal structure of organizations: The diffusion of civil service reform: 1889–1935. *Administrative Science Quarterly, 28,* 22–39.

Tushman, M., & Romanelli, E. (1985). Organizational evolution: A metamorphosis model of convergence and reorientation. In L. L. Cummings & B. M. Staw (Eds.), *Research in organizational behavior* (Vol. 7, pp. 171–222). Greenwich, CT: JAI Press.

Van de Ven, A. H. & Poole, M. S. (1988). Paradox requirements for theory of change. In R. E. Quinn & K. S. Cameron (Eds.), *Paradox and transformation: Toward a theory of change in organization and management* (pp. 19–64). Cambridge, MA: Ballinger.

Walsh, J. P., & Fahey, L. (1986). The role of negotiated belief structures in strategy making. *Journal of Management, 12,* 325–338.

Walsh, J. P., Henderson, C. M., & Deighton, J. (1988). Negotiated belief structures and decision performance: An empirical investigation. *Organizational Behavior and Human Decision Processes, 42,* 194–216.

Watzlawick, P., Weakland, J. H., & Risch, R. (1974). *Change: Principles of problem formation and problem resolution.* New York: Norton.

Weick, K. E. (1979). *The social psychology of organizing.* Reading, MA: Addison-Wesley.

Weick, K. E. (1990, August). *Fatigue of the spirit in organizational theory and organizational development: Reconnaissance as remedy.* Distinguished address presented to the Organizational Development Division of the Academy of Management, San Francisco, CA.

Wiersema, M. F., & Bantel, K. A., (1992). Top management team demography and corporate strategic change. *Academy of Management Journal, 35,* 91–121.

Womack, J. P., Jones, D. T., & Ross, D. (1990). *The machine that changed the world.* New York: Rawson Associates.

6

ORGANIZATIONAL EFFECTIVENESS: OLD MODELS AND NEW CONSTRUCTS

David A. Whetten
University of Illinois

Kim S. Cameron
University of Michigan

INTRODUCTION

More than a decade ago, a symposium at the annual Academy of Management meetings was organized in which several well known scholars discussed the current state of organizational effectiveness. The symposium highlighted the disarray and conceptual confusion that surrounded this construct. The discussion occurred at the height of the scholarly debate over the relative merits of competing models of organizational effectiveness (Goodman & Pennings, 1977; Price, 1982). Seven books and many articles were published on the topic in the late 1970s and early 1980s, most arguing for a particular effectiveness model. None of the competing models of effectiveness emerged as the dominant perspective, and some writers became so frustrated by the confusion that they recommended a "moratorium on all studies of organizational effectiveness, books on organizational effectiveness, and chapters on organizational effectiveness" (Goodman, 1979, p. 4).

In 1983, we countered this recommendation by arguing that "despite its chaotic conceptual condition, organizational effectiveness is not likely to go away" (Cameron & Whetten, 1983a, p. 1). Three main reasons why effectiveness was here to stay were presented. First, organizational effectiveness lies at the center of all models and theories of organizations. That is, all conceptualizations of organizations include some notion regarding the difference between effective and ineffective performance. Second, it logically follows that effectiveness is the ultimate dependent variable in organizational research. Evidence of effective performance is either assumed or required in most research on organizations.

Third, individuals are constantly faced with the need to make judgments about the effectiveness of organizations. Pragmatic choices are continually made about which public school should be closed, which firm will get a contract, in which company an investment will be made, and so on.

Despite our admonition, however, scholarly research nearly ceased on the topic of organizational effectiveness. From a total of more than 20 articles appearing on the topic of organizational effectiveness in the leading organizational science journals from 1975 to 1985, (and several hundred more before that time [see Cameron, 1982 for a review]), only one article (Tsui, 1990) and one book (Denison, 1990) appeared during the next half decade. The conclusion reached by most scholars was similar to that drawn by us in 1983, ". . . multiple viewpoints all may be equally legitimate but under different circumstances and with different types of organizations" (Cameron & Whetten, 1983a, p. 274). The problem was, by concluding that all participants in the effectiveness debates could be right, the bloom was off the "effectiveness rose," and researchers lost interest.

However, it was only the construct of organizational effectiveness that faded away, not the need to assess organizational performance and to make judgments about excellent practice. With the publication of popular books such as Peters' and Waterman's *In Search of Excellence* (1982), Deming's *Out of the Crisis* (1986), Imai's *Kaizen* (1988), and Pascale's *Managing on the Edge* (1990), the emphasis changed from assessing organizational effectiveness to measuring excellence, quality, continuous improvement, transformation, revitalization, and so on. In addition, scholars began to investigate non-normal organizational performance situations that had been largely ignored prior to the mid-1980s. These included, high reliability systems, hyperturbulent environments, one-of-a-kind disasters, and unusually high levels of performance (Perrow, 1984; Weick & Roberts, 1992). These two emergent trends helped fuel the development of new strains of research related to organizational effectiveness.

In retrospect, it appears that our 1983 prediction was half correct. It was correct to argue that there would be ongoing interest in measuring organizational performance. However, we certainly did not anticipate the sudden drop-off in research on the performance measure of choice for several decades.

Therefore, when asked to write this chapter we were faced with a dilemma. We could either craft another wake-up call, of sorts, to again try to stimulate renewed interest in the empirical and conceptual investigation of organizational effectiveness. Or, we could use this opportunity to abstract "lessons learned" from the history of research and theory development on organizational effectiveness that could inform subsequent scholarship on emerging, allied measures of organizational performance, like "total quality."

Given the clearly revealed preferences of our colleagues on the subject, and the unlikelihood that those preferences would be altered by another laundry list of "promising new directions" promulgated by this chapter, we elected the second option. That approach was also attractive, because we were concerned that research on related performance measures was beginning to appear that was seemingly unconnected to the rich tradition of research on organizational effectiveness.

Despite the fact that no general theory of effectiveness emerged from the rancorous debates of the previous two decades, much had been learned about studying organizational outcomes in the process. Given the likelihood that interest in measuring organizational performance would continue, albeit under new titles, we felt it was important to chronicle what had been learned from hundreds of articles and books on organizational effectiveness so that future conceptual and empirical work on related measures of organizational performance might benefit from this intellectual odyssey. We also felt there was an important methodological story to be told. Therefore, in this chapter we include a brief history of the evolution of research designs, highlighting several contemporary methodological issues and interesting research questions that bear further examination in subsequent studies of organizational performance.

THE EVOLUTION OF ORGANIZATIONAL EFFECTIVENESS APPROACHES

In general, the theoretical evolution of organizational effectiveness parallels the evolution of thought about organizations in general. This is not surprising because a theoretical statement about the definition of effectiveness reflects the proponent's theory of organizations in much the same way that a model of motivation reflects the author's assumptions about human nature.

Several thoughtful reviews of the history of general organizational theories serve as a backdrop for a contemporary discussion of the evolution of the effectiveness construct. Perrow (1986), Scott (1992), and Hall (1987) each used a different framework for presenting the "progression" of thought in the field of organizational effectiveness. Perrow grounded his analysis in Weber's bureaucratic model—arguing that subsequent views of organizations were largely attempts to eliminate the perceived weaknesses, or to accentuate the strengths, of this perspective. Scott organized his historical overview around three perspectives: rational, natural, and open systems. He argued that the field has basically evolved through a series of eras, or stages, in which each of these systems dominated contemporary organizational theory. Hall organized his overview using a different set of categories: structures, processes, and outcomes. Our review of the history of theoretical thought on organizational effectiveness will draw heavily on these frameworks.

Ideal Types

The earliest models of organizational effectiveness emphasized ideal types, that is, models of organization that focus attention on salient or distinctive attributes. Weber's (1947) characterization of bureaucracies is the most obvious and well-known example. This "rational-legal" form of organization was characterized by decisions based on rules, equal treatment for all employees, separation of the position from its occupant, staffing and promotions based on skills and expertise, specific work standards, and documented work performance. These characteristics were operationalized as dimensions of bureaucracy, including formalization of procedures, specialization of work, and centralization of decision making (Hall, 1963; Price, 1968).

Early applications of the bureaucratic model to the topic of effectiveness argued that efficiency was the appropriate measure of organizational performance. Given this performance criteria, the more nearly an organization was modeled after the typical bureaucratic characteristics (e.g., specialization, formalization, centralization), the more effective (i.e., efficient) it was. In defense of this perspective, Perrow argued that most of the criticisms of the "sins" of bureaucracy are actually the result of bureaucratic principles not being implemented fully. "Where all organizations strive toward efficiency as defined by the owners, the rational-legal form of bureaucracy is the most efficient form of administration known in industrial societies (1986, p. 4).

Subsequent models of organization began to challenge these assumptions, however, arguing that effective organizations were in fact nonbureaucratic. Barnard's (1938) influential book, *The Functions of the Executive*, argued that organizations are at their core cooperative systems. Furthermore, it was proposed that the role of leaders is to channel and direct those cooperative processes to accomplish productive outcomes. An effective organization, therefore, needs to satisfy the needs of its members by providing adequate inducements to sustain their required contributions. It must also insure that the members' actions are bridled by institutionalized goals and decision making processes. In addition, the organization needed to legitimate its role in society by shrouding its activities in broad social values.

Perrow (1986) argued:

This enormously influential and remarkable book contains within it the seeds of three distinct trends of organizational theory that were to dominate the field for the next three decades. One was the institutional school as represented by Philip Selznick (1948); another was the decision-making school as represented by Herbert Simon (1956); the third was the human relations school (Roethlisberger & Dickson, 1947). (p. 63)

In one sense, each of these schools of thought became a competing ideal type. Although advocates of these perspectives disagreed over the criteria for assessing effectiveness, they agreed that effectiveness should be measured against the standard of an ideal type. As a result, over the years, the "standards" of effectiveness proliferated.

Early researchers used as their standard organizational goal accomplishment (Bluedorn, 1980). Then advocates of what Scott (1992) referred to as the "natural systems" view of organizations proposed that goal accomplishment ultimately depends on controlling critical resources, for example, human and financial capital (Pfeffer & Salancik, 1978; Yuchtman & Seashore, 1967). This challenge to the rational model opened the flood gates of alternative standards, including, the quality of an organization's communication and "interpretive" processes (Weick & Daft, 1983), the satisfaction of members (Schneider, 1983), and the extent to which organizational policies and practices complied with the norms of social equality (Keeley, 1978). The common ingredient during this era was a passion for finding the Holy Grail of organizational theory: the definitive, universal definition of organizational effectiveness.

Contingency Theory

Challenges to the soundness of Weber's reasoning, coupled with mounting frustration over the truth claims of competing models, gave rise to contingency theory. This perspective argued that effectiveness was not a function of the extent to which an organization reflected the qualities of a specific ideal profile, but instead, it depended on the match between an organization's profile and environmental conditions. The challenge for researchers became identifying the relevant environmental and organizational dimensions and building theories of "fit."

Burns and Stalker's (1961) classic treatise on organic versus mechanistic types represented an early bridge from ideal type to contingency theory thinking. They argued that mechanistic organizations (those high on Weber's bureaucratic dimensions) were best suited for highly stable and relatively simple environments. In contrast, organic organizations (those high on Bernard's characteristics list) were better suited for rapidly changing, highly complex situations. This kernel of an idea bore fruits in several large scale studies of congruence between organizational and environmental dimensions during the late 1960s and 1970s. These included Lawrence and Lorsch's (1967) study of multiple industries, the Aston studies in England (Pugh, Hickson, and Hinings, 1969) and Van de Ven and Ferry's (1980) development of the "Organizational Assessment Survey" (OAS).

The critical difference between ideal type and contingency theory thinking was that the former assumed that "one size fits all." That is, effective organizations were distinguished by their fit with a universal set of characteristics, an ideal type. An effective organization emphasized x, y, or z, depending on the theoretical bias. In contrast, contingency theory argued that effective organizations matched their profiles with prevailing environmental conditions. If the organization was in an x type environment, then it emphasized x design features.

These two views shared an emphasis on organizational dimensions. Although the referent for judging effectiveness differed, the way you measured, or assessed, effectiveness was the same. Organizational dimensions like standardization, centralization, satisfaction, and size, and environmental dimensions like simple, dynamic, and patterned were common to both ideal type and contingency theory perspectives.

Multiple Constituents

During the late 1970s and early 1980s thinking on organizational effectiveness entered another evolutionary cycle. Maintaining an external matching perspective, authors began to focus less on the assessment criteria of abstract dimensions and more on the concrete expressions of stake holders' expectations (Connolly, Conlon, & Deutsch, 1980; Zammuto, 1984).

Effective organizations were viewed as those which had accurate information about the expectations of strategically critical constituents and adapted internal organizational activities, goals, and values to match those expectations. Proponents of the stake holders' perspective view organizations as highly elastic entities operating in a dynamic force field which literally pulls the organization's shape and form in different directions—molding the organization to the demands of powerful interest groups, including stockholders, unions, government regulators, competitors, customers, and so forth. Effectiveness is, therefore, a function of organizational qualities like learning, responsiveness, and influence management.

The multiple constituencies model spawned a large number of research studies (Cameron, 1978; Mahoney, 1967; Osborn & Hunt, 1974; Tsui, 1990; Whetten, 1978). Researchers using this approach encountered four difficult theoretical and methodological challenges (Cameron & Whetten, 1983a). First, when asked, individual stake holders have difficulty explicating their personal preferences and expectations for an organization. Second, a stake holder's preferences and expectations change, sometimes dramatically, over time. Third, a variety of contradictory preferences are almost always pursued simultaneously in an organization. Fourth, the expressed preferences of strategic constituencies frequently are unrelated, or negatively related, to one another and to summary judgments made by stake holders about an organization's effectiveness.

The multiple constituencies model is aptly portrayed in Meyer and Zucker's (1989) work on what they call "permanently failing organizations." These authors challenged the basic economic assumption that organizations are driven toward efficiency, arguing instead that organizations tend toward sustained low performance, or, in their terms, "permanent failure."

This occurs in the following manner. When organizations experience poor performance due to shifts in environmental conditions, the interests of various constituencies diverge. Owners want to redeploy their assets to more productive uses (as per standard economic thinking). In contrast, groups who have much to lose if the organization closes (e.g., employees, suppliers, the local community) attempt to block asset redeployment initiatives. According to Meyer and Zucker, because the economic uses of organizations are not always coincidental with their social and political uses, organizational performance is only loosely coupled with organizational persistence.

Paradox Model

The recognition that organizations are simultaneously pulled in opposite directions by the expectations of multiple constituencies lead Quinn and his associates (Quinn & Cameron, 1983, 1988; Quinn & Rohrbaugh, 1981) to introduce the Competing Values Model of Organizational Effectiveness.

This model recognized the inherently paradoxical nature of organizational life. Administrators must not only make tradeoffs between day-to-day competing demands on the organization's resources, but, more importantly, they must balance competing expectations regarding the core identity of the organization as an institution. From this point of view, effective organizations are both short- and long-term focused, flexible and rigid, centralized and decentralized, goal and resource control oriented, concerned about the needs of members and the demands of customers.

The paradoxical model of organizational effectiveness represents the natural, logical extension of earlier eras of thought. It borrows from contingency theory the emphasis on matching external and internal attributes. Like the multiple constituencies model it uses expectations (rather than dimensions) as the criteria for measuring effectiveness. In a sense, the paradoxical model can be viewed as a more complex form of its predecessors—it allows for the likelihood of organizations operating simultaneously in different environmental domains, with each domain conveying different expectations. Whereas contingency theory assumed a single domain, for the sake of matching organizational and environmental characteristics, the paradoxical extension allows for multiple domains requiring multiple, simultaneous, and inherently contradictory matches.

The role of paradoxical logic in organizational effectiveness can best be illustrated by shifting from abstract theoretical constructs to concrete research results. For example, in a study of 14 declining colleges, half of which eventually reversed their declining trends, the major difference between institutions that recovered and those that continued to decline was the presence of paradox: entrepreneurship and conservatism, enacting the environment and buffering against the environment, defensiveness and aggressiveness, and reinforcing and destroying traditions (Cameron, 1986).

The evidence supporting the paradoxical model of effectiveness is summarized by Cameron (1986), "It is not just the presence of mutually exclusive opposites that makes for effectiveness, but it is the creative leaps, the flexibility, and the unity made possible by them that leads to excellence. The presence of creative tension arising from paradoxical attributes helps foster organizational effectiveness" (p. 549).

Proponents of paradoxical thinking use these conclusions to argue that effective organizations are not those that simply match an ideal profile, or personify a universalistic model, nor are they characterized by hyper-responsiveness in juggling competing constituency demands. Instead, they are characterized as hybrid forms, consisting of uncomplimentary elements. They are both large and small, both growing and downsizing, both tightly coupled and flexible, both consistent and inconsistent.

Summary of Current Conceptual Thinking

Looking back over the past three decades, there have been at least three major evolutionary shifts in the prevailing views regarding organizational effectiveness. These are summarized in Table 6.1. This intellectual odyssey has progressively yielded more complex views of organizations as behavioral systems. As a natural consequence, the theories of organizational effectiveness have also increased in complexity. In particular, they reflect more complex and dynamic views of organizational goals, outcomes, and constituencies.

The following four broad conclusions summarize extant thinking regarding organizational effectiveness. *First*, multiple models of organizational effectiveness are products of multiple, often arbitrary models of organization. No model of organization can be argued to be better than any other, so no model of effectiveness has an inherent advantage over any other. *Second*, the construct space (conceptual boundaries) of effectiveness is unknown. It is not clear which criteria are indicators of effectiveness, which criteria are predictors of effectiveness, and which criteria are outcomes of effectiveness. *Third*, the best criteria for assessing organizational effectiveness are unknown and unknowable. Because individuals often cannot identify their own preferences and expectations, because preferences and expectations change over time, and because contradictory preferences and expectations are held by different constituency groups, a stable set of effectiveness criteria simply are not available for organizations. *Fourth*, it is more worthwhile to develop specific frameworks for assessing effectiveness than to try to develop general theories of effectiveness. The issues surrounding effectiveness assessment methodologies are so pivotal, in fact, that they need to be examined in more detail.

ASSESSMENT METHODOLOGY ISSUES

The evolution of the research designs used to study organizational effectiveness has progressed along roughly parallel lines with the development of conceptual thought.

Unfortunately, relatively little sophistication characterized most of the early research. The bulk of empirical assessments in the 1960s, 1970s, and even the early 1980s used generalized summary ratings of overall effectiveness, for example, a single rating of overall performance (Cameron, 1978). When multiple

TABLE 6.1
Evaluation of Approaches to Organizational Effectiveness

	Ideal Types	Contingency Theory	Multiple Constituencies	Paradoxical Model
Examples of authors	Weber Barnard Price	Burns & Stalker Aston Studies Van de Ven & Ferry Seashore & Yuchtman	Pfeffer & Salancik Tsui Connolly, et al. Zammuto	Quinn & Cameron Quinn & Rohrbaugh
Basic Approach	Match between an organization's profile and an ideal type	Match between an organization's profile and environmental conditions	Match between an organization's activities and stake holders' expectations	Combining contradictory elements in an organization and managing inconsistent expectations
Popular Examples of Models	Goals models and internal process models	System resource models	Strategic constituency models	Competing values model

dimensions of effectiveness were assessed, all were measured using question-naires, few empirically identified the relationships among the dimensions or their predictors, and paltry attention was given to their association with objective performance criteria. As reflected in the fact that several efficiency formulas comparing input measures to output measures were introduced as substitutes for effectiveness (e.g., Lewin & Minton, 1986), the reliable and accurate evaluation of effectiveness was almost universally identified as a conundrum. Indeed, by the mid-1980s, one conclusion became clear: Much of the lack of agreement regarding theoretical perspectives had its roots in incomparable research designs.

As effectiveness models began to incorporate elements like congruence, con-stituencies, and paradox, it became clear that research designs needed to become more flexible, complex, and precise. Because no single research design was suitable for the plethora of theoretical perspectives, the key to comparing research findings was to make explicit choices regarding research design parameters. The following seven research design questions were proposed as guidelines for this process (Cameron & Whetten, 1983a, p. 269–274).

1. *What time frame is being employed?* Short-term effects may differ from long-term effects, and different states in an organization's life cycle may produce different levels of performance.

2. *What level of analysis is being used?* Effectiveness at different levels of analysis in an organization (e.g., subunit performance versus organizational adaptation) may be incompatible.

3. *From whose perspective is effectiveness being judged?* The criteria used by different constituencies to define effectiveness often differ markedly and often follow from unique constituency interests.

4. *On what domain of activity is the judgment focused?* Achieving high levels of effectiveness in one domain of activity in an organization may mitigate against effectiveness in another domain.

5. *What is the purpose for judging effectiveness?* Changing the purposes of an evaluation may change the consequence and the criteria being evaluated.

6. *What type of data are being used for judgments of effectiveness?* Official documents, perceptions of members, participant observations, and symbolic or cultural artifacts all may produce a different conclusion about the effectiveness of an organization.

7. *What is the referent against which effectiveness is judged?* No universal standard exists against which to evaluate performance, and different standards will produce conclusions about effectiveness.

The importance of these seven questions for guiding empirical investigations of organizational performance will be illustrated by examining time frame, level of analysis, and constituency and domain, in more detail. This examination will also highlight several important unresolved research issues.

Time Frame

The adage, "Timing is everything," has a special significance for research on organizational effectiveness. The timing of an assessment will effect the outcome of the assessment in two ways. First, short- and long-term measures of effectiveness often produce strikingly different results. For example, in a study of the U.S. tobacco industry, Miles and Cameron (1982) found that one company was the least effective of the six companies studied when short-term criteria were applied, but it jumped to second most effective when long-term criteria were used. Another firm was the most effective in the short-term, but it dropped to fifth in the long-term. Differences in long- and short-term assessments may vary either because the organization is deliberately sacrificing performance in one time frame in hopes of increasing it in the other, or because a study's time frames and outcome measures are incompatible.

The second reason that organizational assessment outcome may be affected by timing is related to the life cycle view of organizations. The application of the biological metaphor to patterns of organizational change (e.g., Katz & Kahn, 1978; McKelvey, 1982), the generalization of small group stage models to organizational development (Cameron & Whetten, 1983b), and the application of product life cycle models to organizational strategy (Child & Kieser, 1981) have led some organizational scholars to conclude that organizations develop through certain identifiable life cycle stages. Cameron and Whetten (1981) found, for example, that the criteria of effectiveness held by participants in simulated organizations changed as the organizations progressed through different life cycle stages. They concluded that, ". . . significant variation existed in the ratings of effectiveness of individual, department, and organizational levels, depending on the organization's stage of development" (p. 537).

There are two residual questions associated with the timing research design parameter that have yet to be empirically addressed in the effectiveness literature. First, what is the optimum time frame for assessing effectiveness in different types of settings and with different types of activities? In a study of organizational change in over 100 organizations, for example, a research team consisting of Huber et al. (1993) assessed organizational performance and change during a 6 month time frame. Each 6 months new data was collected focusing on the previous 6 month period. The assumption was made that this time frame best captured the organizations' change and performance rhythms. The trouble was that very little empirical investigation of differences in time frames has been conducted, so decisions regarding how frequently data should be collected, how long a time horizon should be examined at each interval, and whether multiple time frames (long- and short-term) should be used simultaneously are largely a matter of guess work.

A second research question focuses on the evolutionary processes in organizations: specifically, *what* signals the shift from one organizational life cycle stage to another, and *what* is the best way to match appropriate effectiveness models to an organization's life cycle stage. At least a dozen organizational life cycle models have been proposed in the literature, each with a description of the characteristics typifying different stages. Yet no empirical assessment involving multiple organizations has been made of the fit between different life cycle stages and various models of effectiveness. Simply stated, the change dynamics of organizations and their effectiveness equivalents have not been adequately integrated.

Levels of Analysis

It follows from our understanding of organizations as complex social systems that one's unit, or level, of analysis in assessing organizational effectiveness matters a great deal. Judgments of "organizational" effectiveness can be made at the individual level (e.g., Is the human dignity of organizational members being preserved?); at the unit level (e.g., Is the work group cohesive?); at the organization level (e.g., Does the organization acquire needed resources?); at the population or industry level (e.g., Does the organization's performance enhance the legitimacy of it's industry?); or at the societal level (e.g., What is the effect of the organization's outputs on society?). It is generally the case that assessments of effectiveness at one level do not match assessments made at another level. Indeed, Freeman (1978) argued that selecting the appropriate level of analysis is critical because data on effectiveness at one level is often nonsensical when viewed from another level.

This awareness is critical as we try to accumulate knowledge about organizational effectiveness by pooling the results from studies conducted at different levels of analysis. For example, Tsui has studied effectiveness at the individual (1984) and unit levels (1990), Whetten (1978) and Cameron (1984) focused on the organizational level, and Ehreth (1988) concentrated on the societal level. The well-known, but often overlooked, problems of making comparisons across levels of analysis include lack of construct isomorphism, cross-level effects, and emergent properties (Rousseau, 1985).

These concerns are reflected in what a recent task force of the National Academy of Sciences' Division on Human Factors referred to as the "productivity paradox" (Harris, 1994). That is, when you add up all the dollars that an organization invests in increasing the productivity of its various operations (everything from word processing to CAD-CAM systems) and then compare the aggregate sum with widely accepted measures of organizational-level productivity, the correlation is typically very low.

In the process of analyzing this problem, the task force concluded that our existing models of organizational effectiveness, personal performance, and group productivity were ill-equipped to guide our investigation of the causes of this so-called productivity paradox. The core deficiency with all these models is that they focus on a single level of analysis (either the person, the group, or the organization). Therefore, they are appropriate to answer how the productivity (or effectiveness) of x (where x is a person, group, or organization) can be increased. On the other hand, they shed little light on the question, given an increase in the productivity (or effectiveness) of x (person, group, or organization), under what conditions are we likely to see an increase in the productivity of y (a different level in the organization). The Task Force concluded that very little is known about cross-level processes or their effects.

These observations suggest some interesting and challenging theoretical questions that warrant further investigation. First, from a bottom-up perspective, it is widely accepted that organizational effectiveness is not equal to the sum of the effectiveness of various organizational parts. But little is known about the specific emergent properties and processes that must be factored into our models to account for the differences. Second, taking a top-down view, we know very little about the implications of various models of organizational effectiveness for the performance of encompassed organizational levels (e.g., divisions, work units, and individuals). That is, when specific initiatives are undertaken at the organizational level to increase effectiveness (e.g., downsizing), what intervening properties and processes would allow us to accurately predict their impact on the performance of lower levels in the organization.

Constituencies and Domains

The saying, "Where you stand affects what you see," captures the essence of the current writing on the differences in constituency perspectives. For example, Tsui (1990) examined the effectiveness of the human resources (HR) department in three organizations from the perspective of executives, managers, and employees. She found that the executives were most satisfied, overall, with the HR department's performance. Also, the HR departments' ability to satisfy the expectations of their constituencies varied as a function of the department's resource munificence and the heterogeneity of the membership of their constituents. It appears that the more varied the expectations of an organizational unit's constituents, the more resources it needs to satisfy them.

Scott (1992) expanded the discussion of stake holders' expectations by arguing that various constituencies can be expected to espouse different criteria for measuring organizational performance. These preferences reflect the stake holder's interests in the organization (or organizational unit). For example, he identified four kinds of effectiveness criteria: (a) *Strategic focus*, or direction, has to do with whether the organization is doing the "right things." That is, resources are being deployed to solve the right problems or pursue the right objectives; (b) *Outcomes*, or effects, focus on the quality of the organization's services or products. This criteria examines whether the organization is doing "things right"; (c) *Processes* focus on the quantity or quality of the activities used by the organization to produce its outcomes. Whereas outcome measures effect, process measures effort. It is an assessment of an organization's "throughput";

(d) *Structural capabilities* address the organization's capacity for effective performance. These might include the quality and quantity of a manufacturer's equipment and the technical training of equipment operators. These factors are typically treated as "inputs" in econometric models of performance.

Scott (1992) further argued that administrators tend to focus primarily on capabilities, workers focus on processes, clients or customers focus on outcomes, and regulators (and to some extent stock holders) emphasize strategic focus. He also noted that the interests of researchers tend to be aligned with those of organizational administrators and workers.

This line of reasoning suggests a number of interesting research questions. For example, do the overall effectiveness ratings of these four constituencies in fact correspond with the pattern of specific ratings proposed by Scott? If so, to what extent is it possible for organizational elites to influence the effectiveness ratings of specific constituencies? The typical practice is to share information on all aspects of organizational performance with all constituencies (i.e., through the annual report). What would be the effect of a more targeted strategy, such as highlighting information on the most relevant aspect of the organization for each constituency?

Summary of Assessment Issues

Much progress has been made in the empirical assessment of effectiveness over the past three decades. These developments have roughly followed the major evolutionary stages in the theoretical arena. The first transition involved a shift from single, universalistic evaluations of effectiveness to the identification and assessment of specific effectiveness dimensions. The seven guidelines for research give evaluators of effectiveness research, at a minimum, an apparatus with which to assess the thoroughness, precision, and applicability of effectiveness criteria. Moreover, they help create a boundary for the conceptual definition of effectiveness in particular studies, and thus facilitate the accumulation of comparable results. They also help uncover lingering, but important, issues for which future research attention would prove enlightening.

The shift from thinking of effectiveness as a set of theoretically derived dimensions to a set of politically articulated expectations sensitizes researchers to the fact that the selection of evaluation criteria is an inherently political action. In this regard, three cautions were offered by Scott (1992).

First, the criteria proposed by each group will be self-interested ones. Second, although no criteria are disinterested—each benefits some groups more than others—all will be stated so as to appear universalistic and objective. Third, given multiple sets of actors pursuing their own interests and a situation of scarce resources, we would expect little commonality or convergence and some conflicts in the criteria employed by the various parties to assess organizational effectiveness. (p. 348)

Heeding Scott's counsel subsequent research on organizational performance should be sensitive to the political, as well as the methodological, qualities of their measures—especially given the tendency for researchers' interests to be aligned with those of management.

CONCLUSION

We began this chapter by suggesting that a review of the evolutionary development of organizational effectiveness would help guide future research on this construct. We described the conceptual sophistication that emerged during the formulation of new organizational effectiveness models and the increasing precision provided by the guidelines for empirical measurements. At the same time, we described the significant drop-off in research on effectiveness after the mid-1980s. This was a dramatic statement from the market place of organizational scholarship.

Currently, although interest in effectiveness as a construct is obviously waning, conceptual and empirical work on emerging performance measures, such as "total quality," is picking up. It is beyond the scope of this chapter to systematically compare the attributes of effectiveness with various other performance measures that are currently more fashionable. A reasoned assessment of whether these alternatives are more likely to fizzle as short-term fads, or to replace effectiveness as a construct that has outlived its usefulness is, also, beyond the scope of this treatise. It is obvious, however, that whether or not there is renewed interest in studying organizational effectiveness, there is a new generation of performance measures competing for attention. It seems reasonable, therefore, to focus our concluding recommendations on facilitating the transfer of knowledge from work completed on a mature construct to work underway on newer ones.

First, emerging theories of organizational performance should begin where organizational effectiveness left off, not where it began. Much of the early work on currently fashionable outcomes, like excellence, high performance, high reliability, and quality, has an ideal type orientation. Like previous representations of organizations as bureaucracies or as cooperative systems, a list of attributes for each performance measure has been assembled, and proponents argue that these characteristics apply universally. There is little consideration of the need to vary the attributes to match environmental conditions, or to satisfy the expectations of multiple constituencies. Also, proponents of these models seldom acknowledge that organizations are inherently political institutions characterized by contradiction and paradox.

It is fundamental to our understanding of organizations that they have multiple goals, reflecting the interests of multiple constituencies (with varying degrees of power), that yield multiple outcomes. Furthermore, research on organizational effectiveness has clearly demonstrated that measures of these multiple goals and outcomes are typically either unrelated or negatively correlated. Theoretical and methodological advances in emerging research on various aspects of organizational performance will occur to the extent that authors build on this conclusion from the effectiveness literature.

Second, theories of organizational performance should incorporate organizational processes, outcomes, and effects. Imai (1988) asserted that the most significant difference between Japanese and U.S. models of organizational performance is the prominent emphasis on process criteria in Japan and its absence from U.S. models. Process criteria relate to *how* work is done or *how* performance is accomplished, as opposed to results criteria that relate to *what* is produced or *what* is accomplished. Imai argued that this omission accounts for the competitive success of Japanese organizations over U.S. organizations in the past, as well as the likely triumph of Japanese organizations in the future.

Although we may disagree with Imai's conclusion and prediction, we do agree that much more emphasis is needed on the integration of processes, outcomes, and effects in future organizational performance research. Instead of focusing exclusively on outcomes, as has been traditional, researchers should give equal attention to process criteria and to the *linkages* among processes, outcomes, and effects (i.e., *how* outcomes are produced as well as *what* is produced and its *consequences*).

One characterization of the evolution of effectiveness models is that the ideal type era constituted a *thesis* statement. This was followed by a subsequent articulation of the *antithesis*, in the form of three competing models. The proposal to incorporate processes, outcomes, and effects into subsequent conceptualizations of performance constitutes a form of *synthesis*. It draws from contingency theory attention to fit, both internal and external. Consistent with the multiple constituencies perspective, it acknowledges that each aspect of organizational performance is important to a strategically valuable constituent group. Finally, it follows logically from the paradox model that all elements of an organization must be examined in order to understand the vexing challenge of managing paradoxes and dilemmas.

In conclusion, our 1983 book was published in the midst of the great debates over the relative merits of various models of effectiveness. Therefore, it seemed appropriate to conclude that book with recommendations about selection criteria. Specifically, we argued that the selection of a particular effectiveness model as a guide for research should depend on the specific organizational context under investigation.

Although we still see obvious merit in making informed research design decisions based on explicit criteria, our view today is more holistic, than contingent. It seems that too often even the documented use of explicit selection criteria becomes an exercise in post hoc justification. If there is one lesson to be learned from the organizational effectiveness era it is that studies should be designed to understand organizational phenomena, rather than to collect supporting evidence for an espoused theory. Whether one uses competing conceptual models of organizations (Scott, 1992; Hall, 1987; Morgan, 1986), or the four models of effectiveness discussed herein, multiple perspectives will inherently generate richer views of organizational performance, including its determinants and effects.

REFERENCES

Barnard, C. I. (1938). *The functions of the executive.* Cambridge, MA: Harvard University Press.
Bluedorn, A. C. (1980). Cutting the gordian knot: A Boston consulting group (1970). *The product portfolio.* Boston: BCG.
Burns, T., & Stalker, G. M. (1961). *The management of innovation.* New York: Barnes & Noble.
Cameron, K. S. (1978). Measuring organizational effectiveness in institutions of higher education. *Administrative Science Quarterly, 23,* 604–632.
Cameron, K. S. (1982). *Organizational effectiveness: A bibliography through 1981.* Boulder, CO: National Center for Higher Education Management Systems.
Cameron, K. S. (1984). The effectiveness of ineffectiveness. In B. M. Staw, & L. L. Cummings (Eds.), *Research in organizational behavior* (pp. 235–285). Greenwich, CT: JAI Press.
Cameron, K. S. (1986). Effectiveness as paradox: Consensus and conflict in conceptions of organizational effectiveness. *Management Science, 32,* 539–553.
Cameron, K. S., & Whetten, D. A. (1981). Perceptions of organizational effectiveness over organizational life cycles. *Administrative Science Quarterly, 26,* 525–544.
Cameron, K. S., & Whetten, D. A. (1983a). *Organizational effectiveness: A comparison of multiple models.* New York: Academic Press.
Cameron, K. S., & Whetten, D. A. (1983b). Models of the organizational life cycle: Applications to higher education. *Review of Higher Education, 6,* 269–299.
Child, J. & Kieser, A. (1981). Development of organizations over time. In P. C. Nystrom & W. A. Starbuck (Eds.), Handbook of organizational design (Vol. 1). New York: Oxford University Press.
Connolly, T., Conlon, E. J., & Deutsch, S. J. (1980). Organizational effectiveness: A multiple-constituency approach. *Academy of Management Review, 5,* 211–217.
Deming, W. E. (1986). *Out of the crisis.* Cambridge, MA: MIT Press.
Denison, D. (1990). *Corporate culture and organizational effectiveness.* New York: Wiley.
Ehreth, J. (1988, August). *A competitive constituency model of organizational effectiveness and its application in the health industry.* Paper presented at the Academy of Management Annual Meeting, Anaheim, CA.
Freeman, J. (1978). The unit of analysis in organizational research. In M. Meyer (Ed.), *Environments and organizations* (pp. 335–351). San Francisco: Jossey-Bass.
Goodman, P. S. (1979). *Assessing organizational change: The Rushton Quality of Work Experiment.* New York: Wiley.
Goodman, P. S., & Pennings, J. M., (Eds.). (1977). New perspectives on organizational effectiveness. San Francisco: Jossey Bass.
Hall, R. H. (1987). *Organizations: Structure and process.* Englewood Cliffs, NJ: Prentice-Hall.
Hall, R. H. (1963). The concept of bureaucracy: An empirical assessment. *American Journal of Sociology, 69,* 32–40.
Huber, G. P., Glick, W., O'Rielly, C., Daff, R., Meyer, A., & Cameron, K. (1993). *Organizational change and redesign.* New York: Oxford University Press.
Imai, M. (1988). *Kaizen.* New York: Random House.

Katz, D., & Kahn, R. L. (1978). *The social psychology of organizations.* New York: Wiley.

Keeley, M. (1978). A social justice approach to organizational evaluation. *Administrative Science Quarterly, 22,* 272–292.

Lawrence, P., & Lorsch, J. (1967). *Organization and environment.* Cambridge, MA: Harvard University Press.

Lewin, A. Y., & Minton, J. W. (1986). Determining organizational effectiveness: Another look, and an agenda for research. *Management Science, 32,* 514–538.

Mahoney, T. A. (1967). Managerial perceptions of organizational effectiveness *Administrative Science Quarterly, 14,* 357–365.

McKelvey, B. (1982). *Organizational systematics: Taxonomy, evolution, classification.* Berkeley, CA: University of California Press.

Meyer, M. W., & Zucker, L. G. (1989). *Permanently failing organizations.* Newbury Park, CA: Sage Publications.

Miles, R. H., & Cameron, K. S. (1982). *Coffin nails and corporate strategies.* Englewood Cliffs, NJ: Prentice-Hall.

Morgan, G. (1986). *Images of organization.* Newbury Park, CA: Sage.

Osborn, R. N., & Hunt, J. C. (1974). Environment and organizational effectiveness. *Administrative Science Quarterly, 19,* 231–246.

Pascale, R. T. (1990). *Managing on the edge.* New York: Simon & Schuster.

Perrow, C. (1984). *Normal accidents.* New York: Basic Books.

Perrow, C. (1986). *Complex organizations: A critical essay* (3rd ed.). New York: Random House.

Peters, T., & Waterman, R. H. (1982). *In search of excellence.* New York: Harper & Row.

Pfeffer, J., & Salancik, G. R. (1978). *The external control of organizations.* New York: Harper and Row.

Price, J. L. (1968). *Organizational effectiveness: An inventory of propositions.* Homewood, IL: Irwin.

Price, J. L. (1982). The study of organizational effectiveness. *Sociological Quarterly, 13,* 3–15.

Pugh, D. S., Hickson, D. J., & Hinings, C. R. (1969). An empirical taxonomy of structures in work organizations. *Administrative Science Quarterly, 14,* 115–126.

Quinn, R. E., & Cameron, K. S. (1983). Life cycles and shifting criteria of effectiveness: Some preliminary evidence. *Management Science, 29*(1), 33–51.

Quinn, R. E., & Cameron, K. S. (1988). *Paradox and transformation: Towards a theory of change in organizations.* Cambridge, MA: Ballinger.

Quinn, R. E., & Rohrbaugh, J. (1981). A competing values approach to organizational effectiveness. *Public Productivity Review, 5,* 122–140.

Roethlisberger, F. J., & Dickson, W. J. (1947). *Management and the worker.* Cambridge, MA: Harvard University Press.

Rousseau, D. M. (1985). Issues of level in organizational research: Multi-level and cross-level perspectives. In B. M. Staw, & L. L. Cummings (Eds.), *Research in organizational behavior* (pp. 1–37). Greenwich, CT: JAI Press.

Schneider, B. (1983). An interactionist perspective on organizational effectiveness. In Cameron, K. C., & Whetten, D. A. (Eds.), *Organizational effectiveness: A comparison of multiple models* (pp. 27–54). New York: Academic Press.

Scott, W. R. (1992). *Organizations: Rational, natural, and open systems* (3rd ed.). Englewood Cliffs, NJ: Prentice-Hall.

Selznick, P. (1948). Foundations of a theory of organizations. *American Sociological Review, 13,* 25–35.

Simon, H. (1956). *Models of man.* New York: Wiley.

Tsui, A. S. (1984). A role set analysis of managerial reputation. *Organizational Behavior and Human Performance, 34,* 64–94.

Tsui, A. S. (1990). A multiple-constituency model of effectiveness: An empirical examination at the human resource subunit level. *Administrative Science Quarterly, 35,* 458–483.

Van de Ven, A. H., & Ferry, D. L. (1980). *Measuring and assessing organizations.* New York: Wiley.

Weber, M. (1947). *The theory of social and economic organization.* [A. M. Henderson & T. Parsons Eds. and Trans.]. New York: Oxford University Press.

Weick, K. E., & Daft, R. L. (1983). The effectiveness of Interpretation systems. In K. C. Cameron, & D. A. Whetten (Eds), *Organizational effectiveness: A comparison of multiple models* (pp. 71–94). New York: Academic Press.

Weick, K. E., & Roberts, K. H. (1992). Organizational theories of high reliability [Working paper]. School of Business Administration, University of Michigan.

Whetten, D. A. (1978). Coping with incompatible expectations: An intergrated view of role conflict. *Administrative Science Quarterly, 23,* 254–271.

Yuchtman, E., & Seashore, S. E. (1967). A system resource approach to organizational effectiveness. *American Sociological Review, 32,* 891–903.

Zammuto, R. F. (1984). A comparison of multiple constituency models of organizational effectiveness. *Academy of Management Review, 9,* 606–616.

CONSTRUCT VALIDITY ISSUES IN ORGANIZATIONAL BEHAVIOR RESEARCH

Eugene F. Stone-Romero
State University of New York at Albany

In the past several decades researchers in organizational behavior (including the related fields of industrial and organizational psychology, vocational psychology, occupational psychology, human resources management, and vocational psychology) have devoted a great deal of attention to the development and testing of theories. Progress in such effort hinges on the use of research methods that produce valid findings. Unless studies use appropriate measures, manipulations, statistical tests, subjects, and so forth, inferences that stem from them are of little or no value in theory building, theory testing, or the use of theory based interventions to change individuals, groups, or organizations.

The overall validity of research is a function of internal, external, statistical conclusion, and construct validity (e.g., Cook & Campbell, 1979). As has been noted by Cook and Campbell (1979), research has (a) internal validity to the degree that it provides a sound basis for inferring that one variable (e.g., job design) causes another (e.g., job satisfaction); (b) external validity to the extent that its findings can be generalized to and across different types of persons, settings, time periods, and operational definitions of cause and effect constructs; (c) statistical conclusion validity to the degree that it allows for valid statistical inferences about the degree of association (covariation) between measured or manipulated variables; and (d) construct validity (CV) to the extent that measures or manipulations used in research (i.e., operational definitions of constructs) provide complete and unbiased representations of the underlying constructs. The focus of this chapter is on this latter type of validity. However, this limitation in focus is not meant to imply that the other three facets of validity are of lesser importance. The state of the science in organizational behavior (OB) is a function of research that is strong with respect to all four facets of validity.

A consideration of the literature in OB suggests that many researchers have devoted insufficient attention to CV issues. More specifically, research on a host of topics has used operational definitions (measures and/or manipulations) of constructs that underrepresent or provide for biased empirical realizations of the constructs. As a consequence, serious questions can be raised about the extent to which such research serves as a sound basis for either testing theories or guiding the acts of those who work in organizational settings.

In light of the above, the purpose of this chapter is to consider CV issues in OB research. These issues are addressed in five major sections. The first deals with the general notion of CV and its role in the research process. The second considers CV problems that can be found in OB research conducted over the past several decades. The third deals with the current state of OB research vis-à-vis the issue of CV. The fourth section details strategies that can be pursued to enhance the CV of OB research in future years. The fifth and final section presents some concluding remarks.

THE ROLE OF CONSTRUCT VALIDITY IN THE RESEARCH PROCESS

This section has two major purposes. First, it considers the role of CV in the research process. Second, it presents definitions of key concepts and terms that are used throughout the chapter. The latter purpose is important because there are ongoing debates about various CV issues; and definitions of important CV-related concepts and terms often differ in nontrivial ways from one publication to another.

Overview of the Research Process

An appreciation of the crucial role of CV in OB research can be gained by considering basic elements in an idealized model of the research process (Stone, 1978). The process typically begins with the formulation of research questions. These, along with a knowledge of existing theory and research on a phenomenon, provide a basis for the formulation of hypotheses that are tested through empirical research. It is important to recognize that both hypotheses and theories deal with relationships between constructs (cf. Cook & Campbell, 1979; Kerlinger, 1986; Nunnally, 1978; Stone, 1978). In actually doing empirical research, however, the researcher relies upon operational definitions (i.e., operationalizations) of constructs.[1]

---

[1] I use the terms *operationalization* and *operational definition* as substitutes for one another. Moreover, the use of the latter term is not meant to suggest that any single operational definition or operationalization of a construct bears a one-to-one correspondence with the construct itself and thus is completely valid. That is, no attempt is made here to revive or give legitimacy to the frowned-upon practice of "operationalism" (Campbell & Fiske, 1959; Cook & Campbell, 1979; Cronbach & Meehl, 1955; Webb, Campbell, Schwartz, Sechrest, & Grove, 1981).

In order to test a study's hypotheses the researcher formulates a strategy for gathering and analyzing relevant data. This strategy or research plan includes considerations of such issues as (a) the sampling of units to be studied (e.g., individuals, groups, organizations), (b) the manipulation or measurement of variables that are assumed to be causes (i.e., independent variables), (c) the measurement of variables that are presumed to be effects (i.e., dependent variables), (d) the control of potential confounding or nuisance variables through either experimental or statistical means, and (e) the statistical or other quantitative procedures that will be used in analyzing the study's data.

In designing a study the researcher specifies how focal constructs (FCs), that is, the constructs referenced by his or her hypotheses, will be operationally defined. In experimental or quasi-experimental research (cf. Cook & Campbell, 1979) assumed causal constructs are made real through manipulations; and assumed effect constructs are operationally defined by measures. In nonexperimental research, however, both assumed cause and effect constructs are operationally defined by measures.

Having formulated a research design, the researcher implements it, yielding data from measures of various types of variables (e.g., independent, dependent, moderator, intervening). Then, statistical analyses are performed to assess the degree to which the variables are related to one another. The results of such analyses, as well as other data derived from a study (e.g., manipulation check data, reliability data), provide the researcher with a basis for developing conclusions from a study. In addition, they provide a basis for posing new research questions and the testing of related hypotheses in future studies.

It is important to note that unless measures and manipulations are faithful (valid) representations of a focal construct (FC), valid inferences cannot be made about either the relative standing of individuals on measured FCs, or relationships between the FC and other constructs. Thus, research that lacks CV is of no value whatsoever to either scientists concerned with theory development and theory testing or individuals responsible for guiding the day-to-day operations of organizations.

Two Basic Strategies for Operationally Defining Constructs

Constructs can be operationalized by manipulations and measures. A number of strategies are available for operationally defining FCs through manipulations, all of which involve changing the environment of a research subject. Manipulations are based upon systematic alterations of (a) the physical context of subjects (e.g., ambient temperature, noise level, lighting), (b) the role requirements of subjects (e.g., job duties, responsibilities), (c) the number and types of subjects' social relationships (e.g., by procedures and practices that foster or inhibit social interaction), (d) the policies that serve to govern individual behavior in actual or simulated organizational contexts, (e) the beliefs that individuals have about themselves and their environment (e.g., attitude change programs), (f) the affective states of individuals (e.g., mood inductions), and (e) the knowledge, skills, and abilities of individuals (e.g., training programs).

A second basic strategy for operationally defining FCs is measurement. Among the methods for measuring variables in OB research are questionnaires, interviews, obtrusive observations of behavior, tests of general and specific aptitudes and abilities, projective measures, Q-sorting, sociometry, unidimensional and multidimensional scaling procedures, and unobtrusive measures (e.g., Cook, Hepworth, Wall, & Warr, 1981; Nunnally, 1978; Stone, 1978; Webb, Campbell, Schwartz, Sechrest, & Grove, 1981).

Although OB research relies upon both measures and manipulations of constructs, the remainder of this chapter deals almost exclusively with the CV of questionnaire measures. The primary reason for this is that the examples used in this chapter to illustrate CV problems were drawn from research that has used questionnaire measures. Note, however, that a similar set of examples could be provided for many of the manipulations that have been used is previous OB research.

CONSTRUCT VALIDITY PROBLEMS
IN ORGANIZATIONAL BEHAVIOR RESEARCH

The general purpose of this section is to consider CV problems that exist in previous OB research. In order to do so examples have been drawn from research dealing with such substantive issues as organizational stress, negative affectivity, job satisfaction, organizational commitment, job involvement, and worker personality. Prior to presenting examples of CV problems in previous OB research it is worthwhile to consider a general typology of factors that serve to detract from the CV of measures. At a general level, CV is threatened by operational definitions that (a) are biased, (b) underrepresent the FC, and (c) lack reliability. The nature of these threats is illustrated in Fig. 7.1, which depicts the variance of scores from an actual measure of a FC and the variance of scores from an ideal (i.e., a hypothetical, perfectly valid) measure of a FC. The validity of an actual measure, that is, the variance shared by the ideal and actual measures, is represented by the overlap between the circles. The variance in the actual measure that is not shared with the ideal measure is contamination, which consists of nonsystematic variance attributable to unreliability and systematic variance attributable to bias. An actual measure of a FC is biased to the degree that it systematically measures constructs other than the FC. Both random error and bias detract from the CV of a measure. CV also suffers when items in a measure are an incomplete sample of "items" from the relevant FC's domain. That is, the FC is broader in scope than the items in the measure of it.

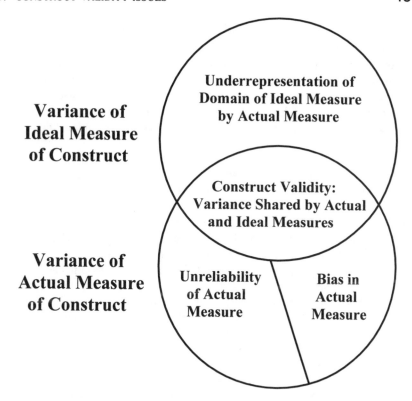

FIG. 7.1.   Construct validity as a function of covariance between an actual measure and an ideal measure of a construct.

In this section, examples are provided of CV problems in selected areas of OB research. However, it deserves stressing that CV problems exist for measures of virtually all constructs referenced in the OB literature. Therefore, it deserves stressing that the specific measures that are considered in this chapter were selected because of my own interest in the constructs, not because the same measures are necessarily poorer than others.

Bias in Measures

The OB literature provides many illustrations of bias in measures. This bias stems from a number of underlying causes, including preoperational and/or operational definitions of FCs (Cook & Campbell, 1979) that confound the FC with other constructs, measures or measurement procedures that are reactive in nature (Webb et al., 1981), and measures of FCs that rely upon a single method of measurement, resulting in the confounding of the FC with method-related irrelevancies (Webb et al., 1981).

Confounded Preoperational and/or Operational Definitions of Constructs.

Preoperational and associated operational definitions of FCs are inappropriate or biased to the extent that they confound the FC with other constructs, even if there is a sound theoretical basis for expecting the FC to correlate strongly with the other constructs. Research in OB provides several notable examples of measures that are based upon inappropriate or confounded preoperational or operational definitions of FCs.

Measures of Negative Affectivity. One vivid illustration of this problem pertains to extant measures of the construct of negative affectivity (NA). As is demonstrated below, many items in popular measures of NA are indices of stress-induced strain. Thus, measures of NA are confounded with strain. In order to better illustrate the nature of the confounding, constitutive and operational definitions of NA and of role related strain are next considered.

Personality psychologists have defined NA in constitutive terms as "a mood dispositional dimension" that "reflects pervasive individual differences in negative emotionality and self-concept: High-NA individuals tend to be distressed and upset and have a negative view of self, whereas those low on the dimension are relatively content and satisfied with themselves" (Watson & Clark, 1984, p. 465). Watson and Clark (1984) further clarified the nature of the NA construct by stating that "the negative mood states experienced by persons high in NA include subjective feelings of nervousness, tension, and worry; thus, NA has as one of its central features what others have called 'trait anxiety' . . . [but is broader than this and] . . . also includes such affective states as anger, scorn, revulsion, guilt, self-dissatisfaction, a sense of rejection, and, to some extent, sadness" (p. 465). Overall, NA is viewed as having two major components, negative emotionality and negative self-concept (Watson & Clark, 1984). In the OB literature, the NA trait has been similarly viewed. For instance, Burke, Brief, and George (1992) noted that NA "entails a generalized negative cognitive set; thus, subjective evaluations of a wide range of potentially negative phenomena are likely to be impacted by the negative interpretive/perceptual orientation characteristic of the high NA individual" (p. 5).

In the physical sciences strain is viewed as "deformation of a body or structure as a result of an applied force" (Random House, 1984, p. 1297). Similar to this view of strain, the OB literature has generally conceived of organizational (work related) strain as a set of psychological and physiological responses to stressors, including long-term problems with physical and mental well-being.[2] Among the

---

[2]Unfortunately, many researchers in OB and related disciplines have not done a good job of distinguishing between the constructs of stress and strain (cf. Schuler, 1980). Thus, in many publications the term stress is used in labeling the *outcomes* that stem from stress (e.g., feelings of tension and anxiety); that is, strain has been erroneously referred to as stress. In addition, there has been a frequent confounding of the concepts of stressors and stress.

concepts that have been used in describing strain are *anxiety, job dissatisfaction, depression, irritation, fatigue, insecurity, hostility, diminished self-esteem, somatic complaints, anger, indecision, physical health problems,* and *role related tension* (e.g., Caplan, Cobb, French, Van Harrison, & Pinneau, 1975; Caplan, Tripathi, & Naidu, 1985; Cooper & Payne, 1978; French, Caplan, & Harrison, 1982; Katz & Kahn, 1978; Kahn, Wolfe, Quinn, Snoek, & Rosenthal, 1964).

From this conceptual definition of strain, it should be obvious that the constitutive definitions of NA and stress induced strain overlap considerably. However, views on the basis for observed differences in self-reported levels of strain differ markedly between researchers. In general, stress researchers (e.g., Caplan et al., 1975; Cooper & Payne, 1978; Frankenhaeuser, 1978; French et al., 1982; Kahn et al., 1964; Kohn & Schooler, 1977, 1982; Lazarus, 1966, 1990; McGrath, 1976) tend to view environmental variables (measured through either self-reports or objective measures) as important determinants of strain (as indexed by psychological and physiological well-being). On the other hand, several OB researchers (e.g., Brief & Atieh, 1987; Brief, Burke, George, Robinson, & Webster, 1988; Brief, Butcher, & George, 1992) tend to view (a) self-reports of stressors and strains and (b) relationships between the two types of variables as an artifact of individual differences in NA. I refer to this explanation as the "NA hypothesis."

The conceptual overlap between NA and stress induced strain is mirrored by a high degree of overlap in popular operational definitions of these constructs. Negative affectivity has typically been measured with such instruments as Taylor's (1953) Manifest Anxiety Scale (TMAS); Welsh's (1965) Anxiety scale; Eysenck and Eysenck's (1968) Neuroticism Scale; and Tellegen's (1982) Negative Emotionality Scale (Watson & Clark, 1984; Watson & Pennebaker, 1989). These measures usually have very high correlations with one another (Watson & Clark, 1984, p. 468).

However, it merits noting that these and other NA measures were not designed for use as measures of personality based confounds in OB research or other fields of research. Instead, most were designed for and have typically been used in the assessment of psychopathology. In addition, one of the most popular of these measures, the TMAS was originally developed for use as a measure of conditionability (cf. Taylor, 1953). Moreover, Taylor (personal communication, June 22, 1992) does not agree with the practice of using the TMAS as a measure of NA. However, because NA is frequently measured with the TMAS or variants of it, to better understand the content of this measure, several items from it are shown below (Taylor, 1953):

I have very few headaches.
I have diarrhea once a month or more.
I am very seldom troubled by constipation.
I have a great deal of stomach trouble.
I frequently find myself worrying about something.

I work under a great deal of tension.
I feel anxiety about something or someone almost all the time.
My sleep is fitful and disturbed.
I have nightmares every few nights.
Life is a strain for me much of the time.
I sometimes feel that I am about to go to pieces.
I find it hard to keep my mind on a task or job.
I cannot keep my mind on one thing.

In research involving human beings, strain has been indexed by three general classes of measures: (a) *Physiological measures* deal with such variables as heart rate, blood pressure, serum uric acid, serum cholesterol, and excretion of such hormones as adrenaline, noradrenaline, and cortisol (e.g., Frankenhaeuser, 1978); (b) *Behavioral measures* typically index such behaviors as the avoidance of stressors, attempts to change the environment so as to reduce stressors, and behaviors designed to reduce the severity of symptoms of strain (e.g., Caplan et al., 1975; Kahn et al., 1964; Karasek, 1979); (c) *Self-report measures* generally deal with such variables as psychological strain (e.g., subjective well-being, emotional distress, anger, negative self-image, depression, anxiety, worry, job satisfaction, life satisfaction, occupational burnout) and physical or physiological strain and its health related consequences (e.g., gastrointestinal problems, pain, weakness, physical illness, arrhythmia, trembling). Because the self-report measures are of greatest importance vis-à-vis the focus of this chapter, a number of measures of this type that have been used in OB research are considered in greater detail below.

Many studies have indexed strain through self-report measures of two general types of tension, job- or role-related tension and general tension/anxiety. Job-related tension has typically been measured by the Kahn et al. (1964) Job-Related Tension Index (JRTI) or variants of it. Items in this index assess perceived incapacities to deal with job-related demands: for example, "Thinking that you will not be able to satisfy the conflicting demands of various people over you" (Kahn et al., 1964, p. 424). In reality many items in the JRTI are more representative of the conceptual domain of stress than they are of strain. In spite of this, numerous researchers have used the JRTI in their studies and referred to it as a measure of role strain (e.g., Berkowitz, 1980; Indik, Seashore, & Slesinger, 1964; Kahn et al., 1964; Snoek, 1966).

Job-related tension/anxiety has also been defined by a 17-item, modified version of the TMAS in which items were rewritten to make clear that the experienced tension was a function of individuals' jobs (House & Rizzo, 1972). The House and Rizzo measure, which assesses the outcomes of job-induced tension, somatic tension, and general fatigue and uneasiness, has been used in a number of studies of stress, including Brief and Aldag (1976) and Frew and Bruning (1987). Thus, the House and Rizzo measure contains *items that are virtually identical to those used by many researchers to operationally define NA*.[3]

Strain has also been operationally defined by several other self-report measures of anxiety, many of which have their origins in the TMAS. Measures of role-related anxiety have, for example, been used in research by Caplan, Tripathi, and Naidu (1985), Karasek (1979), Caplan et al. (1975), Fimian and Fastenau (1990), and Patchen (1970).

In addition, a number of fairly specific indices of strain have been used in stress research. In many studies, strain has been indexed with separate, self-report measures of such constructs as worry, physical health problems, job dissatisfaction, depression, positive and negative affect (as opposed to positive or negative affectivity), anger, self-esteem, irritation, tiredness, fatigue, physical exhaustion, nervousness, problems with sleep, somatic complaints (including, chest pain, twitching muscles, tics, tightness in chest, upset stomach, emotional distress, emotional exhaustion, mental health problems, and problems with concentration (e.g., Caplan et al., 1975; Caplan et al., 1985; Fimian & Fasteneau, 1990; Frone & McFarlin, 1989; House & Rizzo, 1972; Indik et al., 1964; Kahn et al., 1964; Karasek, 1979; Keenan & McBain, 1979; Lehrer & Woolfolk, 1982; Maslach & Jackson, 1981; Parkes, 1990; Patchen, 1970; Quinn & Shepard, 1974; Robertson, Cooper, & Williams, 1990; Warr, Cook, & Wall, 1979).[4]

From the above it should be clear that there is considerable overlap between the operational definitions of NA and strain. Similar to the TMAS and a number of other measures of NA, both general and specific measures of strain have items that deal with such factors as worry, sleep problems, somatic complaints, fatigue, general affect, nervousness, fear, emotionality, self-confidence, excitability, gastric distress, headaches, tachycardia, inability to concentrate, tension, and impatience. The overlap in content is readily acknowledged by NA researchers. For example, Watson, Pennebaker, and Folger (1987) wrote that "The overlap [of the domains] is sufficient to suggest that perceptions of stress, symptoms [of stress, i.e., strain] and negative moods may represent the same basic construct" (pp. 144–145).

In view of the high degree of overlap between the items in many measures of strain and NA, two important questions deserve consideration: Does the overlap suggest that measures of strain lack CV, supposedly because they are confounded

---

[3]It is interesting to note the marked shift in the way that items in measures such as the TMAS have been viewed by Brief (cf. Brief & Aldag, 1976; Brief, Burke, George, Robinson, & Webster, 1988; Burke, Brief, & George, 1992): Items that he once viewed as indices of role-related anxiety/strain are presently regarded as measures of NA.

[4]Stress research has also dealt with a number of other indices of "strain," including self-reports of absenteeism, alcohol consumption, and the use of tranquilizers or sleeping pills (e.g., Karasek, 1979). Although these are interesting and important criteria they are better viewed as responses to strain instead of indices of strain per se.

with NA? Or, does it suggest that measures of what has been labeled NA index something other than a stable tendency on the part of individuals to view all events negatively, and thus to report exaggerated levels of strain? I believe that the latter interpretation is most consistent with the facts (cf. Chen & Spector, 1991; Jex & Spector, in press; Levin & Stokes, 1989).

Measures of Organizational Commitment. Construct validity issues can also be raised in connection with popular conceptualizations and measures of the organizational commitment (OC) construct. The major problem with popular constitutive and operational definitions, as is illustrated below, is that they confound the essence of OC with constructs that are consequences of OC.

One of the most widely used measures of OC is based upon a conception of the FC that was developed and popularized by Porter and his colleagues (e.g., Mowday, Porter, & Steers, 1982; Porter & Smith, 1970). More specifically, Porter and colleagues defined OC in terms of "the relative strength of an individual's involvement in a particular organization. Conceptually, it can be characterized by at least three factors: (a) a strong belief in and acceptance of the organization's goals and values; (b) a willingness to exert considerable effort on behalf of the organization; and (c) a strong desire to maintain membership in the organization" (Mowday et al., 1982, p. 27).

The 15-item Organizational Commitment Questionnaire (OCQ), developed by Porter and his colleagues, has items that reflect these three aspects of the previously noted constitutive definition. Some items from the OCQ that deal with *value acceptance* are "I find that my values and the organization's values are very similar," and "Often, I find it difficult to agree with this organization's policies on important matters relating to its employees." Items that reflect the *willingness to exert effort* component are: "I am willing to put in a great deal of effort beyond that normally expected in order to help this organization be successful," and "This organization really inspires the very best in me in the way of job performance." Finally, items that relate to the *desire to maintain membership* component are "It would take very little change in my present circumstances to cause me to leave this organization," and "I would accept almost any type of job assignment in order to keep working for this organization."

Over the years, a large number of empirical studies have been performed that deal with OC (cf. Cook et al., 1981; Mowday et al., 1982). In many such studies, the OCQ (or a slight modification of it) has been used to measure OC. Unfortunately, the CV of these studies is questionable. The reason for this is that in both the conception of the OC construct and in the empirical realization of the same construct (i.e., the OCQ) there is a serious confounding of the essence of OC (i.e., shared values with the organization) with the action tendencies that are, in reality, the outcomes or consequences of commitment (e.g., the desire to remain a member of an organization).

The nature of the confounding is illustrated by a comparison of two models dealing with the OC construct. In one OC-related nomological network (e.g.,

Mowday et al., 1982) OC is represented as being an *antecedent* of turnover. However, without much seeming consideration of the early conceptualization of OC (e.g., Porter & Smith, 1970) and the principal operational definition of the construct (i.e., the OCQ) several researchers have used the OCQ in studies where one component of the OC construct (i.e., intent to remain with the organization) is also a hypothesized *consequence*. That is, several studies have used scores from the OCQ to predict such criteria as intent to remain with an organization, intent to leave an organization, and intent to re-enlist (for samples of military subjects) (e.g., Hom, Katerberg, & Hulin, 1979; Steers, 1977). Steers (1977), for example, tested a theoretical model in which the focal construct of OC was represented as being an antecedent of intentions to remain with or leave an organization. Unfortunately, Steers' study used the OCQ (including its "intent to remain" items) to predict the outcomes of intent to remain with an organization and desire to remain with the organization. Clearly, the results of this and similar studies are of little scientific value as tests of the criterion related validity of the OCQ in that all that they show is that one measure having a substantial intent to remain component correlates positively with another measure of intent to remain.

Measures of Job Satisfaction. Yet another example of confounding comes from research on job satisfaction. Constitutively, job satisfaction is typically defined as an individual's affective responses to a job, including all of its facets (cf. Cranny, Smith, & Stone, 1992, p. 1). Locke (1976), for example, defined job satisfaction as "a pleasurable or positive emotional state resulting from the appraisal of one's job or job experiences" (p. 1300). However, a very popular measure of job satisfaction, the Job Descriptive Index (JDI) developed by Smith, Kendall, and Hulin (1969) contains items that measure not only the essence of the FC of job satisfaction (i.e., affective responses), but also elements that enter into the appraisal of job satisfaction (i.e., such factors as routineness of work, simplicity of work, repetitiveness of work, feedback from the supervisor, supervisor's job knowledge). Although it is reasonable to argue that such factors may have lawful relationships with affective responses to jobs (cf. Stone, 1986, 1992), the same factors are not part of the conceptual domain of job satisfaction. Moreover, inferences about how such factors may influence satisfaction require information about workers' values (Locke, 1976, p. 1335). Consistent with Locke's (1976) reasoning, Rice, Gentile, and McFarlin (1991) showed that the relationship between the levels of various job facets and satisfaction with such facets was moderated by the importance (value) individuals assigned to the facets.

Reactive Measures or Measurement Procedures

Measures of FCs are also biased to the degree that either the measures or the procedures associated with their use result in reactivity on the part of respondents (Webb et al., 1981). For example, the measurement of some FCs may result in a desire on the part of individuals to respond to items in such a way as to manage the impression that they are well adjusted, emotionally stable, or otherwise normal (Cook & Campbell, 1979; Marlowe & Crowne, 1961; Stone, 1989; Webb et al., 1981). The resulting social desirability bias diminishes the CV of the measures.

Measures of Job-Based Satisfiers and Dissatisfiers. A rather vivid and well-known example of a measure that produces defensive, self-enhancing behaviors on the part of respondents is the critical incidents measurement method used by Herzberg, Mausner, and Snyderman (1959) to identify the attributes of jobs that are responsible for satisfaction and dissatisfaction. A number of studies (e.g., Locke, 1973; Schneider & Locke, 1971) have shown that individuals tend to give credit to themselves for satisfying events and to blame others (e.g., supervisors, co-workers) for dissatisfying events. Moreover, research by Wall (1973) showed direct evidence of an ego-defensiveness bias in the way subjects respond to items in critical incidents measures of satisfiers and dissatisfiers. More specifically, his research showed a positive relationship between scores on a measure of social desirability and an index of the extent to which individuals attributed dissatisfying events to hygiene factors.

Measures of Negative Affectivity. The measurement of NA provides another clear illustration of social desirability contamination. More specifically, Watson and Clark (1984) reported strikingly consistent evidence of a social desirability bias in virtually all popular measures of NA. For example, they reported that a measure of social desirability correlates –.81 with the TMAS, a very popular measure of NA (cf. Watson & Clark, 1984, p. 468). Note, moreover, that there are similarly high levels of correlation between social desirability and other measures of NA. These correlations raise nontrivial concerns about the CV of many popular indices of NA.

Measures of Growth Need Strength. Social desirability biases have also been found in a number of other measures used in OB research. For example, Stone, Ganster, Woodman, and Fusilier (1979) showed evidence of such a bias in the popular, JDS (Hackman & Oldham, 1975) measure of growth need strength. That is, the extent to which individuals prefer enriched jobs over unenriched jobs.

Mono-Method Measurement Biases

Biases in data are often a function of mono-method measurement procedures, that is, the measurement of a FC by only one type of measurement procedure (e.g., questionnaires) (cf. Cook & Campbell, 1979; Webb et al., 1981). This problem appears rather common in previous OB research. Locke (1976), for example, expressed mono-method concerns about the measurement of job satisfaction, because most research on the construct has used questionnaire measures. Unfortunately, similar concerns can be raised about the measurement of the vast majority of constructs measured by OB researchers, because most are measured with questionnaires. One problem with such measures is that they provide individuals with a much greater capacity to dissimulate or manage impressions (Stone, 1989) than do a host of alternative measurement procedures (e.g., unobtrusive measures, psychophysiological measures).

Underrepresentation of Constructs by Measures

Construct validity also suffers when items in a measure are an incomplete sample of items from a FC's domain. The degree to which an actual measure underrepresents a FC is depicted in Fig. 7.1 by that variance in the ideal measure (IM) that does not overlap with variance in the actual measure (AM).

One of the principal causes of construct underrepresentation is research that uses only a single operational definition of a FC (Cook & Campbell, 1979). Note, however, that multiple operational definitions of a construct will not improve representation if they all have items that neglect importance aspects of the FC.

Measures of Job Satisfaction

There are several notable instances of construct underrepresentation problems in OB research. One involves the measurement of facets of job satisfaction. Previous research suggested that there are about two dozen nontrivial facets of job satisfaction. For example Cook et al. (1981) identified such satisfaction facets as supervision, the company, co-workers, working conditions, career progress, promotion prospects, pay, subordinates, job security, general extrinsic, type of work, amount of work, personal growth, and general intrinsic.

Some measures of job satisfaction have items that deal with many of these facets of satisfaction. For example, the Minnesota Satisfaction Questionnaire (Weiss, Dawis, England, & Lofquist, 1967) has subscales dealing with 20 different facets. It is worthy of note, however, that one of the most popular of the facet satisfaction measures, the Job Descriptive Index (JDI) (Smith et al., 1969) has items that deal with only five satisfaction facets (i.e., work itself, present pay, promotion opportunities, supervision, and co-workers). This deficiency may produce several nontrivial problems, two of which are noted here. First, if overall job satisfaction is conceived of as an overall emotional response to a job based upon all of its facets, then a measure such as the JDI is deficient in that items in it underrepresent the FC of overall satisfaction. Second, if individual facets are used as predictors of such criteria as absenteeism and turnover, then a regression equation using only the five JDI facets will explain less criterion variance than an equation involving a greater number of facets.

Measures of the Type A Behavior Pattern

The underrepresentation of FCs is often the result of mono-method measurement practices. Although there are many examples of mono-method-based underrepresentation problems in OB research, the measurement of the Type A behavior pattern (TABP) is worthy of note. For years, OB research on the TABP relied upon the Jenkins Activity Survey (JAS; Jenkins, Rosenman, & Zyzanski, 1974). This is unfortunate because there are serious psychometric problems with the JAS. As has been noted by Matthews (1982, p. 304), not only is the JAS biased by items that reflect the values held by upwardly mobile individuals with white-collar jobs, but it also tends to underrepresent important aspects of the TABP. For example, one important component of the TABP that is not well represented by items in the JAS is anger (Matthews, 1982, p. 304). This speculation was confirmed in a recent study by Edwards, Baglioni, and Cooper (1990). More specifically, the results of their confirmatory factor analysis of data from several TABP measures, including the JAS, showed that only a small proportion of variance in the JAS was anger related. Moreover, the study found that three popular measures of the TABP (i.e. the JAS, Bortner Scale, and Framingham Scale) tended to have low levels of correlation with one another because they are multidimensional, focus on different underlying constructs, and have components with low levels of reliability.

Unreliability of Measures

The CV of a measure of a FC also suffers if the scores produced by it contain high levels of nonsystematic or random variance, resulting in low levels of reliability. As is shown in Fig. 7.1, unreliability is one of the two components of contamination. There are numerous illustrations of unreliability problems in the OB literature.[5]

Job Characteristics Measures

Research on job design provides an example of unreliability problems in OB. More specifically, on the basis of a meta-analytic study, Fried (1991) reported that measures of most constructs considered by the JDS (Hackman & Oldham, 1975) have lower levels of reliability than do measures of the same constructs from the Job Characteristics Inventory (JCI; Sims, Szilagyi, & Keller, 1976). In addition, Stone, Stone, and Gueutal (1990) showed that several subscales of the JDS (e.g., skill variety, task identity, and the job choice measure of growth need strength) had relatively low levels of reliability, especially for individuals with relatively low levels of cognitive ability.

Personality Measures

Growth Need Strength. Measures of personality that have been used in OB research also suffer from reliability problems. For example, Stone et al. (1979)

---

[5]It deserves noting that although a measure of a FC may be perfectly reliable, it may be totally invalid if all of its items pertain to a domain other than that of the FC. Thus, reliability is a necessary but insufficient condition for validity.

showed that the growth-need-strength measures (job choice, would like subscales) of the JDS (Hackman & Oldham, 1975) had relatively low reliability among a sample of college students. In addition, Stone et al. (1990) showed similar reliability problems for the growth need strength measures using data from members of a U.S. Army Reserves unit.

Manifest Needs. Relatively low levels of reliability have also been reported for several other personality measures used in OB research. For example, internal consistency estimates of reliability for three of the four needs measured by the Manifest Needs Questionnaire (MNQ; Steers & Braunstein, 1976) have been found to be rather low. More specifically, coefficient alpha for the need for achievement, need for affiliation, and need for autonomy were estimated to be .66, .56, and .62, respectively (Steers & Braunstein, 1976). Similarly low levels of reliability have been reported in several other studies that have used the MNQ to measure need strengths (e.g., Blackburn, 1981; Brief, Aldag, Darrow, & Power, 1980; Morris & Snyder, 1979).

Managerial Motivation. Reliability problems have also been reported for the multiple-choice version of the Miner Sentence Completion Scale (MSCS; Miner, 1978), a measure of managerial motivation. For example, Stahl, Grigsby, and Gulati (1985) reported that the multiple choice version had an average estimated internal consistency reliability of only .21 across the seven constructs measured by the scale. Moreover, Brief, Aldag, and Chacko (1977) reported reliability problems with the original, subjectively scored version of the MSCS. (However, see Miner, 1978, for a dissenting view on the reliability of the original version of the measure.)

Type A Behavior Pattern. Unreliability is also a problem with several measures of the TABP. For example, research by Edwards et al. (1990) estimated the job involvement scale of the JAS to have an internal consistency reliability of only .472. Their findings led them to conclude that the proportion of true score variance was either unacceptably low or nil for the several subscales of the JAS.

Measures That Tax the Cognitive Abilities of Respondents

Unreliability problems can also stem from items in measures that tax the cognitive capacities (e.g., reading abilities) of respondents. This is a nontrivial issue, because many of the questionnaires used in OB research seem to assume reading abilities that exceed those of substantial proportions of potential respondents. Subjects who have relatively low levels of reading ability may respond to items in such questionnaires in a random or near random fashion, resulting in data that have little or no reliability. For instance, Stone et al. (1990) showed that for several subscales of the JDS there were statistically significant and nontrivial differences between internal consistency reliability estimates across three subgroups of respondents formed on the basis of their level of cognitive ability. In the low cognitive ability subgroup, reliability estimates were below .50 for the JDS measures of skill variety, task, identity, task significance, intrinsic feedback, dealing with others, and growth need strength—job choice.

CONSTRUCT VALIDITY IN CURRENT RESEARCH
IN ORGANIZATIONAL BEHAVIOR

Fortunately, a number of recent studies in OB show evidence of greater concern with the CV of measures. Research on the psychometric properties of measures is one example of this. For instance, results of a study by Edwards et al. (1990) that used confirmatory factor analytic procedures has both clarified the multidimensional nature of TABP and suggested revised measures for the several latent constructs associated with the TABP.

The measurement of role-related conflict and ambiguity is another area in which progress is being made. In previous years, many researchers have used this 14–item measure developed by Rizzo, House, and Lirtzman (1970) to measure what were conceived of as two conceptually distinct dimensions of role-related problems, that is, role stress and role ambiguity (Jackson & Schuler, 1985). Consistent with this conceptualization, two recent studies, using confirmatory factor analytic methods (i.e., McGee, Ferguson, & Seers, 1989; Netemeyer, Johnston, & Burton, 1990), showed evidence supportive of a two-factor model. However, results of the study by McGee et al. also suggested that a method factor (i.e., negative item wording) may serve to explain why all conflict items loaded on one factor and all of the ambiguity items loaded on another. Thus, McGee et al. (1989) called for a moratorium on the use of the Rizzo et al. (1970) scales. To the extent that responses to the role ambiguity scales are contaminated by a method factor, the OB field will benefit from the development and use of alternative measures of role ambiguity.

Yet another area in which progress has been made is in the measurement of job characteristics. For approximately two decades, job design researchers have relied on the conceptualization of job characteristics that was originally proposed by Turner and Lawrence (1965) and later adopted, in slightly modified forms, by Hackman and Oldham (1975) and Sims et al. (1976). Research by Stone and Gueutal (1985), however, has shown that the Turner and Lawrence framework and its derivatives seem to neglect two important dimensions of jobs, (a) the extent to which the job entails work that is physically demanding and dangerous, and (b) the degree to which the job involves direct contact with and service to the public. The benefits of a revised conceptualization of job characteristics were demonstrated in research by Zaccaro and Stone (1988) who showed that measures of job characteristics based upon the revised conceptualization (suggested by

Stone & Gueutal, 1985) did a better job of predicting several outcome variables (e.g., job satisfaction, satisfaction with the work itself) than did the Motivating Potential Score (MPS) conceptualization of job enrichment that is central to the Job Characteristics Model of Hackman and Oldham (1975).

TOWARD IMPROVING CONSTRUCT VALIDITY IN FUTURE RESEARCH IN OB

From the foregoing it should be clear that CV problems are present in many prior OB studies. As was just noted, however, in recent years there are several notable instances of research that should serve to improve the CV of future OB research. The recent progress notwithstanding, subsequent OB research will benefit greatly from increased attention to CV issues. Thus, in the paragraphs that follow, I detail a number of actions that should be taken by researchers to enhance the CV of research in OB.

The CV of measures used in OB research can be improved through the use of sound practices for the development and use of measures. Guidelines that should be followed in developing measures are as follows:

Constitutive Definition of the Focal Construct

In order to develop a valid measure of a FC, the researcher should first define it constitutively (cf. Cook & Campbell, 1979; Kerlinger, 1986). That is, he or she should specify the nature of the construct through references to other constructs (e.g., job satisfaction is a positive attitude towards a job). The more precise this definition, the easier it is to clearly specify the nature of the FC and to differentiate it from other constructs, and develop sound operational definitions of the FC. Developing a sound measure of a FC hinges on the ability of the researcher to clearly and completely specify the FC's conceptual domain and to develop a measure that reflects the domain (Cook & Campbell, 1979; Nunnally, 1978).

Specification of the Nomological Network

Having a constitutive definition of a FC, the researcher should then develop a nomological network for it (Cronbach & Meehl, 1955). That is, he or she should formulate a set of hypotheses about relationships between the FC and other constructs. A good nomological network might be thought of as a mini-theory about the FC. Its usefulness is a function of the degree to which it clearly specifies how the FC is related to hypothesized antecedents, noncausal correlates, and consequences. Had OB researchers in such areas as job satisfaction, job design, job-related stress, and organizational commitment done a better job of specifying relevant nomological networks, many of the CV problems found in past OB research might have been averted.

Item Writing Procedures

The researcher should then write items for the measure that (a) fully reflect the nature of the FC (i.e., have content validity), (b) do not reflect the content of other conceptual domains (including antecedents and consequences of the FC), (c) do not lead individuals to bias or distort their responses (e.g., induce responses that are contaminated by a social desirability response bias), and (d) do not introduce various measurement related artifacts (e.g., underlying methods factors attributable to positive vs. negative wording of items and response formats). Careful work at this stage of the process will prevent the sort of response format problems present in the JDS (cf. Harvey, Billings, & Nilan, 1985) and a number of other measures used in OB research. Such work will also serve to reduce the degree to which data are contaminated by impression management-related biases. This is a nontrivial issue, because it seems likely that most measures used in OB research have the capacity to evoke impression management tendencies on the part of respondents (cf. Stone, 1989). It is crucial, therefore, that researchers consider the degree to which items that they write may evoke such tendencies.

Initial Assessment of Items

Prior to using the items in research designed to test hypotheses from the nomological network, a series of preliminary studies should be conducted to insure that the items can be easily read by individuals who will be expected to respond to them. This will avert the difficulties that result from having individuals with low levels of reading ability respond to items such as those found in the JDS (cf. Stone et al., 1990). Populating measures with items that are easy to read and understand is critical in OB research, especially in light of the fact that approximately one-third of the members of the U.S. workforce are functionally illiterate (Stone et al., 1990, p. 424). To deal with this serious problem, OB researches should consider collecting data through alternatives to questionnaires, such as structured interviews and observations of behavior (Stone et al., 1990).

Preliminary CV-related research should also assess (as appropriate) the measure's internal consistency reliability and its stability over time (cf. Nunnally, 1978). This will help to avert the internal consistency problems associated with such measures as the MNQ (Steers & Braunstein, 1976), the JAS (Jenkins et al., 1974), the JDS (Hackman & Oldham, 1975), and the multiple-choice version of the MSCS (Miner, 1978).

Assessment of Dimensionality

Some FCs may have two or more facets (e.g., job satisfaction). When FCs are hypothesized to be multi-faceted, preliminary research should be done to demonstrate that each of the facets can be reliably measured, and the measured facets are relatively independent of one another. Confirmatory factor analysis procedures (e.g., LISREL, EQS) can be used for this purpose (Bentler, 1985; Jöreskog & Sörbom, 1988). As work of this type proceeds, items in the measure should be rewritten as needed. In addition, if research fails to show support for a priori beliefs about the dimensionality of a FC, constitutive and/or operational definitions of the FC should be revised. For example, the issues that were raised about the JAS provide a vivid example of the need to revise measures and conceptualizations of FCs.

Empirical Studies to Assess Construct Validity

Having a measure of the FC, the researcher should then perform multiple empirical studies to test predictions from the nomological network. This construct validation research should, as appropriate, include: (a) criterion-related validation studies to assess the utility of a measure as a predictor of other variables, (b) convergent validation studies to determine if scores from a measure of a FC correlate in expected ways with scores from alternate measures of the same construct, and (c) discriminant validation research to assess the degree to which a measure is free of irrelevant sources of variance (e.g., bias stemming from the use of a particular type of measurement method).

It is crucial that multiple methods be used in measuring a FC. As has been noted elsewhere, the validity of inferences from research is enhanced to the degree that multiple operational definitions of a FC converge (cf. Cook & Campbell, 1979; Cook & Selltiz, 1964; Webb et al., 1981). The use of multiple measurement methods is important because the types of biases produced by one type of measurement method (e.g., questionnaires) are typically different from those that result from the use of other methods (e.g., interviews, observations, projective measures, psychophysiological measures) (cf. Webb et al., 1981).

A word about exploratory research is crucial at this point. Such research is often of considerable importance in research aimed at identifying problems, formulating research questions, and developing testable hypotheses about phenomena about which little is known. However, exploratory research is of little or no value in attempts to demonstrate the CV of operational definitions of FCs. As previously noted, construct validation efforts presuppose the existence of a theoretical model or a well articulated nomological network. Thus, CV-oriented research should be oriented toward testing predictions stemming from theoretical models or nomological networks. Fortunately, at this point in time there is ample theory and research upon which to base studies of a great many OB phenomena. For example, there are several reasonably well articulated models dealing with stressor-stress-strain relationships (e.g., Caplan, 1983; Caplan et al., 1975, 1985; Kahn et al., 1964).

Assuming that future research is oriented toward testing hypotheses stemming from a nomological network or a theory, researchers should rely upon data from analytic procedures of the confirmatory as opposed to the exploratory variety (cf. Bentler, 1985; Jöreskog & Sörbom, 1988). Thus, for example, rather than trying to "make sense" of entries in a correlation matrix for a large number of variables on a post hoc basis, researchers should test a priori predictions about relationships between variables. In addition, rather than attempting to "discover" the factor structure of items associated with a conceptual domain that is assumed to be multi-faceted, researchers should test the degree to which models having a priori specified factor structures fit empirical data (cf. Ford, MacCallum, & Tait, 1986). The reason for these recommendations is that CV is enhanced more by the confirmation of predictions, than it is by the "discovery" of patterns of covariation among either items in a measure of a given FC or correlation between scores from measures of different constructs.

Revision of Measures and/or Nomological Network

As evidence from construct validation studies accumulates, it may prove necessary to modify either the measure of the FC or the nomological network. One example of a FC for which a revised network is needed is OC. In order to avert the previously noted problems with research on OC (e.g., Steers, 1977; Hom et al., 1979) a revised nomological network (conceptualization) is needed for the OC construct. Under this revised conceptual framework, identification with an organization (i.e., viewing one's own values and goals to be consistent with those of an organization), would be regarded as an *antecedent* of two variables that are now regarded as central to the definition of OC (cf. Mowday et al., 1982): (a) a willingness to exert effort in the service of the organization, and (b) a desire to maintain membership in the organization.

I believe that two lines of actions are needed at this point in time to rectify problems with the conceptualization and measurement of OC. First, the constitutive definition of the construct needs to be changed so as to have it address only identification with the organization. Second, the OCQ measure needs to be revised to eliminate items from it that deal with willingness to exert effort and desire to maintain membership, both of which are consequences of commitment, not commitment per se.

Measure revision is also recommended for the JDI, which as previously noted has items that confound affective responses to jobs with descriptions of the characteristics of jobs. The strategy for overcoming this problem is straightforward. The JDI and similar measures need to be purged of items that are descriptive in nature. These should be replaced with items that are affective or evaluative in nature (cf. Osgood, Suci, & Tannenbaum, 1957).

Use of Measures in Basic and/or Applied Research

Once sufficient evidence on the CV of a measure has accumulated, it can be used in basic and applied research. In general, however, the amount and quality of evidence needed to justify the measure's use in basic research will be less than that required to defend its use in applied research (cf. Nunnally, 1978).

CONCLUSION

In spite of the crucial role that CV evidence plays in building sound OB theories and guiding practice in organizations, an analysis of the OB literature concerned with a large number of FCs reveals that insufficient attention has been paid to CV issues. As a result, tremendous amounts of time, effort, and other resources have been expended on research that has poor conceptual and methodological underpinnings.

The current problems with CV in OB research would appear to be a function of several related practices. First, and perhaps most important, studies of many FCs have been conducted by researchers who did not appear to have based their research on well articulated nomological networks. Second, many researchers have either devoted insufficient effort to developing clear constitutive definitions of FCs or have failed to adopt sound constitutive definitions proposed by others. Third, in the absence of clear constitutive definitions of FCs, many researchers have either developed crude measures of poorly defined FCs or used measures developed by others that appeared, perhaps because of the names of the measures, to be appropriate for the planned research. Clearly, practices such as these are not likely to produce research results that have acceptable levels of CV. They must change.

Fortunately, there are signs of change. Today, more so than in previous years, competent researchers are challenging a number of questionable conceptual frameworks. Moreover, a considerable amount of effort is presently being devoted to assessing and improving the psychometric properties of measures used in OB research. To the degree that these and similarly positive trends continue, there is reason to be optimistic about future OB research vis-à-vis the criterion of CV.

AUTHOR NOTES

I am grateful to George A. Alliger, Jerald Greenberg, Kathryn Kelley, Susan Jackson, Scott O. Lilienfeld, Dianna L. Stone, Kevin J. Williams, and Vincent Fortunato for helpful comments on an earlier version of this chapter.

REFERENCES

Bentler, P. M. (1985). *Theory and implementation of EQS: A structural equations program.* Los Angeles: BMDP Statistical Software.

Berkowitz, E. N. (1980). Role theory, attitudinal constructs, and actual performance: A measurement issue. *Journal of Applied Psychology, 65,* 240–245.

Blackburn, R. S. (1981). An evaluation of the reliability, stability and factor structure of the Manifest Needs Questionnaire. *Journal of Management, 7,* 55–62.

Brief, A. P., & Aldag, R. (1976). Correlates of role indices. *Journal of Applied Psychology, 61,* 468–472.

Brief, A. P., Aldag, R. J., & Chacko, T. I. (1977). The Miner Sentence Completion Scale: An appraisal. *Academy of Management Journal, 20,* 635–643.

Brief, A. P., Aldag, R. J., Darrow, A. L., & Power, D. J. (1980). Examination of responses of registered nurses to Manifest Needs Questionnaire. *Psychological Reports, 46,* 1233–1234.

Brief, A. P., & Atieh, J. M. (1987). Studying job stress: Are we making mountains out of molehills? *Journal of Occupational Behavior, 8,* 115–126.

Brief, A. P., Burke, M. J., George, J. M., Robinson, B. S., & Webster, J. (1988). Should negative affectivity remain an unmeasured variable in the study of job stress? *Journal of Applied Psychology, 73,* 193–198.

Brief, A. P., Butcher, A. H., & George, J. M. (1992). *Integrating bottom-up and top down theories of subjective well being: The case of health* [Working Paper 92–HRMG–02]. Freeman School of Business, Tulane University, New Orleans, LA.

Burke, M. J., Brief, A. P., & George, J. M. (1992). *The role of negative affectivity in understanding relationships between self-reports of stressors and strains: A comment on the organizational literature* [Working Paper 91–HRMG–10]. Freeman School of Business, Tulane University, New Orleans, LA.

Campbell, D. T., & Fiske, D. W. (1959). Convergent and discriminant validation by the multitrait-multimethod matrix. *Psychological Bulletin, 56,* 81–105.

Caplan, R. D. (1983). Person-environment fit: Past, present, and future. In C. L. Cooper (Ed.), *Stress Research* (pp. 35–77). New York: Wiley.

Caplan, R. D., Cobb, S., French, J. R. P., Van Harrison, R., & Pinneau, S. R. (1975). *Job demands and worker health: Main effects and occupational differences* [HEW Publ. No. NIOSH 75–160]. Washington, DC: U.S. Government Printing Office.

Caplan, R. D., Tripathi, R. C., & Naidu, R. K. (1985). Subjective past, present, and future fit: Effects on anxiety, depression, and other indicators of well being. *Journal of Personality and Social Psychology, 48,* 180–197.

Chen, P. Y., & Spector, P. E. (1991). Negative affectivity as the underlying cause of correlations between stressors and strains. *Journal of Applied Psychology, 76,* 398–407.

Cook, J. D., Hepworth, S. J., Wall, T. D., & Warr, P. B. (1981). *The experience of work.* London: Academic Press.

Cook, S. W., & Selltiz, C. (1964). A multiple-indicator approach to attitude measurement. *Psychological Bulletin, 62,* 36–55.

Cook, T. D., & Campbell, D. T. (1979). *Quasi-Experimentation: Design and analysis issues for field settings.* Chicago: Rand McNally.

Cooper, C. L., & Payne, R. (1978). *Stress at work.* Chichester, England: Wiley.

Cranny, C. J., Smith, P. C., & Stone, E. F. (1992). *Job satisfaction: How people feel about their jobs and how it affects their performance.* New York: Lexington Books.

Cronbach, L. J., & Meehl, P. C. (1955). Construct validity in psychological tests. *Psychological Bulletin, 52,* 281–302.

Edwards, J. R., Baglioni, A. J., & Cooper, C. L. (1990). Examining the relationships among self-report measures of the Type A behavior pattern: The effects of dimensionality, measurement error, and differences in underlying constructs. *Journal of Applied Psychology, 75,* 440–454.

Eysenck, H. J., & Eysenck, S. B. G. (1968). *Manual for the Eysenck Personality Inventory.* San Diego, CA: Educational and Industrial Testing Service.

Fimian, M. J., & Fastenau, P. S. (1990). The validity and reliability of the teacher stress inventory: A re-analysis of aggregate data. *Journal of Organizational Behavior, 11,* 151–157.

Ford, J. K., MacCallum, R. C., & Tait, M. (1986). The application of explanatory factor analysis in applied psychology: A critical review and analysis. *Personnel Psychology, 39,* 291–314.

Frankenhaeuser, M. (1978). Psychoneuroendocrine approaches to the study of emotion as related to stress and coping. In H. E. Howe & R. A. Dienstbier (Eds), *Nebraska Symposium on Motivation 1978* (Vol. 26, pp. 123–161). Lincoln, NE: University of Nebraska Press.

French, J. R. P., Caplan, R. D., & Harrison, R. V. (1982). *The mechanisms of job stress and strain.* London: Wiley.

Frew, D. R., & Bruning, N. J. (1987). Perceived organizational characteristics and personality measures as predictors of stress/strain in the workplace. *Journal of Management, 13,* 633–646.

Fried, Y. (1991). Meta-analytic comparisons of the Job Diagnostic Survey and Job Characteristics Inventory as correlates of work satisfaction and performance. *Journal of Applied Psychology, 76,* 690–697.

Frone, M. R., & McFarlin, D. B. (1989). Chronic occupational stress, self-focused attention, and well-being: Testing a cybernetic model of stress. *Journal of Applied Psychology, 74,* 876–883.

Hackman, J. R., & Oldham, G. R. (1975). Development of the Job Diagnostic Survey. *Journal of Applied Psychology, 60,* 159–170.

Harvey, R. J., Billings, R. J., & Nilan, K. J. (1985). Confirmatory factor analysis of the Job Diagnostic Survey: Good news and bad news. *Journal of Applied Psychology, 70,* 461–468.

Herzberg, F., Mausner, B., & Snyderman, B. (1959). *The motivation to work.* New York: Wiley.

Hom, P. W., Katerberg, R., & Hulin, C. L. (1979). Comparative examination of three approaches to the prediction of turnover. *Journal of Applied Psychology, 64,* 280–290.

House, R. J., & Rizzo, A. (1972). Role conflict and role ambiguity as critical variables in a model of organizational behavior. *Organizational Behavior and Human Performance, 7,* 467–505.

Indik, B., Seashore, S. E., & Slesinger, J. (1964). Demographic correlates of psychological strain. *Journal of Abnormal and Social Psychology, 69,* 26–38.

Jackson, S. E., & Schuler, R. (1985). A meta-analysis and conceptual critique of research on role ambiguity and role conflict in work settings. *Organizational Behavior and Human Decision Processes, 36,* 16–78.

Jenkins, C. D., Rosenman, R. H., & Zyzanski, S. J. (1974). Prediction of clinical coronary heart disease by a test for the coronary-prone behavior pattern. *New England Journal of Medicine, 23,* 1271–1275.

Jex, S. M., & Spector, P. E. (in press). The impact of negative affectivity on stressor-strain relations: A replication and extension. *Work and Stress.*

Jöreskog, K. G., & Sörbom, D. (1988). *LISREL 7: A guide to the program and applications.* Chicago, IL: SPSS, Inc.

Kahn, R. L., Wolfe, D. M., Quinn, R. P., Snoek, J. D., & Rosenthal, R. A. (1964). *Organizational stress: Studies in role conflict and ambiguity.* New York: Wiley.

Karasek, R. A. (1979). Job demands, job decision latitude, and mental strain: Implications for job redesign. *Administrative Science Quarterly, 24,* 295–308.

Katz, D., & Kahn, R. L. (1978). *The social psychology of organizations* (2nd ed.). New York: Wiley.

Keenan, A., & McBain, G. D. M. (1979). Effects of Type A behavior, intolerance of ambiguity, and locus of control on the relationship between role stress and work-related outcomes. *Journal of Occupational Psychology, 52,* 277–285.

Kerlinger, F. N. (1986). *Foundations of behavioral research (3rd ed.).* New York: Holt, Rinehart & Winston.

Kohn, M. L., & Schooler, C. (1977). Occupational experience and psychological functioning: An assessment of reciprocal effects. *American Sociological Review, 38,* 197–218.

Kohn, M. L., & Schooler, C. (1982). Job conditions and personality: A longitudinal assessment of reciprocal effects. *American Journal of Sociology, 87,* 1257–1286.

Lazarus, R. S. (1966). *Psychological stress and the coping process.* New York: McGraw-Hill.

Lazarus, R. S. (1990). Author's response. *Psychological Inquiry, 1,* 41–51.

Lehrer, P. M., & Woolfolk, R. L. (1982). Self-report assessment of anxiety: Somatic, cognitive, and behavioral modalities. *Behavioral Assessment, 4,* 167–177.

Levin, I., & Stokes, J. P. (1989). Dispositional approach to job satisfaction: Role of negative affectivity. *Journal of Applied Psychology, 74,* 752–758.

Locke, E. A. (1973). Satisfiers and dissatisfiers among white collar and blue collar employees, *Journal of Applied Psychology, 58*, 67–76.

Locke, E. A. (1976). The nature and causes of job satisfaction. In M. D. Dunnette (Ed.), *Handbook of industrial and organizational psychology* (pp. 1297–1349). Chicago: Rand McNally.

Marlowe, D., & Crowne, D. P. (1961). Social desirability and response to perceived situational demands. *Journal of Consulting Psychology, 25*, 109–115.

Maslach, C., & Jackson, S. E. (1981). The measurement of experienced burnout. *Journal of Occupational Behavior, 2*, 99–113.

Matthews, K. A. (1982). Psychological perspectives in the Type A behavior pattern. *Psychological Bulletin, 91*, 293–323.

McGee, G. W., Ferguson, C. E., & Seers, A. (1989). Role conflict and role ambiguity: Do the scales measure these two constructs? *Journal of Applied Psychology, 74*, 815–818.

McGrath, J. E. (1976). Stress and behavior in organizations. In M. D. Dunnette (Ed.), *Handbook of industrial and organizational psychology*, (pp. 1351–1395). Chicago, IL: Rand McNally.

Miner, J. B. (1978). The Miner Sentence Completion Scale: A reappraisal. *Academy of Management Journal, 21*, 283–294.

Morris, J. H., & Snyder, R. A. (1979). A second look at need for achievement and need for autonomy as moderators of role perception-outcome relationships. *Journal of Applied Psychology, 64*, 173–178.

Mowday, R. T., Porter, L. W., & Steers, R. M. (1982). *Employee-organization linkages: The psychology of commitment, absenteeism, and turnover.* New York: Academic Press.

Netemeyer, R. G., Johnston, M. W., & Burton, S. (1990). Analyses of role conflict and role ambiguity in a structural equations framework. *Journal of Applied Psychology, 75*, 148–157.

Nunnally, J. C. (1978). *Psychometric theory.* New York: McGraw-Hill.

Osgood, C. E., Suci, G. J., & Tannenbaum, P. H. (1957). *The measurement of meaning.* Urbana, IL: University of Illinois Press.

Parkes, K. R. (1990). Coping, negative affectivity, and the work environment: Additive and interactive predictors of mental health. *Journal of Applied Psychology, 75*, 399–409.

Patchen, M. (1970). *Participation, achievement, and involvement on the job.* Englewood Cliffs, NJ: Prentice-Hall.

Porter, L. W., & Smith, F. J. (1970). *The etiology of organizational commitment.* Unpublished manuscript, University of California, Irvine.

Quinn, R. P., & Shepard, L. J. (1974). *The 1972–73 quality of employment survey.* Ann Arbor, MI: Survey Research Center, Institute for Social Research, University of Michigan.

Random House College Dictionary (rev. ed). (1984). New York: Random House.

Rice, R. W., Gentile, D. A., & McFarlin, D. B. (1991). Facet importance and job satisfaction. *Journal of Applied Psychology, 76*, 31–39.

Rizzo, J., House, R. J., & Lirtzman, S. I. (1970). Role conflict and role ambiguity in complex organizations. *Administrative Science Quarterly, 15*, 150–163.

Robertson, I. T., Cooper, C. L., & Williams, J. (1990). The validity of the occupational stress indicator. *Work & Stress, 4*, 29–39.

Schneider, J., & Locke, E. (1971). A critique of Herzberg's incident classification system and a suggested revision. *Organizational Behavior and Human Performance, 6*, 441–457.

Schuler, R. S. (1980). Definition and conceptualization of stress in organizations. *Organizational Behavior and Human Performance, 25*, 184–215.

Sims, H. P., Szylagyi, A. D., & Keller, R. T. (1976). The measurement of job characteristics. *Academy of Management Journal, 19*, 195–212.

Smith, P. C., Kendall, L. M., & Hulin, C. L. (1969). *The measurement of satisfaction in work and retirement.* Chicago: Rand McNally.

Snoek, J. D. (1966). Role strain in diversified role sets. *American Journal of Sociology, 71*, 363–372.

Stahl, M. J., Grigsby, D. W., & Gulati, A. (1985). Comparing the job choice exercise and the multiple choice version of the Miner Sentence Completion Scale. *Journal of Applied Psychology, 70*, 228–232.

Steers, R. M. (1977). Antecedents and outcomes of organizational commitment. *Administrative Science Quarterly, 22*, 46–56.

Steers, R. M., & Braunstein, D. N. (1976). A behaviorally-based measure of manifest needs in work settings. *Journal of Vocational Behavior, 9*, 251–266.

Stone, E. F. (1978). *Research methods in organizational behavior*. Glenview, IL: Scott, Foresman.

Stone, E. F. (1986). Job scope-job satisfaction and job scope-job performance relationships. In E. A. Locke (Ed.), *Generalizing from laboratory to field settings*, (pp. 189–206). Lexington, MA: Lexington Publishing.

Stone, E. F. (1989). Self-presentation biases in organizational research. In R. A. Giacalone & P. Rosenfeld (Eds.), *Impression management in the organization* (pp. 189–202). Hillsdale, NJ: Lawrence Erlbaum Associates.

Stone, E. F. (1992). A critical analysis of social information processing models of job perceptions and job attitudes. In Cranny, C. J., Smith, P. C., & Stone, E. F. (Eds), *Job satisfaction: Advances in theory, research, and applications*, (pp. 21–44). Lexington, MA: Lexington.

Stone, E. F., Ganster, D. C., Woodman, R. W., & Fusilier, M. R. (1979). Relationships between Growth Need Strength and selected individual differences measures employed in job design research. *Journal of Vocational Behavior, 14*, 329–340.

Stone, E. F., & Gueutal, H. G. (1985). An empirical derivation of the dimensions along which characteristics of jobs are perceived. *Academy of Management Journal, 28*, 376–396.

Stone, E. F., Stone, D. L., & Gueutal, H. G. (1990). The influence of cognitive ability on responses to questionnaire measures. *Journal of Applied Psychology, 75*, 418–427.

Taylor, J. A. (1953). A personality scale of manifest anxiety. *Journal of Abnormal and Social Psychology, 48*, 285–290.

Tellegen, A. (1982). *Multidimensional Personality Questionnaire*. Minneapolis, MN: Minnesota Twin/Family Registry, University of Minnesota.

Turner, A. N., & Lawrence, P. R. (1965). *Industrial jobs and the worker*. Cambridge, MA: Harvard University Press.

Wall, T. D. (1973). Ego-defensiveness as a determinant of reported differences in sources of job satisfaction and job dissatisfaction. *Journal of Applied Psychology, 58*, 125–128.

Warr, P., Cook, J., & Wall, T. (1979). Scales for the measurement of some work attitudes and aspects of psychological well-being. *Journal of Occupational Psychology, 52*, 129–148.

Watson, D., & Clark, L. A. (1984). Negative affectivity: The disposition to experience aversive emotional states. *Psychological Bulletin, 96*, 465–490.

Watson, D., & Pennebaker, J. W. (1989). Health complaints, stress, and distress: Exploring the central role of negative affectivity. *Psychological Review, 96*, 234–254.

Watson, D., Pennebaker, J. W., & Folger, R. (1987). Beyond negative affectivity: Measuring stress and satisfaction in the workplace. *Journal of Organizational Behavior Management, 8*(2), 141–157.

Webb, E. J., Campbell, D. T., Schwartz, R. D., Sechrest, L., & Grove, J. B. (1981). *Nonreactive measures in the social sciences*. Boston: Houghton Mifflin.

Weiss, D. J., Dawis, R. V., England, G. W., & Lofquist, L. H. (1967). *Manual for the Minnesota Satisfaction Questionnaire*. Minneapolis, MN: Industrial Relations Center, University of Minnesota.

Welsh, G. S. (1965). MMPI profiles and factor scales A and R. *Journal of Clinical Psychology, 21*, 43–47.

Zaccaro, S. J., & Stone, E. F. (1988). Incremental validity of an empirically based measure of job characteristics. *Journal of Applied Psychology, 73*, 245–252.

8

CAUSAL MODELS IN ORGANIZATIONAL BEHAVIOR RESEARCH: FROM PATH ANALYSIS TO LISREL AND BEYOND

Larry J. Williams
Purdue University

Lawrence R. James
University of Tennessee

Researchers in the field of organizational behavior (OB) have shown a long-standing interest in testing causal hypotheses with correlational data. In the early 1970s, a practice was established of representing these hypotheses graphically and referring to the figure as a "causal model," because paths represented in the figure were presumed to represent influences between variables that were consistent with causal effects.

With this approach, the subsequent evaluation of the causal model was achieved by using statistical techniques to obtain estimates of the magnitude and direction of relationship depicted in the model. The resulting popularity of this methodology may have been because of its easy application to the survey data commonly analyzed by many OB researchers: survey research enabled them to conduct their science with reduced concerns about the external validity of their findings.

Alternatively, OB researchers may have recognized and appreciated the benefit that can be provided when complex processes are presented visually, and this may have contributed to the extent to which this methodology was embraced by organizational scholars. Regardless of the reason for its emergence, it is evident that over the past 20 years, applications of causal modeling in the field of OB have increased dramatically.

At the same time that this interest in causal modeling was developing, there was also an evolution in the data analytic techniques used to evaluate causal models. Early in this literature, OB researchers used partial correlations and, in some cases, simple correlations to obtain estimates of the paths included in a causal model. As time progressed, ordinary least squares regression became

182 WILLIAMS AND JAMES

popular, and this approach became referred to as "path analysis" and the obtained estimates as "path coefficients". Because this methodology made no distinction between the theoretical constructs of interest and the measures used to represent these constructs, research studies adopting the path analytic approach came to be referred to as manifest (observed) variable studies.

An important advancement in causal modeling methodology occurred in the 1980s. A statistical technique that enabled researchers to distinguish between their measures and the theoretical factors or "latent variables" in their model was developed, as was a computer program to estimate the parameters of latent variable models (LISREL: LInear Structural RELations; e.g., Jöreskog & Sörbom, 1989). Conceptually, this development represented an integration of econometric (structural equation) and psychometric (factor analytic) methods into a single, versatile, data analytic approach. Organizational behavior researchers came to recognize the importance of this advancement, and use of this methodology in their substantive research increased dramatically.

Within this context, the first purpose of this chapter is to review the causal modeling efforts that have appeared during this 20-year period. Specifically, the focus will be on models that represent relationships between independent and dependent variables (either manifest or latent), as compared to simple confirmatory factor analysis models that have also become popular. This is not meant to imply that this latter class of models is not important. Instead, the focus reflects the fact that many OB researchers are more interested in relationships between variables in complex models than measurement issues as reflected in confirmatory factor analytic models. The present review will take advantage of the existence of six prior reviews conducted at various times over the 20-year period. This will allow us to see how OB researchers have used causal modeling methodology during this time period and the critical issues underlying this use.

The second objective of the chapter is to provide some guidance as to how OB researchers might improve their causal modeling skills in the future. Advancements in various aspects of latent variable methodology have occurred at an increasing rate, and often they have not been published in outlets regularly read by OB researchers. The technical nature of these developments is another barrier to OB researchers' understanding. Thus, the second section of the chapter attempts to point OB researchers to some of these advancements in a manner that will facilitate understanding of the key issues and promote improvements in future applications of causal modeling in the OB literature.

A REVIEW OF CAUSAL MODELS IN THE OB LITERATURE

Early Issues with Manifest Variable Designs

Feldman (1975). In one of the earliest reviews of causal-correlational techniques in applied psychology, Feldman (1975) noted the increased use of this methodology and attributed this to researchers' desire to test causal propositions in natural (field) settings while maximizing external validity. One technique considered by Feldman was cross-lagged correlation analysis, which involves calculations using correlations among two or more variables based on data collected at multiple time points. He also discussed path analysis, which involves the use of multiple regression techniques to estimate relationships among variables in longitudinal or cross-sectional designs. A particular focus of Feldman's was alternative explanations or competing hypotheses that must be considered when using these two analytical techniques.

Feldman's (1975) concern for alternative explanations and competing theories was based on his review of several studies published during the 1968–1975 time period that used the two causal-correlational techniques. Even at this early stage in the OB modeling literature, a variety of topical areas had been investigated, including expectancy theory, satisfaction-performance relationships, role stress, and leader-subordinate relationships.

In nearly all of the studies examined by Feldman, researchers gave little attention to competing explanations for their empirical findings. As a result of these concerns, Feldman argued that as OB researchers develop causal systems that predict the direction and strength of observed relationships among system variables, they should develop competing theories that predict different patterns of observed relationships. The advantage of this strategy is that the comparative degrees of agreement between the correlations representing the observed relationships and each of the predicted patterns of correlations based on each competing model can serve as criteria for judging the adequacy of the alternative theoretical models. Most importantly, this chapter shows why the issues discussed by Feldman pertaining to the need for alternative causal models remain important in the OB causal modeling literature.

Billings and Wroten (1978). Another review of causal modeling was provided by Billings and Wroten (1978), who examined path analysis in industrial/organizational psychology. Their objective was to translate the procedures, problems, and possible solutions related to path analysis into terms that could be more easily understood by OB researchers. They began their review by summarizing path analysis procedures, including (a) the researcher's specification of direction of relationships among variables, resulting in the identification of independent and dependent variables; (b) the use of multiple regression to estimate the impact of the independent (exogenous) variables on the dependent (endogenous) variables; and (c) the evaluation of the model.

Billings and Wroten (1978) then provided a discussion of applications of path analysis in the industrial/organizational psychology literature, based on a search of path analytic studies appearing in journals from 1970–1978. In considering problems related to the assumptions of path analysis, they first discussed the requirement of uncorrelated residuals: in a model with two or more dependent variables, the application of regression analysis to evaluate the model requires that the residuals or error terms of the regression equations for the dependent variables be uncorrelated. This assumption is not fulfilled if there are any unmeasured variables (not included in the design) that are related to each of the dependent variables, and its violation can result in biased path coefficients. Billings and Wroten further claimed that most existing studies using path analysis had not dealt with this critical assumption adequately.

They next discussed the assumption of correct ordering of variables; in path analysis models the direction of causality must be assumed to be one-way ($x > y$ or $y > x$). They claimed that the issue of correct ordering of variables had been neglected in OB applications of path analysis, with researchers failing to defend their choices of causal order and failing to consider plausible alternative orders. Billings and Wroten (1978) also noted that regression analysis requires the assumption that all variables are perfectly measured (contain no random measurement error), and that the violation of this assumption can either attenuate or inflate estimates of path coefficients, with subsequent effects on Type I and II errors. They claimed that the path analysis studies they reviewed suffered from this problem.

A final aspect of the use of path analysis reviewed by Billings and Wroten (1978) concerned the reproduced correlation matrix used to evaluate path analysis models. If a set of path (regression) coefficients is consistent with the data, the predicted correlations based on the sum of products of direct and indirect paths (as determined by theory) will approximate the sample matrix. Billings and Wroten reported the rule of thumb that the observed and predicted correlations should differ by no more than .05. More importantly, based on their review they observed that most OB examples of path analysis did not attempt to reproduce the correlation matrix as a means of judging the adequacy of the model.

In summary, the review by Billings and Wroten (1978) played an important role in the evolution of causal modeling in OB research. Their encouragement of researchers to consider alternative causal orders was consistent with Feldman's (1975) call for the development of competing causal models. Also, their discussion of random measurement error brought attention to this important problem, which may have helped motivate future use of more advanced techniques with less restrictive assumptions about measurement error. Finally, their encouragement for the examination of reproduced correlation matrices in the model evaluation process was an important step in promoting the assessment of model fit, a key component of current causal modeling efforts.

James and James (1989). A third review that discussed manifest variable causal modeling in OB research was conducted by James and James (1989), who based their comments on articles published during the 1978–1987 time period (thus picking up where the Billings and Wroten, 1978, review ended). James and James identified 39 studies for their review, 28 of which used cross-sectional data, 7 of which used longitudinal data, and 4 of which used a panel design (same variables examined over time). They further reported that 92% of these studies examined recursive (one-way causation) models, whereas 8% examined nonrecursive models, or models that contained a reciprocal relationship. This latter design required complex analytical techniques that go beyond simple path analysis. As a general overview, the studies were based on an average sample size of 287, and each contained about five independent and five dependent variables.

A major issue for James and James (1989) was an evaluation of the extent to which the reviewed studies met the assumptions required for confirmatory analysis. The assumptions examined were those originally proposed by James, Mulaik, and Brett (1982). One important finding of James and James was that only 9% of the studies investigated two or more a priori models. Although most (73%) did specify the causal order for all relations in the model, only 18% even mentioned the self-containment condition (which requires that all important causes of each dependent variable be included in the model). Another dimension upon which the studies were evaluated was the extent that they stipulated the types of environments or subjects to which the model would generalize. James and James found that 25% of the reviewed studies examined moderator effects as a test of generalizability. Regarding the measures used in the studies, James and James reported that 28% of the independent variables and 36% of the dependent variables had reliabilities less than .70, whereas an additional 36% of the independent variables and 29% of the dependent variables had reliabilities between .70 and .80. Thus, approximately two thirds of all measured variables in these studies had reliabilities less than .80.

Another important aspect of the James and James (1989) review was their examination of the inference process used by researchers to evaluate their manifest variable causal models. As one of the conditions needed for confirmatory analysis, James et al. (1982) proposed that confirmation of any causal model requires that paths predicted to be nonzero are statistically significant, and paths predicted to be zero are nonsignificant. They referred to these requirements as Condition 9 and Condition 10, with fulfillment of Condition 9 being based on significance of multiple regression coefficients representing the paths. James et al. (1982) also described two techniques for determining whether Condition 10 had been fulfilled, the first being the reproduced correlation test (based on an examination of the reproduced correlation matrix) and the second being the omitted parameter test (which like the Condition 9 test is based on the significance of the associated regression coefficients).

With respect to these two conditions, James and James (1989) reported that whereas 92% of the reviewed studies contained a test for Condition 9, only 59% contained a test for Condition 10. This finding implies that over 40% of the studies may have contained incorrect zero restrictions of paths that were actually important to the model. More importantly, James and James further noted that many studies mixed exploratory and confirmatory analysis, in the sense that these studies included model modifications (adding or dropping paths) that were not developed prior to the analyses. Specifically, 69% of the studies included specification searches, which resulted in the modification of a model to improve its fit to the data or its parsimony (making it simpler with fewer paths). This latter characteristic is especially important when it is considered that the average study included six modifications, but only one study included an attempt to cross-validate the revised model.

In summary, the James and James (1989) review documented the increased frequency with which causal models were being examined in the OB literature, and it identified several important aspects regarding their use. Their call for increased attention to a priori models and the conditions required for confirmatory analysis paralleled the earlier comments of Feldman (1975) and Billings and Wroten (1978). Also, given the relatively low values for the reliabilities of the measures used in these studies, the need for alternative techniques that can account for the biasing effects of measurement error was made clear. Finally, the results of the review model evaluation strategies used in these studies focused more attention on Condition 10 tests and the cross-validation of revised models.

Williams and Podsakoff (1989).   A fourth review of manifest variable causal models was provided by Williams and Podsakoff (1989), who limited their discussion to research studies using a longitudinal design to investigate reciprocal relationships. They began their review by providing some background on the study of reciprocal causality in OB, which indicated that this type of causal model could be found in many substantive areas, including leadership, employee attitudes, group processes, job design, and work stress. However, they noted also that the time required by researchers and organizations for longitudinal research was a barrier to conducting this research, as was the attrition of sample expected with this type of design. Most importantly, Williams and Podsakoff proposed that the absence of a standard method of data analysis for panel designs was a critical factor limiting this type of research.

Their literature review, which covered the time period 1970–1987, identified 27 studies that used a panel design to investigate reciprocal relationships. Although several data analytic techniques were used in the studies, three were employed most frequently, including cross-lag correlation, dynamic correlation, and path analysis. Williams and Podsakoff (1989) presented the existing critiques of the analytical procedures used in these studies, a review that showed that each strategy suffered from important limitations. Specifically, they noted that the difference in cross-lag correlations (which is the key factor in their interpretation) does not represent a measure of causal effects because it is influenced by properties of the variables being examined (e.g., variances of variables). They also reported that cross-lag correlations are biased by random measurement error and omitted variables. Regarding dynamic correlations (which correlate difference scores between two variables, each measured at two points in time), Williams and Podsakoff reported that they are influenced by factors other than the unique relationship between the involved variables. Path analysis was described as being limited by the presence of random measurement error and the assumption that the residuals for the time two dependent variables are uncorrelated, which frequently runs counter to theory and findings from prior research. Finally, they discussed problems associated with testing for moderators, identifying the appropriate time lag between waves of data collection, and the unmeasured variable problem.

The review by Williams and Podsakoff (1989) shows that because they use time to empirically untangle the issue of direction of relationship between organizational variables, longitudinal designs are valued. As such, the statistical issues addressed were not minor, as they represented a threat to an application of causal modeling that was viewed as having great promise for increasing understanding of complex OB relationships. In some cases, the criticisms of the analysis strategies reported by Williams and Podsakoff had been known for some time by organizational researchers, but were ignored. In other cases the limitations were only recently learned. Regardless, it was clear from their review that an alternative analysis strategy was needed to overcome limitations of prior techniques and allow for the promise of longitudinal designs to be realized.

The Transition to Latent Variable Models

Beginning in the early 1980s, a more sophisticated approach to the evaluation of causal models began to appear in the OB literature. This analytic approach, which will be referred to as *latent variable modeling*, allows for a distinction between the constructs of interest and the indicators used to measure them (a distinction not made with manifest variable designs). Specifically, this type of model allows for the simultaneous estimation of a measurement model, which specifies the relationships between the observed (measured, manifest, indicator) variables and a set of unobserved latent variables (factors), and a structural model. Regarding the measurement model, this methodology provides estimates of factor loadings that indicate the extent to which the latent variables influence the indicators. It also provides estimates of the amount of error variance in the indicators. In cases where multiple indicators are not or cannot be employed, this methodology allows for the use of reliability based information to obtain the measurement parameters. The non-measurement or structural portion of a latent variable model specifies the relationships (a) among latent exogenous variables, (b) between latent exogenous and endogenous variables, and (c) among latent endogenous variables. For the structural model, estimates of these three types of relationships are provided, as are estimates of the amount of variance explained in each of the equations corresponding to the latent endogenous variables.

The capability of accounting for effects associated with random measurement error (and in some cases nonrandom measurement error) has contributed to the popularity of this methodology. However, latent variable models also allow researchers to avoid other restrictive assumptions required of the use of path analysis, such as the assumption that the residuals for the equations of endogenous variables are uncorrelated. Additionally, the fact that these models are so complex requires that more sophisticated parameter estimation techniques be used (as compared to OLS regression to estimate path coefficients), and these techniques often have more desirable statistical properties. Finally, this methodology provides a very powerful way of testing hypotheses about sets of parameters (e.g., that a set of paths equal zero or some nonzero value), something that is not handled very well in path analysis models.

Bentler's (1980) *Annual Review of Psychology* chapter introduced latent variable methodology to the discipline of psychology, and early introductions for organizational researchers were provided by James et al. (1982), Bagozzi and Phillips (1982), and Hunter and Gerbing (1982). As a result of these contributions, applications of latent variable methodology in OB literature began appearing in the mid-1980s. However, for all of the advantages obtained with this methodology, it is also very complex and presents many challenges to individuals wanting to learn about it or apply it to a substantive area. As such, early applications have been characterized by much uncertainty as to which practices should be followed, uncertainty that was magnified by the fact that technical developments were occurring at an increasingly fast rate. The next sections will review these applications of latent variable methodology in the OB field.

James and James (1989). In addition to their review of manifest variable studies, James and James (1989) also reviewed causal modeling articles in OB research that used latent variable methodology. For the 1978–1987 time period, they identified 12 studies using this methodology to evaluate causal models with exogenous and endogenous constructs. Of the 12 studies, 9 utilized a multiple-indicator approach and 3 used reliability information to link the latent variables with their manifest indicators. Across all 16 studies, James and James reported an average of 3.2 latent variables per study and an average of 2.1 indicators per latent variable. James and James also claimed that the models they examined were not very parsimonious, meaning the models contained a large number of structural paths linking the latent variables.

Regarding analysis issues, James and James (1989) noted that 75% of the studies were conducted by analyzing the correlation matrix among indicator variables (as contrasted to the preferred strategy of analyzing the covariance matrix). Additionally, all of the studies employed a full-information, maximum-likelihood-parameter-estimation procedure and LISREL (e.g., Jöreskog & Sörbom, 1989) was the predominant computer program used to obtain the estimates. With respect to establishing the adequacy of the models examined, researchers employed fit indices both with and without known sampling distributions.

From the first of these two categories (indices with known distributions), the chi-square statistic (which reflects the discrepancy between the sample covariance matrix and a predicted matrix based on the model's parameter estimates and, thus, parallels the reproduced correlation matrix mentioned with path analysis studies) was used in nearly all the studies. This statistic can also be used to compare competing nested models (where nested refers to the fact that one model is similar to a second model, except that in the second model certain paths are forced to be zero by the researcher) by examining their difference in chi-square values. This practice was used in about one third of the studies. The significance of the individual parameter estimates was determined in nearly one half of the studies by examining the ratio of the parameter to its standard error, with this ratio being distributed as a *t*-statistic. In the category of *fit indices* with no sampling distribution, James and James reported that nine different indices were used, although none was used in over one half of the studies examined. Of these nine, six were obtained with output from LISREL for a given model, whereas three involved a comparison with a "null" model which proposed that all the variables are uncorrelated. Finally, in the studies reviewed, the common practice was to assess the fit of the measurement and structural models simultaneously. Only two studies assessed the fit of the measurement model before proceeding to test the structural model, a practice that has come to be preferred.

The review of James and James (1989) documented the practices being used by OB researchers as they began to apply latent variable methodology in organizational settings. Based on this review, the authors recommended that increased attention be given to the conditions required of confirmatory analysis, because the review indicated this had not been done in the existing research. They also encouraged researchers to admit to the exploratory nature of their specification searches and provide cross-validation of the models obtained via exploratory model modification. Finally, they strongly urged researchers to develop and evaluate alternative a priori models. As before, many of these issues had been raised in prior reviews, but the recommendations had not been followed.

Harris and Schaubroeck (1989). Another review of latent variable models in OB research was provided by Harris and Schaubroeck (1989). They identified applications of this methodology in several areas including motivation, satisfaction and job stress, commitment, absenteeism, turnover, and leadership. More importantly, they discussed several empirical issues that confront users of latent variable methodology. First, Harris and Schaubroeck discussed the impact of sample size on parameter estimates obtained with these models, and although they noted that parameter estimates are not biased by sample size, other problems can occur if the sample size is not adequate. Examples of these problems include convergence problems, such that the computer program being used does not arrive at a final set of acceptable estimates, and implausible solutions that contain estimates that do not meet logical requirements (e.g., negative measurement error variances).

Harris and Schaubroeck (1989) also discussed the effects associated with the number of indicators used to represent the latent variables in a causal model. They reported that researchers should use three indicators for each latent variable, as various problems were more likely to occur if only two were used. Regarding statistical properties of latent variable models, Harris and Schaubroeck focused on the assumption of multivariate normality required of maximum likelihood estimation. If this assumption is violated, they concluded, the parameter estimates are little affected by skewness and kurtosis. However, they also noted that standard errors may be underestimated when distributional assumptions are not met, which could lead to incorrect inferences about relationships. They further indicated that the chi-square statistic was not reliable when the assumptions were not met.

In addition, Harris and Schaubroeck (1989) reviewed several technical issues involved with latent variable models. They noted that analyses based on a correlation matrix rather than a covariance matrix were likely to have incorrect standard errors for the parameter estimates and an incorrect chi-square statistic. More importantly, they reported that the standard errors were likely to be larger with the analysis of correlations, which would result in a lower likelihood of finding significant parameters. Harris and Schaubroeck discussed potential strategies for dealing with improper solutions and nonconvergence problems as just described.

Regarding assessment of fit, Harris and Schaubroeck (1989) noted the plethora of goodness-of-fit indices being used by OB researchers employing latent variable methodology. They concluded that the normed and parsimonious fit indices reported by James et al. (1982) were used most frequently in OB studies. The normed fit index involves the comparison of a given theoretical model with a null model (which proposed that all variables are uncorrelated), whereas the parsimonious fit index contains an additional component reflecting the number of parameters or the complexity of the model. Interestingly, Harris and Schaubroeck reported that researchers had come to different conclusions about which substantive model was best, depending on the particular index they used. Finally, the review noted that in cases where OB researchers have examined more than one model, model comparisons using chi-square difference tests had become popular and two general approaches had been proposed and used. More will be said about these two approaches in the next section.

The review of Harris and Schaubroeck (1989) drew attention to the increased application of latent variable methodology in OB studies. Their comments on empirical and technical issues has served to provide guidance to researchers who encounter problems with their data and/or models. Also, they provided many useful suggestions related to sample size, number of indicators, distributional assumptions, and choice of matrix to be analyzed. Finally, their comments on the increased number of fit measures at the disposal of OB modelers has helped alert researchers to the complexity of the issues involved in model evaluation.

Medsker, Williams, and Holahan (1994). A final review of latent variable models in OB was conducted by Medsker, Williams, and Holahan (1994). Medsker et al. focused specifically on goodness-of-fit indices and methods used to evaluate causal models. They began their review by describing the various diagnostics provided by LISREL (Jöreskog & Sörbom, 1989). Specifically they presented the chi-square statistic, the Goodness-of-Fit Index (which is conceptually similar to the NFI presented earlier), and the Adjusted Goodness-of-Fit Index (which is conceptually similar to the PFI because it accounts for the number of parameters in the model being evaluated). Also discussed was the root mean square residual, which represents the average of the difference between the sample covariance matrix and the matrix predicted by the model and is based on the logic of the reproduced correlations matrix presented earlier. Finally, the t-values that indicate the significance of each parameter estimate were described. In addition to these basic indices, six other indices based on the information provided by LISREL (Jöreskog & Sörbom, 1989) were described.

Medsker et al. (1994) also reviewed two general strategies (mentioned earlier in the discussion of Harris and Schaubroeck, 1989) for comparing competing theoretical models that had been used in the OB literature. In nearly all cases, the models being compared were nested. The first strategy was provided by James et al. (1982), who discussed the use of chi-square difference tests to compare nested models. According to James et al., when a researcher examines a set of nested models, at the point at which the chi-square comparison is significant (meaning the hypothesized restrictions on the involved parameters are rejected), the process stops and no additional models should be examined. More recently, Anderson and Gerbing (1988) presented an alternative strategy. In addition to emphasizing the assessment and modification of the measurement model prior to examining theoretical models, Anderson and Gerbing recommended that upon obtaining a significant chi-square difference test for two nested models, a more complex sequence of model comparisons should be pursued to demonstrate the adequacy of the retained theoretical model.

Medsker et al. (1994) next reviewed practices being used by OB researchers to evaluate their latent variable models, based on examining the same OB journals that were used by James and James (1989) in their review. It should be noted that although James and James found nine models using multiple indicators to represent latent variables in the 1978–1986 time period, Medsker et al. found 19 studies using this approach published between 1988–1992. Of these studies, about half were cross-sectional and half included some longitudinal data. The average sample size was 454, and the majority of studies had fewer than three indicators per latent variable. Regarding the estimation procedure, nearly half of the studies did not report which technique they used, and there was a greater variety of techniques used than found in the earlier review by James and James. Also, although there was an increase in the percentage of studies basing their analyses on a covariance matrix, a considerable number still used correlation matrices.

Regarding the assessment of fit, all studies conducted both Condition 9 and Condition 10 tests as discussed by James et al. (1982) and nearly all used the chi-square statistic and the t-tests of individual paths in this process. Many of the other fit indices mentioned earlier were also used, and all of the studies used multiple fit indices. Most researchers used both a priori models and hypotheses and post hoc respecifications. Finally, over half of the studies used chi-square difference tests to compare competing models, and a similar percentage assessed the fit of the measurement model before proceeding to test the fit of the structural portion of the latent variable model.

Medsker et al.'s (1994) review documented the rapid rate at which use of latent variable methodology in OB studies has increased. Their comprehensive coverage of goodness-of-fit measures should help bring some clarity to this key aspect of latent variable methodology, an aspect that has gotten increasingly technical, as noted in the prior review of Harris and Schaubroeck (1989). Their review indicated the impact of key articles from quantitative areas, such as Anderson and Gerbing (1988) and Mulaik et al. (1989). Finally, the review indicated some important improvements in OB applications related to larger sample sizes being used, increased analysis of covariance matrices, more attention to Condition 10 tests, more frequent use of chi-square difference tests, and increased attention to initial evaluation of measurement models.

Summary. The preceding reviews suggest that early applications of causal modeling in OB tended to treat such modeling as an extension of multiple regression. Not infrequently, causal models provided a convenient means for interpreting beta weights, now referred to as path coefficients. Slowly, researchers began to realize that the transition to causal modeling, or from exploratory to confirmatory analysis, was more demanding. Conditions must be reasonably satisfied before a causal model can be employed to direct analyses designed to estimate parameters in manifest or latent variable models, where the estimated parameters are used to infer causality.

The reviews indicate a trend toward greater attention being paid to these conditions and to the statistical aspects of causal analysis, which are considerable. However, a trend is not a triumph, and there is much left to be done to achieve truly sophisticated use of causal modeling by the majority of OB users. We thus turn our attention to the future and to suggestions that hopefully will assist in accomplishing this objective.

A GUIDE FOR IMPROVED CAUSAL MODELING IN OB STUDIES

The purpose of this section is to provide guidance for OB researchers as to how they can improve their use of latent variable techniques. Specific recommendations will be offered for each of four stages of the research process: (a) model development, (b) preliminary data analyses, (c) confirmatory analyses, and (d) exploratory model modification. In some cases the recommendations will not be new and will parallel those offered in prior reviews. In other cases, the suggestions will reflect new developments occurring in the quantitative literature. Regardless, it is proposed that increased attention during each of these stages will allow for organizational researchers to more fully utilize this important tool for theory testing and development.

Model Development

A first recommendation for OB researchers using latent variable methodology is that they should devote more effort to model development prior to data collection. Often times, in the latter stages of their investigations researchers may realize the existence of threats to the validity of their conclusions that can only be overcome by examining alternative models requiring additional data. Most importantly, typically these data were not collected, and as a result less confidence can be placed in the conclusions. Gavin and Williams (1993) discussed several issues, which are reviewed in the following section, that should be addressed prior to data collection, which can decrease the chances of this problem occurring. Conversely, failure to attend to these matters may compromise some and perhaps all the interpretations derived from the models and data under consideration.

Satisfy Conditions for Confirmatory Analysis. A first specific suggestion offered by Gavin and Williams (1993) is that increased attention be given to meeting the conditions required for confirmatory analysis. One important consideration involves the specification of the direction of causal relationships in the proposed model. As described by James et al. (1982) and others, researchers must specify whether the relationships among variables are or are not reciprocal (two variables influence each other). In spite of theoretical support in many areas for reciprocal relationships (e.g., Williams & Podsakoff, 1989), James and James (1989) and Medsker et al. (in press) noted the relatively small number of studies examining reciprocal relationships.

Our primary point is that in situations common to many organizational studies that involve cross-sectional data collection, the investigation of reciprocal or nonrecursive relationships requires specific types of predictor variables. As discussed by Bentler and Chou (1987), a nonrecursive model will usually be underidentified unless it contains predictor variables that influence one of the dependent variables involved in the reciprocal relationship but not the other. The underidentification results in an inability to obtain unique parameter estimates representing the relationships of interest. Most importantly, researchers may realize the importance of considering nonrecursive relationships only after their data have been collected, and thus data on unique predictors may not have been obtained. By considering causal direction and the need for reciprocal relationships prior to data collection, OB researchers can help ensure that they will have the data required to test these types of models.

Another requirement of confirmatory analysis that has implications for data collection involves the self-containment condition. As reviewed by Gavin and Williams (1993), a self-contained model requires that there be no omitted variables (James, 1980; James et al. 1982). Thus, with a self-contained model there are no "relevant" causal variables for the endogenous or dependent variables that have been left out. In this case, a "relevant" variable is one that is related to the dependent variable(s) and correlated with other independent variables in the model. If a model is not self-contained, the parameter estimates for the variables included will be biased, thereby threatening the validity of any ensuing conclusions. Most importantly, the reviews by James and James (1989) and by Medsker et al. (1994) have indicated that OB researchers still devote too little attention to the self-containment condition. Thus, at the same time that plans are being made to ensure the capability of investigating nonrecursive relationships, attention should be given to including all predictor variables required for self-containment.

A final condition for confirmatory analysis is that researchers identify the boundaries to which their models will generalize. These boundaries indicate, for example, the types of environments or groups of subjects for which the model will hold true. This search for boundaries is manifested empirically in the search for moderators (James & James, 1989). There are a couple of alternative techniques for testing moderators with latent variable methodology (e.g., multiple-sample analysis, fixed measurement parameters), but an obvious requirement is that data measuring the moderators be available. As with concerns about nonrecursive relationships and self-containment, potential moderator variables should be identified prior to data collection so that required data can be incorporated into the design of the study (Gavin & Williams, 1993).

Give a Priori Consideration to Alternative Models. In addition to giving increased attention to the conditions required for confirmatory analysis with latent variable methodology, Gavin and Williams (1993) also suggested that researchers should take precautions to decrease the possibility that models exist that are "equivalent" to their chosen theoretical model. An equivalent model is one that generates an identical estimated population covariance matrix (e.g., Jöreskog & Sörbom, 1989). It has long been known that equivalent models have identical values on goodness-of-fit indices (e.g., James et al., 1982), and therefore cannot be distinguished from each other on this criterion.

As summarized by Gavin and Williams (1993), to the extent that equivalent models can be generated from the researcher's main theoretical model, alternative explanations or competing models cannot be ruled out. In this case, the suggestion of Lee and Hershberger (1990) is that equivalent models should be retained until each can be specifically examined by more refined theories. With this in mind, it is important to eliminate or minimize the problem of equivalent models in the development of one's main theoretical model. An important way to eliminate the potential for equivalent models is by paying close attention to the variables that are included in the original model (Gavin & Williams, 1993). By understanding the types of models that can result in increased chances of equivalent models (e.g., Lee & Hershberger, 1990), researchers can include alternative variables and relationships that could lessen the likelihood of the equivalent models. Again, the need for these variables should be determined prior to data collection to ensure their availability.

A related suggestion by Gavin and Williams (1993) is that organizational researchers heed recent calls for the development of multiple a priori models (e.g., James & James, 1989; MacCallum, Roznowski, & Necowitz, 1992). Gavin and Williams described a process typically used in organizational studies in which researchers begin with a single a priori model, conduct a specification search, and then add parameters in order to increase the overall fit of the original model. One problem with this approach is that the added parameters often have little theoretical support. A more important problem is that if the theoretical support exists, one might ask why the relationship was not included in the initial model (e.g., MacCallum et al., 1992).

The overriding concern is that models revised using this empirical process often do not cross-validate well across samples (cross-validation will be discussed in greater detail shortly). Given the inherent weakness of post hoc model modification, the development of multiple a priori models that can be directly compared would be an important improvement. As with the other issues discussed by Gavin and Williams (1993), the development of multiple a priori models might require the collection of additional variables beyond those originally planned.

Examine Assumptions of Measurement Model.   A fourth suggestion of Gavin and Williams for organizational researchers during the pre-data collection stage is that the relationship between indicators and constructs be carefully examined. Nearly all organizational applications of latent variable methodology assume that the indicators are "caused" by underlying latent variables, which leads to an expectation of high values for the intercorrelations among the indicators for a given latent variable. However, Gavin and Williams have presented arguments by Cohen, Cohen, Teresi, Marchi, and Velez (1990), which proposed that many constructs should not be thought of as latent variables, but instead should be viewed as "emergent" variables. In this case, instead of the latent variable causing the indicators, the causal direction may be thought of as reversed.

Gavin and Williams (1993) presented an example of this problem from organizational research in which component satisfaction scores (e.g., supervisory satisfaction, co-worker satisfaction) are used as indicators of overall job satisfaction. In this case, it was suggested that overall job satisfaction may be better considered as an emergent latent variable resulting from the indicators, rather than as an underlying cause of the component indicators. Analytically, with an emergent variable there is no reason to expect high intercorrelations among indicators, even though this is an assumption required for the use of the indicators to represent the latent variable. Most importantly, Gavin and Williams summarized different alternative solutions to this problem area, several of which require data beyond that initially collected. By careful consideration of the differences between latent causal and emergent variables, organizational researchers can plan for data collection that is consistent with the assumptions they are making about intercorrelations among indicators.

Preliminary Data Analyses

Consider Alternatives for Missing Data. The next section of this chapter presents suggestions for OB researchers regarding issues in data analysis that should be considered prior to the confirmatory phase of latent variable modeling. A first concern facing researchers is their treatment of missing data, inasmuch as this problem is inherent in the survey designs common to OB research using this methodology. As a result, researchers face a choice between analyzing a covariance matrix based on pairwise deletion and a matrix based on listwise deletion (a strategy resulting in a smaller sample size for the analyses). Unfortunately, an examination of OB applications of latent variable modeling shows that typically researchers do not report the type of matrix that was analyzed. Nevertheless, it is important to consider issues related to the choice of pairwise versus listwise matrices, for reasons that will now be described.

As discussed by Hayduk (1987), the mathematics involved with maximum likelihood estimation (common to most organizational applications of latent variable models) assume a listwise matrix, and this is the preferred strategy. However, there are trade-offs involved with either approach. On the one hand, the costs of using a pairwise matrix increase as the degree of nonoverlap between cases increases and as the size of the smallest n for the covariances decreases. Alternatively, the costs of using a listwise matrix may be that an extremely unusual type of individual may be required to provide a complete set of information. Hayduk's position is that whichever type of matrix is chosen, researchers should reanalyze the final model using the other approach and report any differences in results. Further, it is suggested by Hayduk that if a pairwise approach is going to be used, other alternatives such as mean substitution and regression-based estimates should be carefully considered.

For those situations in which missing data may be a strong concern, recent developments allow for a more sophisticated approach. In a general review of covariance structure models, Kaplan (1990) discussed the differences between data that are "missing-completely-at-random" (MCAR), in which observed responses are a random subsample of the possible responses, and data that are "missing-at-random" (MAR), in which the pattern of missingness may be a function of other variables in the model. Most importantly, Kaplan described the MCAR assumption as being unrealistic in most cases, and then further discussed the approach of Muthen, Kaplan, and Hollis (1987) in which the multiple group feature of the LISREL program is used to test the MCAR model. Bentler (1990b) also proposed an extension of the Muthen et al. strategy that can be more generally implemented. Given that OB researchers may be making the MCAR assumption without being aware when they use listwise matrices, this potential for empirically testing the assumption may be of future value. Additionally, Kaplan further advised that even if direct modeling of missing data patterns is impossible, authors of research papers should share with their readers the rationale underlying their choice of approaches to the missing data issue.

Select Appropriate Parameter Estimation Procedure. In addition to choices about missing data, OB researchers should also take care in examining the distributions of the variables that are going to be used with latent variable models. Reviews of organizational modeling studies by James and James (1989) and Medsker et al. (in press) have shown that researchers typically use the maximum likelihood technique to estimate the parameters of their models. Although this approach requires the assumption that the data follow a multivariate normal distribution, the viability of this assumption is seldom tested. If the assumption is not satisfied, goodness-of-fit values and standard errors of parameter estimates may be biased, and other estimation procedures should be considered (see Jöreskog & Sörbom, 1989 for discussion of the various alternatives). Although it is beyond the purpose of the present chapter to review all the evidence on non-normality (see Gerbing & Anderson, 1992; Kaplan, 1990), the important point is that researchers should examine the skewness and kurtosis of the variables used as indicators, as well as generalized distance functions that may indicate the violation of the multivariate normality assumption (e.g., Johnson & Wichern, 1988). If there is indication that the data are not normally distributed, alternative techniques may be required, some of which involve trade-offs of bias versus sample size requirements. Failure to attend to this issue will likely result in incorrect decisions about the importance of paths in a model and the overall fit of the model.

Once researchers have decided on their approach to missing data and examined the distribution of their variables, an additional problem that can arise is that the sample covariance matrix to be analyzed is not positive definite (which requires all eigenvalues of the covariance matrix to be greater than zero). If this condition is not fulfilled, maximum likelihood and generalized least squares methods cannot be used. Wothke (in press) has presented a general review of nonpositive definite matrices in structural equation modeling that should be of value to organizational researchers confronting this situation. In this review, Wothke discussed the various causes (collinearities among variables, use of pairwise deletion of missing data, use of non-Pearsonian correlations) and possible solutions (dropping variables, smoothing the matrix, changing start values, looking for outliers) to nonpositive definite matrices. While examining organizational applications of latent variable modeling, problems due to failure to have a positive definite matrix are usually not discussed. Nevertheless, our own experience suggests that this problem occurs frequently in the preliminary stages of data analyses. Fortunately, researchers now can consult the article by Wothke for guidance as how to best deal with the situation.

Empirically Examine Measurement Models. Another recommendation for the preliminary phase of data analysis is that greater attention should be paid to the measurement model portion of latent variable models. Anderson and Gerbing (1988) have drawn attention to the importance of this step in a review of structural equation modeling in practice. Specifically, they provided recommendations for the use of several diagnostic indicators of measurement model misspecification, including normalized residuals reflecting the difference between the sample covariance matrix and the predicted matrix based on the model and its parameter estimates. They also discussed different ways in which measurement model respecification might solve problems due to a poor measurement model, with emphasis being given to dropping poor indicators or relating the problem indicators to different factors. This suggestion was based on the fact that these two approaches preserve the potential for unidimensional measurement.

There is some evidence that organizational researchers have paid attention to the suggestion of Anderson and Gerbing (1988) for measurement model evaluation prior to the testing of relationships between latent variables. Specifically, Medsker et al. (in press) have reported that over 80% of organizational studies involving latent variables gave some attention to an initial evaluation of the measurement model with confirmatory factor analysis. However, typically little information was provided as to the specific changes in the measurement model that were made and the reasons for making these changes. Based on our own experience, several additional suggestions can be offered that can help in this last stage of the preliminary analyses.

First, we propose that there still is an important role for exploratory factor analysis as part of causal modeling. Specifically, we propose that an exploratory factor analysis should be conducted using all the items that will represent each of the latent variables (even if these items are going to be combined to form subscales which will be used as indicators). The eigenvalues obtained from such an analysis can give important information regarding unidimensionality that can supplement the interpretation of fit indices obtained from subsequent confirmatory factor analysis. If the pattern of eigenvalues suggests unidimensionality, we further suggest that separate confirmatory factor models be examined in which one-factor models are fit to the indicators of each latent variable in the model. Although we will return to the interpretation of fit indices in the next section, our present point is that if these one-factor models have adequate fit, researchers should proceed with the complete measurement model testing described by Anderson and Gerbing (1988).

Confirmatory Analysis

Assumptions About Unmeasured Variables. Attention to the issues raised in the previous two sections should help OB researchers as they move to the next stage of their research where they examine their theoretical models. As a first step in this process, attention should be given to the assumptions about unmeasured variables that are implicit in the theoretical models. Even if more attention is given to model development, as we suggest, it is very likely that the models examined will suffer from the unmeasured variables problem. That is, at least some important causes will be left out of the model. A special case of this problem comes from models with multiple dependent variables (e.g., job satisfaction and organizational commitment: Farkas & Tetrick, 1989; Williams & Hazer, 1986). When these dependent variables have some common predictors (e.g., Mathieu & Farr, 1991) and not all of these predictors are included in the research design, problems will occur.

Specifically, for every latent dependent variable in a model there is a disturbance term or residual of the associated structural equation that contains the influence of unmeasured causal variables. In the case being considered, with multiple dependent variables and some unmeasured shared predictors, the implication is that there is a common component to the residuals from the multiple equations. The existence of such a component results in correlations among the residuals of the equations, a type of parameter that often can be estimated with latent variable models (although these correlations cannot be estimated with most regression analyses of this type of model). However, despite this potential, most organizational investigators have not questioned assumptions about residuals and possible unmeasured variables. Most importantly, Anderson and Williams (1992) demonstrated that the parameter estimates representing relationships among latent variables can be biased if the residuals are incorrectly assumed to be uncorrelated. As a result, organizational researchers should carefully examine the assumptions they are making about unmeasured variables as a first step in the confirmatory phase of their model testing.

Compare a Priori Models With Chi-Square Difference Test. The second step in the confirmatory phase consists of comparing the various a priori theoretical models identified during the model development phase. The best case for these model comparisons occurs when the models are "nested," which generally means that one model can be obtained from a second model by restricting certain key parameters to zero. The restriction of these parameters to zero represents the test that the involved latent variables are not structurally related. As discussed by Medsker et al. (1994), there have been two general strategies provided for conducting these model comparisons, including approaches presented by James et al. (1982) and by Anderson and Gerbing (1988). For present purposes, several specific suggestions can be provided based on the two general strategies.

In the case where there are multiple competing models, the first test should compare the theoretical model that contains the most structural parameters with a "saturated" structural model (which contains all other possible relationships between latent variables). This comparison provides a test that the parameters that are restricted to zero in the most complex theoretical model are not important, and the researcher hopes to not reject the restrictions based on the chi-square difference test. Assuming this is the case, the researcher next begins to compare the alternative nested theoretical models, which need to be ordered such that the models contain increasing numbers of restrictions on parameters in the original theoretical model. In this second step, it is important to remember that the critical values for the sequential tests are not additive when comparing more than two models. As a result, whatever more restricted theoretical model is identified during this stage of sequential tests, it should also be compared directly with the original theoretical model. Anderson and Gerbing (1988) presented a decision tree that can serve as a guide for how the model comparisons should be conducted. Finally, when the best theoretical model has been identified with the model comparisons, the final test to be examined based on James et al. (1982) involves comparing this theoretical model with a structural null model, which proposes that all latent variables are unrelated. This last test provides information that the structural parameters contained in this theoretical model are in fact significantly different from zero.

Examine Additional Information About the Fit of the Models. A related issue that must be discussed at this stage involves the goodness-of-fit indices that can be used to compare competing theoretical models, as a supplement to the chi-square difference tests described above. Probably no area related to latent variable modeling has generated as much interest and controversy as the use of goodness-of-fit indices (see *Sociological Methods and Research*, 1992, *Vol. 21, No. 2*; *Multivariate Behavioral Research*, 1990, *Vol. 25, No. 2* for special issues devoted to testing structural equation models). Moreover, there has been a wide range of indices and practices used to assess fit in the OB literatures, as discussed in the reviews of James and James (1989) and Medsker et al. (1994). We do not attempt to summarize this voluminous literature (for a useful summary of key issues, see Bollen & Long, 1992). Instead, we provide some suggestions to guide future OB applications of latent variable methodology.

First, it is important to recognize that there can be two uses of these indices: the first being to assess the overall fit of a model, and the second being to assess the relative gain in fit provided by a model compared to an alternative model based on the same data. In the first case, the use of incremental fit indices based on noncentrality parameters is recommended. Specifically, the Relative Noncentrality Index (RNI) developed by McDonald and Marsh (1990), which is comparable to the Comparative Fit Index (CFI) proposed by Bentler (1990a), seems to be most desirable. This recommendation is based on the fact that both are normed with values between 1.0 and 0.0 and are not biased by sample size (see Gerbing & Anderson, 1992, for a review of monte carlo studies of fit indices).

For the second case in which the primary interest is on comparing nested models based on the same data, it is best to use a fit measure that is the most sensitive to differences in the structural portion of the models being compared. Expanding on the discussion of these issues provided by Sobel and Bohrnstedt (1985), Mulaik et al. (1989) proposed the use of relative fit measures that separate the effects due to measurement model specification. More recently, Williams and Holahan (1993) developed a version of the relative fit measure of Mulaik et al. that incorporates the use of noncentrality parameters and is not likely to suffer from the sample size effects expected with the Mulaik et al. version.

In addition to the use of two types of fit indices as just described, a second suggestion concerns the use of parsimonious fit indices by OB researchers. As originally discussed by James et al. (1982), parsimony indices attempt to take into account the complexity of a given model and are based on the recognition that overall good fit can be obtained for a given model simply because it has a large number of freely estimated parameters. Mulaik et al. (1989) provided a more recent presentation of the philosophy behind parsimony indices that has stimulated attention to this aspect of the model evaluation process. However, as reviewed by Williams and Holahan (1993) in the OB literature there have been two distinct uses of these parsimony indices. In the first instance, they have been used to compare models that have different overall fit values, and in the second (and less frequent) case, they have been used to distinguish between two models with equal overall fit. As demonstrated by simulations conducted by Williams and Holahan (1993), the problem with the first case is that this practice can result in the selection of "best" models that have known misspecifications (nonzero parameters inappropriately restricted to zero). This practice runs counter to the use of chi-square difference tests to test for the significance of parameters and should be avoided in the future. Instead, parsimony indices should only be used with models that have been demonstrated to have overall equivalent fit.

Two additional suggestions may be offered that promise to help organizational researchers in the confirmatory stage of their analyses. First, as originally recommended by Wheaton (1987) and by Bentler and Chou (1987), parameter estimates from competing nested models should be compared. To the extent that parameters from a less restricted model change when new parameters are added to the model, and the new parameters are statistically significant, limitations with the original model are suggested. Second, as discussed by Gerbing and Anderson (1992), values of standardized residuals, which reflect the difference between the sample covariance matrix and the matrix predicted by the model, can provide an informal index of fit that also indicates specific problem areas of the model.

Exploratory Model Modification

Remember the Need for Cross-Validation. Even if the recommended increases in attention are given to the three stages of latent variable modeling as presented, OB researchers may still find that the model they have identified as being the "best" does not fit the data very well. Under these conditions, the temptation to revise the model based on statistical diagnostic information is strong, and the most common strategy involves freeing structural parameters that were restricted in the theoretical model. The reviews by both James and James (1989) and Medsker et al. (1994) noted that this type of exploratory model modification is common in organizational research, and typically occurs without any attempt at cross-validation of the resulting model. Recent developments in latent variable methodology provide some suggestions for improved practice at this last stage of the model-evaluation process.

Because the model-modification process described above is data driven, it is likely to be influenced by chance characteristics of the sample data (MacCallum et al., 1992). As such, one must be concerned that the modifications made to the model will not generalize to other samples or to the population of interest. Using sample studies and two large data sets, MacCallum et al. (1992) found that model modifications may be inconsistent and not cross-validate well, if at all. As a result of these findings, they recommended that researchers making model modifications in single samples should make only a few modifications that are clearly interpretable in terms of theory. MacCallum et al. (1992) also described a parallel specification search strategy that should be considered by organizational researchers.

A Strategy for Cross-Validation. With the parallel specification search, the process is to conduct the search process on at least two independent samples and obtain fit measures for each model in each sample. Cross-validation measures are recommended, using a double cross-validation strategy, in which each sample serves both a cross-validation and calibration role. According to MacCallum et al. (1992), any inconsistent results across the two samples would cast doubt on the final models obtained, whereas consistent results would provide strong support. It also should be noted that MacCallum et al. (1992) emphasized the need for theoretical support for all parameters being considered in the modification process.

Another development relevant to the model modification process involves the diagnostic information used in making changes to the original model. As discussed by Kaplan (1990), the modification index (MI) is provided by LISREL and represents the expected drop in chi-square value associated with freeing a restricted parameter. Although the use of MIs is not without controversy (e.g., MacCallum, 1986), it has been recently suggested that they be used in conjunction with the standardized expected parameter change statistic (SEPC). An SEPC gives the approximate magnitude a fixed parameter would assume if it were freed (Kaplan, 1990; MacCallum, 1990). Kaplan (1990) described the advantage of the combined use of the MI and SEPC in that it becomes simpler to identify parameters that will improve the fit of the model and also have large values (indicating their importance). Kaplan (1990) reviewed two studies supporting this practice, and at this point this approach seems to have merit for organizational researchers.

A final caution regarding specification searches based on MIs is related to the problem of equivalent models. As described by Lee and Hershberger (1990), during a specification search it may happen that two or more fixed parameters have the same MI value. As such, if any of these parameters are freed, the resulting models would have equivalent fit. When this happens, existing theory and prior empirical results become even more important in deciding which parameter will be included. Also, researchers should report that this has occurred and discuss the interpretation of the alternative model not chosen.

CONCLUSION

The use of causal models in OB research provides a powerful tool for testing theory in applied settings. This chapter has documented the increased use of this methodology over a 20-year period. During this time, there has been an evolution in the analytical approaches taken. Initially, simple correlation-based procedures were employed; this was followed by the use of a regression-based strategy in the form of path analysis. Currently, latent variable causal models are popular, because of the numerous advantages they possess. As these changes have occurred, OB researchers have faced the challenge of staying informed about which techniques are most desirable and how these techniques can be most effectively implemented in their substantive areas. Based on the reviews, it could be argued that they have been successful.

However, there is also evidence that technical advancements in latent variable methodology will continue to challenge the skills of OB researchers. The second part of this chapter provided some guidance for how the use of this methodology can be improved in future applications. Suggestions were provided for several stages of the research process. Only time will tell if there is as much progress in the effective use of causal modeling methodology in the next 20 years as was true of the past 20 years. It is hoped that this chapter will help ensure that this happens.

ACKNOWLEDGMENTS

The authors would like to acknowledge the helpful comments of Mark Gavin, Gina Medsker, and Peg Williams on earlier drafts of this chapter, and the assistance of Julia Huffer in its preparation.

REFERENCES

Anderson, J., & Gerbing, D. (1988). Structural equation modeling in practice: A review and recommended two-step approach. *Psychological Bulletin, 103*, 411–423.

Anderson, S., & Williams, L. (1992). Assumptions about unmeasured variables with studies of reciprocal relationships: The case of employee attitudes, *Journal of Applied Psychology, 77*, 638–650.

Bagozzi, R., & Phillips, L. (1982). Representing and testing organizational theories: A holistic construal. *Administrative Science Quarterly, 27*, 459–489.

Bentler, P. (1980). Multivariate analysis with latent variables: Causal modeling. In M. R. Rosenzweig & L. W. Porter (Eds.), *Annual Review of Psychology*, (Vol. 31, pp. 419–456). Palo Alto, CA: Annual Reviews.

Bentler, P. (1990a). Comparative fit indexes in structural models. *Psychological Bulletin, 107*, 238–246.

Bentler, P. (1990b). Fit indices, lagrange multipliers, constraint changes and incomplete data in structural models. *Multivariate Behavioral Research, 25*, 163–172.

Bentler, P., & Chou, C. (1987). Practical issues in structural modeling. *Sociological Methods and Research, 16*, 78–117.

Billings, R., & Wroten, S. (1978). Use of path analysis in industrial/organizational psychology: Criticisms and suggestions. *Journal of Applied Psychology, 63*, 677–688.

Bollen, K., & Long, J. (1992). Tests for structural equation models: Introduction. *Sociological Methods and Research, 21*, 123–131.

Cohen, P., Cohen, J., Teresi, J., Marchi, M., & Velez, C. N. (1990). Problems in the measurement of latent variables in structural equation causal models. *Applied Psychological Measurement, 14*, 183–196.

Farkas, A., & Tetrick, L. (1989). A three-wage longitudinal analysis of the causal ordering of satisfaction and commitment on turnover decisions. *Journal of Applied Psychology, 74*, 855–868.

Feldman, J. (1975). Considerations in the use of causal-correlational techniques in applied psychology. *Journal of Applied Psychology, 60*, 663–670.

Gavin, M., & Williams, L. (1993). *Model development in structural equation analysis: Recommendations for organizational research.* Paper presented at the 1993 Meeting of the Society for Industrial and Organizational Psychology, San Francisco, CA.

Gerbing, D., & Anderson, J. (1992). Monte carlo evaluations of goodness of fit indices for structural equation models. *Psychological Bulletin, 21*, 132–160.

Harris, M., & Schaubroeck, J. (1989). Confirmatory modeling in organizational behavior/human resources management: Issues and applications. *Journal of Management, 16*, 337–360.

Hayduk, L. (1987). *Structural equation modeling with LISREL: Essentials and Advances.* Baltimore, MD: Johns Hopkins University Press.

Hunter, J., & Gerbing, D. (1982). Unidimensional measurement, second order factor analysis, and causal models. In L. Cummings & B. Staw (Eds.), *Research in Organizational Behavior* (pp. 267–299). Greenwich, CT: JAI.

James, L. A., & James, L. R. (1989). Causal modeling in organizational research. In C. L. Cooper & I. Robertson (Eds.), *International review of industrial and organizational psychology 1989* (pp. 371–404). New York: Wiley.

James, L. R. (1980). The unmeasured variables problem in path analysis. *Journal of Applied Psychology, 65*, 415–421.

James, L. R., Mulaik, S., & Brett, J. (1982). Causal analysis: Models, assumptions, and data. Beverly Hills, CA: Sage.

Johnson, R., & Wichern, D. (1988). *Applied multivariate statistical analysis.* Englewood Cliffs, NJ: Prentice–Hall.

Jöreskog, K., & Sörbom, D. (1989). *LISREL 7: A guide to the program and applications.* Chicago: SPSS Inc.

Kaplan, D. (1990). Evaluating and modifying covariance structural models: A review and recommendation. *Multivariate Behavioral Research, 25*, 137–155.

Lee, S., & Hershberger, S. (1990). A simple rule for generating equivalent models in covariance structure modeling. *Multivariate Behavioral Research, 25*, 313–334.

MacCallum, R. (1986). Specification searches in covariance structure modeling. *Psychological Bulletin, 100*, 107–120.

MacCallum, R. (1990). The need for alternative measures of fit in covariance structure modeling. *Multivariate Behavioral Research, 25*, 157–162.

MacCallum, R., Roznowski, M., & Necowitz, L. (1992). Model modifications in covariance structure analysis: The problem of capitalization on chance. *Psychological Bulletin, 111*, 490–504.

Mathieu, J., & Farr, J. (1991). Further evidence for the discriminant validity of measures of organizational commitment, job involvement, and job satisfaction. *Journal of Applied Psychology, 76*, 127–133.

McDonald, R., & Marsh, H. (1990). Choosing a multivariate model: Noncentrality and goodness of fit. *Psychological Bulletin, 107*, 247–255.

Medsker, G., Williams, L., & Holahan, P. (1994). A review of current practices for evaluating causal models in organizational behavior and human resources management research. *Journal of Management.*

Mulaik, S., James, L., Van Alstine, J., Bennett, N., Line, S., & Stillwell, C. (1989). An evaluation of goodness-of-fit indices for structural equation models. *Psychological Bulletin, 105*, 430–445.

Muthen, B., Kaplan, D., & Hollis, M. (1987). Structural equation modeling for data that are not completely missing at random. *Psychometrika, 51*, 431–462.

Sobel, M., & Bohrnstedt, G. (1985). Use of null models in evaluating the fit of covariance structure models. In N. Tuma (Ed.), *Sociological methodology* (pp. 152–178). San Francisco: Jossey–Bass.

Wheaton, B. (1987). Assessment of fit in overidentified models with latent variables. *Sociological Methods and Research, 16*, 118–154.

Williams, L., & Hazer, J. (1986). Antecedents and consequences of satisfaction and commitment in turnover models: A reanalysis using latent variable structural equation methods. *Journal of Applied Psychology, 71*, 219–231.

Williams, L., & Holahan, P. (in press). Parsimony based fit indices for multiple indicator regression models: Do they work? *Structural Equation Modeling: A Multidisciplinary Journal.*

Williams, L., & Podsakoff, P. (1989). Longitudinal field methods for studying reciprocal relationships in organizational behavior research: Toward improved causal analysis. In L. Cummings & B. Staw (Eds.), *Research in Organizational Behavior* (Vol. 11, pp. 247–292). Greenwich, CT: JAI Press.

Wothke, W. (in press). Nonpositive definite matrices in structural equation modeling. *Sociological Methods and Research.*

9

The Role of Organizational Behavior in the Business School Curriculum

Milton R. Blood
American Assembly of Collegiate Schools of Business

INTRODUCTION

This chapter advances a particular view of the field of organizational behavior (OB) as it exists in business school curricula. Where are we? How did we get here? Where can we go from here? This chapter represents my experiences and opinions.[1] Readers should be warned at the outset that I will not create an objective history, nor will I try to predict an inevitable future. I will present (a) a personal construction of the activities and dynamics that brought us to the present state of OB, (b) my personal view of the field as it currently exists, and (c) my suggestions for how we can create our future. Other perspectives are possible and supportable. Comparison of a variety of perspectives, on the future of OB, is likely to be healthy for the field. If this chapter generates comparative viewpoints, it will have served a positive function beyond its primary intent to present a view of the curricular role of OB.

---

[1]The author brings a variety of perspectives to bear on the topic, formerly having served as a faculty member and administrator in a management college and currently serving in a management role with the national organization for business schools, the American Assembly of Collegiate Schools of Business (AACSB). The opinions expressed in this chapter are solely those of the author and do not represent an official or unofficial position of AACSB. I gratefully acknowledge the challenging and clarifying comments provided to earlier drafts of this chapter by Roger Atherton, Jeanne Brett, Edward Conlon, André Delbecq, and James Terborg; they are not responsible for any of the chapter's shortcomings.

I begin the chapter with a brief description of how this field of study started. Instruction in OB did not begin with the initiation of business schools (or schools of commerce). It is a relatively recent entrant into the business school curriculum stemming from some very clearly identifiable forces and events in the history of American business education. In this chapter I portray OB's beginning and then trace some forces that forged its current profile. In depicting the present definition of the field, I suggest that its evolution has given it unnecessarily fuzzy form and boundaries. The individuals who developed and moved the field to this point are responsible for its shortcomings and its successes. Because its history is short, many of those same individuals should take the lead to determine future directions.

Next, I discuss the field as it presently exists. My view of extant OB suggests that the discipline needs attention to remain a viable force in the business school curriculum. Simultaneously, OB must focus more and encompass more. It must cut itself loose from its multidisciplinary roots. Also, it must turn its considerable knowledge and skills toward the central issues of the applied world served by business schools. It must reach out to all behavioral disciplines that can contribute solutions to applied management problems.

Finally, I discuss a possible future for the field. There is no time to lose if OB is to make its contribution within the business school. Indeed, if OB faculty members do not accept the challenge of the present, they will likely lose their place in the curriculum. We are at a point in time when universities are restructuring and reorienting. Fields that contribute to the redefined academy will find their position enhanced; others will be displaced. The resulting universities in the next decade will be leaner and more effective.

- Business degree programs will be more focused and pragmatic.
- Instructional goals will compete more forcefully with the research agenda to influence the direction and activity of disciplines.
- Business school curricula will integrate disciplines more thoroughly.
- To insure a place in these integrated curricula, individual fields must delineate their contributions thoughtfully and convincingly.
- Organizational behavior contributors have earned their right to a turn at the pulpit.

Whether their arguments will convince curriculum constructors depends on their ability to define OB as a consequential contributing discipline. This chapter addresses challenges faced by OB faculty in the evolving academy.

THE BIG BANG

In the beginning there were schools of commerce. From the start of the century, major universities began to establish commerce departments and schools of business (Dirksen & Lockley, 1966). In general, their academic contributions were undistinguished. During the first two decades of the 1900s they turned from emphasizing character development to teaching practical skills of commerce (Hugstad, 1983). They prepared graduates to begin working in white-collar office positions that enabled them to work their way into the industrial and corporate hierarchies of the day. With little pretense toward the development of demanding intellectual acumen, these schools provided basic practical tools (knowledge and skills) for employment. They gave little attention to understanding the larger social context for business enterprise. Such learning came, if at all, through the "apprenticeship" provided by early career positions.

By the mid-1950s ferment had begun for these business schools to become more—more legitimate partners in the academic enterprise, more useful contributors to the leadership of corporate America, more of a force in the larger societal context in which business takes place. Two famous reports from 1959 chronicled the weaknesses of the past, reported the nascent intellectual activity, and suggested appropriate directions for development.

Reports by Gordon and Howell (1959) and by Pierson (1959) appeared in the midst of some evolutionary activity already bubbling in business schools. These reports catalyzed the business school changes that were taking place (Schmotter, 1984). The practice-oriented curriculum and pedagogy were under attack from internal revolutionaries who wanted more academically respectable programs. Proponents of theory-based and empirically based approaches challenged the anecdotal content. In the foreword to the Gordon and Howell (1959) report, sponsored by the Ford Foundation, the foundation vice president, Thomas H. Carroll, said:

> The vocational approach that has all too often characterized these schools in the past is now considered inadequate. A few institutions have been experimenting with new curricula designed to provide a more rigorous professional training within the context of a liberal education. The results achieved to date are highly promising. In such programs, increased emphasis is being placed on the application of the fundamental disciplines of the social and behavioral sciences to the problems of business administration. Previously only the relevance of economics had been fully appreciated. Another promising development is the growth in the application of modern mathematical and statistical methods to business problems. (p. v)

The recommendations from this extremely influential report suggested a turning to established disciplinary fields, including the social sciences.

> We also strongly recommend that the business schools take more initiative in establishing closer working relations with other departments and schools on the campus—psychology, sociology, economics (if not a part of the school), mathematics, statistics, engineering, etc. (p. 440)

> Of all the subjects which he might undertake to study formally, none is more appropriate for the businessman-to-be than human behavior. . . . every person

anticipating a responsible position in a modern business enterprise needs a substantial amount of knowledge about human behavior. Thus, we stress human behavior as an element in the undergraduate business curriculum more for its professional implications than for its general education significance, although the latter is far from unimportant. (p. 166)

By human behavior we mean most of the subject matter of the fields of psychology, sociology and (cultural) anthropology. (p. 167)

If psychology or any other discipline is indispensable for the proper preparation of business graduates, the principles of that field should be taught by someone trained in the field, and not by a marketing or management instructor. This is entirely apart from the question as to whether these courses should be offered within the business school or not. (pp. 168–169)

The message was clear. Business schools needed to help students perform the social tasks of management along with the technical tasks of business functions such as accounting, finance, marketing, and production management. For that, the curriculum should include the social sciences. Business students should receive fundamental knowledge from theoretically and empirically based social sciences disciplines, not just anecdotal guidance of applied management. This was a call for insertion of social science materials into the curriculum.

There were suggestions to develop the theoretical and empirical underpinning of the business curriculum by enhancing research programs in business schools. These suggestions were important. They influenced the evolution of instructional content in business programs and enhanced the fulfillment of the service function of the business school enterprise. The development of the research program also greatly strengthened the position of the business school as a legitimate university unit. This chapter does not develop the specifics of those recommendations or trace their fulfillment as changes in the scholarly activities of business schools. Here, they emerge only as they affect the curricular role of OB.

AFTER CREATION, EVOLUTION

The widely circulated appeals of the Gordon and Howell (1959) and Pierson (1959) reports and funding to leading schools for implementation of the reports' recommendations, led to widespread change. Flowing from the impetus of the reports and from the influence of changes taking place in "lead" institutions, business curricula incorporated courses from social science departments, and business schools hired social scientists. Industrial psychologists made the crossover to business schools among the earliest hires and in the largest numbers. Industrial sociologists and social psychologists also moved from their disciplinary departments in liberal arts colleges or took joint appointments.

This infusion of social scientists into the business school created the field of OB. Topics of OB courses became the management-oriented versions of applied psychology (or sociology) courses. A range of topics was imported (or bolstered with disciplinary support), stretching from the macro-orientation of organizational theory to the individual differences outlook of personnel practices. Often, the idiosyncratic scholarly interests brought from their disciplinary backgrounds determined the topics and focus of courses of these newcomers to the business school faculty. "Organizational behavior" as a designator for these offerings differentiated them from industrial psychology and industrial sociology as taught in their home disciplines and differentiated them from management and management theory as taught in the business school.

Tensions between the new settlers fencing off intellectual territory for OB and established management faculty members must have existed from the start. The field of management was based on anecdotal and experientially derived knowledge; the new OB faculty came from empirically-based social science disciplines. Industrial psychologists brought in their penchant for individual differences research, their correlational approaches to knowledge creation, and their disdain for knowledge that is not empirically authenticated. The clash of epistemologies must have created as many agreements-to-disagree as it created opportunities to pool perspectives. At any rate, in some schools OB supplemented an existing management department. In others, OB supplanted management. In still others, OB grew up as a separate, parallel field that competed for the same topic areas under different names and approaches.

Soon after social scientists were added to business school faculties, OB doctorates began to appear. The appellation "organizational behavior" served to differentiate its bearers from scholars produced in the disciplines of origin of the faculty guiding the degrees. However, the apprentice nature of doctoral education meant that many OB doctorates simulated doctorates coming from social psychology, industrial psychology, and industrial sociology programs. The earning of these degrees often included considerable academic work pursued in the base discipline.

CURRENT STATUS OF THE FIELD

A look at the current field of OB shows a lack of focus. There's no discipline in the discipline. Compared to other subject areas, schools use a remarkable variety of approaches to include OB into the business curriculum. The way curricula include OB varies both within and between schools.

Some schools offer a course with content reflecting the chapter headings of a basic OB text. Others stress human resource management issues. For others, certain OB topics have been added to a "principles of management" course. Still others send students to the psychology department for a course in industrial or organizational psychology. Some schools approach OB with a menu of the topics above from which students may choose.

My position with the American Assembly of Collegiate Schools of Business provides an opportunity/responsibility to review curricula and syllabi of 40 to 50 business schools annually. That review reveals no canon of commonly agreed on topics that constitutes the general OB knowledge students should master to acquire a business degree.

Perusal of lists of available electives shows an even greater variation from school to school. This diversity in electives often reflects the interests of the particular faculty members at a school, and it shows the positive dynamism of the field. But lack of agreement on what constitutes the core knowledge of OB shows the difficulty faculty manifest when defining the field and its contributions.

Business leaders and academics agree that both knowledge and skills are important in behavioral topics. Earlier studies documented this need (Gordon & Howell, 1959; Pierson, 1959) and the comprehensive study of management education and development conducted by Porter and McKibbin (1988) reiterated it. Commenting on "undernourished emphases in the curriculum," Porter and McKibbin noted the continuing need for what they called "soft" or "people" skills.

> . . . this need—as it relates to management education—has been documented repeatedly throughout our data. Corporate respondents showed an overwhelming preponderance of opinion that behaviorally oriented subject matter should receive more attention in the curriculum. Deans and faculty members themselves perceive a gap between how much "soft" skills and personal characteristics are currently emphasized in the curriculum versus how much they "should be." Also, and perhaps most important, the corporate sector gives business school graduates relatively low ratings in terms of the strength (or lack thereof) of their leadership and interpersonal skills. (p. 324)

To be sure, much of the criticism of business graduates in the behavioral area has been skill-, rather than knowledge-oriented. Defenders of OB could argue that their curricular and pedagogical goal has been knowledge instead of skills. Such an argument comes up short. Graduates of business schools should be prepared to do things, not just know about things. This is a difference from a liberal arts college presentation of the originating social science disciplines. Knowledge about interpersonal behavior will be of little use in a business or management career if it does not change a graduate's interpersonal behavior. The ambivalence within the field in choosing between knowledge and skills may be one force slowing the progress of OB in asserting its right to a focused place in the business school curriculum.

Critics identified the need for more attention to OB topics before the 1960s. Why is there still a need? Why has this need not been fulfilled? It cannot be lack of effort. Professional associations, conferences, course listings, and degree programs all attest the wealth of activity in OB. However, a look at the nature of the activity demonstrates that the field's definition is extremely indistinct. Pirsig (1991) differentiates "static quality" (forces holding characteristics in place) from "dynamic quality" (forces moving to new patterns). Throughout its history OB has suffered(?) from a surfeit of dynamic quality and has resisted most of the normal academic and societal forces that create static quality. No orthodoxy has emerged. Thus, a look to discern the role of OB in the business curriculum finds indeterminate and changing boundaries, expectations, and ambitions.

Who defines OB in business school curricula—customers or producers? Clearly, customers (however defined) have had little to say. One set of customers is the business school faculty, usually represented by a curriculum committee. Unfortunately, in most schools the curriculum setting process is primarily an exercise in dividing into separate fields the "turf" of credit hours required for graduation from the program. What gets planted within each field is seldom considered within the jurisdiction of the committee.

Sometimes, an interdisciplinary group convenes to integrate the different fields. Such groups usually confine their activity to coordinating content, not creating or prescribing content. Often, these efforts align work in related fields (e.g., accounting, finance, and economics or production and marketing) and omit OB from the integrated curriculum package. This kind of coordination, when it includes OB, is rare, and it is commendable. However, even this seldom occurring interdisciplinary attention to the OB curriculum doesn't go far enough. Although it brings broader business school faculty attention to OB, it stops short of using the faculty as a customer to define what to include in OB. At best, it rearranges the presentation order so OB topics fit with issues as they occur in other disciplines.

Similarly, employers of graduates and students themselves rarely have an opportunity to define OB curricular needs. As happens in most academic disciplines, the self-contained OB faculty overwhelmingly decides OB offerings. On the one hand, this situation should be "excusable" as no better or worse than other disciplines. On the other hand, we, of all disciplines, should know better. We should know that the vested interests of OB faculty members will be different from, and will take precedence over, the interests of employers, students, and the broader faculty.

The major failing of the resultant current state of OB is that it fits Gertrude Stein's (1937) classic description of Oakland, California "There is no there there." The streams of scholarship that have entered the OB pool have maintained their separation. Enrichment could result from more thorough integration of the various specialties and disciplines. Instead, meccas of activity attract those who are already believers around increasingly specialized journals, Academy of Management divisions, single topic research institutes, and the like.

Two phenomena display these separate tracks in business school curricula. First, different facets of OB show up in interschool comparisons of what travels under the OB banner. Second, multiple OB tracks occur within a single school. For example, a human resource management track, an organizational theory track, an OB track, and an organizational communications track. Despite our claim to a greater understanding of human behavior, we have not found ways to avoid the generally decried splintering of academic endeavor. Indeed, given the particular circumstances of the origin and development of OB, we pass up a marvelous opportunity to meld several academic streams into an integrated, action oriented, problem directed force.

Several social science disciplines have converged in the business school curriculum drawn by the need for understanding of behavioral problems confronted in business organizations. Combining insights and tools from psychology, sociology, anthropology, and other fields could create an amazingly well armed attack on those problems. However, streams of teaching (and research) have tended to maintain, not merge, the originating disciplines. I consider this a failure of OB doctoral programs. This shows up in the communication difficulties encountered within OB. Colleagues sometimes find they do not have a common core of knowledge and language.

Faculty members in OB programs often come from a base social science discipline. It is not surprising when they maintain allegiance to that discipline in their own scholarly activity. However, when doctoral graduates from OB programs identify with one of the base disciplines when building their own careers, it is a missed opportunity. They should be prepared to pull broadly from the paradigms, methodologies, and content of many social sciences as they define the discipline of OB. When describing organizational change, for example, they should be able to discuss incentives, learning, individual differences, communications, interpersonal roles, group dynamics, norms, organizational and societal cultures, political forces, and other phenomena that have practical and theoretical implications for the change process.

Further, it is a failure of OB that there is no widely accepted "basic" OB learning. In Pirsig's (1991) terms, OB's role in the curriculum is all dynamic quality and no static quality. If it is possible to argue that every business school graduate should have some behavioral learning, then it should be possible to say that there are some essential parts to that learning. If none of the parts is essential, how do we justify requiring "some"? The prevalence of menu-satisfied OB "requirements" in curricula suggests that a canon of essential elements is not accepted (or even proposed!).

CURRENT SCOPE OF THE FIELD

As presently manifest, OB brings to the business school curriculum "applied" representations of a plethora of topics from basic social science disciplines. The many topics have varying histories in OB. Some disciplinary topics come to the business school with little adjustment to their disciplinary incarnation or to the vocabulary used to discuss them. This is true, for example, for job attitudes and for methodological issues such as measurement and data analysis. Other social science topics are translated into business settings with accompanying changes in language, for example, communications issues and topics pertaining to rewards and incentives. Still other topics have been treated by OB writers and researchers over an extended time. These topics have developed their own history, and they have evolved into OB topics, that is, topics that (a) have their intellectual life primarily among OB writers and (b) evolve independently from root topics in the originating disciplines. Examples would include leadership and organizational commitment.

Several issues have come from areas of applied psychology, such as social psychology, personnel psychology, industrial psychology, and organizational psychology. Examples of OB topics that have such psychology based roots are: selection, promotion, and other human resource management issues; work and organizational satisfaction studies; motivation, rewards/goals/incentives; leadership; group and interpersonal interaction; organizational commitment; decision making; and social perception.

Some other OB topics have sprung from concerns of the academic field of management. These include such topics as influence and control, job structure and reward contingencies, organizational structure and communications, and some parts of the topic of leadership.

Sociology also has provided topics for the OB palette. Some OB versions of sociology originating issues include boundary spanning mechanisms, influences of indigenous and exogenous entities, organizational development issues, and group membership dynamics.

Other social science disciplines bring in additional insights. Political science has contributed to the study of membership, alliances, and political forces within organizations. Anthropology has donated the notion of corporate cultures and the methodology of participant observation. Economics has been a parallel, though seldom cross-pollinating, contributor to issues of incentives and control.

AN APPROPRIATE SCOPE FOR THE FIELD

Clearly, OB has a rich larder of intellectual sustenance from which to derive its activities and its role in the business curriculum. The question, however, is not "What are the allowable topic areas?," or even "What are the intellectually interesting topic areas?" Those questions appropriately influence the scope of OB research. However, for purposes of this chapter, the fitting question is "What topic areas define a proper scope for organizational behavior as a component of the business school curriculum?"

To the relief of most readers (and certainly to my relief), I will not attempt to define a proper scope for OB in the curriculum. Instead, I will suggest the basis for such a definition. The definition itself should not come from one person, nor should it come exclusively from active participants in OB. It should be forged from a contemplation of OB that includes several constituencies. The field of OB must establish its own curricular agenda. It is time to stop borrowing and importing the OB agenda from other social science disciplines.

The primary principle in the definition of OB in the curriculum is recognition that it is an applied field. The needs of application come first. Practitioners of management, graduates from business school curricula, need the knowledge they can receive from studying the field of OB. To create a definition of the field, those needs must form the base. Information about current and future practitioner needs can come from informed conversation among several constituencies including business school students and graduates, OB faculty members, other business school faculty, employers of business school graduates, intellectual leaders in the practice of management, and informed observers of societal evolution. These combined perspectives should be directed to the task of defining the purpose and the content of "basic" or "essential" behavioral knowledge and skills for effective management.

In developing such a definition, questions and needs of application should be the driving force, not theories and methods that OB researchers have brought from the social sciences. Remember, this chapter concerns the curricular contribution of OB, not the research contribution. Theoretical perspective should and will continue to influence the development of new knowledge. It is critical that the knowledge base of OB derives from careful empirical and theoretical foundations in the social sciences. However, it is equally critical for the effectiveness of OB that the instruction provided to future managers gains its definition from applied concerns. The definition for instructional purposes should not come from the structure and needs of current research in the contributing disciplines. Further, pedagogy must address the applicability of the information received by students. For example, leadership sounds like an applied topic, but its classroom presentation can leave students no better prepared to lead.

Basing the discipline on applied needs may help overcome misdirection and lag now evident in many OB offerings. Examples of misdirection and lag in current OB syllabi are easy to find. I will furnish some such examples, and most readers will find it an easy exercise to provide more.

One example of misdirection of effort is the amount of class time spent on historical depiction of the development of certain OB areas. To prepare a student to motivate peers and subordinates, there is little need to equip that student to recite the history of Theory X and Theory Y. When preparing a student to lead, it is not necessary to trace the history of leadership studies through their many steps and missteps. When transferring from the basic social sciences, OB faculty members often fail to recognize the change in the student body and the teaching task. The business school graduate needs to lead, not trace the history of leadership research. The graduate needs to motivate, not compare and contrast six different theories of motivation, and needs to design and evaluate training programs, not recite once-popular learning theories.

I recognize that a curricular focus on relevance can go too far. I do not advocate a return to the trade school mentality that prevailed in business schools through the 1940s. To the contrary, I believe that OB teaching requires solidly supported social science findings (and I include OB as one of the social sciences). However, priorities of social science theories should not determine the content of OB teaching. The needs of management application should form it.

These suggestions are for undergraduate and masters degree students who plan careers in business and management. For doctoral students pursuing academic careers and for individuals wishing to be students of the field, an entirely different approach is necessary. For this clientele a more historic presentation of knowledge for its own sake is suitable.

Examples of lags in the OB curriculum component are equally easy to designate. Faculty members structure most OB courses on topics coming from the base social sciences, rather than on the excitement of the behavioral challenges faced by managers. Because of this, many important topics are left out of OB until they literally force themselves onto a syllabus from sheer brute obviousness. Hence, OB faculty members rarely lead managers into new realities. They scramble to catch up.

Usually, practicing managers learn to deal with behavioral phenomena from private consultants long before the topics make their way into the business school classroom. This results from the stronger necessity for consultants to find and satisfy the requirements of their customers. Instances where this has been true in recent years include such topics as the increasing cultural heterogeneity of the American workforce, social dislocations caused by corporate mergers, cultural heterogeneity of globalized corporations, influence of information access on organizational functioning, and structural changes caused by technological change. Although business school graduates struggle with these issues, business school students learn to distinguish drive theories from need theories.

I do not aver that learning about things is bad, nor that having a sense of the history of an intellectual field does not impart a deeper understanding. It is a question of priorities with a limited resource—the time and effort of business school students. Business graduates will not become producers of social science. They will be users of social science. Their exposure to OB in the business school curriculum should make them knowledgeable and skilled users.

THE FUTURE OF ORGANIZATIONAL BEHAVIOR

What part does organizational behavior have in the future business school curriculum? If I were a pessimistic person, it would be easy to create the following negative future for OB. The field succumbs to its own lack of focus. Continued attentiveness to topics coming from the base social science disciplines leads to increasing irrelevance in the eyes of the rest of the business school. Continued allegiance to the concerns of the separate base social science disciplines and an unwillingness to create an alloy from them lead to unsustainable fragmentation in the already unstable multidisciplinary business school enterprise. In his review of the Porter and McKibbin (1988) report, Cummings (1990) described institutional political and motivational forces that hinder change in business schools.

I believe such pessimism is unwarranted. In relative terms, the field is young. Although faculty members maintain strong ties to "home" disciplines, hardening of the categories has not reached fatal levels. Increasingly, there are signs of attention to the concerns of practitioners.

One of the most heartening signs of dynamic quality is the gradual incursion of new disciplines and new ideas into the OB portfolio. Some recent additions offer exciting directions, and further, have the potential to push the field toward increasing relevance to management practitioners. For example, Jeanne Brett, Leonard Greenhalgh, and Roy Lewicki have moved the topics of negotiation and conflict resolution into OB.[2] Students no longer study only their game theoretic and industrial relations import. With this work, students can gain experience with their behavioral implications. Anthropological insights have been directed toward organizational issues by Michael Tushman. Such understandings will be critically important as mergers and globalization confound the effects of intercorporate cultures and international cultures. Wayne Cascio has brought utility assessments to bear on human resource activities. This valuable tool will arm graduates to make more informed judgments about personnel policies and practices. Fred Luthans has imported behavior modification perspectives to business school course offerings. This provides an important approach to graduates as they attempt to manage behavioral change and provides methodology for assessing organizational change in single organization studies.

Perhaps, one of the most telling developments for relevance in OB has been the development of "management vérité" as pioneered in the scholarly work of Henry Mintzberg (1973). The work of Whetten and Cameron (1991) epitomized the pedagogical rendition of this approach. They provided a curricular contribution that follows the same research/theory impetus as Mintzberg; that is, "Let's see what managers really do in their natural habitat." Whetten and Cameron go the additional pedagogical step by supplying textual materials toward what managers need to know and what behavioral capacities managers need. Their work and a substantial proportion of the work in the *Journal of Management Education* display the positive attention being given by some OB faculty members to application.

These are encouraging signs that OB is a field ready to get its second breath. Timing could not be better. Higher education is going through a restructuring that will eventuate in (among other things) a greater concern for accountability, relevance, and attention to instruction. Business education is going through an exaggerated version of the transformation taking place in higher education (American Assembly of Collegiate Schools of Business, 1992). The technological and global evolutions going on in the world of business reinforce the urgent need to reconsider business education simultaneously with the current reevaluation of higher education.

---

[2]The following examples are meant to be illustrative, not exhaustive. Many individuals could be noted who have brought specific topics into organizational behavior instruction at a particular institution or who have prepared textual materials available to the field.

Nearly every business school in America is (or recently has been, or soon will be) engaged in a serious and thorough review and revision of its curriculum. This creates an opportunity for OB to claim its worth in the education of business students. We must bring the combined richness of the disciplines we represent to the crucial problems of human behavior faced by our graduates. Then, we can substantially enrich the lives of our students and ourselves. If we let this opportunity escape, we will lose our place in the business school curriculum. We will deserve that fate for our inattention to what is important, but our students will not deserve the opportunity loss they will suffer as a result.

Of course, rethinking what we do is never without risk. Breaking away from safer harbors of the base disciplines will not be comfortable, nor will it always pay off. However, overcoming the inertial features of academe described by Cummings (1990) and Oviatt and Miller (1989) can save OB faculty members from themselves. They must be saved from natural tendencies toward academic fragmentation and practical irrelevance. They must trust in the resource already incorporated in a diverse and intellectually active professional population. They must reach out to welcome more participation and ideas from disciplines that, until now, have made only marginal contributions (anthropology, political science, demographics, and behavioral economics readily come to mind).

Most of all, OB faculty members must take their place as the embodiment of a business school discipline that has its own boundaries and focus. So long as faculty members define themselves, and evaluate themselves, in terms of the social science disciplines from which they came, they create their own self-defeating boundaries. When they declare independence and purpose for OB, they invite a future of excitement, positive surprises, and meaningful contributions.

REFERENCES

American Assembly of Collegiate Schools of Business. (1992). *Crisis and survival* [Special Report]. St. Louis, MO: Author.

Cummings, L. L. (1990). Management education drifts into the 21st century. *Academy of Management Executive, 4*(3), 66–67.

Dirksen, C. J. & Lockley, L. C. (1966). Development of collegiate schools of business and activities of AACSB. In *The American Association of Collegiate Schools of Business 1916–1966* (pp. 1–18). Homewood, IL: Irwin.

Gordon, R. A., & Howell, J. E. (1959). *Higher education for business.* New York: Columbia University Press.

Hugstad, P. S. (1983). *The business school in the 1980s: Liberalism versus vocationalism.* New York: Praeger.

Mintzberg, H. (1973). *The nature of managerial work.* New York: Harper & Row. Englewood Cliffs, NJ: Prentice–Hall, 1980.

Oviatt, B. M., & Miller, W. D. (1989). Irrelevance, intransigence, and business professors. *Academy of Management Executive, 3*(4), 304–312.

Pierson, F. C. (1959). *The education of American businessmen.* New York: McGraw–Hill.

Pirsig, R. M. (1991). *LILA: An inquiry into morals.* New York: Bantam.

Porter, L. W., & McKibbin, L. E. (1988). *Management education and development: Drift or thrust into the 21st century?* New York: McGraw-Hill.

Schmotter, J. W. (1984, Spring). An interview with Professor James E. Howell. *Selections*, pp. 9–14.

Stein, G. (1937). *Everybody's autobiography.* New York: Cooper Square.

Whetten, D. A., & Cameron, K. S. (1991). *Developing management skills* (2nd ed.). New York: HarperCollins.

TECHNIQUES FOR TEACHING OB
IN THE COLLEGE CLASSROOM

Craig Lundberg
Cornell University

The title of this chapter will appear to most readers as both ambitious and foolhardy, yet welcome. The field of organizational behavior (OB) is currently taught in nearly all professional schools and programs at both the undergraduate and graduate levels, as well as to executives. For numerous reasons it is predictable that OB will be taught in an almost bewildering number of ways. Some of these reasons include: the relative recency and the enormous breadth of subject matter in OB (as evidenced in the other chapters of this volume); OB's multiple overlaps with management generally and the several functional areas of business, the variety of backgrounds, training and experience of OB faculty; the heterogeneity of institutional purposes and values where OB teaching occurs; and the pressures—organizational and personal—for reputation, visibility and security, and so on. Given OB's subject matter, it is not surprising that OB instruction often utilizes, clearly more than any other business field, a more reflexive, more process and context sensitive, and learning centered set of classroom methods. Unfortunately, to date, there have been no attempts to describe or assess OB's instructional methods. Yet, because OB's diverse and evolving knowledge is consciously disseminated, there is a need to highlight both the variety and the vitality of OB instruction. This task is undertaken in this chapter.

This chapter is organized into four major sections. The first sketches the brief, but multifaceted history of teaching OB in the college classroom. The second section describes the rather wide array of classroom teaching techniques currently in use. The third section discusses several ideas and values underlying the design and assessment of teaching methods. The final section offers a number of suggestions for enhancing and extending OB teaching methods in the future.

THE EVOLUTION OF OB CLASSROOM INSTRUCTION

Teaching techniques in all academic fields and disciplines appear over time as a response to an interacting set of factors, including levels of student sophistication and demand, technological and facility innovation, instructional objectives and prevailing educational philosophy, the number and heterogeneity of ideas and theories, the rewards for innovation and reform, and the like (Lundberg & Motamedi, 1978). Organizational behavior is no exception. An appreciation of a particular OB classroom teaching technique, therefore, requires as a backdrop, a consideration of the times in which it first appeared and the conditions receptive to its acceptance and diffusion. This section will sketch the evolution of OB classroom instruction over four time periods, each of which contributes to our discussion of contemporary teaching methods.

At the Outset: Tensions of Focus

The field we now know as OB had its origins in the teaching area once broadly referred to as *administration*. Not surprisingly, opinion initially differed widely about whether or not the practice of administration, later termed *management*, was teachable and, if so, how. According to one school of thought, people either were or were not born having management skills—or more accurately, people may have such latent talents but they flower only when challenged by job experience (e.g., Dale, 1960). Another, highly favored view was that managerial talents could be nurtured by appropriate coaching and by being given progressively greater levels of responsible experience on the job. With the popularity of scientific management, human behavior at work was deemed analytical and hence teachable. And when successful executives (e.g., Barnard, 1938) began to publish sensitive accounts of their experiences, interested observers began to attempt normative generalizations about their practice, that is, principles and universals that were didactically taught. This early history of seeking the "one best way" and the abstract lessons of success in business was of course predated by advisors and participants in the public realm (e.g., Machiavelli, 1958; Waldo, 1948). When the focus shifted away from managers to include workers, probably most noticeably in the famous Hawthorn Studies (Roethlisberger & Dickson, 1939), and soon thereafter by the Human Relations in Industry studies at Chicago (Muhs, 1989), the previous normative literature was quickly augmented by descriptive literature. Human relations training then took two distinct forms. One continued the didactic teaching of micro "how–to–do–its" (e.g., leadership), and the growing body of applied knowledge (e.g., personnel psychology). The other human relations training method promoted the acquisition of generalized human relations skills (Roethlisberger, Lombard, & Ronken, 1954) via role-playing, clinical experiences, and the case method. Thus, what was to become OB instruction had at the outset a set of diverging streams of topics and teaching methods.

Borrowings From the Social Sciences

During World War II, all kinds of social scientists were called upon to do applied research. From that time psychologists, sociologists, anthropologists, economists, political scientists, and others found a receptivity to their work in business, industry, and the professions, and more and more their work also found its way into texts and lectures (e.g., Costello & Zalkind, 1963; Miller & Form, 1951; Viteles, 1953). It was the appearance of two separate reports on business education sponsored by the Carnegie Foundation and Ford Foundation (Gordon & Howell, 1959; Pierson, 1959) however that stimulated much of the subsequent use of behavioral and social science ideas and findings. These reports unequivocally recommended that business schools expand their instruction about human behavior in organizations. Psychologists and sociologists were added to business faculties and ideas and theories from applied psychology, social psychology, industrial sociology, and cultural anthropology were applied to organizational, managerial, and industrial relations courses. Although didactic teaching continued in force, texts became more and more catalogues of borrowed ideas (e.g., Leavitt, 1958) and readers both "practical" (e.g., Leavitt & Pondy, 1964) and "scientific" (e.g., Scott & Cummings, 1969) began to appear. In addition, new teaching methods were invented such as replicating experiments in the classroom (e.g., communication networks), and the adaptation of games (e.g., prisoners' dilemma). Organizational behavior as we now understand it, began to flower with borrowings from both faculty and ideas.

Reformers and Respectability

As OB fully separated itself more and more from management and organization theory and personnel, OB faculty sought academic respectability. Although this search for respectability was seen primarily in terms of research endeavors (e.g., experimental designs and sophisticated analyses), in the classroom, respectability was sought in three overlapping ways. First, the majority of OB teaching focused on managerial behavior (respectability through association with organizational elites). Second, much of the content of OB courses was derived from the research literature (respectability through association with "science"). Third, the classroom theme of relevance showed students that OB ideas and findings enhanced understanding of themselves and revealed powerful organizational dynamics that called common sense into question (respectability through association with the pragmatic values of business). Organizational behavior courses proliferated and differentiated. Organizational behavior had, by the mid-1960s, earned a place in the required curriculum—taught more and more with multiple pedagogies—and elective specialties appeared reflecting important managerial concerns. Significantly, the field also began to grow its own faculty through doctoral programs in OB. Although most OB teaching seemed to reflect the unquestioned belief that with OB knowledge student career behavior would be enhanced, a small number of OB faculty began to apply OB knowledge to OB teaching. Some of this self-reflexive work was descriptive, seeking the contingencies associated with effective teaching (e.g., Clark, 1962; Orth, 1963), and other work was primarily critical (e.g., Finney & Siehl, 1985–1986; Nord, 1972; Vaill, 1979). In response, OB teaching began to change in several ways: it became to be more self-conscious about learning styles and processes (e.g., Kolb, Rubin, & McIntyre, 1974); it began to experiment with learning from experience technologies (e.g., Randolph & Miles, 1979; Sata, 1978); alternatives to the case method were invented (e.g., the predictive case series, Sieler, 1967); and it began the use of the classroom as a total learning context (e.g., Balke, 1981).

The Diversity of the Present

OB teaching for a decade or more has exhibited several trends—the continuing innovation of classroom techniques, a shifting focus on core subject matter, and the building of bridges to other fields.

All of the teaching methods noted earlier continue to be used. Each also has been extended (e.g., lectures into lecturettes, texts into primers and fiction, role-playing into experiential exercises, written cases into multimedia cases, etc.). In addition, visual media have been incorporated into OB teaching, as have many other ways of creating and utilizing student experiences in the service of learning. As the next section will show, the inventory of OB instructional methods has become almost bewilderingly large.

At present, the diversity of OB teaching methods in part reflects the variety of core subject matter as well as alternative teaching objectives. On the one hand, there is micro-OB and on the other, there is macro-OB, and of course various micro-macro ratios. Associated with these foci are OB courses that emphasize one or more learning objectives among the major categories of knowledge acquisition, skill enhancement, and attitude change (Summer, 1956). Organizational behavior courses also may be crudely distinguished in terms of whether they are organized by academic topics or by practitioner problems and issues. Organizational behavior teaching methods and materials now obviously serve many different learning purposes, foci, and emphases.

As OB has acquired an identity, a sophisticated knowledge base, many educator adherents and advocates, and subspecialties, (i.e., it has become differentiated from other fields), it has become a source that other fields borrow from and build upon. All of the contemporary texts in OB's sister organizational science fields (i.e., organizational theory, organizational communication, organizational development, human resource management, and management itself) now contain OB material. Contemporary OB texts likewise now often incorporate materials from each of these fields. The ever-expanding inventory of OB teaching methods are also freely borrowed by other business fields—from operations management to strategic management—and other disciplines as well (e.g., public administration, health sciences, social work, and psychology). The educational use of small groups, for example, first common in OB, now appears in all other business courses.

THE CONTEMPORARY ARRAY OF METHODS AND TECHNOLOGIES

As we have seen, the relatively young field of OB has increasingly differentiated itself from its sister fields. The field has progressed rapidly and gained reputation, adherents, enthusiasts, and reformers. The teaching of OB has likewise developed enormously, sharing the general rise in popularity of business education. At present OB educators may draw upon a truly wide array of classroom techniques. The use of these techniques is, of course, dependent on contextual and resource constraints, beliefs about the teaching–learning process, and a variety of instructional purposes. Hence, I shall outline the present inventory of classroom pedagogies and methods—roughly corresponding to their appearance over time, with the exception of the case method, which is discussed last.

Traditional Methods: Knowledge Delivery

The lecture is probably the major classroom pedagogy in OB for presenting the substantive material—as it is for most fields and disciplines. Lectures vary from formal speeches to informal conversations in form (Odiorne, 1976). Although the art of lecturing was originally developed for large classes before good texts were available, lectures are now used for classes of all sizes—typically augmenting and providing emphasis beyond assigned reading. Lecturettes, short, one topic presentations, are common also. To stimulate interest and guide student attention, lecturers do all kinds of things. For example, they hand out or project outlines of their presentation, punctuate the lecture with examples, instructor experiences (e.g., "war stories," Grover & Greenberg, 1983), and ask provocative questions (Kriger, 1989–1990), invite student questions and feedback (Ewans, 1985–1986; Gioia, 1986–1987), and utilize modern communication technology.
   Another major OB knowledge delivery method is assigned reading in the form of texts, readers, and instructor designed packets. The diversity of OB reading materials is enormous in their scope, level of sophistication, degree of integration, and focus. Texts range from primers (e.g., Bowditch & Buono, 1990; Robbins, 1992) to those topically organized replete with illustrative materials, exercises, and short cases or problems (e.g., Greenberg & Baron, 1993; Moorhead & Griffin,

1989) to those written around a particular conceptual approach (e.g., Klein & Ritti, 1980; and Whyte, 1969). Short, one topic texts are also readily available, works intended to be used in sets or as supplements to a main text. There are also several shorter practice-oriented texts available (e.g., Ritti & Funkhouser, 1987).

Readers, collections of previously published materials of all types, are also prevalent. These typically are collections of practitioner articles (e.g., Gabarro, 1991), "classic" academic OB articles (e.g., Natemeyer, 1978) and, more recently, samples of OB "reality," (e.g., Frost, Nord, & Mitchell, 1992). Several firms now offer the service of assisting instructors in creating personalized "texts" of items in the literature. The academic literature has, of course, been exploited for years for class work (e.g., Weick & Orton, 1986–1987). A wide range of training films and audio tapes are now available that inform about particular phenomena, for example, the Abilene paradox, or provide instruction in various behavioral practices (e.g., counseling subordinates, developing teamwork, etc.).

Experience-Loaded Learning

As we have seen, the traditional techniques for teaching OB are used primarily for the delivery of knowledge. When skill acquisition is added as a course objective, instructors turn to a variety of techniques in which experience is the learning vehicle. Each of the techniques described below share an instructor designed activity that provides students with the opportunity to experience some OB phenomenon or practice, thereby "seeing" it better and/or gaining practice with it.

Role-playing is the oldest and best known of these techniques (e.g., Maier & Solem, 1951). Here, students interact, playing the parts of people in particular situations to either acquire a sense of the behavioral demands or to practice some preferred performance. Role-play may deal with contrived or actual situations and involve two or more students. They may range from being careful scripted to completely unscripted. Some are focused on common practices (e.g., performance appraisal), others on current issues (e.g., dealing with sexist behavior). Another early method was the incident process (Pigors & Pigors, 19661), a technique in which a brief statement of a situation is used by students to question the instructor for additional information, thereby promoting discovery skills. Replicating experiments in and out of the classroom with students as subjects is another experience-loaded method (e.g., Ambuske, Locke, & Manning, 1987–1988). Here, the patterned behavior is produced to be experienced and later discussed—often in conjunction with a lecture or reading. The effects of alternative communication networks is an example. Closely related to experiments are behavioral simulations (Greenhalgh, 1979; Paul & Barbato, 1984–1985; Seltzer, 1988–1989), a one to three day role-playing exercise that simulates situations encountered in real organizations. Behavioral simulations often contain a formal hierarchy and division of labor, realistic information provided in the form of an "in" basket, standing committees and scheduled committee meetings, and incoming and outgoing mail

(Strumph & Dunbar, 1990). Simulations can take many forms, from one phenomenon (e.g., Bolman & Deal, 1979) through combinations of two or three variables (such as management style, job design, and type of task), to complex organizational settings (e.g., Bretton, 1991; Clawson & Pfeifer, 1989–1990), and even culture (e.g., Bafa–Bafa, Shirts, 1977). Complex competitive computer games are also sometimes utilized to provide experiences to be analyzed with OB concepts and theories (e.g., Sherman, 1988–1989; Solomon, 1979).

Field projects of several kinds also are used to provide students with opportunities to observe OB knowledge in action (Guest, 1976). All sorts of college activities and local organizations are often readily accessible to students who are assigned observation and description tasks using OB knowledge. These can range greatly in scope, such as from interviewing someone about his or her work to the comprehensive analysis of a neighborhood franchise outlet. Student work experience and internships (Kaupins, 1989–1990) are also often relied upon for this purpose.

In the past decade, experiential exercises have become a popular and widely used classroom technique (Bowen, 1980; Whetten & Cameron, 1984). These are typically short, phenomena-focused, well structured exercises in which students behave as themselves to do something, and then analyze it to learn from it. At present, nearly every OB topic can be taught experientially (e.g., Hall, Bowen, Lewicki, & Hall, 1982). Again, the range of topics for these experiential exercises varies considerably—from active listening to planned change. Experiential exercises also vary about whether there is a "proper" lesson to be learned. The high degree of focused involvement within well-defined behavior parameters is attractive to students, who view them as fun and as job relevant as well. Organizational behavior educators, likewise, find experiential exercises attractive for a variety of reasons: they are popular with students, are easy to use, fit easily within standard class sessions, teach by doing, and are readily available.

A long-standing set of OB teaching methods utilize drama, film, video, and literature—both fiction and nonfiction—to provide vicarious learning experiences for students (e.g., Cowden, 1989–1990; Marx, 1985–1986; Vaill, 1981). Classics such as *King Lear, Billy Budd, Henry V,* or *For Whom the Bell Tolls* are used to examine issues of authority, leadership, and change. Biographies of managers, for example, *Iacocca,* descriptions of supervisors (e.g., *Bosses,* Wall, 1986) and workers (e.g., *Working,* Terkel, 1972) and firsthand accounts of work units (e.g., *Soul of the New Machine,* Kidder, 1981), all provide meaningful materials for OB teaching that can capture student interest and provide opportunities for students to identify with. A few novels have even been written just for OB usage (e.g., *Stephanie's World,* Stevens, 1991). Short stories can illustrate a variety of OB topics (e.g., Puffer, 1991). Films have long been used to illustrate OB phenomena and analysis—from old standbys such as *Twelve Angry Men* and *Twelve O'Clock High* to more recent movies like *Moby Dick* and *Top Gun.* Plays ranging from Arthur Miller's *Death of a Salesman* to Mamet's *Speed the Plow* have been used similarly to explore issues from work lives to ethics. Popular television programs often explore organizational behavior in the workplace (Marx, Jick, & Frost, 1991)—two now defunct television series such as *St. Elsewhere* and *Hill Street Blues*, illustrated a range of issues, from decision making in crisis, to how organizations respond to contexts and constituents to professional roles, team work, mentoring, and even MBWA (Management by Walking Around)! With the accessibility of equipment increasing, student video projects also are appearing also (Maier, 1989; Weber, 1976).

Finally, mention should be made of those other methods perhaps less utilized, that also enhance OB education through experience loaded learning. We speak here of using articles in the business press to draw attention to OB phenomena and practices, debates among students on alternative theories, projects where students design activities highlighting OB topics, keeping a journal (e.g., Allen & Enz, 1986–1987; Porras, 1975), inviting guests to class to share their experiences with reoccurring behavioral problems or new practices, and the use of experiential activities to initiate courses and classes (e.g., Rasmussen, 1986–1987).

Experience that Counts

There is a set of OB teaching techniques that goes beyond the sorts of artificial and secondhand experiential techniques just described in that they ask students to learn from their own firsthand experiences. These techniques utilize either special circumstances or task contexts for students to apply OB concepts and models to, thereby enhancing student's phenomenological sensitivity and/or skill development. They typically are used with readings and lectures keyed to them, although the instructor's assumptions about learning may dictate such cognitive inputs either before the experience (to sensitize students to their experiencing) or after (to aid in making sense of their experience).

Organizational behavior courses, as noted above, commonly use groups of students for a variety of instructional tasks. When the group is asked to focus on their own experiences, that is, their own member dynamics and the group's activities—this self-reflection supposedly contributes to both heightened awareness and enhanced competency. Such focusing can be accomplished either regularly through instrumental feedback (e.g., Dyer, 1987) or verbal processing (e.g., Schein, 1969) for team development purposes or just once or twice more analytically (e.g., Lundberg & Lundberg, 1992).

The "laboratory method" (Bradford, Gibb, & Benne, 1964; Nath, 1975) is less frequently seen today than a decade or two ago. Here, small groups without agendas are formed and facilitated to provide a "here and now" focused experience for members. When the phenomena of interest are the group's dynamics and development, they are called T-groups or human interaction groups. When the phenomena of interest are self-insight and interpersonal behaviors, they are called sensitivity training, encounter or personal growth groups, or leadership laboratories. The laboratory method is an unusually potent technique, because it legitimizes and encourages the expression of affect, giving and receiving descriptive feedback between members, and countervenes members' habitual expectations about task group leadership and structure. Such groups may meet almost continuously for just a few days or up to 2 or 3 weeks. Alternatively, such groups may meet regularly for a few hours once or twice a week for periods extending up to a semester. In academe, laboratory groups are usually semi-structured, with some experiential exercises, instrumented self-diagnostic devices, and lecturettes and reading periodically inserted into the group's life. The facilitation of "lab" groups requires a trainer/facilitator of considerable self-insight and small group skills whose cardinal rule is not to try to make things happen in the group.

Organizational behavior courses and laboratory groups sometimes use a "micro-lab" as an event, to get acquainted or as a sampler of things to come. A micro-lab is a set of instructor-led, short, structured, verbal and nonverbal activities in which constantly changing pairs, trios, or very small groupings of students are invited to cyclically experience and then discuss common OB phenomena in new ways. Typical activities might include: introducing oneself in unconventional ways, experimenting with physical proximity in conversation, expressing positive and negative feelings nonverbally, orchestrated self-disclosure and its impact on trust development, short-guided fantasies, and the like.

Some OB instructors structure and manage their courses to resemble actual organizations—either for one or a few classes or for the whole term (Putzel, 1992; Schwartz, 1984–1985). Most organizational phenomena can be then experienced by the students—to focus upon periodically as examples of cognitive learning, or to practice OB and managerial skills. Common topics examined through this class–as–organization methodology are the effects of goals, reward systems, managerial style, hierarchy, coordination and conflict, attributions, leadership, and alternative tasks and technologies. Thematic in this technique is learning to learn from experience that counts–now in an OB course that resembles a real organization and later from a real organization that hopefully resembles the OB course.

Organizational behavior instructors have been unusually creative in exploiting all sorts of real experiences for OB learning. Many students have work experience, often current, that when understood by means of OB concepts and models, becomes especially meaningful. The same is true for internships, living and athletic experiences, student-run businesses (e.g., Miller, 1991), student consulting projects (e.g., Tubbs, 1984–1985), Outward Bound excursions (Lewicki, 1975), and student field work and case writing, almost any experience that incorporates responsibility and accomplishment. All sorts of personally meaningful student out-of-class experience can be used to illustrate OB ideas and findings, discover constraining contingencies, and otherwise solidify OB knowledge. The commonality in each of the techniques briefly mentioned above is the student learning opportunity from their own firsthand experience where they are involved in the situation for some meaningful purpose other than studying OB.

The Case Method

The major alternative to all of the techniques discussed earlier, both from a pedagogical and a usage point of view, is the case method of instruction. It is probably the major teaching technique in most executive programs and many graduate business programs, and to a lesser extent in undergraduate programs, which attempt to link the classroom to the realities of business by engaging the student in a practice-oriented, problem-solving modality. The case method has, from its inception 75 years ago, been used for all business subjects.

The case method originated at the Harvard Business School in the early 1900s under its first two deans, Gay and Donham (Christensen, 1989). It began simply enough with executives invited to come to class with a write-up of their own company problems to lead the class in a discussion of them. Soon, however, cases written by faculty and research assistants became the dominant source as they are today at Harvard and several other schools. Cases attempt to mate knowledge and action, not by first passively learning knowledge and then applying it, but in accordance with the principles elucidated by John Dewey, that is, education consists of the cumulative and unending acquisition, combination, and reordering of learning experiences. In Dewey's (Soltes, 1971) words, "Only by wrestling with the conditions of the problem at hand, seeking and finding his own way out, does he think. . . . If he cannot devise his own solution . . . and find his own way out he will not learn, not even if he can recite some correct answer with one hundred percent accuracy" (p. 83).

The case method recognizes that managers must be able to meet in action the problems arising out of new situations in an ever changing environment. As an early Harvard professor, Dewing (1931) stated, a proper business education ". . . would consist of acquiring facility to act in the presence of new experience. It asks not how a man be trained to know, but how a man be trained to act" (p. 49). The origins, educational philosophy, and development of the case method are chronicled by Andrews (1953), Christensen (1989), Erskine, Leenders, and Maufette-Leenders (1981) and Towl (1969). The case method has not, of course, been without criticism and debate. See, for example, articles by Argyris (1980), Berger (1983), Reynolds (1978), and Turner (1981).

The Basic Case and Its Use.   A written case is most usually a description of an actual situation, commonly involving one or more decisions or problems, and normally written from the viewpoint of the decision makers involved. Cases allow students to figuratively step into the shoes of the managers involved. A typical case is, therefore, a record of some situation actually faced by a manager with the facts, opinions, prejudices upon which decisions depend. In this regard, Lawrence (1953) noted:

> A good case is the vehicle by which a chunk of reality is brought into the classroom to be worked over by the class and instructor. A good case keeps the class discussion grounded upon some of the stubborn facts that must be faced in real life situations.

It is the anchor on academic flights of speculation. It is the record of complex situations that must be literally pulled apart and put together again for the expression of attitudes or ways of thinking brought into the classroom (p. 215).

A true case is not a fictional account (so-called armchair cases), or simply a set of data, or a journalistic account. A real teaching case is the product of careful field work. The case method uses a clinical approach of learning by doing, blending both cognitive and affective learning. It has a compelling power to involve students in a highly personal learning experience as a consequence of several reasons. Students have to repeatedly confront the intractability of reality (e.g., the absence of needed information, the ever present conflict of objectives, and the imbalance between needs and resources). There is the imperative of relating analysis and action (the application of always partial knowledge to the complexities of a situation that requires doable, concrete action). The discussion provides students with practice in managerial skills (observation, listening, diagnosing, deciding, persuading, and intervening in group processes). Students also acquire a general, managerial perspective (where a person accepts responsibility for action with a sense of what is critical and possible in an interconnected, bounded specific context).

The role of the instructor for effective case teaching is crucial. Foregoing the role and status of a center stage, intellectually superior authority figure, a case discussion leader guides a process of discovery. Facilitating a case discussion is an act composed of asking questions that reveal the relevance of the discussion and invite advances in thinking, weaving together individual contributions into patterns that all can perceive, and intervening to speed up, slow down, and focus the discussion. At present, the artistry required for case discussion leadership is often aided by detailed case teaching notes, written conceptual and industry notes, phenomenon-focused modules (a sequential set of cases and readings), and a few models for analyzing cases and guiding case discussions (e.g., Clawson & Frey, 1986–1987; Hogan, 1984; Lundberg, 1993).

Use of the case method began before the emergence of OB. In the beginning, the phenomena of OB were addressed in all functional business courses. Then, more and more, OB became the province of courses on general administrative practices. As the human side of enterprise became more appreciated, what we now term as *OB* surfaced and coalesced in a field termed *human relations*. Both "administrative practices" and "human relations" were nearly pure case courses initially, but began to add substantive readings on OB ideas as they appeared in the literature. This model of teaching, for example, the classroom devoted to cases, with conceptual readings as additional homework, is still popular. Yet, for all of its distinctiveness, the classic case method, especially in OB, has spawned many variations.

Variations of the Case Method. The most frequently seen OB case is a relatively short, topic-focused one—the sort of case seen at the end of a text chapter. Ostensibly offering an opportunity for problem solving, these short cases are actually devices for sensitizing students to the phenomena on which the chapter focuses conceptually—a far cry from the classic case as described earlier. A related case variation focuses on some innovative managerial technique or practice (e.g., executive compensation), describing it and its implementation in a specific situation—providing diagnostic practice and new knowledge. Other special purpose cases are written from a practitioner's perspective. These are designed to give students practice in problem identification. There are also data rich cases without a decision maker used to provide practice in applying a conceptual scheme or model.

Organizational behavior cases vary from narrow to wide in phenomenological scope or issue complexity on the one hand, and from short to long in terms of their time frame. At one extreme there are "iceberg" cases that describe some symptomology and a situation in outline at a point in time asking of students to specify what other information they wish to have and why, in order to do an adequate analysis. At the other extreme are series of cases in which a case is given and is followed by another case at a later time—sometimes over many years of real time—where students can see the consequences of predicted action recommendations. There has been and continues to be innovation in case teaching. Gadon (1976), for example, introduced case discussions designed to generate some of the same issues as in the case, thereby raising students' level of involvement and experiential learning. Gallos (1992) used the same case repeatedly but asked her students to use different perspectives each time. Molstad and Levy (1987–1988) developed experiential analogues to cases, and Lundberg (1989–1990) created realistic action experiences in role-plays following case endings. Cases also have been developed utilizing multiple media (e.g., a written case with audio and/or video parts).

CONCEPTUAL CONSIDERATIONS

Our inventory of OB classroom teaching techniques has shown that their adoption mostly depends, in large part, on the learning objectives sought. OB courses, like most management curricula, emphasize knowledge acquisition, skill development, or attitude change (Summer, 1956), or some combination of these. Traditional techniques tend to be used for knowledge acquisition. Experience-loaded techniques are used for particular knowledge and skill acquisition. Experience that counts is used for attitude change as well as knowledge and skill learning. The case method is used for teaching more generalized managerial skills and perspectives. In this section I highlight several fundamental considerations that influence and constrain OB course design and teaching technique selection.

Fundamentals About Learning

Behind the adoption of a teaching technology is some belief about how students learn. Although the distinction is, no doubt, overdrawn, there seem to be three quite different assumptions. The first, probably prevalent assumption, holds that students need to have knowledge before they can apply it. The second assumption holds that with appropriate experiences, particularized knowledge is easier to acquire and use. The third assumption holds that general competencies (combinations of skills and practical knowledge) are best acquired through repetitive, meaningful experiences. At the root of these three different assumptions is the relationship between knowledge and behavior. Although few OB instructors would argue that knowledge equals behavior, the degree to which knowledge is presumed to influence behavior is debated. In part, this debate hinges upon the nature of the knowledge being discussed—whether abstract, conceptual knowledge, or concretized, factual knowledge. To a large extent, contemporary OB educators have sidestepped these debates by adopting the general, cyclic model of learning most clearly explicated by Kolb, Rubin, and McIntyre (1974). This cycle encompasses four elements—in order: active participation in a new experience ("concrete experience"); examination of that experience ("reflective observation"); integration of conclusions based on the new experience into workable models ("abstract conceptualization"); and application of the model to new situations ("active experimentation"). All OB teaching techniques may be conceived of emphasizing one or more parts of this model, initiating learning at different points in the cycle, and encompassing the whole cycle or some portion of it.

Organizational behavior teaching techniques also may or may not take account of other fundamental considerations. One major consideration has to do with students' maturity and/or their level of cognitive development (e.g., Gallos, 1988–1989). Here, teaching techniques should be congruent with students' needs to dependently acquire facts, interdependently explore ideas, independently develop judgment, and so forth. Learning for adult students is likewise presumed to reflect their stage of moral development (e.g., Torbert, 1987). Another consideration is the degree to which the learning activity holds the potential to upend or upset the student (Shaw, 1957). Upending refers to the degree to which any new piece of knowledge is consistent with what is already known. If it is close, then knowledge is easy to accept but little real learning occurs. If it is different, then more real learning occurs. If there is a large degree of incongruency, there is the risk of no learning because students will likely be upset and revert to defensive behavior and rationalizations. A third fundamental consideration has to do with the effectiveness of vicarious learning (Bandura, 1977) and cooperative learning (Johnson & Johnson, 1987). A fourth, and some would say the most critical, consideration has to do with the level of authoritarianism inherent in the structure of the teaching technique (e.g., Berg, 1984). When the instructor specifies the learning objectives, structures the activity, and predetermines what correct learning is, regardless of the content, the meta-learning may be the reinforcement of dependency and obedience and the subtle legitimation of hierarchical, superordinate relationships, as well as the implicit affirmation that might is right. Still another fundamental consideration is whether or not the analytic process of knowledge discovery (i.e., the scientific practice of breaking phenomena into analytically separable parts to enhance rigorous research), if reflected in teaching, handicaps meaningful learning. The assumption that students can or will assemble separate OB skills or bits of OB knowledge into coherent, meaningful wholes has been questioned (e.g., Vaill, 1989). A related consideration is whether the piecemeal approach taken in OB courses (and courses taken in other subjects) actually prepares students for the " . . . messiness, contingency, sprawl, and indeed, danger of the real managerial world" (Vaill, 1992, p. 133). Most OB teaching, it appears, presumes a degree of pattern and consistency of phenomena that may not reflect the randomness of some realities. Finally, there is the fundamental consideration of ideology. Organizational behavior knowledge mostly presumes to be neutral in value, yet OB teaching as a professional practice, is never completely value free. Organizational behavior teaching implicitly adopts one or more ideological stances—ideology, here following Gouldner's (1979) meaning that it serves the material and ideal interests of the group that espouses it. At least three ideologies are implicit in OB teaching: managerial (knowledge developed and appropriated in service of the managerial and capitalistic elite to improve productivity, control, and ultimately, profitability), humanistic (knowledge used to develop human potential by promoting emotional maturity, open communication, ethical behavior, etc.), and, to a lesser extent, critical (knowledge used to challenge the exploitation and domination of the less powerful by the more powerful).

Training Versus Education

Underlying the choices implicit in the several considerations above, is a still more basic design issue. Some OB instructors believe that the field has developed to the stage where we know, in large part, not only what causes behavior but what practices are most effective. These educators tend to view OB instruction as training—teaching techniques are selected that ostensibly enable students to learn how to perform some activity correctly.

Alternatively, some OB instructors believe that the field is such that we are just beginning to really understand the causes and consequences of behavior. These educators tend to view OB instruction as education—selecting those classroom techniques that promote thinking better and learning how to learn. Professional students are thus encouraged to be "tough minded" (McNair, 1954) and engage in meta-learning (i.e., learning to continuously learn about OB phenomena from ongoing experience in and beyond the classroom).

Although the distinction just drawn no doubt both oversimplifies and exaggerates, woven into it are other seldom considered beliefs that condition OB classroom pedagogy, instructional design, and teaching performance. It makes a difference whether an OB educator believes OB should be taught as a science or as a field of applied practice; whether OB should be taught as a static body of knowledge emphasizing order and predictability or dynamically emphasizing conflict, messiness and change; and whether OB should promote student professional development or personal growth (Walter & Marks, 1981).

FUTURE DIRECTIONS OF OB CLASSROOM TEACHING

In this last section I turn to the future. Organizational behavior classroom instruction from its inception has continuously evolved. Although we now have a sizable inventory of teaching techniques upon which to draw, and a growing awareness of their manifest and latent functions, OB instruction, at present, is easily characterized as a field in transition. There are several disturbing trends in OB education that, if continued on their present course, may make OB teaching increasingly irrelevant for future managers.

1. The teaching process is becoming increasingly mechanized as evidenced by large classes, low instructor contact, computer scored objective exams, complete publisher teaching packages, little student writing, trivialization of competency development, and the analytic separation of topics and issues.
2. Teaching materials continue to ignore or downplay contexts (especially international and industrial contexts), as well as continue to emphasize industrial era examples and findings.
3. Knowledge is taught as objective truth, both theory and prescription tends toward overgeneralization as well as oversimplification and abstraction, and OB knowledge is becoming relatively self-sealed, that is, there is relatively little connection to OB's underlying behavioral science disciplines.
4. Management is too often narrowly conceived as an organizational "role" that downplays the whole person, the manager's peer and superordinate relationships, part in the community and society, and his or her own developmental processes.
5. There is an emphasis on well structured and familiar problems handled in rationalistic ways. Messy, complex, interrelated problems in situations of uncertainty and ambiguity (dilemmas, predicaments, and paradoxes) tend to be underrepresented.

Three questions will guide the following discussion: What can or should be taught and how? What is required of OB educators in the coming years? What does the future hold for classroom techniques?

Topics and Course Emphasis

The contemporary content of OB is both wide and deep. We have many ideas, models, and theories about the major units of analysis (e.g., the person, small groups, multigroup contexts) and the processes within and between these units. This content continues to be refined and extended as the work in this volume aptly demonstrates. In the future, we anticipate that some ideas that have fallen out of fashion (e.g., status, social class, semantics), will be reinserted back into OB courses. We may also anticipate that many relatively new topics and issues will get even more attention (e.g., empowerment, international OB, Adler, 1986; culture, McCarthy & Trice, 1985–1986; emotions, Lindsay, 1992; gender, Sullivan & Buttner, 1992; ethics, McCormick & Fleming, 1989–1990; race, Waters, 1991; diversity, and so on). No doubt we will see increasing attention given to studying OB in a greater variety of contexts, such as family enterprises, service professions, Third World organizations, and the like. It seems probable too that OB educators will turn to basic processes (e.g., attention, the honing of judgmental skills, creative abilities, and moral values), common but as yet not well understood situations (e.g., paradox, Berg & Smith, 1987–1988), ill-structured or divergent problems (Cameron, 1986), and seriously introduce new perspectives (e.g., feminism and post-modernism). The time also seems ripe to once again begin to borrow ideas and models form OB's underlying disciplines.

With an increasing awareness of the conceptual considerations in teaching OB, several emphases may be predicted. The micro-macro distinction is likely to continue to blur. There probably will continue to be an emphasis on OB competency acquisition but with more attention to their integration and contextual contingencies. Analysis for analysis' sake is probably a thing of the past, with analysis in service of action much more common. Organizational behavior courses and modules are also likely to be more carefully differentiated for the type of the student audience (e.g., Neilsen, 1986–1987; Payne & Brannen, 1989–1990; Rahim, 1986), whether course purpose is training or education, and whether they prepare students for their first, second, or later career positions. We can also anticipate that OB texts, now all too frequently look-alike inventories of all possible ideas, will become increasingly differentiated. For example, we need some texts that are a lot more practitioner relevant as well as some academically sophisticated, that are better attuned to different levels of student experience, and that illustrate the negative side of organizational behavior as well as the positive.

Course emphasis and content coverage are features of OB teaching that, in conjunction with resource availability, instructor training and proclivities, and curricular thrust, get reflected in the choice of classroom techniques.

Faculty Development

The several topical and course emphasis choices just outlined suggest that OB faculty development will become more important. To meet the increasing demands for relevance by our naive, as well as sophisticated, students will require that OB educators go beyond teaching as they were taught, or using whatever technique is currently in vogue. Instead, with a deep and thorough knowledge of OB, an increased repertoire of teaching methods, and instructional competencies, the OB educator will be better able to design teaching–learning situations and continue to learn as an OB educator.

As the other chapters of this volume attest, OB knowledge and its production is swiftly moving forward. OB teachers will have to work hard to just keep up with their field. Perhaps just as important, however, will be the need to "deepen" their knowledge in three ways. One way is to become informed about the historical roots of developing knowledge—knowing original sources instead of interpretive summaries. Another is to know the philosophy behind ontological and epistemological debates instead of blindly accepting today's ascendant favorite (Morgan & Smircich, 1980). The third type of deep knowledge will be the ability to identify OB theory and findings paradigmatically and ideologically.

Acquiring a large "tool kit" of classroom techniques also will be required. Without an appreciation of their strengths and weaknesses, it is too easy to violate students' developmental needs and the evolving professional requirements of the emerging postindustrial society. Given OB's subject matter, we might expect OB faculty to have formally addressed issues of technique effectiveness, alternative learning styles, written assignments, grading systems, test formats, and the like, but this has not been the case. It's as if either some OB faculty feel these issues should be farmed out to the faculty of schools of education or fervently, if amateurishly, tackled. The time seems ripe for OB's research and assessment sophistication to be applied to OB teaching technologies and practices.

OB teachers, to be more than just knowledge disseminators or to simply teach a subject, need training in course design, implementation of alternative pedagogies, and so forth; that is, research training does not suffice. Organizational behavior faculty also have to go beyond the technical skills of teaching (e.g., setting behavioral objectives and structuring learning activities), to being able to authentically develop a repertoire of classroom management styles and roles as each new situation demands. Here, the images of the OB educator as a clinician, a role model, a designer, and an action researcher will become increasingly relevant. By "clinician" I am referring to a sensitivity to ongoing classroom dynamics (including those in oneself) in situo—that is, being continuously aware of situational demands, indicators of student reactions, alterations in classroom climate, and so on. By "role model" I am referring to consciously and appropriately performing several roles (e.g., manager, learner, team member, etc.), for the purpose of demonstrating useful behavior to students. By "designer" I am referring to combining our understanding of the teaching-learning and developmental processes with available classroom techniques and technologies to optimize student learning. By "action-researcher" I am referring to learning from classroom interventions to continuously improve practice (Lundberg & Westacott, 1982).

Classroom Techniques

Classroom techniques are selected to reflect a set of factors such as resources, facilities, constituencies, purposes, and learning models (e.g., Lundberg & Motamedi, 1978) according to some sequencing and combinatorial model (e.g., Posner & Randolph, 1978; Randolph & Posner, 1979) resulting in configurations and applications of an amazing variety (e.g., Schwindt, 1990). Two ongoing developments will no doubt complicate what we know about course design and technique adaption and innovation. I am referring here to videos and computers. Today's students are sometimes called "the video generation" because almost every student has grown up with television, with its potential for dramatizing. Not surprisingly, students have become accustomed to the passivity of being in an audience. Does the OB educator teach to countervail television's impact or attempt to exploit it? To what extent can written, audio, and experiential teaching materials be effectively substituted with video? The answers to these and similar questions are as yet unclear, but considerable innovation and experimentation is beginning to take place.

As students gain familiarity and confidence with computers, all sorts of computer-assisted instructional methods have emerged. Statistical programs make the analysis of data quite easy, thereby encouraging student research, diagnosing their work groups, speeding up case analysis, and so on. Computer-assisted simulations are appearing, as are interactional problem sets and cases (Rude, 1988–1989) and computerized tutors (Bigelow, 1988–1989). New uses and creative materials are appearing continuously.

For all of the development in OB teaching methods and materials, however, several gaps exist that beg to be examined in future work. OB educators are presently designing their courses and selecting both teaching materials and methods primarily in terms of topics and ideas and secondarily in terms of contexts. Needed, it seems, are issue-focused materials and methods aiding exploration of organizational decline, crises, shortened product life cycles, technological change, organizational injustice, and the like. Although many organizational practices are now being examined and experienced (e.g., performance appraisal, enriched job design, participative decision making, etc.), there is much room for practice-focused innovation (e.g., the service encounter, alternative human resource strategies, flexitime, quality circles, boundary-spanning roles, devolutionary teams, most sense making activities, etc.). We also need to create learning situations that enable students to learn to grapple with organizational realities (e.g., being really responsible for outcome consequences, a workforce highly variable in terms of literacy, conflicts in basic assumptions about worker–manager relations, and the like). In part, these gaps just mentioned require a reorientation or retranslation of OB knowledge for instructional purposes from neutral science to an actor perspective.

Classroom techniques also need exploration and trials in terms of how and with what consequences they deal with students as individuals, as small and large batches, and in general audiences. We know very little, for example, about the uses and limitations of self-paced instruction, the structures and conditions for self-learning groups, or the impact on attitudes and behavior in vicarious learning situations. We need to experiment with and learn from alternative ways to move from knowledge acquisition to analytical maturity to judgment enhancement and even wisdom (e.g., Gentry & Burns, 1981). These and other cracks in our pedagogical knowledge beg innovation and research.

CONCLUSION

In this chapter, I endeavored to do several things: sketch the historical circumstances of OB classroom teaching, describe the rich and expanding array of OB teaching techniques currently available, suggest several fundamental conceptual considerations behind OB's classroom pedagogies and materials, and offer some conjecture of where OB teaching is and should be going. Organizational behavior classroom teaching is an unusually challenging endeavor. Choices abound—for content, methods, and course design—exacerbated by a growing knowledge base, new pedagogical innovations, new and differentiated student populations, curricular reforms, and changing organizational and societal contexts. Although OB may lead other business fields in terms of the vitality and variety of its instruction, much still needs to be learned about what is appropriate and effective. The early aspiration of OB classroom teaching has been clearly met; the present is exciting; and the future of OB teaching is promising indeed.

REFERENCES

Adler, N. J. (1986). *International dimensions of organizational behavior.* Boston: Kent.

Allen, B., & Enz, C. (1986–1987). Journal writing: Exercises in creative thought and expression. *Organizational Behavior Teaching Review, 11*(4), 1–14.

Ambuske, G., Locke, K., & Manning, M. P. (1987–1988). Replication: One pedagogical approach for teaching research methods. *Organizational Behavior Teaching Review, 12*(3), 45–53.

Andrews, K. R. (1953). *The case method of teaching human relations and administration.* Cambridge, MA: Harvard University Press.

Argyris, C. (1980). Some limitations of the case method: Experience in a management development program. *Academy of Management Review, 5,* 291–298.

Balke, W. M. (1981). The policy learning co-op: Treating the classroom as an organization. *Exchange, 6,* 27–32.

Bandura, A. (1977). *Social learning theory.* Englewood Cliffs, NJ: Prentice-Hall.

Barnard, C. I. (1938). *The functions of the executive.* Cambridge, MA: Harvard University Press.

Berg, D. N. (1984). Authority and experiential methods. *Organizational Behavior Teaching Methods, 9*(1), 36–41.

Berg, D. N., & Smith, K. K. (1987–1988). The management of paradox in the educational process. *Organizational Behavior Teaching Review, 12*(1), 1–15.

Berger, M. (1983). In defense of the case method. A reply to Argyris. *Academy of Management Review, 8*, 327–333.

Bigelow, J. D. (1988–1989). A computerized management readiness tutor: Development and implementation. *Organizational Behavior Teaching Review, 13*(1), 48–57.

Bolman, L., & Deal, T. E. (1979). A simple–but powerful–power simulation. *Exchange, 4*(3), 38–41.

Bowditch, J. L., & Buono, A. F. (1990). *A primer on organizational behavior* (2nd ed.). New York: Wiley.

Bowen, D. D. (1980). Experiential and traditional teaching in OB: A dubious distinction. *Exchange, 5*(3), 7–12.

Bradford, L. P., Gibb, J. R., & Benne, K. D. (1964). *T–group theory and laboratory method.* New York: Wiley.

Bretton, J. H. (1991). Simulating organizations: A student-documented history of emergent behavior. *Journal of Management Education, 15*(2), 193–205.

Cameron, K. S. (1986). Effectiveness as paradox: Consensus and conflict in conceptions of organizational effectiveness. *Management Science, 35*(5), 539–553.

Christensen, C. R. (1989). *Teaching and the case method.* Boston: Harvard Business School.

Clark, J. V. (1962). *Education for the use of behavioral science.* Los Angeles: Institute of Industrial Relations, University of California at Los Angeles.

Clawson, J. G., & Frey, S. C. Jr. (1986–1987). Mapping case pedagogy. *Organizational Behavior Teaching Review, 11*(1), 1–8.

Clawson, J. G., & Pfeifer, P. E. (1989–1990). Global markets. *Organizational Behavior Teaching Review, 14*(2), 70–81.

Costello, T. W., & Zalkind, S. S. (1963). *Psychology in administration.* Englewood Cliffs, NJ: Prentice-Hall.

Cowden, A. C. (1989–1990). Mystery novels as organizational context. *Organizational Behavior Teaching Review, 14*(2), 93–101.

Dale, E. (1960). *The great organizers.* New York: McGraw-Hill.

Dewing, A. S. (1931). An introduction to the use of cases. In C. E. Fraser (Eds.), *The case method of instruction* (pp. 1–5). New York: McGraw-Hill.

Dyer, W. G. (1978). *Team building: Issues and alternatives.* Reading, MA: Addison–Wesley.

Erskine, J. A., Leenders, M. R., & Mauffette-Leenders, L. R. (1981). *Teaching with cases.* London, Canada: Research and Publications Division, School of Business Administration, The University of Western Ontario.

Ewens, W. (1985–1986). Teaching using discussion. *Organizational Behavior Teaching Review, 10*(3), 77–80.

Finney, M., & Siehl, C. (1985–1986). The current MBA: Why are we failing? *Organizational Behavior Teaching Review, 10*(3), 1–11.

Frost, P. J., Nord, W. R., & Mitchell, V. (1992). *Organizational reality: Reports from the firing line* (4th ed.). New York: HarperCollins.

Gabarro, J. J. (1991). *Managing people and organizations.* Boston, MA: Harvard Business School.

Gadon, H. (1976). Teaching cases experientially. *Exchange, 2*(1 & 2), 20–24.

Gallos, J. V. (1988–1989). Developmental diversity and management education: Implications for teaching and learning. *Organizational Behavior Teaching Review, 13*(4), 33–47.

Gallos, J. V. (1992). Revisiting the same case: An exercise in reframing. *Journal of Management Education, 16*(2), 257–261.

Gentry, J. W., & Burns, A. C. (1981). Operationalizing a test of a model of the use of simulation games and experiential exercises. *Developments in Business Simulation and Experimental Exercises, 19*, 54–57.

Gioia, D. A. (1986–1987). Contribution! Not participation in the management education classroom. *Organizational Behavior Teaching Review, 11*(4), 15–20.

Gordon, R. A., & Howell, J. E. (1959). *Higher education for business.* New York: Columbia University Press.

Gouldner, A. W. (1979). *The future of the intellectual and the rise of the new class.* New York: Continuum Press.

Greenberg, J., & Baron, R. (1993). *Behavior in organizations* (4th ed.). Needham Heights, MA: Allyn & Bacon.

Greenhalgh, L. (1979). Simulating an ongoing organization. *Exchange, 4*(3), 23–27.

Grover, R. A., & Greenberg, J. (1983). A note on the role and potency of "War Stories" in teaching organizational behavior. *Exchange, 8*(4), 38–40.

Guest, R. H. (1976). Teaching OB through field research and consultation projects. *Exchange, 2*(1 & 2), 13–19.

Hall, D. T., Bowen, D. D., Lewicki, R. J., & Hall, F. S. (1982). *Experiences in management and organizational behavior* (2nd ed.). New York: Wiley.

Hogan, E. (1984). Using a model for case analysis in case method instruction. *Organizational Behavior Teaching Review, 9*(2), 38–48.

Johnson, D. W., & Johnson, R. T. (1987). *Learning together and alone: Cooperative, competitive, and individualistic learning.* Englewood Cliffs, NJ: Prentice–Hall.

Kaupins, G. E. (1989–1990). Ideas for integrating organizational behavior into internships. *Organizational Behavior Teaching Review, 14*(4), 39–45.

Kidder, T. (1981). *The soul of a new machine.* New York: Avon Books.

Klein, S. M., & Ritti, R. R. (1980). *Understanding organizational behavior.* Boston: Kent.

Kolb, D. A., Rubin, I., & McIntyre, J. M. (Eds.). (1974). *Organizational psychology: A book of readings* (2nd ed.). Englewood Cliffs, NJ: Prentice-Hall.

Kriger, M. P. (1989–1990). The art and power of asking questions. *Organizational Behavior Teaching Review, 14*(1), 131–142.

Lawrence, P. (1953). The preparation of case material. In K. R. Andrews (Eds.), *The case method of teaching human relations and administration* (pp. 215–224). Cambridge, MA: Harvard University Press.

Leavitt, H. J. (1958). *Managerial psychology.* Chicago: University of Chicago Press.

Leavitt, H. J., & Pondy, L. R. (1964). *Readings in managerial psychology.* Chicago: The University of Chicago Press.

Lewicki, R. J. (1975). Outward bound and sensitivity training: Experiential learning in the wild. *Exchange, 1*(2), 20–24.

Lindsay, C. (1992). Learning through emotion: An approach for integrating student and teacher emotions into the classroom. *Journal of Management Education, 16*(1), 25–38.

Lundberg, C. (1989–1990). Case follow-up role plays: One way of creating realistic action experiences. *Organizational Behavior Teaching Review, 14*(1), 157–158.

Lundberg, C. (1993). A framework for student case preparation. *Case Research Journal, 2,* 132–144.

Lundberg, C., & Lundberg, J. (1992). Student team analysis: An experiential task. *Journal of Management Education, 16*(3), 371–373.

Lundberg, C., & Motamedi, K. (1978). Toward extending the teaching of organizational behavior. *Exchange, 3*(1), 14–20.

Lundberg, C., & Westacott, G. A. (1982). Enhancing instructional practices: Models and methods of self-research. In C. Cooper, R. Freedman, & S. Strumph (Eds.), *Management education* (pp. 59–85). New York: Wiley.

Machiavelli, N. (1958). *The prince.* London: J. M. Dent & Sons.

Maier, M. (1989, June). *The academic applications of video.* Paper presented at the 16th Organizational Behavior Teaching Conference, Columbia, MO.

Maier, N. R. F., & Solem, A. R. (1951). Audience role-playing: A new method in human relations training. *Human Relations, 4,* 279–294.

Marx, R. D. (1985–1986). In search of excellence: How to use a bestseller in the OB classroom. *Organizational Behavior Teaching Review, 10*(3), 87–92.

Marx, R., Jick, T. D., & Frost, P. J. (1991). *Management live! The video book.* Englewood Cliffs, NJ: Prentice-Hall.

McCarthy, S., & Trice, H. M. (1985–1986). Teaching about organizational cultures: The field format. *Organizational Behavior Teaching Review, 10*(3), 19–29.

McCormick, D. W., & Fleming, J. (1989–1990). Teaching ethics means practicing ethics. When a student says his company is breaking the law. *Organizational Behavior Teaching Review, 14*(3), 14–21.

McNair, M. P. (1954). Tough-mindedness and the case method. In M. P. McNair (Ed.), *The case method at the Harvard Business School* (pp. 15–24). New York: McGraw-Hill.

Miller, D. C., & Form, W. H. (1951). *Industrial sociology.* New York: Harper & Brothers.

Miller, J. A. (1991). Experiencing management: A comprehensive, "hands-on" model for the introductory undergraduate management course. *Journal of Management Education, 15*(2), 151–169.

Molstad, C., & Levy, S. (1987–1988). Developing experiential analogs to cases. *Organizational Behavior Teaching Review, 12*(2), 28–32.

Moorhead, G., & Griffin, R. W. (1989). *Organizational behavior* (2nd ed.). Boston: Houghton Mifflin.

Morgan, G., & Smircich, L. (1980). The case for qualitative research. *Academy of Management Review, 5*(4), 491–500.

Muhs, W. (chair). (1989, August). *The Committee on Human Relations in Industry of the University of Chicago.* Symposium conducted at the meeting of the Academy of Management, Washington, DC.

Natemeyer, W. E. (1978). *Classics of organizational behavior.* Oak Park, IL: Moore.

Nath, R. (1975). The management training laboratory: An experiential orientation to the MBA program. *Exchange, 1*(2), 10–15.

Neilsen, E. H. (1986–1987). Two roles, four realities in the executive classroom. *Organizational Behavior Teaching Review, 11*(3), 1–15.

Nord, W. R. (1972). *Concepts and controversy in organizational behavior.* Santa Monica, CA: Goodyear.

Odiorne, G. S. (1976). The role of the lecture in management education. *Exchange, 2*(3), 7–14.

Orth, C. D. III. (1963). *Social structure and learning climate: The first year at the Harvard Business School.* Boston: Division of Research, Graduate School of Business Administration, Harvard University.

Paul, K., & Barbato, R. (1984–1985). The organization game: Its use and life cycle. *Organizational Behavior Teaching Review, 9*(3), 53–59.

Payne, S. L., & Brannen, D. E. (1989–1990). Doctoral programs in management and business administration: Investigation of criticisms and reforms. *Organizational Behavior Teaching Review, 14*(3), 1–13.

Pierson, F. C. (1959). *The education of American businessmen.* New York: McGraw-Hill.

Pigors, P. J. W., & Pigors, F. (1961). *Case method in human relations: The incident process.* New York: McGraw-Hill.

Porras, J. I. (1975). Using personal journals in cognitive and experiential courses. *Exchange, 1*(2), 30–33.

Posner, B. Z., & Randolph, W. A. (1978). A decision tree approach to decide when to use different pedagogical techniques. *Exchange, 3*(2), 16–19.

Puffer, S. (1991). *Managerial insight from literature.* Boston: PWS-Kent.

Putzel, R. (1992). "Experience base" learning: A classroom-as-organization using delegated, rank-order grading. *Journal of Management Education, 16*(2), 204–221.

Rahim, R. A. (1986). Organizational behavior courses for graduate students in business administration: Views from the tower and battlefield. *Psychological Reports, 49*, 583–592.

Randolph, W. A., & Miles, R. H. (1979). The organization game: A behaviorally played simulation. *Exchange, 4*(2), 31–34.

Randolph, W. A., & Posner, B. Z. (1979). Considerations in the design of learning situations. *Journal of Experiential Learning and Simulation, 1*, 267–276.

Rasmussen, R. V. (1986–1987). Starting off with a "bang!" rather than a whimper: The first lecture in the introductory OB course. *Organizational Behavior Teaching Review, 11*(3), 16–28.

Reynolds, J. I. (1978). There is method in cases. *The Academy of Management Review, 3*, 129–133.

Ritti, R. R., & Funkhouser, G. R. (1987). *The ropes to skip and the ropes to know* (3rd ed.). New York: Wiley.

Robbins, S. P. (1992). *Essentials of organizational behavior* (3rd ed.). Englewood Cliffs, NJ: Prentice–Hall.

Roethlisberger, F. J., & Dickson, W. J. (1939). *Management and the worker.* Cambridge, MA: Harvard University Press.

Roethlisberger, F. J., Lombard, G., & Ronken, H. (1954). *Training for human relations: An interim report.* Boston: Division of Research, Harvard Business School.

Rude, D. E. (1988–1989). Hardware, software and (soft stuff): Review of *Interactive Cases in Organizational Behavior. Organizational Behavior Teaching Review, 13*(3), 146–147.

Sata, L. S. (1978). Experiential methods in a large classroom setting. *Exchange, 3*(1), 31–33.

Schein, E. H. (1969). *Process consultation: Its role in organization development.* Reading, MA: Addison-Wesley.

Schwartz, R. M. (1984–1985). Grounded learning experiences: Treating the classroom as an organization. *Organizational Behavior Teaching Review, 9*(3), 16–30.

Schwindt, R. (1990). *Organizational behavior: Business administration reading lists and course outlines (Vol. 7).* Durham, NC: Eno River Press.

Scott, W. E., Jr., & Cummings, L. L. (1969). *Readings in organizational behavior and human performance.* Homewood, IL: Irwin.

Seltzer, J. (1988–1989). Experiences with Looking Glass. *Organizational Behavior Teaching Review, 13*(1), 58–65.

Shaw, F. J. (1957). Transitional experiences and psychological growth. *ETC, 15*, 39–45.

Sherman, D. (1988–1989). Interactive cases for introductory courses in organizational behavior: An emerging computer-aided instructional technique. *Organizational Behavior Teaching Review, 13*(4), 112–120.

Shirts, R. G. (1977). *Bafa Bafa: A cross culture simulation.* Del Mar, CA: Simile II.

Sieler, J. A. (1967). *Systems analysis in organizational behavior.* Homewood, IL: Irwin.

Solomon, G. T. (1979). A computer simulation exercise to acquire interpersonal competence. *Exchange, 4*(2), 25–36.

Soltes, J. (1971). Dewey, John. *Encyclopedia of Education* (pp. 81–85). New York: MacMillan.

Stevens, J. (1991). *Stephanie's world.* Philadelphia: St. Cecilia Press.

Strumph, S. A., & Dunbar, R. L. M. (1990). Using behavioral simulations in teaching strategic management processes. *Organizational Behavior Teaching Review, 14*(2), 43–62.

Sullivan, S. E., & Buttner, E. H. (1992). Changing more than the plumbing: Integrating women and gender differences into management and organizational behavior courses. *Journal of Management Education, 16*(1), 76–89.

Summer, C. E., Jr. (1956). *Factors in effective administration.* New York: Graduate School of Business, Columbia University.

Terkel, S. (1972). *Working.* New York: Ballantine.

Torbert, W. R. (1987). *Managing the corporate dream: Restructuring for long-term success.* Homewood, IL: Dow Jones–Irwin.

Towl, A. R. (1969). *To study administration by cases.* Boston: Graduate School of Business Administration, Harvard University.

Tubbs, S. L. (1984–1985). Consulting teams: A methodology for teaching integrated management skills. *Organizational Behavior Teaching Review, 9*(4), 52–57.

Turner, A. N. (1981). The case method revisited. *Exchange, 6*(3), 6–8.

Vaill, P. B. (1979). Cookbooks, auctions, and claptrap cocoons: A commentary on the field of organizational behavior. *Exchange, 4*(1), 3–6.

Vaill, P. B. (1981). Thoughts on using poetry in the teaching of OB. *Exchange, 6*(3), 50–51.

Vaill, P. B. (1989). *Managing as a performing art.* San Francisco: Jossey-Bass.

Vaill, P. B. (1992). Notes on "running an organization." *Journal of Management Inquiry, 1*(2), 130–138.

Viteles, M. S. (1953). *Motivation and morale in industry.* New York: Norton.

Waldo, D. (1948). *The administrative state.* New York: The Ronald Press.

Wall, J. A. (1986). *Bosses.* Lexington, MA: D.C. Heath.

Walter, G. A., & Marks, S. E. (1981). *Experiential learning and change: Theory, design and practice.* New York: Wiley.

Waters, H., Jr. (1991). Introducing race into the undergraduate organizational behavior course. *Journal of Management Education, 15*(4), 447–464.

Weber, R. J. (1976). Using videotape to teach organizational behavior. *Exchange, 2*(1 & 2), 37–42.

Weick, K. E., & Orton, J. D. (1986–1987). Academic journals in the classroom. *Organizational Behavior Teaching Review, 11*(2), 27–42.

Whetten, D. D., & Cameron, K. S. (1984). *Developing management skills.* Glenview, IL: Scott, Foresman.

Whyte, W. F. (1969). *Organizational behavior: Theory and application.* Homewood, IL: Irwin.

11

I/O AND OB IN THE MILITARY SERVICES: PAST, PRESENT, AND FUTURE

Delbert M. Nebeker*
Navy Personnel Research and Development Center,
San Diego, CA
and
California School of Professional Psychology, San Diego, CA

Industrial/organizational (I/O) psychology and organizational behavior (OB), as applied sciences, have many ties to subspecialties in psychology as well as other disciplines. Also, they have many ties to institutions and industries that have provided impetus and opportunity for them to develop. None of these ties, however, are as strong as the tie between I/O psychology and the military (Driskell & Olmstedt, 1989). In many respects the early history of I/O Psychology is simply the history of military psychology. Without support from the military, one can only speculate about whether I/O psychology would have thrived or died. There can be little doubt, though, that if I/O psychology had developed apart from the military it would be very different from what it is today.

Beginning with psychologists' efforts to aid the military in "the war to end all wars" (World War I) I/O psychology was born of necessity. Problems in military organizations needed the solutions offered by psychology. The size and nature of military organizations gave unique opportunities for the field to grow. Its development continued through World War II, the Korean and Vietnam conflicts, and most recently in Operation Desert Storm. Each of these events spurred the application of psychology to the performance problems of individuals, small groups or teams, and large military organizations. Today as the collapse of the Soviet Block signals Western victory in the cold war and the U.S. budget deficit sends shock waves through the U.S. economy and government, the legacy

---

*The views expressed in this chapter are those of the author, are not official and do not necessarily represent those of the Department of the Navy.

continues. These monumental events demand that the role of the U.S. Armed Forces be redefined; redefined to operate in a different and uncertain world—a world that may be more uncertain than at any time since the Civil War. Industrial/organizational psychology and organizational behavior will help create the military that will operate therein.

GOALS FOR CHAPTER

With these facts in mind I have four goals for this chapter. First, I describe the similarities and differences between nonmilitary and military organizations. Second, I review briefly the major forces and events that have shaped the history of I/O psychology and OB in the military. Third, I describe the current state of I/O psychology and OB in the military. Finally, I look to the future and provide some thoughts on where I/O psychology and OB in the military are likely headed and where I think they should be headed. In this chapter I attempt to provide a broad view of the state of I/O psychology and OB research and development (R&D) in the military. Space limitations make it impossible to provide a detailed account of even a small portion of the I/O and OB work currently underway in the military services. Also, my focus will be on the U.S. Military Services. Good I/O and OB work exists in the military services of most European nations and Israel (e.g., Gal & Mangelsdorff, 1991). Technical cooperative programs with participating countries and publications in the open literature make much of this work available. However, because the U.S. efforts generally outnumber and lead these other countries, little will be done to describe them. Eastern Bloc countries are a different matter, however. We know very little about what role psychology played in the military of the former Soviet Union and its satellites.

The reader should know that what I have written is to a large extent interpretive. I will present facts and examples to support my points; but I have no choice but to report only a small, selected portion of the literature and practice. Not everyone will agree with all my choices. Honest differences of professional opinion stimulate the discipline. My views on the history, current state of the field, and hopes for its future may be controversial among my colleagues. Critical discussion and self- assessment are the lifeblood of innovation, growth, and renewal in any discipline.

THE NATURE OF MILITARY ORGANIZATIONS

To understand I/O psychology and OB in the military, it is necessary to understand the nature of military organizations. How similar are military organizations to private business and nonmilitary government organizations? In what ways are they different? Are the differences important to the study and practice of I/O psychology and OB?

Measures of Performance

Military definitions of organizational performance are remarkably similar to those used in the private sector. At a conceptual level the definitions really do not differ at all—the key concept is *effectiveness*. Organizational effectiveness is defined as the extent to which an organization accomplishes its goals or mission (Cameron & Whetten, 1983; Tuttle, 1983). Modern military organizations consider themselves most effective (i.e., they accomplish their goals or "do the right things") if they deter aggression. That is to say they are most effective if they never have to perform the functions they spend years preparing to execute. If they do have to go to war, they seek to win swiftly, decisively, and with a minimum of casualties (General Accounting Office, 1993). It can be likened to a football team that practices all week long for the "big game" but has no opponent. How do you know how good they are if they never or only rarely play a game? Can you afford to wait until then to find out? Competing arguments hold that having a military that never fights a war is very inefficient. If you believe a standing military does nothing to protect your national interests and prevent hostility, never fighting is terribly inefficient because resources are wasted. On the other hand, if you believe that (a) wars are much more expensive than peace, and (b) having an excellent military deters war while promoting national interests, then a standing military is very efficient.

What substitutes for organizational effectiveness in the military? "Readiness" is the primary criterion used as a substitute any time a unit is not actually fighting. Expert judges evaluate a combat unit's readiness to fulfill any mission it may be assigned. Readiness is a surrogate for capability. Usually the judgments are made by external judges during inspections and exercises before a unit deploys. Once a unit is deployed, some aspects of its readiness are reported following self-assessments. Even when the judgments can be applied objectively, readiness still represents standardized expert judgment about how the unit would perform in a real combat situation. For example, the readiness of a naval ship may be assessed based on several factors. Are its equipment and weapon systems properly maintained and in good working order? Is the ship properly manned with qualified personnel in all key positions? Has the crew demonstrated proper preparation for battle or other missions by completing training cycles satisfactorily? Is the ship complying with all fiscal and procedural regulations?

Often an operational unit's effectiveness is evaluated during battle exercises and war games. Sometimes these exercises are against a computer enemy and at other times against members of own or allied forces operating as opponent forces with computers and other devices scoring the outcome (e.g., the Navy's Top Gun School).

For noncombat military organizations (e.g., maintenance, supply, logistics, training, etc.), the primary "customers" for their products and services are the combat units. It is to these and other customers that they are accountable. Like business organizations, noncombat support organizations must deliver: (a) quality products or services, (b) on time, and (c) at the lowest possible cost. Measures of these categories are similar to those found in private sector organizations where productivity, product quality, timeliness, and measures of process quality are used to evaluate effectiveness.

Measuring individual performance in the military raises many of the same issues mentioned for organizational performance, although to a lesser extent. It also raises criterion issues that are problematic in any setting (Borman, 1991). For combat personnel, effectiveness in battle is an important criterion. For the individual combatant, however, much greater weight is given to adherence to proscribed actions than for the results of those actions. The effectiveness of strategy, tactics, equipment, or planning is not typically part of the performance assessment of those on the front lines. What can be assessed is the quantity and quality of their knowledge and execution compared to the standards for the task (Wigdor & Green, 1991). In addition, almost all combat personnel have significant noncombat duties besides their combat tasks (e.g., maintenance of equipment). For these reasons, assessment of individual performance can be assessed more directly than organizational performance. Still, the measurement of individual performance, as currently practiced, is mostly a judgmental process. Supervisors still rate an individual's performance on a number of different dimensions. As in the private sector, the reliability and relevance of supervisor performance ratings can be questioned (Landy & Farr, 1983; Wigdor & Green, 1991).

Recently a 10-year project was undertaken to develop job performance measures for 30 military jobs (Wigdor & Green, 1991). The Joint Service Job Performance Measurement/Enlistment Standards Project (JPM) developed a broad spectrum of measures for these military jobs as the basis for validating selection and classification standards and was intended to establish criteria that would identify the necessary and sufficient level of ability for these jobs. It showed both the value and the expense of obtaining these kinds of measures. Building on this effort, the Army's Project A also used sophisticated methods to develop multiple and composite criteria for soldiers (Borman, 1991).

Besides ratings, two additional measures of individual performance are used. Successful completion of training, and length of service completed (retention), are valuable measures because of cost considerations. These criteria represent indirect assessments of individual job performance. Before individuals can be successful on the job they must successfully complete initial job training. Once initial training is completed, the longer they remain on the job the greater utility for the services. Both measures, alone and in combination with job performance ratings, are used as criteria in validating selection and classification procedures (Wigdor & Green, 1991).

Member Profile and Transitions

Although military institutions may be old and traditional, the members within military organizations are young and transient. Planned, frequent rotation is typical among all uniformed personnel. Two to four years in a given job or organization is the norm. Uniformed personnel average less than 30 years of age, which is almost six years younger than the rest of the U.S. workforce. Although women's roles in the military have expanded rapidly over the last 20 years, they still represent only approximately 11% of uniformed personnel (Department of Defense, 1992b). Each service differs in its gender and racial mix. African-Americans and Hispanics are overrepresented in the U.S. Army, and Marine Corps. In the U.S. Navy, African Americans are overrepresented, whereas Hispanics are underrepresented. The U.S. Air Force has the largest percentage of women in uniform among the U.S. services—over 15%. Of all large national armed forces, only Israel has a larger percentage of women in its military than the U.S. (Hoiberg, 1991). This is due to the Israeli mandatory conscription laws that require military service of both men and women. Contrary to popular belief, the Israel Defense Force (IDF) has not allowed women to occupy combat positions since 1949.

The military services operate chiefly as open systems (Katz & Kahn, 1978; Miller, 1978). Their personnel systems, however, differ from most other organizations. They only allow personnel entry in low level positions (young recruits and almost equally young junior officers). Personnel are moved through a complex system of training and rotational job assignments to prepare them for more responsibility and leadership. All uniformed mid-level and upper level positions are filled by individuals who entered at the bottom of either the officer or enlisted pipelines. Only a miniscule number of individuals enter the system at any level above the lowest entry points. Even those who enter at higher levels do so near the bottom of the authority hierarchy. The exception to this rule is in civilian leadership. The U.S. President, Secretary of Defense, and service secretaries are filled by "outside" personnel.

More than other organizations, a combat organization cannot depend upon outside training or experience to prepare personnel to function in its jobs. Movement out of the system is not completely free either. Individuals entering the services incur an obligation to remain for a contracted period. However, because most recruits enter the military to get postsecondary education and job training, they leave the service to pursue civilian careers after the minimum obligation. As a result, flow through the system is heavy and unflagging. The U.S. military conducts the largest job training programs in the world. This places a tremendous logistical burden on the training and job rotational systems. Consequently, most military organizations are the antitheses of the stability Japanese business organizations strive for. This makes it very difficult to provide continuity in behavior and leadership in any particular unit. At a more global level, however, some continuity is achieved through standardization of training, procedures, policy and tradition.

This standardization creates some interchangeability of personnel that helps an organizational unit adapt to change. Both planned and unintended change (e.g., rapid turnover or casualties in war) create uncertainty that can be disruptive. In other respects, the military acts like other open systems. They take in resources, transform them, and then deliver them as outputs to their customers.

Uniformed Versus Civilian Members of the Military

Until now, I discussed the human resources of military systems from the perspective of uniformed personnel. United States military organizations, however, fill many essential jobs with federal civilian employees and private civilian contractors. These civilians serve in positions ranging from the President (Commander-in-Chief) to custodial workers. Many of these positions are in industrial organizations in which over 90% of the personnel are civilians. Shipyards, aircraft, and motor vehicle depots that repair and overhaul military equipment and weapons systems (e.g., ships, aircraft, tanks, and missiles) are examples of these kinds of organizations. Industrial and logistical organizations throughout the Department of Defense (DoD) employ over 350,000 civilians in jobs nearly identical to those found in the private sector. Without their services the military could not operate. Often these organizations are required to compete with each other and private sector firms to win their workload. Consequently, these organizations have much in common with organizations doing the same kind of work in the private sector.

A SYSTEM FOR CATEGORIZING I/O PSYCHOLOGY ISSUES

The volume of literature and practice in I/O psychology and OB in the military is so large that an efficient method of classifying and organizing this work is necessary. This taxonomy will be used throughout this chapter to organize my presentation of issues important to I/O psychology and OB. The method I chose is rooted in both theory and practical application. Following the seminal work of Lewin (1951) and Vroom (1964), my taxonomy specifies that aspects of ability and motivation are found in both the person and in the work environment. One useful way of thinking of the relationship among these categories of variables is to present them in a two-by-two matrix.

Figure 11.1 presents such a taxonomy for performance variables. Some examples of the variables represented in the two-by-two classification system are also given. The person–ability cell of the taxonomy shows some personal characteristics or individual differences that enhance or limit the capacity of individuals to be productive. Individual intelligence, knowledge, physical aptitudes, and skills have an impact upon the ability of individuals to be productive. This list illustrates the kinds of variables that fall in this cell. Tests of these aptitudes, skills, and abilities are generally considered tests of maximal performance.

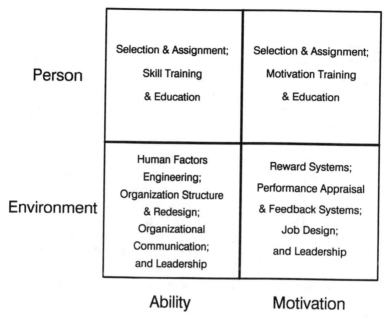

	Ability	Motivation
Person	Selection & Assignment; Skill Training & Education	Selection & Assignment; Motivation Training & Education
Environment	Human Factors Engineering; Organization Structure & Redesign; Organizational Communication; and Leadership	Reward Systems; Performance Appraisal & Feedback Systems; Job Design; and Leadership

FIG. 11.1.   Taxonomy of variables affecting performance.

Environmental attributes that have a major influence on individual and group ability to perform are shown in the environment–ability cell. These include the way an organization or work group is organized and managed; the tools and equipment available to reduce effort and increase capability; the efficiency of task methods; and the physical conditions of the work environment (heat, noise, vibration, motion, lighting, etc.).

The person–motivation cell represents the attributes that workers carry from situation to situation that help motivate them to be productive. Measures of these individual differences are often labeled measures of values, beliefs, attitudes, and personality. When correlated with job performance they are considered measures of typical performance. An individual's desire to excel (need for achievement), general beliefs in his or her own competence (self-efficacy), value placed on outcomes, and generalized beliefs in the consequences of his or her actions are examples of variables associated with motivation (Kanfer, 1991) and are included in this cell.

Finally, the environment–motivation cell lists those variables that are part of the work situation that have a major influence on motivation. These variables include the norms and sanctions of the work group toward high and low performers, financial and nonfinancial rewards, and other consequences administered by the organization or work group. The design of the task or job itself is also an environmental factor in motivation.

Categorizing I/O and OB Techniques

This taxonomy provides a useful system for generating and categorizing the variables that are important determinants of performance not only in military organizations but in all organizations. In addition, it provides a useful scheme for categorizing the various techniques developed to improve performance. There are many different forms of these techniques. Most of them attempt to change one or more of the variables in the taxonomy's cells. Some prominent techniques (e.g., leadership activities) attempt to influence multiple cells at the same time. This complicates classifying techniques cleanly in only one cell. Usually, however, most techniques have a primary emphasis. Another complicating factor is a level of analysis problem. For example, suppose a leadership training technique is primarily intended to increase the skill of identified leaders. The expected effect is to change leader capability. This is a person–ability technique. When, however, these behaviors are actually used with the leader's subordinates the technique's classification changes because the leader is part of the subordinate's environment. If the leader's behavior improves *subordinate* motivation it becomes an environment–motivation technique. Figure 11.2 lists a few examples of different types of techniques and shows their relationship to the performance determinants' taxonomy. The categories of techniques shown in Figure 11.2 are now discussed.

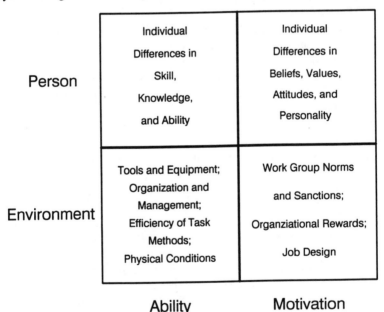

FIG. 11.2. Taxonomy of techniques to improve performance.

Person–Ability Techniques. These techniques usually emphasize classical personnel psychology. The selection of individuals based on tests of job relevant aptitudes and skills have positively contributed to the improvement of performance in organizations (Ghiselli, 1966; Guion, 1991; Schmitt, Gooding, Noe, & Kirsch, 1984). When those individuals most likely to succeed are brought into the organization, performance is enhanced. Training programs to improve employee knowledge, skill, and ability in accomplishing their jobs also have a positive effect on performance (Cascio, 1991; Goldstein, 1991).

Environment–Ability Techniques. In addition to I/O psychology and OB, professionals in a variety of other fields have often developed techniques for this cell. Industrial engineers, management scientists, and operations research analysts have all made contributions to improving ability through the variables in this cell (Hodson, 1992; Salvendy, 1992). Some techniques in this cell use new technology. Often they improve the tools, equipment, and methods used in productive activity. Mechanized or automated equipment and tools, robots, computers, and so forth, are just a few obvious examples. Organization designs, work methods, or equipment that eliminate unnecessary steps and motion or fit human capabilities better can also increase worker ability and hence performance. Organization design methods including sociotechnical systems design (Davis, 1983) and mechanisms to differentiate and integrate (e.g., division of labor and coordination) functions and activities are some examples. Techniques that improve the information available for planning and decision making belong here because they are designed to increase people's ability to be productive.

Person–Motivation Techniques. These techniques are logically similar to those used in the person–ability cell but with a different focus. Some techniques identify highly motivated individuals (or individuals likely to be more motivated than others in specific occupations) so they can be selected or matched to jobs. Others are designed to train or develop motivation directly in the individual. Informal methods (e.g., "pep talks"), as well as formal methods (e.g., motivation seminars and need achievement training) fall into this category. These techniques are frequently used with sales personnel in the civilian world. The documented benefits of these programs in the military (Braun, Weigand, & Aschenbrenner, 1991) have not been as strong as the techniques in the other cells.

Environment–Motivation Techniques. These techniques are designed to change the motivating potential of the work environment. They recognize the importance of the environment in influencing individual motivation. These techniques are developed with the understanding that changing the environment can produce substantial changes in the direction and intensity of effort. Incentive plans,

MBO/goal setting, and performance appraisal are all aimed at altering the consequences of performance so that improvement "counts" toward things of value to the individual. Job enrichment seeks to influence performance by making high performance more interesting, fun, and challenging, thereby enhancing individual efforts to do well. Support for the effectiveness of some of these methods is substantial. Improvements in performance often exceed 40% (Gerhart & Milkovich, 1992; Locke, Feren, McCaleb, Shaw, & Denny, 1980; Shumate, Dockstader, & Nebeker, 1978).

A BRIEF HISTORY OF I/O PSYCHOLOGY IN THE MILITARY

World War I to 1939: Beginnings

Prior to World War I, psychology began exploring the development of tests to measure differences in human abilities. Of particular interest were intelligence tests with their primary application to educational problems. Alfred Binet and later Lewis M. Terman saw them as a means of classifying students to increase school efficiency (Freeman, 1939). However, even as early as 1908 Binet had urged the testing of conscripts to eliminate "defectives" in the military. About this same time, industrial applications were being suggested by Munstererberg and others (Viteles, 1932). In 1917 as the United States entered World War I, Robert M. Yerkes, then the president of the American Psychological Association, volunteered the services of psychologists to aid the Army in the classification of draftees' fitness for duty (Wigdor & Green, 1991). Thus began the association of psychology and the U.S. military. Yerkes, Terman, and five of their associates developed the first ever multiple choice test, a test for intelligence called the Army Alpha. This test along with a nonverbal companion, Army Beta, were also unique because they were designed to be administered to groups. Before the end of the war, these tests were administered to over 1,750,000 men (Wigdor & Green, 1991). They were used to screen men for minimum service eligibility and qualify them for jobs. During this period some noncognitive tests were also developed to help select individuals for specialized jobs (e.g., aircraft pilots).

In the years between World War I and World War II the use of intelligence tests in America flourished. The development and use of the army tests permitted easy transition to the private sector (Freeman, 1939). Extensive refinement of test items, procedures, and calibration increased their reliability and validity. Military use of the tests, however, declined until the military buildup began again in the late 1930s (Jones, 1991). This early work was devoted exclusively to the person–ability cell of the taxonomy presented above. Both cognitive and noncognitive testing of abilities were used to identify which individuals were capable of performing military jobs.

World War II to 1965: Expanded Influence

By 1939 as war broke out in Europe, selection testing was firmly established in the American military. Military leaders of the time anticipated American entry into the war in Europe, which would require a rapid mobilization of manpower. With washout rates exceeding 75% in pilot training, new emphasis was given to the problems of selecting those who could succeed in those programs (DuBois, 1947). Early in 1940 selected psychologists were invited to join the U.S. Army Air Force to assist with the development of new selection tests for pilots. Some of the great names of I/O psychology eventually accepted the invitation and spent the war years developing selection tests for the Army Air Force. J. P. Guilford, S. Rains Wallace, Edwin E. Ghiselli, Paul Horst, and Robert L. Thorndike were among the 100 plus who worked on the project (DuBois, 1947).

Tests in this period looked not only at intellectual predictors of pilot success but also at a wide variety of additional predictors. These included such things as: perception, psychomotor skills, complex coordination, emotion, temperament, and personality. Later, additional predictors of adjustment were added including biographical and life experience measures. The target population also expanded to include all members of air crews such as navigators and bombardiers. Again testing in this period was primarily designed to identify individual differences in ability that predicted performance (the person–ability cell). Also during this period the first studies in the person–motivation cell were undertaken. The inclusion of measures of adjustment and personality were intended to identify interest and motivation to become a pilot. Their addition expanded the scope of I/O psychology in the military. Personality tests, however, were not always used as person–motivation measures. Sometimes they were evaluated to determine if individual temperament gave some people the ability to cope with the rigors of flying.

The success of these combined efforts to reduce pilot attrition was quite remarkable. Pilot attrition during training at the beginning of the war exceeded 75%; by 1945 it was reduced to 33% (Davis, 1947). A validation experiment was conducted in 1943 to evaluate the success of the procedures. A sample of over 1300 applicants took the full test battery and were allowed to attempt pilot training. Eighty percent failed to completed the training. The validity of the total test battery used was calculated to be .66 (DuBois, 1947). This was a powerful demonstration of the value of selection based on test scores.

Personality measures, however, failed to contribute to this success in pilot selection. No personality tests accounted for unique variance in the criterion. In spite of the failure of standard paper and pencil personality tests, assessment center type situational tests were being developed and tested successfully for other jobs. The British military developed the first assessment centers to identify potential leaders (Jones, 1991). Shortly thereafter, situational tests were used in assessment centers established in the United States by the Office of Strategic Services (1949). These proved so successful that AT&T built on these efforts to develop managerial assessment centers.

During this same period the Army had developed the Army General Classification Tests (AGCT), which consisted of vocabulary, arithmetic reasoning, and block counting items (Harrell, 1992; Uhlaner & Bolanovich, 1952). This test was used as both a screening test and a classification test. Because the demand for personnel was so heavy during the war, the screening standards for the AGCT were very low. Therefore, the primary use of the AGCT was for classifying inductees into job categories. The primary criterion for validation again was training success. By the end of the war a new test had been developed, the Army Classification Battery (Uhlaner & Bolanovich, 1952). It continued in use until 1951 when it was replace by the Armed Forces Qualification Test (AFQT). A variant of the AFQT remains today as part of the more comprehensive Armed Services Vocational Aptitude Battery (ASVAB). The ASVAB is used to screen and classify applicants into the U.S. Armed Forces. Again this work predominately occurred in the person–ability cell of the taxonomy. A small amount of work began in the person–motivation cell. All of this research work, however, was aimed at selecting people who would succeed in training.

Research supporting the development of training techniques and instructional technologies was a late entry into I/O in the military. As mentioned previously, the military services are extremely dependent on an internal "grow your own" training philosophy. Ventures into training research began in part as a response to the heavy use of training results as the criterion for selection efforts. Not until the 1950s did the military earnestly begin its own research to improve training methods.

Improved selection and training are ways of providing people who can fulfill the requirements of military jobs. Quite a different approach comes from work to change jobs so they can be performed more easily by everyone. With roots in the work of Frederick W. Taylor, industrial engineering, and ergonomics, the field of human factors engineering in the military began about 1940 (Bernotat, 1991). As the technology of weapon systems advanced military jobs became more and more complex. Complexity in engineering design led to complexity in human operations and maintenance. With this complexity, human operators had more and more difficulty achieving the performance capabilities of the systems they operated. Selection of capable operators alone was not enough. The increased use of sophisticated weapons demonstrated the need for a good fit between machines and those who operate and maintain them.

One of the first places this became apparent was in the design of aircraft cockpit layouts. As a new technology it was open to innovation. Studies of the human sensory, perceptual, and physical capabilities made it possible to design equipment that fit the operators rather the other way around (Bernotat, 1991). Aircraft cockpit design was a major aim of this early work. In the jam packed cockpit the following questions should be asked: What instruments are necessary? Where should the instruments be placed? How large should instrument faces be for proper reading? What should the color contrast be? Should they have digital or analog readouts? What should be the relationship between displays and controls? Where should the controls be located? What human actions should manipulate them? Up to this point the decisions about these issues were left to the personal preferences or traditions of the aircraft design engineers. This was the first systematic research work in the military that focused on the environment–ability cell of the taxonomy.

About this same time a second new area of research began that had little to do with psychology. Eventually, however, it has come to play a significant role in the techniques that are used to allocate and assign personnel to training and jobs. This area is operations research. Employing mathematical techniques associated with linear programming, military planners originally used them to optimize solutions to logistic distribution problems. Like statistics in agriculture before, personnel researchers recognized operations research as a useful tool to deal with the massive problems created when trying to efficiently and optimally manage the movements of hundreds of thousands of personnel through entry, training, and frequent job rotation. Again this new area of research focused on improving performance by reducing the effort required to perform tasks. In this case the tasks of the manpower planners. Again this work was in the environment–ability cell.

The final area of research started during this era was in the environment–motivation cell. Stouffer, Suchman, DeVinny, Star, and Williams (1949) and others began looking at organizational- and group-based influences upon individual motivation. They found that group structure and cohesion had a profound effect upon a soldier's motivation to fight. Toward the end of this period work also began to look at the impact of leader behavior upon the motivation of military personnel. Up to this time leadership research had been attempting to identify the traits of leaders so those who had leadership ability or potential could be selected for leadership assignments (Mann, 1959; Stogdill, 1949). Following the work of Stogdill (1963) and his associates, leadership research started looking for behaviors that leaders could be taught to improve their effectiveness. During this period the U.S. military services adopted a philosophy of leadership training rather than leadership selection.

1965 to the Present: Change and Diversification

Beginning in the late 1960s fundamental changes in U.S. society and the military influenced the work of I/O psychology and OB in the military. Anti-Vietnam War sentiment, the racial tensions of the 1960s and the abolition of the draft in 1973 had profound impacts on the services. The need to depend on volunteers increased the costs of recruitment and personnel salaries, which in turn led to changes in priorities. Rates of premature attrition from training and service obligations, along with retention of quality personnel became key indicators of effectiveness during this era. In turn, recruitment, selection and classification, training effectiveness, and organizational development all became more important. Productivity and cost efficiency received added emphasis.

Work in the person–ability cell continued to focus on testing. A selection and classification test common across all the services (the ASVAB) was introduced in 1976. This cognitive test is an expansion of the AFQT. Altogether it contains the following 10 subtests: (a) general science, (b) arithmetic reasoning, (c) word knowledge, (d) paragraph comprehension, (e) numerical operations, (f) coding speed, (g) auto shop and information, (h) mathematics knowledge, (i) mechanical comprehension, and (j) electronics information (Wigdor & Green, 1991). From these 10 subtests each of the services creates their own composites to determine individual eligibility for different jobs.

Also in the person–ability cell, training was becoming a substantial effort. An Instructional Systems Development (ISD) model was espoused with primarily military applications in mind (e.g., Ellis, 1985; Reigeluth, 1983). All standard military training courses are required to be created with ISD procedures.

The environment–ability cell saw the development of large-scale manpower models to forecast personnel inventory and requirements, and to evaluate policy in terms of driving inventory to meet requirements. In the Navy it was discovered that even very small errors in forecasting personnel end strength (those individuals on the payroll at the end of a year) results in large financial losses. For example, a 1% error in forecast currently results in an $8 million loss. It was also during this period that large scale organizational development efforts were first tried in the Army and the Navy only to be abandoned several years later (Lenz & Roberts, 1991).

During the mid-1970s the environment–motivation cell saw the first projects directed at improving civilian industrial organizations. My colleagues and I developed and tested the first successful productivity based financial reward systems (e.g., Nebeker & Neuberger, 1985; Shumate et al., 1978). The use of these systems typically improved productivity 10% to 30% and in one case 70%.

It was during this time that the present structure for conducting I/O and OB R&D stabilized. The services expanded their in-house civilian R&D organizations. The remainder of this chapter will address the current state of the science being conducted in these laboratories and their prospects for the future.

I/O PSYCHOLOGY AND OB IN THE MILITARY: THE CURRENT STATE

Who is Doing the Work? The Role of Scientific Offices and Military Laboratories

Even though the size of the active duty military forces is shrinking rapidly, they are still very large organizations. The DoD has assistant secretaries to the Secretary of Defense to oversee and coordinate all personnel and human resources related policy and R&D. In turn each of the separate services at their secretariat level also has an office that does the same for that particular service (Defense

Technical Information Center [DTIC], 1992). Each of the military services has one or more organizations devoted to the development of science and technology related to personnel and human resources. In the Army the largest of these organizations are: The U.S. Army Research Institute for the Behavioral and Social Sciences (ARI), The Human Engineering Laboratory (HEL), and the U.S. Army Training and Doctrine Command (TRADOC). The Air Force has combined all of their manpower, personnel, training, and human factors R&D into the Armstrong Laboratory, with directorates dealing with human resources and crew systems. The Navy and Marine Corps get their R&D support from the Navy Personnel Research and Development Center (NPRDC), the Naval Training Systems Center (NTSC), the Naval Command, Control and Ocean Surveillance Center (NCCOSC), and the Office of Naval Research (ONR). Over the past 5 years the amount of money spent on all I/O psychology and OB related R&D has been approximately $100 million per year. This is a great deal of money, but to put it in perspective one needs to consider the scale of personnel related activities in the military and the potential payoff for systems improvements. Currently the military has over 1.75 million personnel in uniform and slightly less than 1 million civilian employees (Department of Defense, 1992a; 1992b). Each year all of the approximately 300,000 people who enter the uniformed service must be trained. About 60% of these will leave by the end of their initial term of obligation (Wigdor & Green, 1991). The services have a continuing need for new personnel and must provide proper training for them. I/O psychology and OB R&D are needed to improve the use of these human resources.

In 1992 the DoD, either directly or through its separate services, supported over 790 R&D projects in I/O and OB (Defense Technical Information Center, 1992). Over 900 professionals and support staffs are *directly* employed by the DoD and its separate services to do much of that work. Also many more professionals in 150 to 200 non-DoD institutions (mostly universities and private contracting firms) provide additional professional support. With numbers this large it is easy to understand how the volume of literature produced by these professionals can become gigantic. To review it all is an impossible task.

Some of this work is found in the open literature. However, the majority is not published in professional journals but rather in technical publications produced by each of the R&D organizations. Although some of this work has limited appeal outside the military, much of it addresses problems common to large, technically sophisticated organizations. For a small fee most of these reports are available from the DTIC or the National Technical Information Service (NTIS).

Trends in Military R&D

A search of the DTIC electronic data bases for published technical and research reports, as well as PsychINFO for journal articles, books, and book chapters that acknowledges a military corporate author (i.e., identifies a military institution as the affiliation of the first author or references one of the military services in the abstract) found over 8,900 citations to military I/O psychology and OB work. These data bases are not exhaustive sources of all reports and articles ever published because they have not attempted to recover all the work completed before 1967. Furthermore, countless additional citations could be linked to the military. If journal articles and book chapters partially supported by the services could be reliably identified the number would grow substantially.

Nevertheless, the large volume of manpower, personnel, training, and human factors literature from military R&D organizations since 1967 provides an excellent opportunity to examine the trends in the type of R&D being done. To do this, all citations in the data bases were searched for keywords and descriptors associated with each of the four cells in my classification taxonomy. Furthermore these searches were repeated for different time periods and for the different branches of service. Over 90% of the citations could be classified into one or more of the four cells. Absolute and relative frequencies in each cell of the taxonomy were then examined for differences. With ns this large almost all differences were found to be significant by x^2 tests. Therefore, what I report are some of the most interesting differences.

Several things were revealed by these analyses. First, the services differ in the number of citations found in the databases. The differences are related to the differences in the size of each service and the size of their R&D staffs. The U.S. Army is the largest contributor, the U.S. Navy the second largest, and the U.S. Air Force the smallest. When all the work in the DoD is combined and viewed across time some interesting patterns emerge. Figure 11.3 shows several things. First, the work is not evenly distributed across the four cells. Across all time periods, work that focuses on improving ability (84.9%) has greater support than improving motivation (15.1%). Also work that focused on changing the

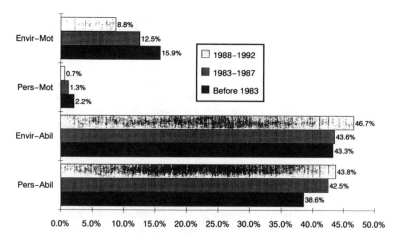

FIG. 11.3. Change in all DoD work over the years.

environment (57.6%) has an edge over work focusing on personal characteristics (42.4%). Although one might argue with the wisdom of these choices, nevertheless, they represent what has been supported in the past by the military services. It is also apparent that the proportion of work in some cells of the taxonomy is increasing and some decreasing. Again the work in the ability cells has been increasing at the expense of work in the motivation cells. This has been a real decline as well as a relative decline.

Figure 11.4 shows the results from the classification across all years by service. These results show that there are substantial differences between services on the amount of work supported in each category. The army has the greatest emphasis upon both ability and environment variables. Over the years only 11.2% of its work has focused on motivation. By contrast the Navy is the highest supporter of motivation R&D and has almost double the Army amounts. The Navy is also different from the other services in the distribution of work among the person and the environment categories, particularly among the ability variables. Whereas the Army places strong emphasis on R&D that focuses on changing ability through changes to the environment, the Navy reverses this emphasis. The Air Force falls between these two extremes.

Finally, Fig. 11.5 shows the splits between the different services over only the last 5 years. The differences seen earlier between the Army and the Navy have become even more extreme. The Army remains most committed to the environment–ability cell. The Air Force placed significantly more emphasis on the work in the environment–ability cell than in previous periods and is closing on the Army. Meanwhile the Navy has increased its lead in the person–ability cell and continues to show the greatest support for the environment–motivation cell. With these trends in mind we turn to a discussion of some examples of projects or efforts in each cell.

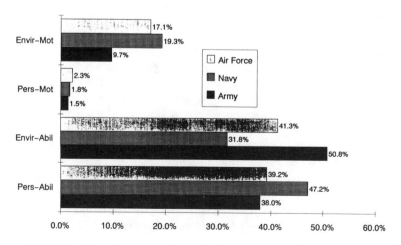

FIG. 11.4. Comparison among the services in work emphasis over all the years.

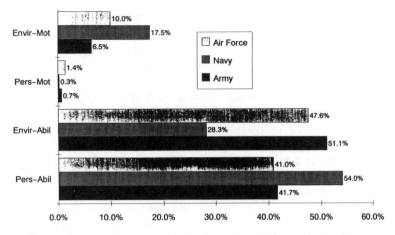

FIG. 11.5. Comparison among services in work emphasis over the last 5 years.

Work in the Person–Ability Cell

Tests. Using test results from the ASVAB all the services must attempt to assign individual enlistees to job categories and training where they are best qualified and where they will be most satisfied. This assignment must not only consider the aptitudes and interests of the individuals but also simultaneously consider military needs and school vacancies. This becomes a difficult optimization problem. Each service has developed computer algorithms to help do this. In the Navy the system used is the Classification and Assignment Program (CLASP) (Kroeker, 1989). Work continues to make these algorithms more flexible and to take a broader spectrum of variables into consideration.

The Services are also attempting to develop new tests to increase selection validities. The Air Force has been experimenting with a number of new tests in their Learning Abilities Measurement Program (LAMP) project (Kyllonen & Cristal, 1989). So far only very modest improvements in validities have been reported, but with the number of people being selected it doesn't take much improvement to make a big difference in utility.

The Army has been attempting to create some new tests, including new noncognitive tests, in Project A (Campbell, 1990). A special issue of *Personnel Psychology* was devoted recently to describing these extensive efforts. The most surprising results are the added utility of temperament and personality scales in predicting some aspects of job performance (e.g., effort, leadership, personal discipline, and physical fitness) (McHenry, Hough, Toquam, Hanson, & Ashworth, 1990). An important difference between these and previous efforts in validation is in the criteria chosen. Actual job performance, rather than success in training, was used to obtain these results.

Computerized Adaptive Tests (CAT). The DoD is just beginning to implement in Military Entrance Processing Stations a new version of the ASVAB—CAT-AS-VAB. The ASVAB has been redesigned to capitalize on Lord's item response theory (Drasgow & Hulin, 1990), branching, intelligent item selection, and a computer interface. The CAT-ASVAB is not just a page turning program for the old tests. It has a number of desirable features (Steege & Fristcher, 1991). First, because it is adaptive, it takes less time to administer, because only those items of appropriate difficulty are presented to a taker. Second, it is more reliable in the tails of the distribution. Third, it is more secure because no two examinees will get the same test. Fourth, it can accommodate new dynamic tests that could not be given by paper and pencil methods. Fifth, it is no longer necessary to administer the test in large groups because it can be administered and scored individually by the computer. Finally, it is attractive to potential recruits as evidence of the high technology used in the military.

Work is already underway for an Enhanced CAT. New tests are being evaluated for target tracking, fluid and crystallized intelligence, and reaction time, to name a few. The nonmilitary applicability of CAT type tests in applications is enormous. This is an area of wide interest.

Instructional Systems. Picture a training school were Marines go house to house in an urban sweep up operation. They will face and return "live" fire without any potential harm to themselves or to expensive equipment. Sound like "Star Trek" or a dream? Virtual reality is coming. In one project, Military Operations in Urban Terrain (MOUT), a virtual reality simulator is being developed for the marines to practice house to house fighting. The services are counting on this technology to provide realistic training and at the same time reduce the costs and risks of live training exercises. A joint effort between engineers, computer scientists, psychologists, and educational specialists from all the services will make this possible.

Consider also a student's Electroencephalogram (EEG) waves and Event Related Potentials (ERP) being analyzed by computer to tell when a student has lost attentiveness or when a critical skill has become automatic. The Neurosciences Division at NPRDC is exploring these possibilities.

The above technologies attempt to improve efficiency of what is learned by the student. Another approach is also being tried by the services. Training aids such as electronic hypertext equipment repair manuals, multimedia technology, and video teletraining are being evaluated. These approaches take rich training to the student to reduce the costs associated with school houses. The evidence so far suggests that these techniques are useful for some training, but where dangerous or expensive equipment is necessary for hands-on training centralized or supervised training may still be necessary. A final new approach is to decrease the time it takes to update training courses and manuals in schools. In the past the rapid replacement of equipment with new and more advanced technology created great challenges in keeping the technical manuals and training course materials current. Often a student would learn in school on equipment that was no longer being used in the field. Projects at NPRDC entitled Authoring Instructional Material (AIM) and the Paperless Classroom are designed to speed the development of course materials.

Work in the Person–Motivation Cell

All of the services are very concerned about the loss of personnel prior to completing their first term enlistment. These losses, or attrition, are estimated to cost more than $200 million each year because of the high cost of recruiting, training, and benefits (Trent & Laurence, 1993). Historically, in addition to any minimal test scores required for enlistment, other screens have been used to eliminate those who are high risks for attrition. The best available predictor has been whether or not the recruit held a diploma from a regular high school. Currently it is very difficult for nongraduates to enlist. However, this is politically sensitive because GED and Adult Education programs, with congressional supporters, do not want to see their graduates less able to enter military service. Adaptability Screening (Trent & Laurence, 1993) is a joint service project designed to evaluate the reliability and validity of the noncognitive Armed Services Applicant Profile (ASAP). The ASAP is a biodata and life experiences form used to predict first term attrition. It is hoped to be a replacement for the high school diploma as a screening device. The validities for the instruments developed so far have been significant and somewhat better than for the high school diploma alone (.32 vs. .24). Although the Navy has implemented a compensatory screening model based on these findings, DoD-wide implementation of the instrument has been delayed. Political issues, concerns about forgery, and stability of validities have been the chief concerns.

Work in the Environment–Ability Cell

The Navy and the Air Force are leading the military services in adopting new methods of process improvement and quality management know as Total Quality Leadership (TQL) or Total Quality Management (TQM). Based upon the work of Deming (1986) and others, NPRDC in the early 1980s began to experiment with the management philosophies of Deming in Navy Aviation Depots. These largely civilian organizations overhaul and repair naval aircraft and components. Early success in trials with quality methods and principles led NPRDC to coin the Term Quality Management and advocate its wider use (Walton, 1991). The Navy recently modified the name to Total Quality Leadership to broaden its appeal to military units as well as civilian organizations. Currently the Navy has adopted a top down approach for implementing TQL and is in the midst of a large-scale program to train a critical mass of Navy leaders, managers, and internal advisors in the principles of TQL. The Air Force has taken a less top down approach and is encouraging bottom up adoption of a less structured approach to TQM.

Teams play a central role in American industry. The same is true for the military. Recent work has been undertaken at the Naval Training Systems Center to understand and improve team functioning. Team decision making is critical in military team functioning. Errors in this process have been blamed for the Iranian Airbus incident and the Iraqi missile attack on a naval ship in the Persian Gulf in the late 1980s. These problems have led to a Tactical Decision Making Under Stress (TADMUS) project, which has as a goal designing better methods of communication and coordination among teams in the combat information centers aboard ships (Salas, Cannon–Bowers, & Price, 1990).

Work in the Environment–Motivation Cell

Recently all the services have begun large-scale efforts to scientifically survey their members' attitudes and perceptions. These surveys are intended to "take the pulse" of the personnel and identify trouble spots that can effect performance and retention. The surveys also provide a way to get grassroots feedback to decision makers who must make personnel policy and allocate resources. Job satisfaction, equal employment opportunity, sexual harassment, rotational practices, and leadership practices are just a few of the issues that have been included in recently surveys. In the current "drawdown" or "downsizing" climate, the military services see this kind of information as vital to good decision making. Akin to these regular surveys is quality of life research that is underway in the Army and the Navy. This research is designed to evaluate the impact of serving in the military and the effects military programs have on individual and organizational outcomes. The Army has been using the life course perspective (Gade, 1991) to follow Army personnel longitudinally to determine if the military is a "good place to start." The Navy is focused on using Structural Equation Modeling to assess the impact of different work, nonwork factors, and benefit programs on quality of life, readiness, and retention.

I previously mentioned the positive effects productivity based reward systems had on civilian productivity (e.g., Nebeker & Neuberger, 1985). Although these demonstrations were typically successful, widespread adoption was not realized. Some reasons for such limited adoption are: (a) difficulty in developing adequate individual performance measures on all jobs, (b) a desire to cover all employees rather than just selected employees, and (c) a desire to create cooperative rather than independent employee efforts. Currently, productivity gain sharing is being evaluated in a number of Navy organizations as an alternative to individual, productivity based reward systems. With the assistance of NPRDC, the DoD is preparing new guidance on the design of gain sharing plans for organizations with primarily civilian employees. Currently federal law does not permit financial rewards to be paid to uniformed personnel for productivity improvement.

During the implementation and field testing of different reward systems, it became evident that many design decisions about reward systems had inadequate empirical research to guide action. To counter this lack of information, NPRDC developed an Organizational Systems Simulation Laboratory (OSSLAB). This lab simulates a data entry organization of 10–12 people. Workers are hired temporarily to do real work at computer work stations. The computers automatically collect a large amount of performance information from each worker so different treatment conditions can be evaluated. Alternative designs for performance monitoring, feedback, and reward system have been evaluated with better experimental control than found in the field and with more fidelity than found in most experiments (e.g., Nebeker & Tatum, 1993). The results from these simulations have helped guide decisions and recommendations in field testing different reward alternatives and addressed important theoretical questions about motivation and cognition.

THE FUTURE OF I/O PSYCHOLOGY IN THE MILITARY

For more than 75 years military problems have been and continue to be solved by I/O psychology and OB. In turn I/O and OB have benefited by what has been learned in solving these military problems. What does the future hold for this union?

With the end of the cold war, the military services are undergoing the most radical change since the end of World War II. The drawdown is making the size of the forces smaller, and the chief threat to American defense is no longer the Soviet Union. The military forces of the future must prepare for potentially more, but less capable, enemies. The services must be more mobile while operating with fewer bases and personnel overseas. Budget plans call for the DoD to reduce its budget by 37% in real terms over 1985. The 1997 defense budget outlays will be less than 3.4% of the gross national product. This is less than half the rate in 1985 and the lowest percent in over 50 years (General Accounting Office, 1993). Additional cuts are likely before these projections take effect.

These changes will affect not only U.S. soldiers, sailors and airmen but also I/O psychologists and OB scientists. Weapon systems will change and with them, military jobs. There will be fewer strategic weapon systems and fewer people to operate and maintain them. The gender and racial composition of the forces will become more diverse. More women and minorities will enter the services. United States women will be the first among free world nations to be approved for some combat positions since Israel banned women from combat in 1949. Issues of cultural and ethnic diversity will become center stage. Budget deficit problems will exacerbate all these changes. For the I/O psychologist and OB scientist these changes mean new opportunities. How should new tasks, jobs, and occupations be designed? What predicts success in these new jobs? How should people be trained to perform them? How can they be motivated? How can all these things be done at a lower cost? The problems caused by all these changes increase the need for the expertise of I/O psychologists and OB scientists. However, I/O psychologists and OB scientists must be seen as having the right solutions when they are required. If we are going to meet the challenges before us we must anticipate what will be needed and be ready to respond. The following are some of my views on what should be on the agenda for I/O psychology and OB in the military over the next several years.

General Issues

Systemic Solutions. A strength of I/O psychology and OB in the past has been its problem focus. We have solved many significant problems, but many of the problems, as well as the solutions, have been narrow. In the future we must take a more systemic view of organizations if we are going to make a meaningful contribution to the military. Military systems and organizations are becoming more multifunctional, technically integrated, and complex. Something done to one part of the system has greater significance to the rest of the system than ever before. Problems can't be seen just as selection problems or training problems. Because military I/O psychology and OB applications have often led applications in other settings, I believe this should be a trend for the field as a whole. To take a more systemic view, we need more comprehensive theories or models of organizational functioning. These models need to consider the organization as system and provide a way to integrate most if not all of the traditional I/O psychology and OB issues. Some total quality approaches already take this position.

As previously mentioned the military services currently have a heavy emphasis on work in the ability cells of my taxonomy. A more integrated approach demands that increased emphasis be placed on the motivation cells. The JPM project and the Army's Project A have suggested that large portions of reliable variance remain unexplained by the current predictors of actual job performance (Wigdor & Green, 1991). Although the current cognitive and maximum performance tests used for selection and classification do predict actual job performance as well as training performance. It is also true that additional variables are reliably associated with factors such as effort, leadership, personal discipline, and military bearing. Person–motivation factors such as personality, temperament, and achievement orientation can and do predict meaningful variance in job performance (McHenry et al., 1990). No doubt environment–motivation factors also play a significant role in determining the performance of military personnel on the job. It is time to increase the attention paid to these cells of the taxonomy.

Greater Joint Service Cooperation. Efforts to increase cooperation between the services are currently underway. This will continue to increase in the future. The relentless pressure to reduce costs will require that each of the R&D organizations in the separate services become more specialized and work on problems across the services. A Training and Personnel Systems Science and Technology Evaluation and Management (TAPSTEM) Committee has been formed to provide the coordinating mechanism for increased cooperation. Over time the I/O psychology and OB R&D in the different service labs will become more specialized and distinct while applications in each service will become more similar. This greater cooperation will extend to other branches of the Federal Government as well.

Dual Use Technologies. President Clinton and Vice President Gore (1993) have initiated a program to convert a substantial portion of the military Science and Technology laboratories to dual use activities. Dual use means that the labs will seek private sector applications for work on both military technologies. Technology that has been developed in the services will be available for licensing to private sector firms. In addition, private sector organizations are now allowed to contract with the military labs to develop technology or provide professional services to them. The legal mechanism to establish these relationships is a Cooperative Research and Development Agreement (CRADA). The CRADAs may change the laboratories' methods of getting their workload. If CRADAs become a significant portion of the workload in the military labs in the future they will have a profound effect upon their work. Because of these relationships, more attention will be paid to the civilian component of the military services. The job design, selection, training, motivation, and assessment of civilians should become a more important activity in military labs.

Specific Issues

From a more specific perspective I view a number of topics as important to the future of I/O psychology and OB in the military. Space limitations prevent detailed discussion of the topics but their enumeration can be useful.

Under the heading of *methodology* a number of topics will be important in the future. These are:

1. Increased use of Linear Structural Equation Modeling (LISREL) and other methods of estimating complex causal relationships should, and will, play an important role in the future of I/O psychology and OB in the military.
2. As a related development Artificial Neural Nets and Artificial Intelligence will find wide acceptance as a technology to help solve problems and be used as a method for discovering embedded structure and meaning in complex data.
3. As we gain a better understanding of complex systems we should develop computer simulations of these systems. These simulations will allow tests of system manipulations and theory propositions.

Person–Ability topics will continue to be extremely important. The following areas should be emphasized:

1. Enhanced Computer Adaptive Testing should place a high priority on developing new tests of abilities. Perceptual–motor tests as well as other dynamic tests will be valuable for classification of recruits into a number of different jobs.

2. Reduction of training costs will receive a higher priority. School house training methods will be de-emphasized. *In situ* training will be emphasized.

3. Neuroscience and brain wave applications will aid in better understanding human cognition and brain function. This will in turn lead to important breakthroughs in training evaluation and student competency certification.

4. Virtual reality will revolutionize training devices and simulations. With these technical improvements we must also increase our training validation against on-the-job performance criteria. We must improve our ability to evaluate the cost effectiveness and utility of training against on-the-job performance criteria.

5. Increased emphasis should be given to officer selection and placement. The matching of an officer to an assignment is too important to leave to the informal and subjective methods that now prevail. Formal assessment center methodology should be evaluated for the services. Most of the attention should be in the area of abilities but some attention should be given to motivation also.

Added emphasis should be given to *Person–Motivation* topics. The following two recommendations are made:

1. The recent success of personality tests in Project A suggests that this area may be an important addition to all testing. Achievement orientation and other constructs such as the "Big Five" personality dimensions have the potential to aid selection decisions.

2. Biographical and life experience data represents a second area of continued value in selection decisions.

A systems approach to organizational improvement (see previous discussion) along with changes in the nature of military demographics will demand some new topics be emphasized in the *Environment–Ability* area. These are:

1. A systems approach to task improvement generally means that the first step in long term improvement of a process is reducing task difficulty

(Davis, 1983; Driskell & Salas, 1991). Once the task has been improved, the training, selection, and motivation of personnel will have a much better result. Therefore the initial task of any improvement effort should be to improve the task process. This approach is consistent with Total Quality Management or Leadership. Methods and techniques to make process improvement available to military organizations are needed.

2. Increased diversity among military personnel is a certainty. The effects on organizational performance, however, are uncertain. Cultural diversity programs typically emphasize the positive aspects of increased diversity, whereas the literature on group heterogeneity suggests that these changes will be more difficult than some expect (Gottfredson, 1992). It is important for the military services to understand what can be done to help more diverse organizations improve their performance.

3. Military organizations need the capability to assess themselves in terms of their culture and climate for improvement. Instruments and methods to provide such assessments need to be developed. Organizations will need to have tools to assist them in understanding where their strengths and weaknesses are. Armed with this information they will be better able to plan effective change strategies.

Under the heading of *Environment-Motivation* work on the following topics is needed:

1. Continued development of measures of productivity and effectiveness is needed. Such measurement is essential to goal setting and productivity gain sharing systems. As the civilian parts of the military cope with demands to be more productive, the work force will need clear direction about what changes are required. They will also be more motivated to achieve them when they can see some benefit to themselves.

2. If an added emphasis on motivation is going to bear fruit we need to have a better understanding of the cognitive processes involved in human motivation. New approaches to work motivation including cognitive resource approaches, should be evaluated in a military context.

3. An almost universal complaint in organizations is the performance appraisal system. Years of effort have yielded only modest, if any, improvements in supervisor ratings of individual performance. It may be time for a completely different approach. Perhaps we need to reconsider the role of individual appraisal in the larger scheme of providing control and direction for employees in a system.

At the beginning of World Wars I and II psychologists were ready with solutions when needed. To be any less prepared for the world of tomorrow would be a calamity. I'm confident professionals in I/O psychology and OB will respond to the challenge as they have in the past.

REFERENCES

Bernotat, R. K. (1991). Human-machine systems: Research and application. In R. Gal & A. D. Mangelsdorff (Eds.), *Handbook of military psychology* (pp. 195–208). West Sussex, England: Wiley.

Borman, W. C. (1991). Job behavior, performance, and effectiveness. In M. D. Dunnette & L. M. Hough (Eds.), *Handbook of industrial and organizational psychology, Vol. 2* (2nd ed., pp. 271–326). Palo Alto, CA: Consulting Psychologists Press.

Braun, P., Weigand, D., & Aschenbrenner, H. (1991). The assessment of complex skills and of personality characteristics in military services. In R. Gal & A. D. Mangelsdorff (Eds.), *Handbook of military psychology* (pp. 37–62). West Sussex, England: Wiley.

Cameron, K., & Whetten, D. A. (1983). *Organizational effectiveness: A comparison of multiple models.* New York: Academic Press.

Campbell, J. P. (1990). An overview of the army selection and classification project (Project A). *Personnel Psychology, 43,* 231–240.

Cascio, W. F. (1991). *Applied psychology in personnel management* (4th ed.). Englewood Cliffs, NJ: Prentice-Hall.

Clinton, W. J., & Gore, A., Jr. (1993, February 22). *Technology for America's economic growth, a new direction to build economic strength.* Washington, D.C.: Office of the President of the United States of America.

Davis, F. B. (1947). *The AAF qualifying examination* U.S. Army Air Force Aviation Psychology [Tech. Rep. No. 6, AD 651 782]. Washington, DC: Government Printing Office.

Defense Technical Information Center (1992). *Research directory for manpower, personnel, training, and human factors.* San Diego, CA: Manpower and Training Research Information System (MATRIS) Office.

Deming, W. E. (1986). *Out of the crisis.* Boston, MA: Massachusetts Institute of Technology, Center for Advanced Engineering Study.

Department of Defense. (1992a, December 31). *Civilian manpower statistics.* Washington, DC: Washington Headquarters Services (DoD), Directorate for Information, Operations, and Reports.

Department of Defense. (1992b, December 31). *Military manpower statistics.* Washington, DC: Washington Headquarters Services (DoD), Directorate for Information, Operations, and Reports.

Driskell, J. E., & Olmstedt, B. (1989). Psychology and the military: Research applications and trends. *American Psychologist, 44,* 43–54.

Driskell, J. E., & Salas, E. (1991). Overcoming the effects of stress on military performance: Human factors, training and selection strategies. In R. Gal & A. D. Mangelsdorff (Eds.), *Handbook of military psychology* (pp. 183–194). West Sussex, England: Wiley.

DuBois, P. H. (Ed.). (1947). *The classification program* (U.S. Army Air Force Aviation Psychology Program Research Report No. 2). Washington, DC: U.S. Government Printing Office.

Ellis, J. (Ed.). (1985). *Military contributions to instructional technology.* New York: Praeger.

Freeman, F. N. (1939). *Mental tests, their history, principles and application* (rev. ed.). Boston: Houghton Mifflin.

Gade, P. A. (Ed.) (1991). Military service and the life-course perspective [Special issue]. *Military Psychology, 3*(4), 185–267.

Gal, R., & Mangelsdorff, A. D. (Eds.) (1991). *Handbook of military psychology*. West Sussex, England: Wiley.

General Accounting Office. (1993). *Force structure: Issues involving the base force* (NSIAD–93–65). Washington, DC: Author.

Gerhart, B., & Milkovich, G. T. (1992). Employee compensation: Research and practice. In M. D. Dunnette & L. M. Hough (Eds.), *Handbook of industrial and organizational psychology* (2nd ed.) (Vol. 3, pp. 482–569). Palo Alto, CA: Consulting Psychologists Press.

Ghiselli, E. E. (1966). *The validity of occupational aptitude tests*. New York: Wiley.

Goldstein, I. F. (1991). Training in work organizations. In M. D. Dunnette & L. M. Hough (Eds.), *Handbook of industrial and organizational psychology* (2nd ed.) (Vol. 2, pp. 507–619). Palo Alto, CA: Consulting Psychologists Press.

Gottfredson, L. S. (1992). Dilemmas in developing diversity programs. In S. Jackson (Ed.), *Diversity in the workplace* (pp. 279–305). New York: Guilford.

Guion, R. M. (1991). Personnel assessment, selection, and placement. In M. D. Dunnette & L. M. Hough (Eds.), *Handbook of industrial and organizational psychology* (2nd ed.) (Vol. 2, pp. 327–397). Palo Alto, CA: Consulting Psychologists Press.

Harrell, T. W. (1992). Some history of the army general classification test. *Journal of Applied Psychology, 77*(6), 875–878.

Hodson, W. K. (Ed.). (1992). *Maynard's industrial engineering handbook* (4th ed.). New York: McGraw-Hill.

Hoiberg, A. (1991). Military psychology and women's role in the military. In R. Gal & A. D. Mangelsdorff (Eds.), *Handbook of military psychology* (pp. 725–739). West Sussex, England: Wiley.

Jones, A. (1991). The contributions of psychologists to military officer selection. In R. Gal & A. D. Mangelsdorff (Eds.), *Handbook of military psychology* (pp. 63–80). West Sussex, England: Wiley.

Kanfer, R. (1991). Motivation theory in industrial and organizational psychology. In M. D. Dunnette & L. M. Hough (Eds.), *Handbook of industrial and organizational psychology* (2nd ed.) (Vol. 1, pp. 75–170). Palo Alto, CA: Consulting Psychologists Press.

Katz, D., & Kahn, R. L. (1978). *The social psychology of organizations*. New York: Wiley.

Kroeker, L. P. (1989). Personnel classification/assignment models. In M. F. Wiskoff & G. M. Rampton (Eds.), *Military personnel measurement, testing, assignment, evaluation* (pp. 42–73). New York: Praeger.

Kyllonen, P. C., & Cristal, R. E. (1989). Cognitive modeling of learning abilities: A status report of LAMP. In R. F. Dillon & J. W. Pelligrino (Eds.), *Testing: Theoretical and applied perspectives* (pp. 146–173). New York: Praeger.

Landy, F. J., & Farr, J. L. (1983). *The measurement of work performance: Methods, theory, and applications*. New York: Academic Press.

Lenz, E. J., & Roberts, J. R. (1991). Consultation in a military setting. In R. Gal & A. D. Mangelsdorff (Eds.), *Handbook of military psychology* (pp. 671–688). West Sussex, England: Wiley.

Lewin, K. (1951). *Field theory in the social sciences*. New York: Harper.

Locke, E. A., Feren, D. B., McCaleb, V. M., Shaw, K. N., & Denny, A. T. (1980). The relative effectiveness of four methods of motivating employee performance. In K. D. Duncan, M. M. Grunberg, & D. Wallis (Eds.), *Changes in working life* (pp. 360–388). New York: Wiley.

Mann, R. D. (1959). A review of the relationships between personality and leadership and popularity. *Psychological Bulletin, 56*, 241–270.

McHenry, J. J., Hough, L. M., Toquam, J. L., Hanson, M. A., & Ashworth, S. (1990). Project A validity results: The relationship between predictor and criterion domains. *Personnel Psychology, 43*, 335–366.

Miller, J. G. (1978). *Living systems*. New York: McGraw-Hill.

Nebeker, D. M., & Neuberger, B. M. (1985). Productivity improvement in a purchase division: The impact of a performance contingent reward system. *Evaluation and Program Planning: An International Journal, 8*, 121–134.

Nebeker, D. M., & Tatum, B. C. (1993). The effects of computer monitoring on work performance, job satisfaction, and stress. *Journal of Applied Social Psychology, 23*(7), 508–536.

Office of Strategic Services. (1949). *The assessment of men: Selection of personnel for the Office of Strategic Services.* New York: Rinehart.

Reigeluth, C. M. (Ed.). (1983). *Instructional-design theories and models: An overview of their current status.* Hillsdale, NJ: Lawrence Erlbaum Associates.

Salas, E., Cannon–Bowers, J. A., & Price, C. (1990). Team training and performance research: Research challenges for the 90's. *The Industrial-Organizational Psychologist, 28*(2), 50–52.

Salvendy, G. (Ed.). (1992). *Handbook of industrial engineering* (2nd ed.). New York: Wiley.

Schmitt, N., Gooding, R. Z., Noe, R. A., & Kirsch, M. (1984). Meta-analyses of validity studies published between 1964 and 1982 and the investigation of study characteristics. *Personnel Psychology, 37*, 407–422.

Shumate, E. C., Dockstader, S. L., & Nebeker, D. M. (1978). *Effects of a performance contingent reward system on worker productivity: A field study* (Tech. Rep. No. 78–34). San Diego, CA: Navy Personnel Research and Development Center.

Steege, F. W., & Fristcher, W. (1991). Psychological assessment and military personnel management. In R. Gal & A. D. Mangelsdorff (Eds.), *Handbook of military psychology* (pp. 7–36). West Sussex, England: Wiley.

Stogdill, R. M. (1949). Personal factors associated with leadership: A survey of the literature. *Journal of Psychology, 25*, 35–71.

Stogdill, R. M. (1963). *Manual for the leader behavior description questionnaire, Form XII.* Columbus: Ohio State University, Bureau of Business Research.

Stouffer, S. A., Suchman, E. A., DeVinney, L. C., Star, S. A., & Williams, R. M., Jr. (1949). *The American soldier: Adjustment during army life.* Princeton, NJ: Princeton University Press.

Trent, T., & Laurence, J. H. (1993). *Adaptability screening for the Armed Forces.* Washington, DC: Office of Assistant Secretary of Defense (Force Management and Personnel).

Tuttle, T. C. (1983). Organizational productivity: A challenge for psychologists. *American Psychologist, 38*, 479–486.

Uhlaner, J. E., & Bolanovich, D. J. (1952). *Development of armed forces qualification test and predecessor army screening tests, 1946–1950* (PRS Report No. 976). Washington, DC: Department of the Army, Personnel Research Section.

Viteles, M. S. (1932). *Industrial psychology.* New York: Norton.

Vroom, V. (1964). *Work and motivation.* New York: Wiley.

Walton, M. (1991). *Deming management at work.* New York: Perigee.

Wigdor, A. K., & Green, B. F., Jr. (Eds.). (1991). *Performance assessment for the workplace, Vol. I & II.* Washington, DC: National Academy Press.

12

THE PAST, PRESENT, AND FUTURE OF OB APPLICATIONS BY CONSULTING ACADEMICIANS

Milton D. Hakel
Bowling Green State University

Organizational behavior (OB) is a broad and inclusive field, covering any intervention that influences the behavior of one or more people working in a group. This definition therefore includes both selection and organizational development, topics in which the modal organizational behaviorist may have limited interest. OB is not limited to particular types of organizations (e.g., corporations) or even to monetarily compensated activity. The definition uses the word *intervention* to emphasize both causal and applied views of the phenomena we study. The purpose of this chapter is to examine how we might learn more from attempts at application, and thus become more effective at both studying and intervening.

By way of preface, please note that none of the world's problems come in neatly partitioned packages, subdivided in correspondence to the disciplinary and subdisciplinary affiliations of researchers. Organizational problems do not know the sociological structure of academia, and effective solutions to them may not respect that structure either.

OB APPLICATIONS: PAST, PRESENT, AND FUTURE

The Past

The field has a long history of contributions by academicians working as consultants toward the solution of organizations' problems. There is no need to attempt to review all of them, but rather it is sufficient to note only a few to serve as exemplars of what consulting academicians have accomplished. The Army Alpha (Yerkes, 1921) was created and pilot tested by a committee of consulting academicians in only 4 months, and was used to classify 1,700,000 Army recruits during World War I. The Hawthorne Studies (Roethlisberger & Dickson, 1939), after 1927, resulted from a collaboration of academicians and corporate managers, and pioneered the core of what is now known as OB. The Ohio State Leadership Studies (Fleishman, Harris, & Burtt, 1955) and the research at the University of Michigan's Institute for Social Research on leadership (Bowers & Seashore, 1966) and organizational development based on survey feedback (Likert, 1967) involved leading academicians in field research and consultation. AT&T's Management Progress Study (Bray, Campbell, & Grant, 1974) was conducted mainly by staff researchers, but it also drew strategically on consultants from academia. These examples illustrate a distinguished past record.

The Present

Today consulting academicians are applying their knowledge throughout the length and breadth of OB. Organizations' concerns about topics such as career development, customer service, performance enhancement through goal setting, employee recruitment and selection, management development, gain sharing, outplacement, right sizing, and workforce diversity are being addressed not only by staff specialists but also by consultants, some of whom are academicians. This is as it should be. As a field, we are not learning from this work as fully or as rapidly as we should. The key question is "What should we do differently tomorrow?"

The Future

Looking ahead can involve confronting issues one would rather avoid, and making forecasts runs the risk of being flat-out wrong. And sometimes it is difficult to see the forest because of the trees. In such cases, looking at what is apparently someone else's forest can be helpful as a means of suggesting ways to scrutinize our own. Few organizational behaviorists would identify ergonomics as the sum and substance of our field, yet it may be so. De Montmollin (1992) discussed trends in ergonomics, particularly the rise of macroergonomics—an emphasis on factors beyond the work station such as the technical system, the social system, cultural and ideological aspects, and the general organization and environment. It looks remarkably like the forest of applied organizational behavior:

> Ergonomics is first and foremost a technology before being a "discipline." Ergonomics cannot exist without the prospect of action, and it is this action that permits evaluation. In short, the Macroergonomics trend recalls that basic but so often forgotten truth: ergonomics is problem–oriented. This implies that it is not the solution that should seek the problem but the problem that should guide the search or finding of a solution (hence the necessity of a preliminary diagnostic).

The idea—unformulated but certainly implicit—that by some miraculous pre-established harmony, the endeavours of laboratory researchers will end up with a catalogue of data which will make it possible to solve all the problems of organizations is violently refuted by actual practice. Genuine problems have genuine solutions, that is to say, comprehensive solutions which do not neglect the main points under the pretext that it is beyond the competence of the discipline as scientifically laid down by the old academic traditions. Thus, Macroergonomics offers the possibility for ergonomics to finally become a "science of work" on its own merit, an *Arbeitwissenschaft* defined by its object and not by the assorted collection of "applications" of "pure" sciences which have never shown much concern for the real needs of ergonomists working in the field.

The new hero of this type of ergonomics, therefore, is not the scientist, who nevertheless still maintains his authority at congresses, but the *consultant*, capable of carrying out a dialogue at the highest levels of the hierarchy and convincing the managers through broader, and therefore more realistic, perspectives. (de Montmollin, 1992, p. 176.)

Setting aside the question of whether OB and macroergonomics are one discipline with two names, de Montmollin's comments suggest three issues that need confrontation. These issues are overcoming the disadvantages of specialization, sharpening the focus on important research questions, and learning more from consultants.

How Can We Overcome the Disadvantages of Specialization? As noted at the outset, problems do not come in neatly partitioned, discipline-tagged packages. The prospect of action, indeed, the imperative of action was emphasized by de Montmollin (1992). One factor standing against effective action is the historic trend toward more and more specialization. I see no evidence that this trend is slowing, let alone reversing. One disadvantage of specialization is the compartmentalization of knowledge. Another is fragmentation. Both of these constrain the correct formulation of the problem and the discovery or invention of a comprehensive solution. The most obvious evidence of growing specialization is sociological—divisional structures appear within scholarly societies and professional associations, and new groups form either *de novo* or phoenix–like from the ashes of internal conflict in older groups.

A further disadvantage of specialization is most easily seen from outside the field–it is that outsiders don't know how to select wisely among the competing groups of insiders. A century ago if one had a medical problem, one was visited by a doctor. Today many Americans have access to a dazzling array of medical specialists, and if the self-diagnosis leading to the initial selection of a specialist is accurate, they have quick access to effective treatment. But if the initial selection is not accurate, or if the medical problem is multifaceted, the owner of the problem is in for considerable frustration, or even mistreatment. With regard to the application of programs based on OB research results, the owner of the problem faces a similar array of choices. Although OB consultants are not yet licensed, or board-certified as are medical specialists, don't be surprised if this eventually happens. Note that all states require licensure for psychologists who offer services to the public, and that the American Board of Industrial and Organizational Psychology conducts examinations for diplomate status for psychologists who provide what is here included in "applied organizational behavior" services. Some holders of these credentials feel that they provide a competitive advantage, and so do some employers. But credentials cannot substitute for competence, nor can they solve the problem-owner's dilemma in selecting a specialist.

In part the disadvantages of specialization are buffered by publication, because the open literature makes ideas and findings widely available. At least, that's the theory. In practice, the "open" literature is tough to get into—witness the occasional editorials in the major journals reporting their rejection rates. This becomes a point of pride in some quarters, with promotion and tenure committees and merit review committees giving greater credit for publication in more selective journals. These same committees usually also give less credit for publication in mass circulation magazines.

To some extent the research literature is incomprehensible, not only for its elegant multivariate statistical analyses but also for its lexical obfuscation. Hayes (1992) measured word usage patterns, and found that scientific journals are increasingly typified by rare words. He concluded that more expertise than ever is required to understand published research and theory in other fields, and therefore ideas flow less freely across and within the sciences. Hayes noted that this raises the cost of becoming expert in additional fields, and may diminish the public's trust because scientific work will appear to be less open to outside examination and appraisal.

The open research literature is not widely read in any case. Tulving and Madigan (1970) formally rated 540 published articles in terms of their contribution to knowledge (of memory and verbal learning), and judged two-thirds of them to be "utterly inconsequential." Only about 10% were judged as worthwhile. Garvey and Griffith (1963) estimated that 50% of the articles published in APA journals are read by fewer than 200 people, and that two-thirds of them are never cited by another author. Of late there has been an explosion of new journals in the broad domain of OB, and it will be interesting to see whether the increase in printed pages produces a corresponding increase in useable knowledge.

Further increases in specialization appear to be inevitable, and this will surely pose an even more significant challenge to those who aspire to use scientific knowledge in the future.

How Can We Sharpen the Focus on Important Research Questions? De Montmollin's (1992) long view raised the question of what it is that we are trying to do, and the natural response is that we are trying to answer important questions. There is no uniform view of which questions are important, however, nor is there a shortage of views on the many facets of the general issue of purpose. One need only sample from Argyris, Putnam, and Smith (1985) on action research; Campbell,

Daft, and Hulin (1982) on research topics; Campbell (1990b) on the role of theory; Cook and Campbell (1979) on research design; Hakel, Sorcher, Beer, and Moses (1982) on designing research with implementation in mind; Hakel (1991) on consulting academicians; Lawler, Mohrman, Mohrman, Ledford, and Cummings (1985) on doing research that is useful for theory and practice; Lindblom and Cohen (1979) on useable knowledge, Locke (1986) on generalizing from laboratory research; and the almost annual appraisals offered by society presidents (e.g., Aldag, 1992; Klimoski, 1992) to see the diversity of views. I won't attempt to resolve this; we need only to note the continuing vigor of healthy debate about where the field should go and how it should attempt to get there. Three points warrant mention, however, with regard to sharpening the focus on important problems.

First, the greater the importance of the question, the greater the possibility of marshalling significant resources to investigate it. Thus, one way to gauge the relative importance of specific research is on the basis of the relative resources allocated to it. This necessarily will involve researchers in the marketing and sales of research ideas.

Second, multi-investigator longitudinal research teams are likely to grow in importance in the coming decades. Teams allow the pooling of talent, perspectives, and resources. The Army Research Institute's Project A is by far the largest example of team effort to date. At times this 10-year, $27 million project had a staff of 200 collecting data worldwide from over 50,000 soldiers. Initial results are reported by J. P. Campbell (1990a) and colleagues. Single investigator research is likely to decline in importance. This trend surely has implication for doctoral level training, where the emphasis is still placed on preparation for functioning as a solo researcher.

Third, consensus among investigators may soon play a bigger role in judging the importance of research questions. The recent publication of *The Human Capital Initiative* (Spence & Foss, 1992) represented a novel departure from the conduct of research as usual. Over 100 representatives from 70 research societies and federal agencies attended two summit meetings that debated the need for a national research agenda and authorized the publication of a document that outlines broad themes for basic and applied research and development in service of the nation's needs. Representatives from the Academy of Management, the Society for Industrial and Organizational Psychology, and the Human Factors Society were among the participants. *The Changing Nature of Work* (Greeno & O'Leary, 1993), the first of a series of companion documents, elaborates the productivity in the workplace theme from the first document. What is novel is the consultation between groups on research needs and priorities. This can help to identify issues that groups of researchers regard as important, and single investigators and research teams alike can use these documents in the quest for attracting research resources.

Sequencing the human genome and pursuing the Higgs particle with the superconducting supercollider are "big science." Biologist Lewis Thomas wrote,

The social scientists have a long way to go to catch up, but they may be up to the most important scientific business of all, *if and when they finally get to the right questions.* Our behavior toward each other is the strangest, most unpredictable, and almost entirely unaccountable of all the phenomena with which we are obliged to live. In all of nature there is nothing so threatening to humanity as humanity itself. (Thomas, 1980, p. 23, emphasis added)

Organizational behavior is at the heart of "the right questions," and we need to start asking them loudly.

How Can We Learn More From the Consultant? We need to figure out how to get more out of the consultant, as de Montmollin (1992) said, the "new hero." This need is especially great with regard to the consulting academician. Can consulting and action research contribute to useable knowledge? They can and do, as shown in the field's history, but very little of today's consultation will show up in tomorrow's open literature. There are many reasons for this.

First, for many of us it is more fun to plan and to execute the next project than to write up the last one. Second, a lot of consulting and field data collection is not addressed to conceptual or general questions. But more researchers nowadays are becoming effective at combining "academic" research questions with "applied" (field or consulting) data collection opportunities (e.g., Harrison & McLaughlin, 1993; Schmit & Ryan, 1992; Schwarzwald, Koslowsky, & Shalit, 1992; Williams & Levy, 1992), and this trend needs to be encouraged.

Third, time and budget pressures are chronic. Organizational problem solving is often characterized as "quick and dirty," but academically respectable research seldom gets described with these attributes. Academic respectability is gained through publication, and publication requires both time and financial resources of an order not often granted in consulting projects. The client's need for useable answers *now*, and the client's access to other vendors who will provide them *now*, put significant pressure on the consulting academician to work as quickly and inexpensively as possible. What gets sacrificed is the possibility of collecting data that could contribute to scientific understanding.

Fourth, consulting academicians and consultants have unique viewpoints. Behling (in press) suggested that we as academicians need to clarify our expectations and focus our roles. He elaborated on ideas from Mitroff and Kilmann (1978), arguing that academicians need to concentrate on (a) conceptualizing in response to problems, (b) theorizing from a world view that encompasses the problem situation, and (c) validating theories by testing them in problem situations. It is left to others such as change agents and managers, or consultants and consulting academicians, to emphasize other aspects of organizational problem solving—(d) describing and explaining the problem, and (e) applying and implementing solutions. All five of the elements of organizational problem solving are part of applied science. The academic consultant's role is interesting and challenging because it encompasses all of the elements. We can only hope that our proficiency in performing each of these elements will grow rapidly, even though as individuals we might choose to specialize in or to emphasize one or another of them.

Fifth, much applied work in our field does not fit the standard format for research articles (e.g., literature review, hypothesis, method, results, discussion). Not all useable knowledge is scientific, and not all scientific knowledge is useable. In passing, note that *Personnel Psychology* in 1994 began publishing a new section of the journal called "Innovations in Research-Based Practice." The section is intended to provide a written forum for descriptions of hands-on attempts at implementing research findings, case examples of practical issues confronted in applying research, real world tests of ideas and theories, and examinations of innovative practices. Consultants and consulting academicians encounter these issues all the time.

Sixth, significant proprietary and commercial interests are at stake. This is most obvious for organizations; some believe that work by OB consultants gives them strategic advantages against their competitors. It is also a problem for consultants, however, as they have a vested interest in exploiting whatever competitive advantages they might possess. There is little or no personal advantage in giving away "trade secrets." This, though, slows the growth of the research literature for the scientists among us, and slows the diffusion of OB innovations for the managers among us, a factor that in turn slows overall economic development.

When all is said and done, it is the consultant, nevertheless, who offers the greatest chance of integrating diverse fields of knowledge, and of overcoming the disadvantages of specialization, because the practical problem being addressed in the real world demands a genuine solution. We need to learn how to learn more from consultants and consulting academicians.

SUPPOSE WE WERE CONSULTANTS TO OURSELVES

There's nothing like a tangible problem to provide a stiff dose of multi-faceted reality testing. Consulting bluntly teaches us the limits of our knowledge. As a consultant, whether one is selling a specific solution or diagnosing a general problem, whether one is embroiled in the conflicts between academic and practitioner roles, or whether one is searching for academically respectable or organizationally acceptable answers, consulting is a blunt teacher. Let us briefly examine how our knowledge of OB relates to management education and development, as though we were consultants to ourselves. My point here is not to divert attention from Blood's (chapter 9, this volume) writing on this topic (indeed, I hope to call *more* attention to it), but to make a few closing points about future contributions to useable knowledge of OB by consulting academicians.

Background Information

First, as a consultant one acquires a tremendous amount of background information. So, to illustrate this for management education and development, here's a sample: Joseph Wharton invented the idea of university-based business education in 1881 by giving $100,000 (worth $1.4 million according to 1992 standards) to the University of Pennsylvania, making a major change in the academy. At the turn of the century, separate colleges of business were just beginning to emerge as entities within universities. Pierson (1959) summarized the origins and early growth of business schools from 1880 to 1914, their expansion and diversification from 1914 to 1940, and the reassessment and reorganization of their curricula from 1940 to 1959. Porter and McKibbin (1988) brought the picture up to date in a book subtitled "Drift or Trust into the 21st Century?". Business education has come a long way since the days of high school and college courses in secretarial, typing, and commercial skills.

But it still has a long way to go. Of late there has been a spate of criticism of contemporary management education and development. At a recent conference, a colleague noted that the MBA degree had probably reached the end of its productive life cycle, citing as evidence the recent creation by Oxford and Cambridge Universities of MBA-like programs. Americans aren't the only critics—England's Department of Education and Science released a survey suggesting that most British employers think that MBA courses are irrelevant (On Harvard's heels, 1992). The issue for learning from the consulting academician is how to capture and transmit relevant background information.

Needs Assessment

Second, consultants conduct needs assessments. Much of the needs assessment, or in de Montmollin's (1992) terminology, the "preliminary diagnostic," has already been completed for management education and development. Porter and McKibbin (1988) identified several specific criticisms, noting after their analysis that many of them are well warranted. Two are reported here because of their obvious overlap with the preceding critique of applied OB.

Lack of Integration Across Functional Areas. This concern is as convincing now as when it was expressed by Bossard and Dewhurst (1931), "One wonders whether much of the purported specialization in the collegiate business schools, most of it perhaps, is not mere window dressing designed to impress students and businessmen. . ." (p. 313). Pierson (1959) argued, "The besetting weakness . . . is the tendency to build up areas and subareas far beyond their true academic worth. What may have once been a pioneering effort to increase the scope and depth of a field too often turns into an elaborate departmental structure with a variety of prerequisites, course requirements, and specialized electives" (p. xi). Gordon and Howell (1959) noted, "the time has come to face up to the fact that 'specialization has been running riot' in American business schools" (p. 217). Neither awareness of the need for integration, nor the use of the case method introduced at Harvard in 1920 and now widely used, has led to the creation of meaningfully integrated educational programs. Porter and McKibbin (1988) viewed this as one of the most critical issues for us as educators to face in the future.

Lack of Management and Leadership Skills Development. Pierson (1959) noted, "employers tend to look for qualities of integrity, vigor, resourcefulness, and general intelligence in new recruits" (p. xiii). Porter and McKibbin (1988) repeatedly documented the need for "soft" or people skills, and concluded that "business schools will need to be both aggressive and inventive in attacking the overall problem" (p. 324). They noted the great difficulty of this challenge, but observed that skill development in these domains is not impossible because both the military and industry have had some success.

Both of the knowledge integration and "soft skills" problems are thoroughly saturated with the content of OB. Their solvers can't help but apply OB principles, some of which have already been enshrined in theory, and others of which may be discovered in the real world of solving today's management education and development problems.

The issue for learning from the consulting academician is how to capture and convey the detailed and specific substantive content of the problem in question.

Constraints

Third, consultants also need to identify major constraints. For management education and development, three key constraints are politics, publication, and scheduling.

Inertia and Academic Politics. Both Smith and Martin wrote lovingly but devastatingly about the faults of the modern American university. In *Killing the Spirit*, Smith (1990) surveyed the history and the current circumstances of universities from his dual perspectives as an historian and as the founding provost of the University of California at Santa Cruz. In *To Rise Above Principle*, Martin (1988) viewed the same domain from his perspective as a dean. Both authors offered detailed glimpses of the rich social and institutional context within which OB research and teaching are pursued: publish or perish, the social nonsciences, the inhuman humanities, what the dean wants, conflicts of interest, and the tricks of the trade, for example. Both give far more sobering and entertaining commentaries than could be given here, and because this essay is not likely to be read by many people outside of academia, you've probably already experienced all this, from the inside, so it doesn't need elaboration. I will note only that the political context is a crucial constraint.

Systemic and Personal Publication Pressure. Arrowsmith wrote,

At present the universities are as uncongenial to teaching as the Mojave desert to a clutch of Druid priests. If you want to restore a Druid priesthood you cannot do it by offering prizes for Druid-of-the-year. If you want druids, you must grow forests. There is no other way of setting about it. (quoted in Smith, 1990, p. 219)

Research productivity (grants and publications) counts tangibly and assures career mobility, whereas teaching and course development count for far less (in a quarter-century in university teaching, I heard of only one person being hired solely for teaching excellence). Career mobility is at the heart of the matter—without sufficient research productivity there is no hope of moving up. Curricula will not change without a systemic change in this constraint—otherwise we will continue the folly of rewarding A while hoping for B (Kerr, 1975).

Class Schedules, Courses, and Academic Calendars. Teachers almost never have access to students for large, uninterrupted blocks of time. I know of only two schools that organize their curricula into month-long blocks of full-time concentration on a single subject, but these schools prove that it *can* be done. Some subjects, music performance for example, do not lend themselves well to this regime, but most do. When studying geology, students at Colorado College, for example, can explore around the Rockies without the constraints of a 50–minute hour, three–meetings–a–week format. What a wonderful way to be able to encounter the "wholeness" of a subject. But even in this scheme, knowledge is compartmentalized into subjects and the approach is still discipline-oriented rather than problem-oriented. Fragmentation is a fact of curricular time and content, but it is one we should find a way to circumvent.

The constraints facing academicians who aspire to reform management education are immense. They are so big that as between Porter and McKibbin's (1988) "drift" and "thrust," this commentator is betting on "drift."

So, what's this got to do with consulting academicians? In any consulting management there are vested interests and stakeholders together with real (e.g., economic, motivational) constraints of every sort. They are more salient when we experience them ourselves, but in any case they are always there. Designing and executing a successful laboratory experiment is neither a simple matter nor a small accomplishment. Designing and executing a successful field intervention is no less demanding, nor should it be accorded less status.

Intervention

Finally, the consultant recommends an intervention. Sooner or later, the consultant needs to propose a solution. Concerning the knowledge integration and "soft skills" problems, and in the spirit of a fearless forecast, I expect to see market forces propel the appearance of a management "finishing school & boot camp" as a supplement to traditional academic programs. Imagine a full-time, month-long, computer-driven simulation featuring models of effective performance together with specific and copious individual feedback and coaching. Think of simulated organizational problems that challenge participants to integrate and use the facts and principles they absorbed as BBA and MBA students. Put this together with follow-up coaching once participants start on regular full-time jobs.

Precursors of this imaginary program already exist, and can be seen in the feverish market that has sprung up in leadership and management development. Many large corporations have in-house programs, with GE and Ford being among those most often noted for excellence. Many consulting houses provide specially tailored development programs to organizational clients, and a few even provide publicly available programs that are well suited for smaller organizations and individuals who seek self-development. Conger (1992) reported on five such leadership development programs. It is easy to see how these programs contrast with the typical classroom based university approach—there is next to no declarative knowledge transmitted by them (nor do they intend to transmit any). They vary widely with respect to the transmission of procedural knowledge, but I would bet on any of them over the typical MBA approach as a means to improve leadership *performance*. They are intensive, and therefore costly. Wouldn't it be interesting to see research and application proceed concurrently on this front? Management education and development would be the richer for it, as would the discipline of OB.

Management education and development is discussed here only as a vehicle for making the general point that we need to be learning far more about behavior in organizations, and that some of what needs to be learned can be learned from consulting.

CONCLUSION

By now my view of our field should be clear—we can be and should be a whole lot better than we are at discovering knowledge *and* at using it. We have not tended our shop well. We've ignored some of our "customers." The gap between theory and action is large, and appears to be growing. We cannot afford to let the academic demand for rigor lead the field into rigor mortis. In 11 years as a journal editor, I rejected hundreds of manuscripts for too little rigor. One can only be sad to see such a waste. There were a few manuscripts, however, that were so rigorous that there was no substance left, and they were rejected as well.

The general lament for academicians was expressed bluntly by Wassily Leontief, 1982 Nobel Laureate in Economics: "Year after year economic theorists continue to produce scores of mathematical models and to explore in great detail their formal properties; and the econometricians fit algebraic functions of all possible shapes to essentially the same sets of data without being able to advance, in any perceptible way, a systematic understanding of the structure and the operations of a real economic system" (Leontief, 1982, p. 107). The substitutions needed to make this lament apply to us are simple. We've got at least as long a way to go as do the economists, probably longer. We as a field cannot afford to confine ourselves in an ivory tower behind a barricade of arcane statistical techniques bordered by a moat of obscure theoretical conundrums in a forest of impenetrable prose.

Will change come? Clark Kerr (Otis, 1990, p. 166) once observed that 66 Western institutions have existed continuously since 1530: The Roman Catholic and Lutheran Churches, the Parliaments of Iceland and of the Isle of Man, and 62 universities. Kerr's observation is a fitting place to conclude this exploration of the state of the academy-based OB consultant's art, because it is both comforting and daunting. It is comforting to know that little of what happens in the chaotic swings of history will wipe out the academy, so if I spend too much time on consulting and too little on impression management with my colleagues and the dean, the world won't fall apart (though mine, the dean's, or the faculty's might). It is daunting because OB needs to change, and Kerr's observation suggests that we are not going to change much, easily, or quickly.

REFERENCES

Aldag, R. J. (1992). Images of the Academy. *The Academy of Management News, 22*(4), 1–5.

Argyris, C., Putnam, R., & Smith, D. M. (1985). *Action science.* San Francisco: Jossey-Bass.

Bossard, J. H. S., & Dewhurst, J. F. (1931). *University education for business.* Philadelphia: University of Pennsylvania Press.

Bowers, D. G., & Seashore, S. E. (1966). Predicting organizational effectiveness with a four-factor theory of leadership. *Administrative Science Quarterly, 11*, 238–263.

Bray, D. W., Campbell, R. J., & Grant, D. L. (1974). *Formative years in business.* New York: Wiley.

Campbell, J. P. (1990a). An overview of the Army selection and classification project (Project A). *Personnel Psychology, 43*, 231–240.

Campbell, J. P. (1990b). The role of theory in industrial and organizational psychology. In M. D. Dunnette & L. M. Hough (Eds.), *Handbook of industrial and organizational psychology* (2nd ed.) (Vol. 1, pp. 39–73). Palo Alto, CA: Consulting Psychologists Press.

Campbell, J. P., Daft, R. L., & Hulin, C. L. (1982). *What to study: Generating and developing research questions.* Beverly Hills, CA: Sage.

Conger, J. A. (1992). *Learning to lead: The art of transforming managers into leaders.* San Francisco: Jossey-Bass.

Cook, T. D., & Campbell, D. T. (1979). *Quasi-experimentation: design and analysis issues for field settings.* Chicago: Rand McNally.

de Montmollin, M. (1992). The future of ergonomics: hodge podge or new foundation? *Le Travail humain, 55*, 171–181.

Fleishman, E. A., Harris, E. F., & Burtt, H. E. (1955). *Leadership and supervision in industry.* Columbus, OH: Ohio State University, Bureau of Educational Research.

Garvey, X., & Griffith, Z. (1963). *Reports of the project on scientific exchange in psychology.* Washington, DC: American Psychological Association.

Gordon, R. A., & Howell, J. E. (1959). *Higher education for business.* New York: Columbia University Press.

Greeno, J., & O'Leary, V. (Eds.). (1993). *The changing nature of work.* Washington: American Psychological Society.

Hakel, M. D. (1991). The consulting academician. In Bray, D. W. (Ed.), *Working with organizations and their people* (pp. 151–171). New York: Guilford.

Hakel, M. D., Sorcher, M., Beer, M., & Moses, J. L. (1982). *Making it happen: Designing research with implementation in mind.* Beverly Hills, CA: Sage.

Harrison, D. A., & McLaughlin, M. E. (1993). Cognitive processes in self-report responses: Tests of item context effects in work attitude measures. *Journal of Applied Psychology, 78,* 129–140.

Hayes, D. P. (1992). The growing inaccessibility of science. *Nature, 356,* 739–740.

Kerr, S. (1975). On the folly of rewarding A, while hoping for B. *Academy of Management Journal, 18,* 769–783.

Klimoski, R. J. (1992, April 30). *Presidential address.* Paper presented at the 7th Annual Convention of the Society for Industrial and Organizational Psychology, Montreal.

Lawler, E. E. III, Mohrman, A. M., Mohrman, S. A., Ledford, G. E., & Cummings, T. G. (1985). *Doing research that is useful for theory and practice.* San Francisco: Jossey-Bass.

Leontief, W. (1982). Academic economics. *Science, 217,* 104–107.

Likert, R. (1967). *The human organization.* New York: McGraw-Hill.

Lindblom, C. E., & Cohen, D. K. (1979). *Usable knowledge.* New Haven, CT: Yale University Press.

Locke, Edwin A. (Ed.). (1986). *Generalizing from laboratory to field settings.* Lexington, MA: Lexington.

Martin, J. (1988). *To rise above principle: The memoirs of an unreconstructed dean.* Champaign, IL: University of Illinois Press.

Mitroff, I. I., & Kilmann, R. H. (1978). *Methodological approaches to social science.* San Francisco: Jossey-Bass.

On Harvard's heels. (1992, August 1). *The Economist,* p. 55.

Otis, Harry B. (Ed.). (1990). *Simple truths: The best of the cocklebur.* Kansas City: Andrews & McMeel.

Pierson, Frank C. (1959). *The education of American businessmen: A study of university–college programs in business administration.* New York: McGraw-Hill.

Porter, L. W., & McKibbin, L. E. (1988). *Management education and development: Drift or thrust into the 21st century?* New York: McGraw-Hill.

Roethlisberger, F. J., & Dickson, W. J. (1939). *Management and the worker.* Cambridge, MA: Harvard University Press.

Schmit, M. J., & Ryan, A. M. (1992). Test-taking dispositions: A missing link? *Journal of Applied Psychology, 77,* 629–637.

Schwarzwald, J., Koslowsky, M., & Shalit, B. (1992). A field study of employees' attitudes and behaviors after promotion decisions. *Journal of Applied Psychology, 77,* 511–514.

Smith, P. (1990). *Killing the spirit.* New York: Penguin.

Spence, J., & Foss, D. (Eds.). (1992). *The human capital initiative.* Washington, DC: American Psychological Society.

Thomas, L. (1980). *Late night thoughts on listening to Mahler's Ninth Symphony.* New York: Viking.

Tulving, E., & Madigan, G. (1970). Memory and verbal learning. *Annual Review of Psychology, 29,* 437–484.

Williams, J. R., & Levy, P. E. (1992). The effects of perceived system knowledge on the agreement between self-ratings and supervisor ratings. *Personnel Psychology, 45,* 835–848.

Yerkes, R. M. (1921). *Psychological examining in the United States Army.* Washington, DC: National Academy of Science.

Author Index

289

SUBJECT INDEX

A

Absenteeism
  definition of, 86–87
  Fitchman's theory on, 96
  as withdrawal behavior, 93
Academic calendars, 284
Academic politics, inertia and, 283
Academic respectability, in teaching
    organizational behavior, 223–224
Academicians, *See* Consulting academicians
Accepting, opposition between differentiating
    and, 118–119
Actions
  proactive versus reactive, 103–104
Adaptability, in effective leadership, 65–66
Analysis, levels of, 146–147
Application contributions, to cognitive
    organizational behavior research, 14
Appraisal process, 6–7
Armed Services Applicant Profile (ASAP), 264
ASAP, *See* Armed Services Applicant Profile
    (ASAP)
Assessment
  of dimensionality for measures, 172–173

initial, of items for measures, 172
  of needs, by consultant, 282–283
Attitudes
  description of, 32
  hypothetical relations among, 91*f*
Attribution theory, 4

B

Background information, by consultant,
    281–282
Behavior of leaders, 48–51
Behavioral measurement bias, 162
Biographies, in teaching organizational
    behavior, 227
Biological approach to job design, 28–30
Business press, in teaching organizational
    behavior, 228
Business school curriculum, organizational
    behavior in, 207–208
  current status of, 211–214
  evolution of, 210–211
  future of, 217–219
  origin of, 208–210
  scope for, appropriate, 215–217
  scope of, current, 214–215

303